1·29·96

A Guide

to Wil

in W

D0863606

A Guide to Wildflowers in Winter

Herbaceous Plants of Northeastern North America

Carol Levine

Illustrations by Dick Rauh

Photographs by Samuel Ristich

Additional Illustrations by Redenta Soprano

Yale University Press / New Haven and London

Published with assistance from the foundation established in memory of
Calvin Chapin of the Class of 1788, Yale College.

Designed by Deborah Dutton.
Set in Sabon type by The Composing Room of Michigan, Inc.
Printed in the United States of America by BookCrafters, Inc., Chelsea, Michigan.

Library of Congress Cataloging-in-Publication Data
Levine, Carol, 1928–
    A guide to wildflowers in winter : herbaceous plants of
northeastern North America / Carol Levine ; illustrations by Dick
Rauh ; photographs by Samuel Ristich ; additional illustrations by
Redenta Soprano.
        p.   cm.
    Includes bibliographical references and index.
    ISBN 0-300-06207-9 (alk. paper). — ISBN 0-300-06560-4 (pbk. : alk. paper)
    1. Wild flowers—Northeastern States—Identification.   2. Wild
flowers—Canada, Eastern—Identification.   3. Plants in winter—
Northeastern States—Identification.   4. Plants in winter—Canada,
Eastern—Identification.   5. Wild Flowers—Northeastern States—
Pictorial works.   6. Wild flowers—Canada, Eastern—Pictorial
works.   7. Plants in winter—Northeastern States—Pictorial works.
8. Plants in winter—Canada, Eastern—Pictorial works.   I. Title.
QK117.L48   1995
582.13'0974—dc20   94-46215
                                                                    CIP

A catalogue record for this book is available from the British Library.

The paper in this book meets the guidelines for permanence and durability of the Committee
on Production Guidelines for Book Longevity of the Council on Library Resources.

10 9 8 7 6 5 4 3 2 1

Contents

Acknowledgments

This book could not have been written without the advice and support of many people. I remain grateful to and inspired by Dr. Sam Ristich, whose broad knowledge of natural history and endearing sense of humor are unique, who is an inspiration to all who have had the privilege of learning from him, and without whom I could not have created this book; Walter and Mary Plant, who introduced me to the wonders of botany and started my life in this direction; Robb Reavill, for being the first to have faith in this undertaking and getting this project off the ground; Dr. Andrew Greller, Karl Anderson, and Glenn Dreyer, who took time from their very busy lives to review the manuscript and offer much-appreciated insights and corrections; Dr. Mark McDonnell, director of the University of Connecticut's Bartlett Arboretum, for his enthusiastic encouragement; my teachers and co-instructors at the New York Botanical Garden, where I received my botanical education; Laura Jones Dooley, manuscript editor, who is a joy to work with; Dan Cassel, whose computer wizardry was of inestimable help; and most of all, my editor, Jean Thomson Black, who guided this book to completion and has become my good friend—she has my everlasting gratitude.

Wildflowers
in Winter: An
Introduction

What remains of wildflowers once the blooming season has passed? Gone are the spectacular flowers, along with their distinguishing features. Left behind are forms that may not typify the families to which the plants belong. This makes the identification of wildflowers out of season a challenge, but with the right clues, it is an experience that will reward the winter naturalist. Pause awhile and examine plants' remains. These winter leftovers have their own tales to tell. In studying them, you will discover their unique beauty. No, you will not be dazzled by a riot of colors like those that spring and summer bring, but you will find a quiet purity and simplicity that can be experienced only in fall and winter.

This book fills a gap in the field guides of northeastern North America. Little has been written to guide the amateur naturalist in identifying the remnants of nonwoody plants in fall and winter. With *A Guide to Wildflowers in Winter* you will discover that the study of winter botany can be as exciting as the study of wildflowers in bloom.

When we speak of nonwoody plants, we mean herbaceous plants—those that die down to the ground in winter and then either die off completely or winter over by means of live underground stems and roots. Parts of the plants often remain standing aboveground either as dried remnants of stems, leaves, and fruits or as low-growing rosettes of living green leaves. In contrast to woody plants, these aboveground remnants of herbaceous plants are not alive (the basal rosettes are an exception). It can be difficult to tell whether a particular plant is woody or herbaceous. To make this identification in winter, scrape the stem. If the inside is green rather than brown, the plant is alive, though in a dormant state, and it is a tree or shrub or woody vine and will not be found in this book. If the scraping shows tan or brown, the material is not living and probably belongs to an herbaceous plant. The remnants of herbaceous plants look quite different from the flowering forms. They lack flowers, of course, and the leaves, if they remain, are shriveled and dry, their green color turned to beige or gray. The flowers have gone to fruit, and the fruit and seeds may still cling to the stems. This fruit may be of help in identification, although in many cases it will have been dispersed, leaving behind dried-up receptacles and perhaps calyx remnants.

Herbaceous plants are categorized by three kinds of life cycles: annual, biennial, or perennial. Most annuals complete their life cycles in less than twelve months. They sprout from a seed, bloom, produce seed, and die within one growing season. Winter annuals produce seeds that germinate in late summer, sprouting a plant that winters as a leafy, low-growing rosette before growing forth, blooming, and dying the following spring. Common ragweed (*Ambrosia artemesifolia*) is a well-known annual.

Biennials, in contrast, usually spend an entire year as basal rosettes of leaves. In their second summer, they sprout, bloom, produce seed, and die. Queen Anne's lace, or wild carrot (*Daucus carota*), is a familiar example.

Perennials live on from year to year through their underground stems and roots, sending up shoots to flower and produce seed each year. One common perennial is the spring woodland wildflower red trillium (*Trillium erectum*). The roots and underground parts of annuals and perennials differ from one another and can be of help in identification. Since the underground parts of a perennial live over the winter and initiate spring growth, they must be large enough to store food for this growth. An annual's roots are seldom much enlarged and lack special food-storage structures.

A Guide to Wildflowers in Winter concentrates on plants of the northeastern United States and adjacent Canada. It would be impossible to describe each of the thousands of species that live in this area, so the guide is necessarily selective, and the most representative herbaceous species have been chosen. The perimeters of the area covered are western Illinois, Wisconsin, and Tennessee to the west; Virginia and Kentucky to the south; the Atlantic coast to the east; and Ontario and Quebec to the north. However, the emphasis is on plants growing near the East Coast. Although many species in this book are also found in the Midwest, some Midwestern species are not included.

The section titled "General Guidelines for Identification," below, will tell you what to look for when identifying a plant. Most species described in the guide are detailed according to the following: Key Impressions, Fruit, Leaves, Stem, Life Cycle Type (annual, biennial, or perennial), Habitat, and Range. These features are easily observed. The Illustrated Glossary at the back of the book defines terms used in the species descriptions.

Once you are familiar with the features of the specimens you are trying to identify, you should turn to the dichotomous key, in the section titled "The Illustrated Key," below. The key should enable you to find the page on which your specimen is described and illustrated. The plants are grouped according to an outstanding character; there are, for example, "Twining or Climbing Vines," "Plants Bearing Berrylike Fruits or Seeds," and "Plants with 1-chambered Fruits (Pods) That Split on 2 Sides and Hairless Seeds."

Plants in this guide are listed by scientific name, common name or names, and family. The scientific name, used throughout the world, is established according to the International Rules of Botanical Nomenclature. It is a binomial: the first word names the genus, the second the specific epithet. The genus and the specific epithet make up the full name of the species. Common names are also given, but be aware that confusion can arise with their use—a number of different and unrelated species of plants may bear the same common name, and names can vary from region to region.

A Guide to Wildflowers in Winter generally follows the nomenclature of Henry A. Gleason and Arthur Cronquist, *Manual of Vascular Plants of Northeastern United States and Adjacent Canada,* second edition. John T. Mickel, curator of ferns at the New York Botanical Garden, was consulted for names of ferns and fern allies. Other sources used for obtaining information on morphology, habitat, and range are Lauren Brown, *Weeds in Winter;* Merritt Lyndon Fernald, *Gray's Manual of Botany,* eighth edition; Henry A. Gleason, *The New Britton and Brown Illustrated Flora of the Northeastern United States and Adjacent Canada,* third revised edition; Lawrence Newcomb, *Newcomb's Wildflower Guide;* Roger Tory Peterson and Margaret McKenny, *A Field Guide to Wildflowers of Northeastern and North-central North America.* For information on goldenrod galls I used E. P. Felt, *Plant Galls and Gall Makers.*

General Guidelines for Identification

Each species description consists of a series of headings. To make the best use of these headings you should bear in mind certain guidelines about what to observe in plants out of season. The following characters should prove valuable both in using the Illustrated Key and in reading the species descriptions.

Key Impressions describes the outstanding features of the species. Look for the following:

Height	Odor	Inflorescence
Mode of growth	Minty (may be in Mint Family	Attachment
Upright	[Lamiaceae] if it has a square stem)	Spike
Sprawling	Wintergreen	Raceme
Creeping by rhizomes or	Spicy	Panicle
stolons	Unpleasant	Umbel
Viny	Carrot or parsley (may be in	Head
General shape	Carrot Family [Apiaceae],	Remnants
Wandlike	especially if fruits are	Calyx
Elmlike	in an umbel)	Bracts
Flat-topped		Receptacles
Bushy		Ovaries
Unbranched		

Fruit describes the fruit and the seeds within. The term *fruit* encompasses the ripened ovary and any other structures that enclose the ovary at maturity. Plants have many ways of packaging and dispersing their seeds and fruits. Some species retain fruits or parts of fruits and even seeds in winter. (See the section entitled "Classification of Fruits," below, for a more detailed description of the various kinds of fruits.) Look for:

Fruit texture	Seed shape	Seed texture
Smooth	Round	Smooth
Hairy	Flat	Ridged
Spiny	Triangular	Hairy
Bristly	Ellipsoid	Spiny
Fleshy		Attachments
Dry		

Leaves are described even though they may have fallen or appear dry and shriveled if remaining on the stem. In the absence of leaves, scars on the stem may indicate whether the leaves were opposite or alternate. For example, all members of the Mint Family (Lamiaceae) and Pink Family (Caryophyllaceae) have opposite leaves; all members of the Carrot Family (Apiaceae) and Smartweed Family (Polygonaceae) have wraparound leaf scars.

Remaining leaves may be gently uncurled to obtain any distinguishing characters. Floating a dried leaf in warm water will help uncurl it. Some biennials or perennials have basal leaves that survive winter. If you find basal leaves and you are familiar with the plant in summer, the leaves might help you identify the species. Look for:

Presence or absence	Alternate	Texture
Attached	2-ranked	Smooth
Simple	3-ranked	Hairy
Compound	Basal rosettes	Spiny
Lobed	Margins	
Phyllotaxy	Smooth	
Opposite	Toothed	
Simple	Lobed	
Decussate		
Whorled		

Stem describes branching patterns, shapes, texture, thorns, and other characters. Look for:

Branching patterns	Texture	Pith
Single stem	Smooth	Solid
Branched	Hairy	Hollow
Shape	Spiny	Chambered
Round with nodes	Thorny	
Round without nodes	Bristly	
Triangular		
Flat		
Square		

Perennial, annual, and *biennial* are indicated along with descriptions of underground stems and roots. Look for:

Rhizome (underground stem)	Root
Elongated and stringy	Taproot
Elongated and thick	Fibrous-thin
Onion-shaped	Fibrous-thick
Spherical	Tuberous
Tuberous	

Habitat is an important character; many species are limited to their adapted location, and this can narrow and confirm the choices for identification. Look for:

Woodlands	Roadsides	Wetlands
Wood edges	Waste areas	Swamp
Thickets	Dry and sandy	Freshwater marsh
Fields and meadows	soil	Saltwater marsh
		Bog
		Streamside

Range describes the geographic limits of the species.

Classification of Fruits

I. Fleshy fruit—pericarp mostly fleshy.

  A. Berry—pericarp fleshy throughout.

    1. Typical berry—pericarp fleshy throughout, e.g., grape, tomato.

    2. Pepo—hard rind, e.g., watermelon, cucumber.

    3. Hesperidium—leathery rind and parchmentlike partitions, e.g., citrus fruits.

  B. Drupe—endocarp stony, forming a pit that contains a single seed, e.g., cherry, peach, plum.

  C. Pome—endocarp papery, forming a core with several seeds, e.g., apple, pear.

II. Dry fruit—pericarp dry.

  A. Dehiscent fruit—opening and releasing seeds when ripe.

    1. Legume—1 chamber splitting along 2 sutures, e.g., pea, bean.

    2. Follicle—1 chamber splitting along 1 suture, e.g., milkweed.

    3. Capsule—2 or more chambers.

      a. Typical—dehiscing either by pores, along a line of fusion, or around the middle, e.g., iris, lily.

      b. Silique—elongate, narrow capsule; pericarp falls off, leaving seeds on partition, e.g., mustard.

      c. Silicle—similar to silique but shorter, e.g., shepherd's purse.

  B. Indehiscent fruit—remaining closed when ripe, with few or solitary seeds.

    1. Achene—solitary seed lightly attached to pericarp, e.g., dandelion, buttercup.

    2. Caryopsis—grain; pericarp and seed coat firmly united, e.g., grasses.

    3. Samara—pericarp extending into a thin, flat wing or sometimes duplicate halves, e.g., ash, elm, maple.

    4. Nut—like an achene but with a larger, thicker, and harder wall, e.g., acorn, hazelnut.

    5. Schizocarp—2 chambers splitting apart at maturity but remaining closed around a solitary seed, e.g., carrot, parsley, parsnip.

Examples of Seeds and Achenes

The following families and genera have seeds or achenes that typify the plants
throughout the grouping and can be a helpful guide in identification.

Polygonaceae, the Smartweed Family

Achenes either lens-shaped or 3-angled;
shiny black or brown.

Clusiaceae, the Mangosteen Family
Genus *Hypericum*, St. John's-wort

Seeds short and cylindrical, rounded on
ends, with longitudinal lines and cross
walls; gold to tan to blackish.

Caryophyllaceae, the Pink Family

Seeds kidney-shaped with concentric rounded blunt projections; gray to grayish brown
to black.

Scrophulariaceae, the Figwort Family
Genus *Verbascum*, mullein

Seeds elongate, flat at both ends, longitudinally ridged, with cross wrinkles; brown.

Asclepiadaceae, the Milkweed Family

Seeds round to elongate with tuft of hair
(coma) at the apex; reddish brown.

Amaranthaceae, the Amaranth Family

Seeds lens-shaped; shiny black.

Juncaceae, the Rush Family
Genus *Juncus*, rush

Seeds elliptic or spindle-shaped, with parallel ridges and cross walls, tapered at both
ends, sometimes with each end prolonged
into a slender tail that may be longer than
the body; yellow to light tan.

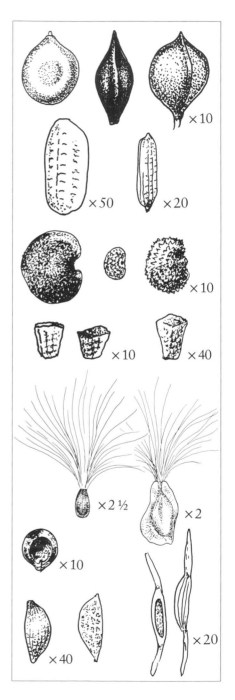

Guide to the Use of Keys

The dichotomous key that follows (as well as the several family keys elsewhere in the guide) is a logical device for the identification of unknown plants. It consists of a series of paired, contrasting statements that describe one or more features of a group of plants. The two halves of each pair are mutually exclusive; the unknown can fit under only one of the two descriptions. Begin with the first pair of statements and decide which statement best describes your specimen. Go to the next appropriate statement and again make a choice. Each statement leads either to a subsequent pair or to an answer with a page number next to it. When you arrive at a choice with a page number, turn to that page and compare your specimen with the drawings and descriptions found there. If they match, you have identified your plant. If they do not, you have probably made a mistake somewhere in the key.

If you are unfamiliar with a term in the key, check the meaning in the Illustrated Glossary at the back of the book.

The best of keys can be hard to use. Keys to winter remnants can be frustrating because certain elements that characterize a family may be absent from the plant. This key, therefore, is not organized according to traditional, botanically correct family groups. Instead, plant remnants are gathered according to similarities of obvious characters, for example, "Stems and other parts with spines, barbs, or bristles," "Climbing vine," and "Fruits with 1 chamber (pod) that splits completely on 2 sides; seeds without silky hairs."

It is important to add, however, that certain plants will be found grouped more or less together as families because of the similarities in their winter characters. One family in particular is grouped as a unit in this book. This is the Daisy Family (Asteraceae), with its unique pappus attachments to the fruits for dispersal. With the Daisy Family there is also a special guide to goldenrod galls. In addition, grasses, sedges, and rushes are described and grouped as families, as are ferns, clubmosses, and horsetails. However, in a book of this size these very large families can be given only cursory treatment.

This visual system of arrangement is admittedly artificial, but it offers a handy approach to the difficulties in dealing with plant remnants.

Here are some tips and suggestions:

Leaves: To better observe the characters of dried leaves, float the leaves in warm water; they will revive enough to show their original appearance.

Stems: Roll stems between your fingers to feel if they are round, square, or 3-sided.

The Illustrated Key

Not included here are ferns, clubmosses, and horsetails, found on pp. 254–260, and grasses, sedges, and rushes, found on pp. 260–305.

1a Plants of aquatic areas, freshwater and salt-water marshes, beaches, and wet or damp places 2
1b Plants of dry land 3
    2a Plants of beaches and salt marshes p. 14
    2b Plants of freshwater and wet or damp places p. 20
3a Climbing vine or trailing groundcover 4
3b Upright plant 5
    4a Climbing vine p. 28
    4b Evergreen or trailing groundcover p. 34
5a Short with basal leaf rosette, leafless stem 6
5b Not as above 7
    6a Basal leaf rosette evergreen, found in woodlands p. 38
    6b Basal leaf rosette found in fields, open spaces p. 44
7a Barbs, burs, needles, or spines present 8
7b Not as above 9
    8a Stems without spines, barbs, or bristles p. 48
    (See also Daisy Family [Asteraceae] p. 206)
    8b Stems and other parts with spines, barbs, or bristles p. 56
    (See also Daisy Family [Asteraceae] p. 204)
9a Plant remnants small, fine, delicate p. 60
9b Plant remnants robust, not delicate 10
    10a Opposite or whorled branches and leaves 11
    10b Alternate branches and leaves 15
11a Opposite branching with square stems 12
11b Opposite branching with round stems 13
    12a Flower and fruit remnants in leaf axils p. 78
    12b Clusters, spikes, or panicles terminal p. 64
13a Opposite branching, swollen nodes p. 84
13b Opposite branching, nodes not swollen 14
    14a Opposite branching, fruits with bristly hairs p. 196

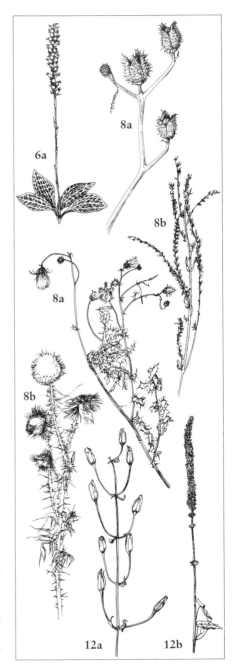

14b Opposite branching, no hairs attached to fruits p. 90

(See also Daisy Family [Asteraceae] p. 200)

15a Fruits appear as a string of beads p. 100

15b Fruits not beaded **16**

    16a Berrylike fruits or seeds p. 100

    16b Not as above **17**

17a Flowers aromatic; leaves aromatic and lobed or dissected, white or silvery beneath, persistent in winter p. 190

17b Leaves not as above **18**

    18a Fruits with 1 or more chambers or sections that split open **19**

    18b Fruits not obviously divided into regular chambers or sections that split open **27**

19a Fruits with 1 chamber **20**

19b Fruits with 2 or more chambers (capsules) **22**

    20a Fruits with 1 chamber (pod) that splits completely on 2 sides; seeds without silky hairs p. 108

    20b Not as above **21**

21a Fruits with 1 chamber (follicle) that splits on 1 side; seeds with silky hairs [*Note:* seeds may be gone, leaving only papery fruit remnants] p. 116

21b Fruits with 1 chamber that opens along side slits; seeds minute, without hairs: Orchid Family (Orchidaceae) p. 114

    22a Fruits with 2-chambered capsules **23** (See also **36a** Mustard Family [Brassicaceae])

    22b Fruits with 3 or more chambers **24**

23a 2-chambered heart-shaped fruits p. 122

23b 2-chambered fruits not heart-shaped p. 124

    24a Fruits with 3 chambers **25**

    24b Fruits with 4 or more chambers **26**

25a Fruits with 3-chambered capsules of 1–3in (2.5–7.5cm) p. 128

25b Fruits with 3-chambered capsules of less than 1in (2.5cm) p. 130

    26a Fruits with 4 chambers p. 132

    26b Fruits with 5 or more chambers; capsules or follicles p. 134

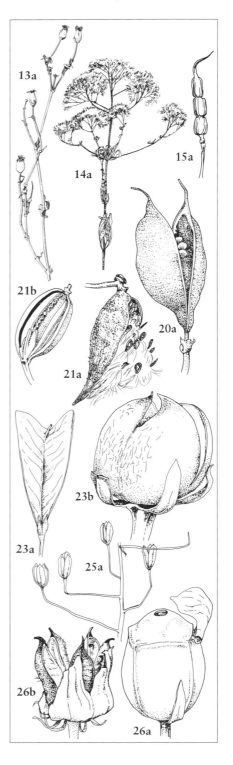

27a Fruits or seeds with bristly, silky, or woolly
    hairs attached 28
27b Not as above 31
    28a Fruit heads round with beaked hairs p.
        220
    28b Fruit heads with hairs attached that
        are not beaked 29
29a Receptacles not star-shaped p. 140
(See Daisy Family [Asteraceae] p. 208)
29b Receptacles star-shaped 30
    30a Receptacles tiny, less than ½in (1cm),
        star-shaped in dense clusters, plants
        2–5ft (.6–1.8m) tall: Goldenrod—*Sol-
        idago* p. 232 and *Euthamia* p. 194
    30b Receptacles ½in (1cm), star-shaped,
        not in dense clusters; 1–4ft (.3–1.3cm)
        tall: *Aster* p. 242
31a Flower remnants nearly stemless (sessile)
    along main stem p. 142
31b Flower remnants with stems 32
    32a Flower and fruit remnants on umbrel-
        lalike branches (umbels); umbels em-
        anate from a single point 33
    32b Not as above 34
33a Umbrella branches inverted p. 144
33b Umbrella branches not inverted p. 154
    34a Flower and fruit remnants in spikes,
        racemes, or panicles 35
    34b Not as above 37
35a Flower and fruit remnants in panicled
    clusters p. 170
35b Flower and fruit remnants in spikes or
    racemes 36

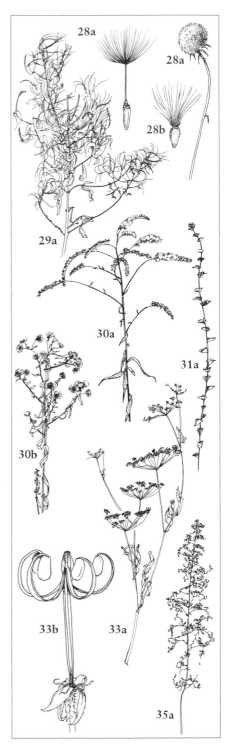

36a Spikes or racemes with hang-ons of translucent fruit partitions (septa); basal rosette of leaves sometimes present: Mustard Family (Brassicaceae) p. 156

36b Spikes or racemes not as above p. 166

37a Flower and fruit remnants in cupped, globular, or oval heads of dried bracts 38

37b Not as above 40

    38a Cupped heads of dried bracts p. 228

    38b Globular or oval heads of dried bracts or calyxes 39

39a Heads of white or brown papery bracts, with white woolly stems p. 222

39b Dense rounded heads of fruits and bracts; heads not white, stems not woolly p. 174 (See also Daisy Family [Asteraceae] p. 224)

    40a Stems with wraparound leaf scars; fruits 3-winged or lens-shaped p. 180

    40b Not as above 41

41a Receptacles appear as long, needlelike spikes at terminal ends p. 192

41b Not as above 42

    42a Flower and fruit remnants in flat-topped clusters; cluster branches slightly alternating p. 194

    42b Not as above 43

43a Fruits enclosed in an inflated, papery calyx p. 184

43b Short plants sometimes parasitic on tree roots or living on decayed plant litter of forest floor; no leaves p. 184

See also: Ferns, fern allies pp. 254–260
        Grasses, sedges, and rushes pp. 260–305

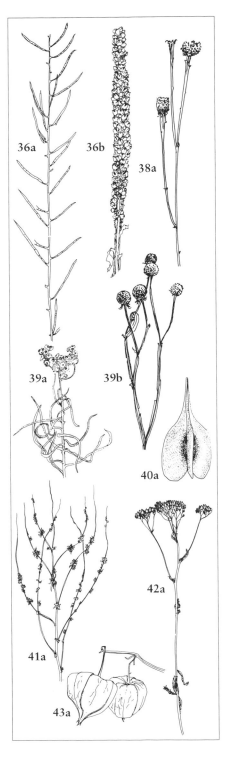

The

Field

Guide

Plants of Salt Marshes and Beaches
(Marine Edge Habitat)

See also *Solidago sempervirens* p. 236, *Aster tenuifolius* p. 252, *A. subulatus* p. 252, *Spartina alterniflora* p. 278, *S. patens* p. 276, *Ammophila breviligulata* p. 278, *Distichlis spicata* p. 280, *Xanthium* spp. p. 52, *Oenothera humifusa* p. 58, *Lathyrus maritimus* p. 112

Salicornia europaea L.
Glasswort, samphire
Goosefoot Family (Chenopodiaceae)

KEY IMPRESSIONS Grows 4–20in (10–50cm). Partially erect and partially spreading plant of salt marshes, with jointed stems that bear spikes with rounded tops. Succulent when ripe. Leaves minute, barely visible scales.
FRUIT Enclosed in calyx. Seed brown, vertical, oval, with short curved hairs.
LEAVES Reduced to minute, opposite scales.
STEM Jointed, branching, erect, and sprawling. Joints 2–4mm, longer than wide.
ANNUAL From fibrous roots.
HABITAT Very common in coastal salt marshes.
RANGE Que. to Fla.
SIMILAR SPECIES
  S. bigelovii Torr. Dwarf glasswort. Stems erect. Joints wider than long. Salt marshes. N.S. to Tex.
  S. virginica L. Perennial glasswort. Grows 4–12in (10–31 cm). Stems hard or woody, prostrate, rooting at nodes, forming mats from which ascend unbranched stalks. Salt marshes. Mass. to Tex.

Salsola kali L.
Common saltwort, Russian thistle
Goosefoot Family (Chenopodiaceae)

KEY IMPRESSIONS Grows 1–2ft (to 40cm). Exceedingly spiny plant of sandy beaches.
FRUIT 1-seeded bladdery fruit (utricle) enclosed in 5-lobed calyx; at maturity, segments incurve over fruit, tips joining. Seeds conical in outline, with transparent seed coat and embryo in form of 2 coils, one inside the other.
LEAVES Upper leaves short, stiff, dilated at base, long-spined at tip.
STEM Loosely branched.
ANNUAL
HABITAT Coastal beaches.
RANGE Nfld. to La.

Suaeda maritima (L.) Dumort
White sea-blite
Goosefoot Family (Chenopodiaceae)

KEY IMPRESSIONS Low-growing plant of salt marshes that forms mats with spreading ascendant and decumbent branches.
FRUIT Bladdery fruit (utricle) enclosed in 5-parted capsule, found in leaf axils. Seeds 1.5–2mm wide, red-brown or black, with flat, spiral embryo.
LEAVES Alternate, linear. Upper leaves reduced to bracts that form terminal spikes.

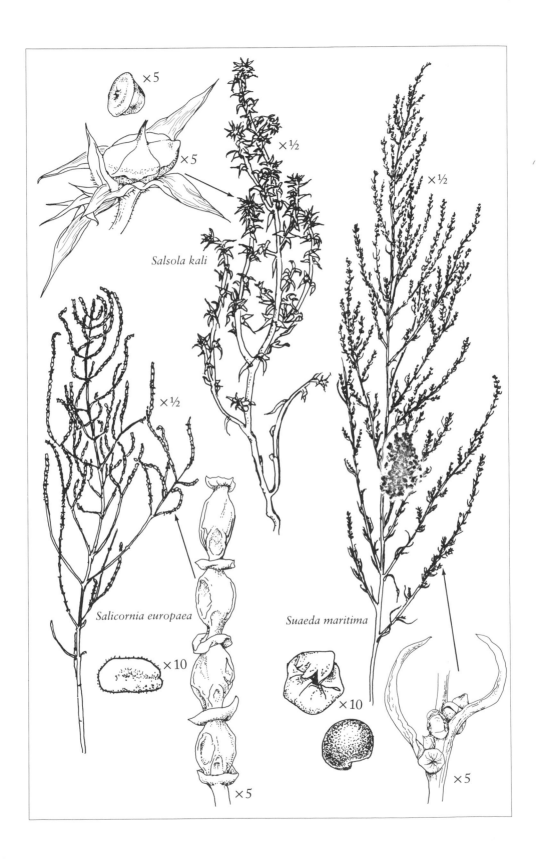

×5

×5

×½

Salsola kali

×½

×½

Salicornia europaea

×10

Suaeda maritima

×10

×5

×5

Stem Branches spreading, ascendant and decumbent.
Annual or Perennial
Habitat Salt marshes.
Range Que. to N.J.

Artemisia stelleriana Besser
Dusty miller, beach-wormwood
Daisy Family (Asteraceae)

Key Impressions Grows 8–24in (30–70cm). Matted, creeping, whitish plant of beaches and dunes. Leaves deeply lobed, white, downy. Remnant narrow, elongate.
Fruit Achenes smooth, narrowed to base, rounded at summit. Seeds oval. No pappus.
Leaves White, downy on both sides, rounded lobes.
Stem Simple to fruit remnants, white, downy.
Perennial From creeping underground stems.
Habitat Beaches, dunes.
Range Native to Japan, escaped from cultivation; St. Lawrence Gulf to Va.

Cakile edentula (Bigelow) Hook.
Sea-rocket
Mustard Family (Brassicaceae)

Key Impressions Grows 6–12in (10–80cm). Seaside mustard with branching stems and fruits transversely divided into 2 parts of different shape. Lower joint persists in winter, but upper falls off.
Fruit Lower joint persists in winter, top-shaped, to 8mm, 1-seeded or seedless. Upper joint usually 1-seeded, always much larger than lower joint.
Leaves Spatula-shaped, succulent.
Stem Branched.
Annual
Habitat Coastal sands.
Range S. Lab. and south; local on Great Lakes shores.

Plantago maritima L.
Seaside-plantain
Plantain Family (Plantaginaceae)

Key Impressions Stem rises 2–8in (5–20cm) from basal leaf rosette. Plant of salt marshes and beaches. Spikes terminal to stem, ¾–4in (2–10cm), loosely or densely flowered.
Fruit Oval capsule rises above stem, splitting near middle. 2–4 seeds, about 2mm, brown, elliptical, with longitudinal groove on inner face.
Leaves Basal rosette to 6in (15cm), thick and fleshy, linear, toothless.
Stem Erect, ¾–4in (2–10cm).
Perennial From stout, short underground stem.
Habitat Salt marshes, beaches, coastal rocks.
Range Circumboreal, extending south along coast to N.J.

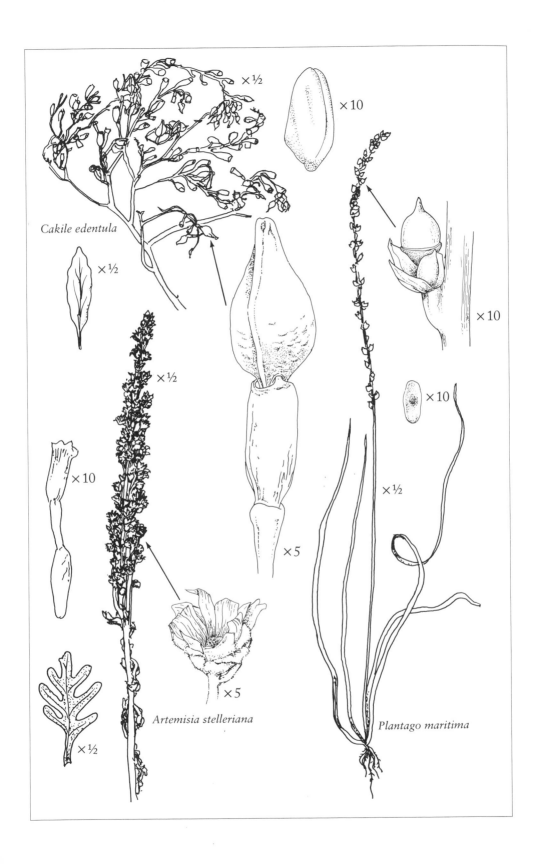

Cakile edentula

×½

×10

×½

×½

×10

×5

Artemisia stelleriana

×5

×10

×½

×10

Plantago maritima

×½

Limonium carolinianum (Walter) Britton
Sea-lavender
Leadwort Family (Plumbaginaceae)

KEY IMPRESSIONS Grows 8–24in (20–70cm), widely branched. Plant of eastern coastal salt marshes. Fruits in stemless clusters. Leaves, if present, long and tapering, found at base.
FRUIT Small, dry, 1-seeded, sealed within persistent calyx.
LEAVES Basal leaves 2–6in (5–15cm), gradually tapering into a stem usually longer than blades.
STEM Widely branching.
PERENNIAL From thick, stout, woody underground stem.
HABITAT Salt marshes.
RANGE Lab. to ne. Mexico.

Althaea officinalis L.
Marsh-mallow
Mallow Family (Malvaceae)

KEY IMPRESSIONS Grows 1½–4ft (.5–1.3m). Stems almost white, erect, branched, hairy. Circular fruits in upper axils.
FRUIT 2¾in (7cm) diameter. 1-seeded chambers numerous, in a circle, 15 or more falling away from central axis at maturity.
LEAVES Velvety, alternate, oval, toothed, shallowly 3-lobed.
STEM Erect, branched, hairy, almost white.
PERENNIAL
HABITAT Salt marshes.
RANGE Native to Europe; naturalized from Mass. to Va., locally inland.

Triglochin maritimum L.
Common arrow-grass
Arrow-grass Family (Juncaginaceae)

KEY IMPRESSIONS Grows to 2½ft (20–80cm). Erect, grasslike leaves. Fruits scattered in a raceme that rises above leaves.
FRUIT Elongated, oval. Cluster appears narrowly 12-winged. Seeds cylindric.
LEAVES Basal, long, narrow, grasslike blade with evident sheath.
STEM Erect, leafless, unbranched.
PERENNIAL From underground stems.
HABITAT Coastal brackish or freshwater marshes and bogs.
RANGE Circumboreal, south to Pa., Ind., Iowa, Nebr., and N.Mex.

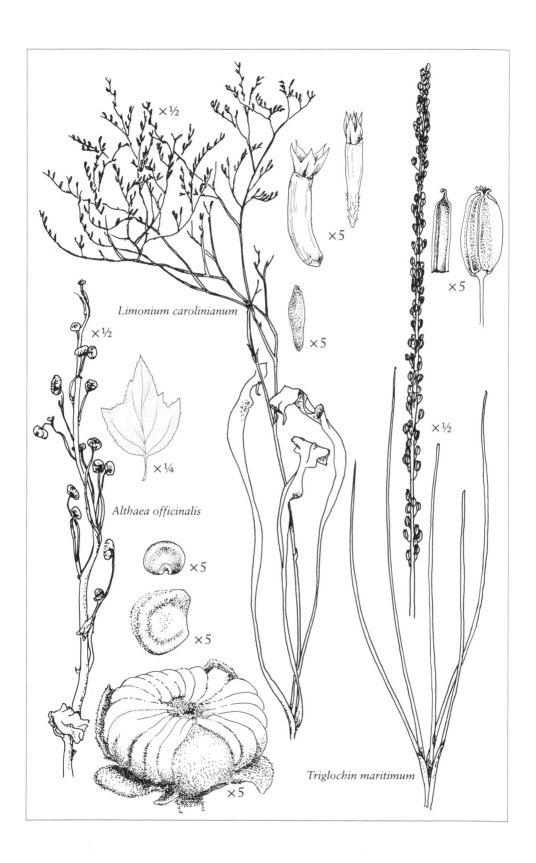

×½

Limonium carolinianum

×5

×5

×½

×¼

Althaea officinalis

×5

×5

×5

×5

×½

×½

Triglochin maritimum

Plants of Freshwater Wet or Damp Areas, Freshwater Marshes, Swamps, and Bogs

See also *Iris* spp. p. 128, *Lysimachia terrestris* p. 96, *Lythrum salicaria* p. 74, *Mimulus* spp. p. 78, *Boehmeria cylindrica* p. 84, *Triglochin maritimum* p. 18, *Chelone glabra* p. 72, *Rhexia* spp. p. 74, *Gentiana andrewsii* p. 92, *Polygonum sagittatum* p. 58, *Triadenum virginicum* p. 98, *Lathyrus maritimus* p. 112

Alisma L. spp.
Water-plantain
Water-plantain Family (Alismataceae)

KEY IMPRESSIONS Grows to 3ft (1m). Plant of aquatic or marshy areas. Fruits arranged in clusters within 3-pointed sepals but fall off in winter, leaving sepals behind. Fruit stalks grow in whorls of 3–10 that re-divide into further whorls; whole inflorescence appears as panicle on upper part of triangular stem.

FRUIT Few to many achenes, 2.5–3mm, small, flat, rounded on back. Found in circular clusters on flat doughnut-shaped receptacle. 3-pointed sepals at base. Seeds curved, hooked.

LEAVES Elliptic to broadly oval with parallel veins, heart-shaped at base. Long stems separate at base.

STEM Triangular.

PERENNIAL From underground stems that often produce tubers. Roots fibrous.

HABITAT Wet places, standing water, shallows, freshwater marshes, ponds, streams.

RANGE Throughout region.

Sagittaria latifolia Willd.
Common arrow-head
Water-plantain Family (Alismataceae)

KEY IMPRESSIONS Grows to 3½ft (.1–1.3m). Plant of wet areas. Fruits aggregated onto sub-globose heads on stalks. Separate male flower remnants are sometimes found above female parts.

FRUIT Achenes 2.3–3.5mm, oval, flat, long with broad marginal wings but no facial wings.

LEAVES Resemble arrowheads (sagittate), with basal lobes directed downward. Basal, sheathing, with parallel veins.

STEM Soft, watery. Tends to fall over when mature.

PERENNIAL From underground stems that form stolons; tubers at stem ends. Roots fibrous.

HABITAT Shallow water, muddy areas, river edges, swamps, ponds, streams.

RANGE Throughout region.

SIMILAR SPECIES

S. engelmanniana J. G. Smith Acid-water arrow-head. Leaves, if present, much narrower than in *S. latifolia*. Achenes with marginal and facial wings.

S. graminea Michx. Grass-leaved sagittaria. Leaves, if present, rarely arrow-shaped. Achenes with marginal and facial wings.

S. rigida Pursh. Sessile-fruited arrow-head. Fruit heads lack stalks. Achenes with marginal wings.

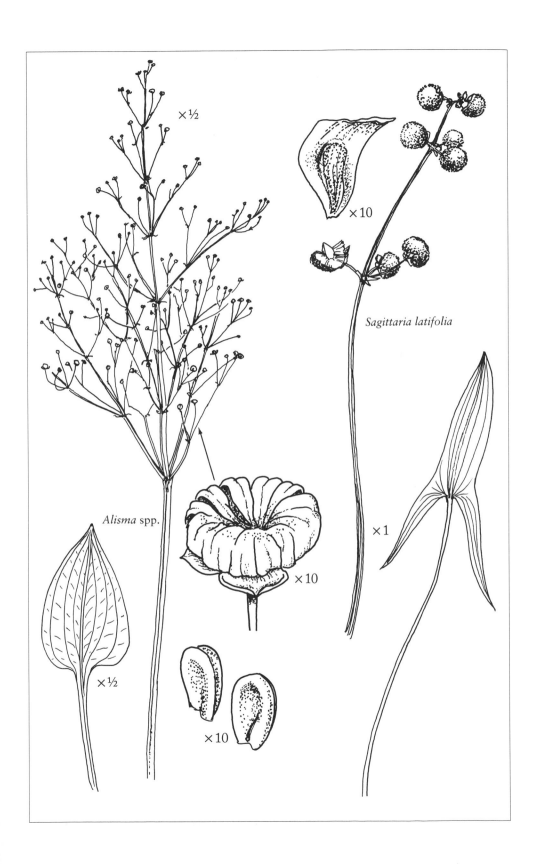

×½

Sagittaria latifolia

×10

×10

Alisma spp.

×10

×1

×½

×10

Sparganium americanum L. spp.

Bur-reed

Bur-reed Family (Sparganiaceae)

KEY IMPRESSIONS Grows to 4ft (.3–1.4m). Fruits, in axils, are round heads of packed, beaked achenes.

FRUIT Achenes dull, dark brown, distinctly beaked, subtended by persistent sepals, and packed into a round head 1in (2.5cm) or less diameter. 1–2 seeds in each achene.

LEAVES Ribbonlike, alternate, stemless, sheathing stem.

STEM Erect when alive. In winter, likely to be found limp and trailing in water.

PERENNIAL From creeping, horizontal underground stems. Roots fibrous.

HABITAT Mud, shallow water.

RANGE Throughout region.

SIMILAR SPECIES

S. androcladum (Engelm.) Morong Achenes shining, light brown. Que. to Va., Ohio to Minn. and Mo.

Typha latifolia L.

Common cat-tail

Typha angustifolia L.

Narrow-leaved cat-tail

Cat-tail Family (Typhaceae)

KEY IMPRESSIONS Grows to 9ft (3m). Stem terminates in densely packed cylindrical spikes. Spike consists of innumerable fruits, each attached by a minute stalk. The compacted fruits have rusty hairs attached, giving the spike its rust color. Atop the spike is a narrow, bare spike, a remnant indicating where male flowers were attached. *T. latifolia* has thicker, larger spikes than *T. angustifolia*.

FRUIT Linear achenes, ½in (1 cm), with copious white hairs near base. When ripe, fruits explode and hairs fluff out and carry them away.

LEAVES *T. latifolia* has long, broad leaves, linear, stemless, sheathing at stem. *T. angustifolia* has narrower leaves.

STEM Single, jointless, erect.

PERENNIAL From spreading underground stems.

HABITAT Fresh or brackish water and marshes. *T. angustifolia* is more tolerant of salt and alkali than *T. latifolia*.

RANGE Throughout region.

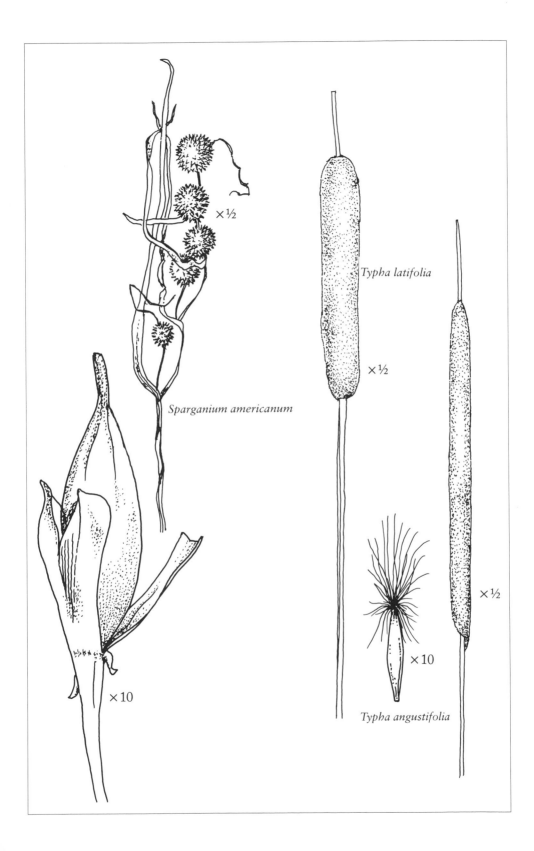

Sparganium americanum

×½

×10

Typha latifolia

×½

Typha angustifolia

×10

×½

Sarracenia purpurea L.
Pitcher-plant
Pitcher-plant Family (Sarraceniaceae)

KEY IMPRESSIONS Grows 12–20in (30–50cm). Plant of sphagnum bogs and other acidic wet places. Leaves hollow, pitcher-shaped, with broad wings extending into a hood. In winter, 5 spreading sepals remain, forming a 5-lobed umbrella-shaped body. Flower remnant on separate stem from leaves.

FRUIT Capsule splits between septa. Seeds small, numerous, 1.9 × 1.0 × .6mm, oval, with narrow, winglike ridge on 1 margin.

LEAVES Pitcher-shaped, hollow, basal, with broad wings extending into a hood.

STEM Single leafless stem, terminating in flower remnant.

PERENNIAL

HABITAT Sphagnum bogs, sandy acid shores, other wet areas.

RANGE Lab. and Nfld. to n. Fla. and s. La., restricted to coastal states southward, but far inland northward to Man., Minn., Ill., Ind., and Ohio.

Decodon verticillatus (L.) Elliott
Water-willow, swamp loosestrife
Loosestrife Family (Lythraceae)

KEY IMPRESSIONS Grows 3–9ft (1–3m). Branches often arch over into water or mud and send out new roots; often forms large patches. Leaves are whorled, and flower remnants or fruits are densely clustered in leaf axils. Calyx surrounds fruit with 5–7 erect teeth interspersed with longer hornlike processes in sinuses.

FRUIT Globose capsule within calyx, 5mm diameter, 3–5 chambered, splitting between septa.

LEAVES Lance-shaped, usually 3–4 in a whorl.

STEM 4–6-sided, recurved.

PERENNIAL

HABITAT Swamps, shallow pools, lakeshores, streams.

RANGE Minn., Wis., s. Ont., n. N.Y., New Eng., and south.

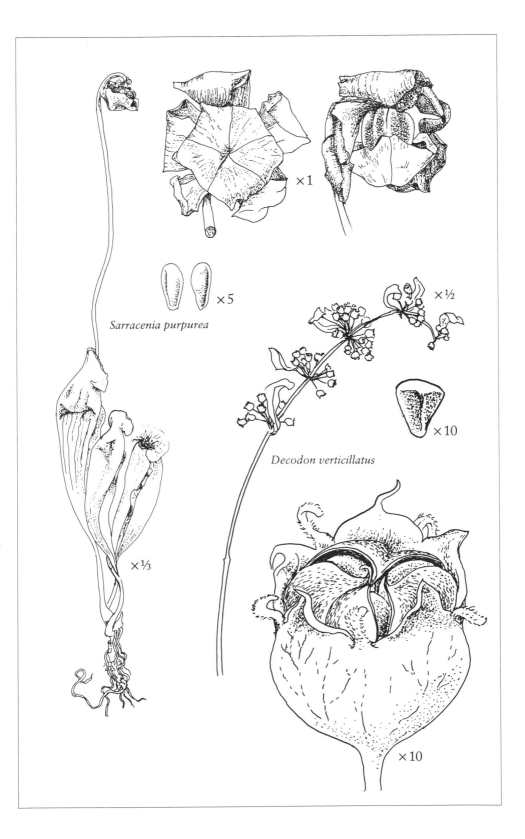

×1

×5

Sarracenia purpurea

×½

Decodon verticillatus

×10

×⅓

×10

Symplocarpus foetidus (L.) Nutt.
Skunk cabbage
Arum Family (Araceae)

KEY IMPRESSIONS Strong odor in all parts, to some resembling a skunk's smell. From fall through winter, 2 types of buds visible: a leaf bud, a light green pointed cone, 4–6in (10–15cm), and a flower bud, rounded, with a mottled purple-brown and yellow overhanging bract (spathe). Flower bud enlarges and produces heat in late winter. When in bloom, spathe opens and club-shaped receptacle with flowers (spadix) can be seen inside.
FRUIT Globular mass composed of enlarged spadix enclosing spherical seeds. (Fruit looks like a dark brown hand grenade.) Seeds usually disperse in late summer, but fruit can sometimes be found in winter.
LEAVES Appear in spring after flowers are pollinated. Large, ovate, heart-shaped at base, with large ribbing.
STEM Stout, vertical underground stem.
PERENNIAL From underground stems. On large plants, underground stems about 2in (5cm) diameter and 2–12in (5–30cm) long. Roots light colored, thick, with encircling ridges, radiating out from stem.
HABITAT Swamps, wet meadows.
RANGE Que. and N.S. to N.C., west to Minn. and Iowa.

Orontium aquaticum L.
Golden club
Arum Family (Araceae)

KEY IMPRESSIONS Clublike spadix erect, ¾–2in (2–5cm). Spadix has yellow flowers in summer but appears tan in winter.
FRUIT Green or brown, small, thin-walled, 1-seeded, slightly inflated (utricle).
LEAVES Basal with thick, dilated stems. Blades floating or submerged.
STEM 8–12in (20–30cm), round, flattened above.
PERENNIAL
HABITAT Swamps, streams, shallow water, especially on coastal plain.
RANGE Mass. to Fla., west to c. N.Y., sw. Pa., e. Ky., w. Tenn., and La.

Drosera spp.
Sundew
Sundew Family (Droseraceae)

KEY IMPRESSIONS Grows 7–8in (18–20cm). Small plant of boggy and acidic swampy areas. Fruiting stalk arises from basal leaf rosette that may remain in winter. Capsules arranged on short spike.
FRUIT Capsules 3-valved. Seeds minute, 1mm, elliptic.
LEAVES Basal rosettes covered with sticky gland-tipped hairs that entrap insects. Several species of sundew, distinguished mainly on basis of leaf shape—some narrow, others elliptic, as shown here.
STEM Erect, leafless.
ANNUAL TO PERENNIAL
HABITAT Bogs, swamps, wet meadows.
RANGE Throughout region.

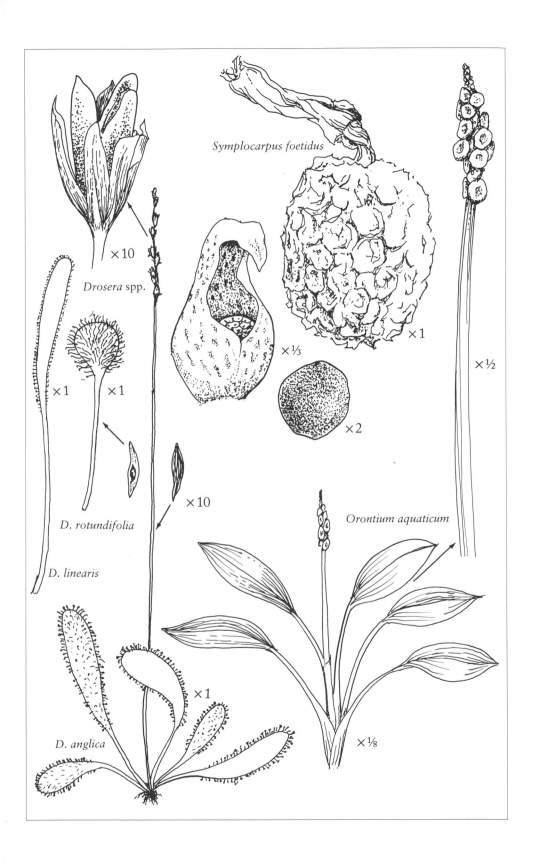

×10

Drosera spp.

×1   ×1

×10

D. rotundifolia

D. linearis

D. anglica   ×1

Symplocarpus foetidus

×⅓

×1

×2

×½

Orontium aquaticum

×⅛

Twining or Climbing Vines

See also *Vincetoxicum nigrum* p. 120, *Polygonum sagittatum* p. 58

Cuscuta L. spp.
Dodder
Dodder Family (Cuscutaceae)

KEY IMPRESSIONS Thin, twining vine, gold-colored when fresh and parasitic on other herbaceous plants. Singular in appearance because it contains no chlorophyll. Globular masses of fruits on stems.

FRUIT Capsules round, whitish, 2-chambered, with 4 seeds. Seeds 1.1–1.6mm, tan, oval.

LEAVES None or minute scales.

STEM Threadlike, intensely orange when fresh, twining on other plants, attaching by suckers (haustoria).

ANNUAL Small roots underground until plant establishes itself on a host by twining tightly. Roots then die out.

HABITAT Parasitic on wide range of hosts.

RANGE Throughout U.S.

Echinocystis lobata (Michx.) T. & G.
Wild cucumber, balsam-apple
Gourd Family (Cucurbitaceae)

KEY IMPRESSIONS High-climbing vine with 3-forked, tightly coiled tendrils. Fruits spiny, oval.

FRUIT 1¼–2in (3–5cm), oval, bladdery. Fleshy when formed, becoming dry. Outer layer weakly spiny, papery, wrinkled. Inner layer white, elaborately decorated with fibrous, netted material. 2 chambers, 4 seeds. Seeds 18–20mm, broadly oval, flattened, with thickish, hard, roughened coat, resembling large squash seeds. Face has light brown border, reddish brown center.

LEAVES Alternate, deeply and sharply 5-lobed on long stems.

STEM Climbing vine with 3-forked tendrils.

ANNUAL

HABITAT Moist ground, thickets.

RANGE Throughout region.

SIMILAR SPECIES

   Sicyos angulatus L. Bur-cucumber. Distinguished from *E. lobata* by its clustered fruits, each with 1 seed. Fruits covered with barbed, prickly bristles that are readily detached. Streambanks, thickets. Maine and Que. to Minn., south to Fla. and Ariz.

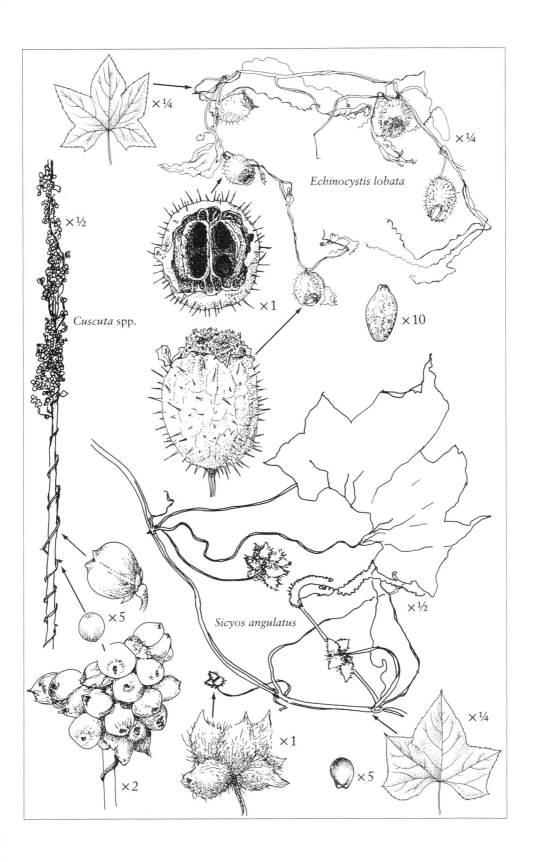

×¼

×¼

Echinocystis lobata

×½

Cuscuta spp.

×1

×10

×5

Sicyos angulatus

×½

×¼

×2

×1

×5

Dioscorea villosa L.

Wild yam, colic-root

Yam Family (Dioscoreaceae)

KEY IMPRESSIONS   Grows to 4ft (1.3m). Twining vines. 3-winged fruits in spikes growing in axils.

FRUIT   Capsules 16–26mm, tan, 3-winged, semicircular, 3-valved, heart-shaped. Seeds 8–18mm, dark brown, flat, winged. 1–2 seeds per cavity.

LEAVES   Alternate, heart-shaped.

STEM   Twining vine.

PERENNIAL   From large, hard underground stem with hairy roots.

HABITAT   Wet areas, moist open woods, thickets, roadsides.

RANGE   Conn. and N.Y. south to Fla. and Tex.

Smilax herbacea L.

Carrion flower

Catbrier Family (Smilacaceae)

KEY IMPRESSIONS   Grows to 6ft (2m). Freely branched herbaceous vine that clings to other plants with tendrils that disappear. No prickles. Fruits in round umbels on axillary stems. Umbel stalk persists when berries are gone.

FRUIT   Berry ½in (1cm) in diameter, blue, 3-chambered, containing 3–4 brown, round seeds.

LEAVES   Oval, heart-shaped base, pale beneath, toothless.

STEM   Herbaceous vine.

ANNUAL   From branching underground stems.

HABITAT   Moist soil of open woods, roadsides, thickets.

RANGE   Throughout region.

SIMILAR SPECIES

> *S. rotundifolia* L.   Catbrier, horsebrier, greenbrier. Woody, perennial vine with thorns or prickles along quadrangular stem. Berries blue-black, in umbels, mostly 2–3 seeded. Leaves oval, bright green on both sides, toothless, rounded, with parallel veins. Stems woody, high-climbing vines, quadrangular. Perennial from long, slender, much-branched underground stems. Open woods, thickets, roadsides. N.S. to n. Fla., west to Mich., se. Mo., e. Okla., and Tex.

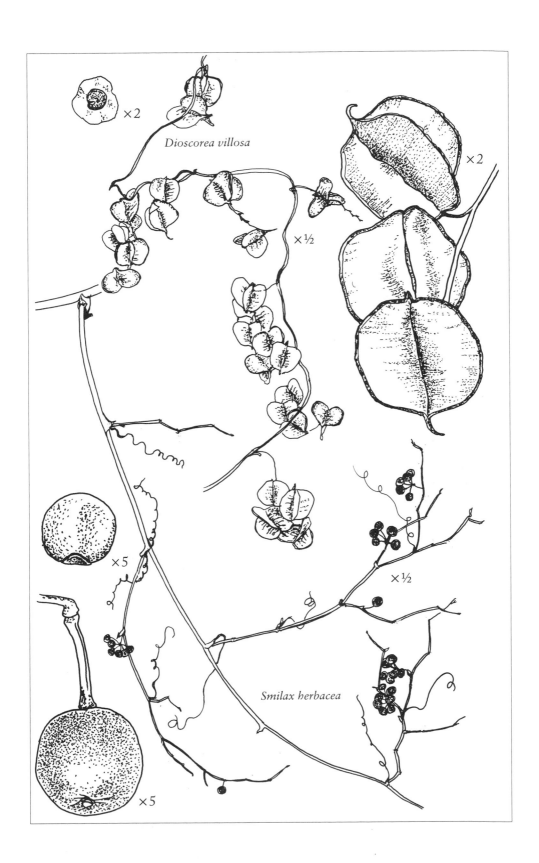

×2

Dioscorea villosa

×2

×½

×5

×½

×5

Smilax herbacea

Polygonum scandens L.
Climbing false buckwheat
Smartweed Family (Polygonaceae)

KEY IMPRESSIONS   Twining vine that grows to 15ft (5m). Racemes on long stems, made up of achenes surrounded by calyx. 3 outer sepals winged.

FRUIT   Achenes 3.5–6mm, glossy black, surrounded and exceeded by pale brown calyx, 8–10mm. Outer 3 sepals broadly winged. Whole fruit, from joint up, grows to 15mm.

LEAVES   Oval to heart-shaped, alternate, sharp at tip.

STEM   Twining brown vine, to 15ft (5m).

PERENNIAL

HABITAT   Moist woods, thickets, roadsides.

RANGE   Que. to N.Dak., south to Fla. and Tex.

SIMILAR SPECIES

  P. cilinode Michx.   Fringed bindweed. Calyx keeled but not 3-winged. Ocrea oblique, reflexed, bristly at base. Achenes dull black.

  P. convolvulus L.   Black bindweed. Calyx keeled but not 3-winged. Ocrea reflexed, bristly at base. Achenes shiny.

Clematis L. spp.
Clematis
Buttercup Family (Ranunculaceae)

KEY IMPRESSIONS   Climbs 6–9ft (2–3m). Somewhat woody vine. Branches whorled with fruits in whorls. Fruits have long, feathery plumes attached.

FRUIT   Achenes numerous, small, brown, 1-seeded, retaining styles (or beaks), which are prolonged into trailing plumes. Achenes in spiral on central receptacle.

LEAVES   Opposite, with 3–5 toothed leaflets.

STEM   Mostly woody vine, climbing by clasping action of leaf stalks.

PERENNIAL

HABITAT   Moist soil, low grounds, thickets, wood edges.

RANGE   Some species found throughout region.

Polygonum scandens

×5

×½

×5

×½

Clematis spp.

×5

Lathyrus latifolius L.

Everlasting pea

Pea or Bean Family (Fabaceae)

KEY IMPRESSIONS Vine with broadly winged stems and pods that are twisted when open. Leaves in 2 leaflets.

FRUIT Pods 2–4in (5–10cm), forming tight spiral corkscrews when open. Seeds have small projections on surface.

LEAVES Alternate, 2 leaflets at each node, lance-shaped to oval with winged stem.

STEM Climbing or trailing vine, terminated by tendril. Stems broadly winged. Can use but does not need other plants for support.

PERENNIAL

HABITAT Garden escapee; waste areas, roadsides.

RANGE Native to Europe, escaped from cultivation; Ind. to New Eng., south to Mo. and Va.

Mikania scandens (L.) Willd.

Climbing hempweed

Daisy Family (Asteraceae)

KEY IMPRESSIONS Grows to 15ft (5m). Twining, herbaceous vine. Numerous fruit heads on stems in axils.

FRUIT Achenes 1.5–2.5mm, with pappus of capillary bristles.

LEAVES Opposite, simple, heart-shaped, with stems.

STEM Twining vine.

PERENNIAL From fleshy, bundled roots.

HABITAT Climbing on bushes in moist areas.

RANGE On or near coast from Maine to Fla., s. Ill., and Tex.; locally inland to Mich., Ind., and Ky.

Evergreen Trailing Groundcover
Vinca minor L.

Periwinkle, myrtle

Dogbane Family (Apocynaceae)

KEY IMPRESSIONS Evergreen, somewhat woody plant with glossy green leaves. Forms a ground cover with trailing stems that grow to 3ft (1m), creating mats.

FRUIT Follicles ¾–1in (2–2.5cm), abruptly beaked. Seeds rough.

LEAVES Glossy, evergreen, opposite, oval to oblong, toothless, ½–1¼in (1.5–3cm).

STEM Trailing, scrambling to 3ft (1m).

PERENNIAL From fibrous roots.

HABITAT Roadsides, woods.

RANGE Native to Europe, escaped from cultivation; common garden escapee.

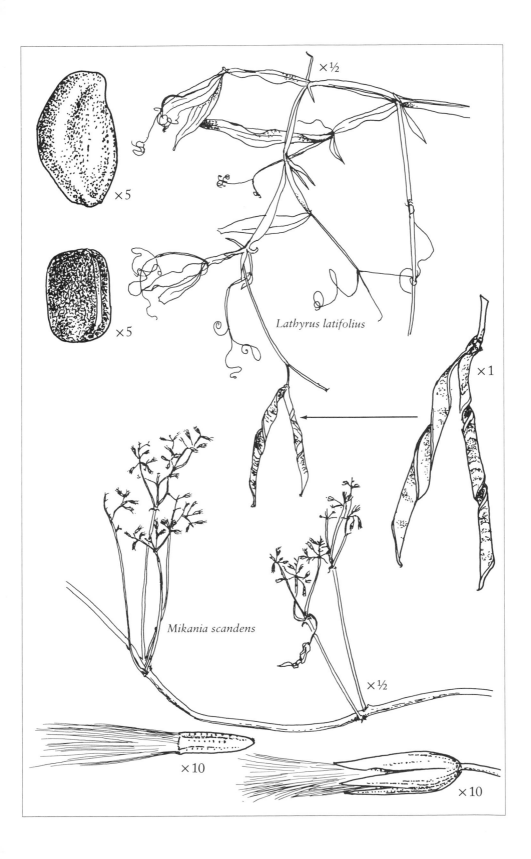

×½

×5

×5

Lathyrus latifolius

×1

Mikania scandens

×½

×10

×10

Mitchella repens L.

Partridge-berry

Madder Family (Rubiaceae)

KEY IMPRESSIONS Trailing small, evergreen woodland plant. Red berries remain over winter.

FRUIT Twin red berry with 8 seeds.

LEAVES Small, paired, roundish.

STEM Trailing on ground, rooting at nodes, and forming mats.

PERENNIAL

HABITAT Woods.

RANGE N.S. to Ont. and Minn., south to Fla. and Tex.

Glechoma hederacea L.

Gill-over-the-ground, ground ivy

Mint Family (Lamiaceae)

See pl. 8a

KEY IMPRESSIONS Creeping, ivylike plant with scalloped, rounded, or kidney-shaped leaves that remain on ground throughout winter.

FRUIT 4 minute nutlets.

LEAVES Scalloped, roundish to kidney-shaped, opposite, stemmed.

STEM Creeps along ground.

PERENNIAL From fibrous roots and slender creeping stems.

HABITAT Moist woods, varied disturbed habitats.

RANGE Native to Eurasia; throughout region.

Gaultheria procumbens L.

Wintergreen, checkerberry

Heath Family (Ericaceae)

KEY IMPRESSIONS Evergreen plant with thick, shiny, elliptic leaves on creeping stems along ground.

FRUIT Red "berry" (capsule surrounded by thickened fleshy calyx).

LEAVES Elliptic, thick, shiny, evergreen, fragrant.

STEM Creeping on or below surface, slender.

PERENNIAL

HABITAT Dry or moist woods in acid soil.

RANGE Canada and n. U.S., south in mountains.

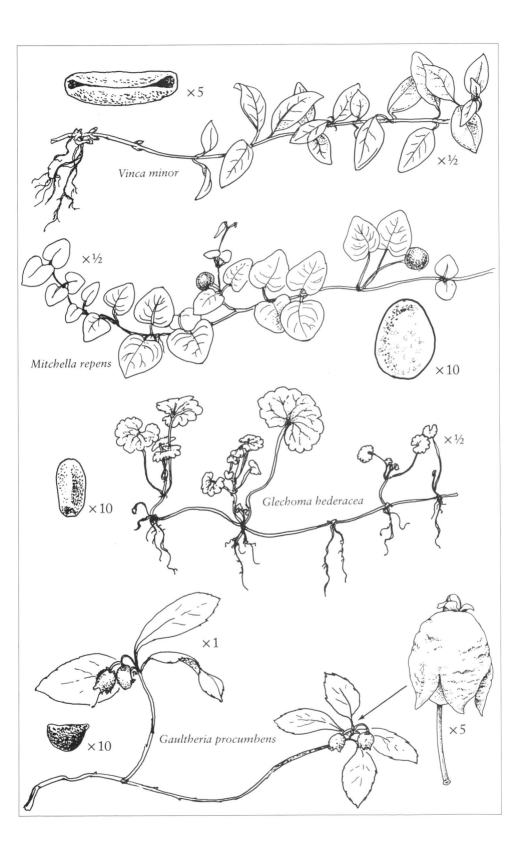

×5

Vinca minor

×½

×½

Mitchella repens

×10

×10

Glechoma hederacea

×½

×1

Gaultheria procumbens

×10

×5

Short Woodland Plants with Evergreen Basal Leaf Rosettes

See also *Gaultheria procumbens* p. 36

Goodyera pubescens (Willd.) R. Br.
Downy rattlesnake-plantain
Orchid Family (Orchidaceae)

See pl. 5b

KEY IMPRESSIONS Fruiting stalk grows to 16in (40cm), with terminal spikelike raceme. Raceme 1½–4in (4–10cm), dense, cylindric. Often colonial. Distinctive basal leaves last through winter.

FRUIT 1-chambered capsules, 6mm, closed at each end and opening by 3 slits on side. Linear seeds minute, dustlike.

LEAVES Basal leaves oval, dark green, with netted pattern of white veins.

STEM Erect, leafless.

PERENNIAL From thick fibrous roots that extend from creeping underground stem. Slender stolons.

HABITAT Dry or moist woods.

RANGE Minn., Ont., Maine, and south.

SIMILAR SPECIES

G. *repens* (L.) R. Br. Lesser rattlesnake-plantain. Smaller, grows to 12in (30cm). Raceme 1¼–2½in (3–6cm), loosely flowered, 1-sided. Dry or moist woods. Canada, northern states, south in mountains.

G. *tesselata* Lodd. Checkered rattlesnake-plantain. Grows 6–16in (15–40cm). Raceme 1½–4in (4–10cm), loosely fruited, often spiral. Rich forests. Canada, northern states.

Chimaphila maculata (L.) Pursh.
Spotted wintergreen
Shinleaf Family (Pyrolaceae)

See pl. 5a

KEY IMPRESSIONS Grows under 1ft (30cm). Single stem stiffly erect in fruit, with 1–5 capsules grouped on terminal end. Leaves dark green with white veins, remaining throughout winter. Half shrubby.

FRUIT 5-parted, round capsule, splitting on midline of chambers. Seeds minute, numerous.

LEAVES Evergreen, remotely toothed, dark green with white veins, in a whorl, oval to lance-shaped on short stems.

STEM Erect, leafless.

PERENNIAL From long, extensively trailing underground stems.

HABITAT Dry, acidic oak, hickory, or coniferous woods.

RANGE Mich., Ont., Maine, and south.

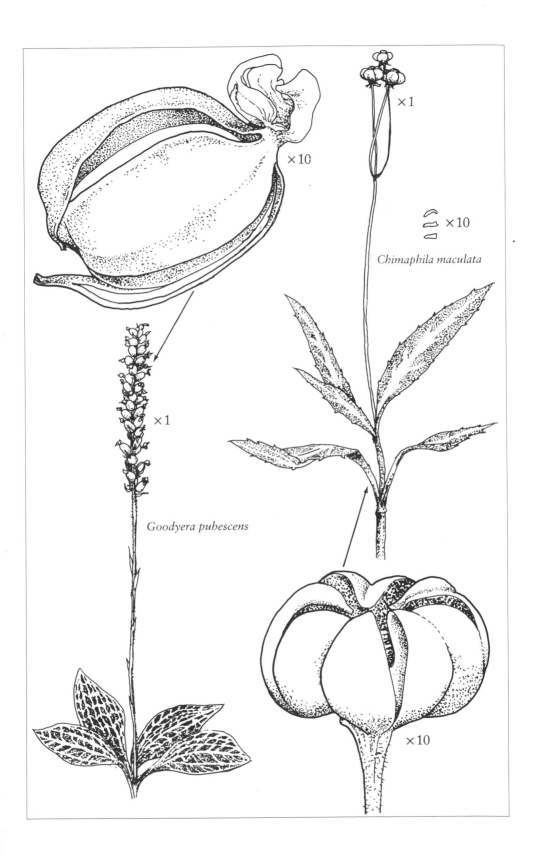

×10

×1

×10

Chimaphila maculata

×1

Goodyera pubescens

×10

Chimaphila umbellata (L.) Barton
Pipsissewa, prince's pine
Shinleaf Family (Pyrolaceae)

See pl. 10b

KEY IMPRESSIONS   Similar in many respects to *C. maculata*, but with solid dark green leaves (no white veins). Leaves relatively long, thin. Half shrubby.

FRUIT   Similar to that of *C. maculata*. 4–8 capsules at terminal end of flower stalk.

LEAVES   Sharply toothed toward summit, but nearly smooth below midline. Solid dark green, no white veins. Single leaves whorled on stem.

STEM   Erect.

PERENNIAL   From long, creeping underground stems.

HABITAT   Dry woods, sandy soil.

RANGE   Ont., Que., and south to n. U.S., in mountains to Ga.

Pyrola elliptica Nutt.
Shinleaf
Shinleaf Family (Pyrolaceae)

See pl. 2c

KEY IMPRESSIONS   Grows to 1ft (30cm). Small plant with single stem and raceme of ascending fruits. Basal leaves evergreen, broadly elliptic.

FRUIT   Capsules round, 5-chambered, drooping in raceme and splitting on midline of chamber upward from base. Valves have cobwebby margins. Seeds numerous, minute, dust-like.

LEAVES   Evergreen, rounded at summit, broadly elliptic, basal, dull green, with stems.

STEM   Single, erect.

PERENNIAL   From creeping underground stems.

HABITAT   Dry or moist upland and mountain woods.

RANGE   Canada to Minn., south to Del., W.Va., and Iowa.

SIMILAR SPECIES

P. rotundifolia L.   Rounded shinleaf. Usually larger than *P. elliptica*. Leaves rounder, more leathery. Leaf stems often as long as leaf blades, whereas blade is usually larger than leaf stem in *P. elliptica*. Woods, bogs. Across Canada and n. U.S., south to N.C., Ky., Ind., and Minn.

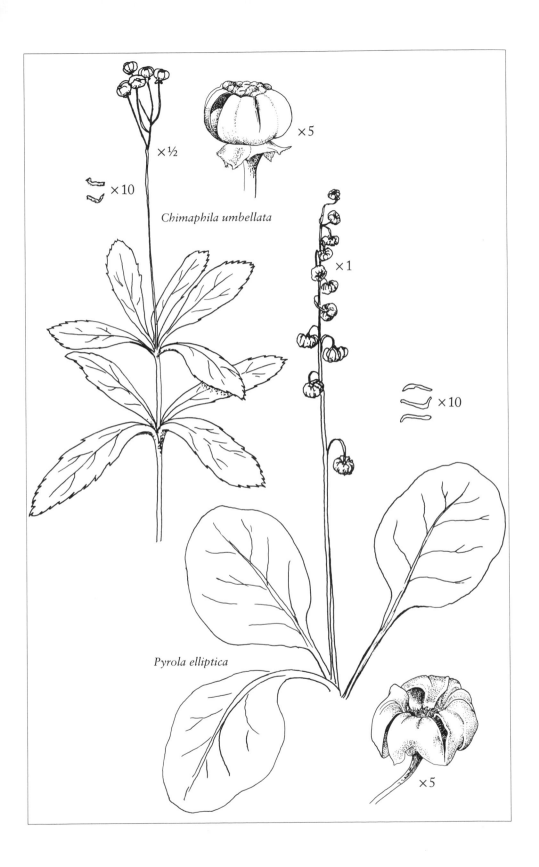

×½

×10

×5

Chimaphila umbellata

×1

×10

Pyrola elliptica

×5

Coptis trifolia (L.) Salisb.

Gold thread, canker root

Buttercup Family (Ranunculaceae)

KEY IMPRESSIONS   Grows to 6in (15cm). Small evergreen plant with naked stem, 1 fruit. Basal leaves shiny, with 3 leaflets.

FRUIT   3–7 follicles, 5–9mm. Fruits beaked, in an umbel. 4–8 seeds, 1.2 × .6mm, about half filling follicles, glossy black, oval to elliptic.

LEAVES   Basal, shiny, evergreen, trifoliate. Leaflets rounded, toothed.

STEM   Fruits and leaves on separate stems.

PERENNIAL   From golden underground stems with bitter taste, hence common names.

HABITAT   Mountains, damp northern woods, bogs.

RANGE   Canada, n. U.S., and south in mountains.

Hepatica americana (DC.) Ker Gawler

Round-lobed hepatica

Buttercup Family (Ranunculaceae)

KEY IMPRESSIONS   3-lobed leaves remain on ground through winter until new flowers come up in spring.

FRUIT   Not available in winter.

LEAVES   3-lobed, lobes broadly rounded, terminal leaf often wider than long.

STEM   Not available in winter; leaves basal.

PERENNIAL

HABITAT   Dry or moist upland woods.

RANGE   Que. and N.S. to Minn. and Man., south to Ga., Tenn., and Mo.

SIMILAR SPECIES

H. acutiloba DC.   Sharp-lobed hepatica. Leaves deeply heart-shaped at base, lobes broad and acute at tip.

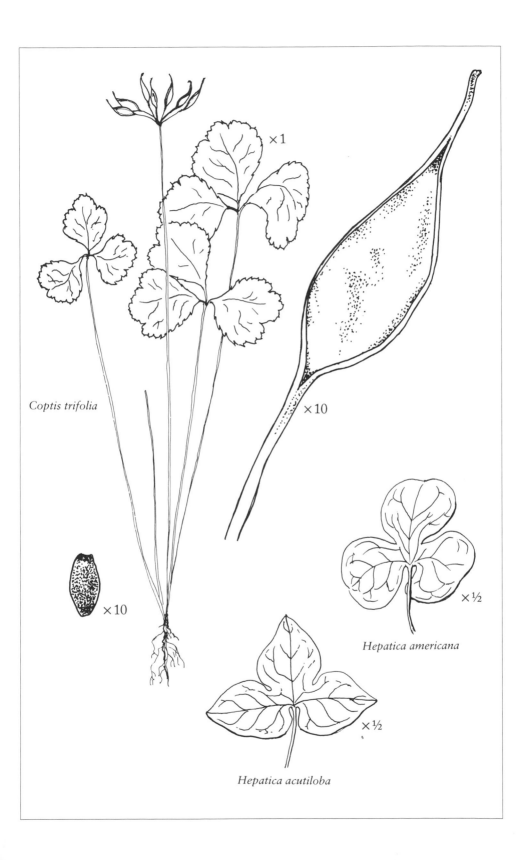

×1

Coptis trifolia

×10

×10

×½

Hepatica americana

×½

Hepatica acutiloba

Short Plants with Evergreen Basal Leaf Rosettes in Fields and Open Spaces

The following are but a few examples of the many species that present rosettes of green leaves in winter.

See also *Antennaria* spp. p. 208, *Taraxacum officinale* p. 220, *Salvia lyrata* p. 84, Mustard Family (Brassicaceae) p. 156

Plantago major L.
Common plantain
Plantain Family (Plantaginaceae)

See pl. 1b

KEY IMPRESSIONS Fruiting stalk grows erect from basal leaf rosette. Stemless fruits run length of stem.
FRUIT 2-chambered elliptical capsule, 3–4mm. Capsule circumsissile—top falls off, leaving behind rounded bottoms of seeds. Seeds light to dark brown, with lighter stripe on dorsal side. Shape variable, surface granular or wrinkled.
LEAVES Basal rosette broadly elliptic, toothless, thick. Found in winter.
STEM Erect, with capsules all along length.
ANNUAL OR PERENNIAL From short, erect underground stem with fibrous roots.
HABITAT Lawns, gardens, roadsides.
RANGE Native to Eurasia; throughout U.S.

Plantago lanceolata L.
English plantain
Plantain Family (Plantaginaceae)

See pl. 1b

KEY IMPRESSIONS Fruiting stalks grow 6–8in (15–20cm) above basal leaf rosette. Fruits crowded into small spike terminating stem.
FRUIT Similar to *P. major*. Seeds 2.1–2.6mm, glossy light to dark brown, with broad yellow stripe on dorsal side, boat-shaped, oval to elliptic. Ventral side deeply grooved.
LEAVES Basal rosette lance-shaped, ribbed, toothless, stemless. Found in winter.
STEM Erect, bare, terminating in fruit.
ANNUAL BECOMING PERENNIAL From stout, short underground stem. Roots fibrous.
HABITAT Common in lawns, roadsides.
RANGE Native to Eurasia; throughout U.S.

Plantago aristata Michx.
Buckhorn
Plantain Family (Plantaginaceae)

KEY IMPRESSIONS Grows to 10in (25cm). Capsules on terminal 1–1½in (2.5–4cm) of single, leafless stem. Bracts beneath capsules extend outward like whiskers.
FRUIT Capsules split at or below middle. 2 seeds, 2–3mm, brown, elliptic, boat-shaped, very convex on outer side, concave on inner.

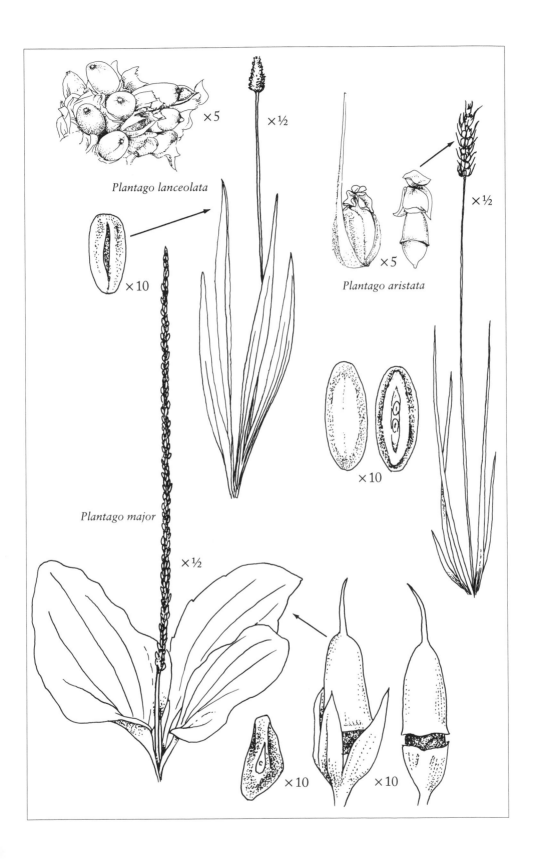

×5

Plantago lanceolata

×½

×½

Plantago aristata

×5

×10

×10

Plantago major

×½

×10

×10

LEAVES   Basal, linear.
STEM   Erect, leafless.
ANNUAL   From taproot.
HABITAT   Disturbed habitats.
RANGE   Naturalized over most of e. U.S. and adjacent Canada.

Hedyotis caerulea (L.) Hook (*Houstonia c.*)
Bluets, Quaker ladies
Madder Family (Rubiaceae)

See pl. 4b

BASAL LEAVES   Lance-shaped, broadest above middle, tapering to base, narrowed to stem often as long. Finely hairy.
PERENNIAL   From slender, fragile underground stems.
HABITAT   Moist soil, meadows.
RANGE   N.S. and Que. to Wis., south to Ga. and Ark.

Ranunculus acris L.
Common buttercup, meadow buttercup
Buttercup Family (Ranunculaceae)

See pl. 9a

BASAL LEAVES   Palmately lobed, segments deeply cleft into oblong or linear lobes.
PERENNIAL
HABITAT   Fields, meadows, roadsides.
RANGE   Native to Europe; widely introduced throughout region.

Tussilago farfara L.
Coltsfoot
Daisy Family (Asteraceae)

See pl. 10a

BASAL LEAVES   Large, wide, 2–8in (5–20cm), heart-shaped, long-stemmed, with white woolly hairs on underside; leaf edge lightly toothed.
PERENNIAL   From underground stems.
HABITAT   Disturbed areas, waste areas, wood edges.
RANGE   Native to Eurasia; naturalized in ne. U.S. and adjacent Canada.

Chrysanthemum leucanthemum L.
Ox-eye daisy
Daisy Family (Asteraceae)

See pl. 13c

BASAL LEAVES   Lance-shaped, broadest above middle, somewhat lobed or cleft.
PERENNIAL   From underground stems.
HABITAT   Fields, roadsides, waste areas.
RANGE   Native to Eurasia; naturalized throughout most of temperate N. Am.

Plate 1. Smooth Edge

1a. English plantain (*Plantago lanceolata*)

1b. Common plantain (*Plantago major*)

1c. Heal-all (*Prunella vulgaris*)

Plate 2. Smooth edge

2a. Common evening-primrose (*Oenothera biennis*)

2b. Seaside-goldenrod (*Solidago sempervirens*)

2c. Shinleaf (*Pyrola elliptica*)

Plate 3. Smooth edge, finely hairy

3a. Common mullein (*Verbascum thapsus*)

3b. Pussytoes (*Antennaria* spp.)

3c. Black-eyed Susan (*Rudbeckia hirta*)

Plate 4. Smooth edge, finely hairy

4a. Yellow king-devil (*Hieracium caespitosum*)

4b. Bluets (*Hedyotis caerulea*)

Plate 5. Smooth edge, white veins

5a. Spotted wintergreen (*Chimaphila maculata*)

5b. Rattlesnake-plantain (*Goodyera* spp.)

Plate 6. Wavy edges

6a. Great burdock (*Arctium lappa*)

6b. Chicory (*Cichorium intybus*)

Plate7. Wavy edges

7a. Broad dock (*Rumex obtusifolius*)

7b. Curly dock (*Rumex crispus*)

Plate 8. Scalloped edges, palmate veining

8a. Gill-over-the-ground (*Glechoma hederacea*)

8b. Common mallow (*Malva neglecta*)

8c. Garlic-mustard (*Alliaria petiolata*)

Plate 9. Palmately lobed

9a. Common buttercup (*Ranunculus acris*)

9b. Motherwort (*Leonurus cardiaca*)

Plate 10. Leaf edge lightly toothed

10a. Coltsfoot (*Tussilago farfara*)

10b. Pipsissewa (*Chimaphila umbellata*)

Plate 11. Spiny leaves

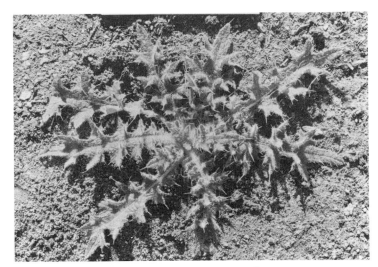

11a. Bull-thistle (*Cirsium vulgare*)

11b. Common teasel (*Dipsacus sylvestris*)

Plate 12. Basal lobes

12a. Yellow rocket (*Barbarea vulgaris*)

12b. Purple avens (*Geum rivale*)

Plate 13. Deeply lobed, pinnatifid

13a. Lousewort (*Pedicularis canadensis*)

13b. Fall-dandelion (*Leontodon autumnalis*)

13c. Ox-eye daisy (*Chrysanthemum leucanthemum*)

Plate 14. Deeply lobed, pinnatifid

14a. Common dandelion (*Taraxacum officinale*)

14b. Shepherd's purse (*Capsella bursa-pastoris*)

Plate 15. Opposite leaflets

15a. Common St. John's-wort (*Hypericum perforatum*)

15b. Speedwell (*Veronica officinalis*)

15c. Pinweed (*Lechea* spp.)

Plate 16. Opposite leaflets

16a. Common chickweed (*Stellaria media*)

16b. Celandine (*Chelidonium majus*)

Plate 17. Trifoliate and cinquefoliate

17a. Strawberry (*Fragaria virginiana*)

17b. Red clover (*Trifolium pratense*)

17c. Dwarf cinquefoil (*Potentilla canadensis*)

Plate 18. Palmately compound leaf and fernlike leaf

18a. Wild lupine (*Lupinus perennis*)

18b. Common yarrow (*Achillea millefolium*)

Plate 19. Finely dissected leaves

19a. Wild carrot (*Daucus carota*)

19b. Common tansy (*Tanacetum vulgare*)

19c. Pineapple weed (*Matricaria matricarioides*)

Chelidonium majus L.
Celandine
Poppy Family (Papaveraceae)

See pl. 16b

BASAL LEAVES   Compound with deeply lobed leaflets. Markedly yellow juice when stem is broken.
BIENNIAL
HABITAT   Moist soil.
RANGE   Native to Eurasia; well established from Que. to Iowa, south to Ga. and Mo.

Fragaria virginiana Duchesne
Wild strawberry
Rose Family (Rosaceae)

See pl. 17a

BASAL LEAVES   3 leaflets, toothed.
PERENNIAL
HABITAT   Open fields.
RANGE   Throughout much of U.S. and s. Canada.

Potentilla canadensis L.
Dwarf cinquefoil
Rose Family (Rosaceae)

See pl. 17c

BASAL LEAVES   5 leaflets, oval, wider at upper end, toothed. More wedge-shaped than in *P. simplex.*
PERENNIAL   From short underground stems.
HABITAT   Dry woods, fields.
RANGE   N.S. and N.B., south in coastal states to Ga., inland to s. Ont., s. Ohio, and e. Tenn.

Plants Bearing Fruits with Barbs, Burs, Needles, or Spines and Stems without Spines or Bristles

See also *Osmorhiza claytonii* p. 150, *Aralia hispida* p. 154, Daisy Family (Asteraceae) p. 206

Datura stramonium L.
Jimson-weed, thorn apple
Nightshade Family (Solanaceae)

KEY IMPRESSIONS Varies in size from 6–8in (15–20cm) to 5ft (1.5m). Fruits erect, spiny capsules on short stems in branch axils. All parts narcotic and poisonous.

FRUIT 4-chambered, sub-globular capsule covered with spines, opening in 4 parts longitudinally by valves. Lacy membrane divides sections. Calyx leaves collar under fruit. Seeds numerous, 2.5–3mm, black, flat, ear-shaped, with wavy margins. Surfaces broadly wrinkled, with network of veins.

LEAVES Alternate, ovate, angular-toothed.

STEM Stout, hollow, opposite branched.

ANNUAL

HABITAT Varied; barnyards, roadsides, seashores, waste areas.

RANGE Throughout region.

Circaea lutetiana L. (*C. quadrisulcata*)
Enchanter's nightshade
Evening-primrose Family (Onagraceae)

KEY IMPRESSIONS Grows to 3ft (1m). Plant of woodland patches. Fruits numerous, in terminal racemes up to 10in (25cm). Fruits covered with hooked bristles.

FRUIT Capsules grow to 6mm, oval, teardrop-shaped. Surface has 3–5 ridges covered with stiff, hooked little bristles. Chambers 1-seeded, indehiscent.

LEAVES Opposite, petioled, oblong to ovate, undulate.

STEM Firm, glabrous below.

PERENNIAL From slender horizontal underground stem and narrow aboveground stolons, forming patches.

HABITAT Rich woods, thickets, ravines.

RANGE Que. and N.B. to N.Dak., south to N.C., Tenn., and Okla.

Agrimonia L. spp.
Agrimony
Rose Family (Rosaceae)

KEY IMPRESSIONS Grows to 3ft (1m). Plant of open woods. Terminates in spikelike racemes bearing turbinate (top-shaped) fruit structures topped by hooked bristles.

FRUIT Capsule turbinate. The outer part, dried calyx tube, is grooved and topped by hooked bristles. Each pointed tip consists of closed sepals containing 1–2 achenes.

LEAVES Alternate, with stipules, toothed, pinnately compound.

STEM Usually hairy.

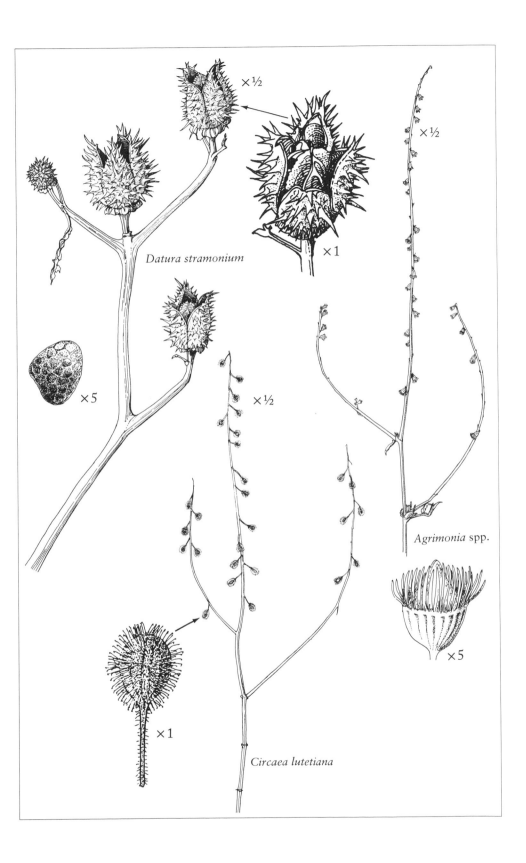

×½

×1

Datura stramonium

×5

×½

×½

Agrimonia spp.

×½

×5

×1

Circaea lutetiana

PERENNIAL   From stout underground stems with fibrous roots on tuberous thickenings.
HABITAT   Thickets, open woods.
RANGE   Most of region.

Geum canadense Jacq.
White avens
Rose Family (Rosaceae)

KEY IMPRESSIONS   Grows 18–30in (45–75cm). Numerous hooked fruits cluster on bristly, ovoid receptacle, snagging passersby.
FRUIT   Achenes tipped by long, persistent hooked styles.
LEAVES   Commonly with 3 oval leaflets.
STEM   Slender, smooth.
PERENNIAL   From underground stems.
HABITAT   Wood edges, thickets.
RANGE   N.S. to Minn. and S.Dak., south to Ga. and Tex.
SIMILAR SPECIES

See pl. 12b. There are a number of species of *Geum*, variable as to foliage but closely resembling each other in the fruiting body.

Arctium minus Schk.
Common burdock
Daisy Family (Asteraceae)

KEY IMPRESSIONS   Grows 2–4ft (.6–1.2cm) wide and 2–5ft (.6–1.5m) tall. Large, widely branching and bushy, full of burs.
FRUIT   Achene, 4.6–6mm, 5-angled, ribbed, elongated, dark, mottled, topped by pappus of numerous short scales. Achenes set in densely bristly receptacle subtended by bracts with protruding hooked bristles, making a round sticky bur.
LEAVES   Oval, large, to 18in (46cm), alternate. Basal rosette in first year.
STEM   Hollow, unfurrowed.
BIENNIAL, SOMETIMES PERENNIAL   From deep, thick taproot to 1ft (30cm). Starchy and edible in first year, tough and woody in second.
HABITAT   Waste areas.
RANGE   Native to Eurasia; widespread throughout region.
SIMILAR SPECIES

A. lappa L.   Great burdock. See pl. 6a. Grows 4–9ft (1.3–3m). Burs few, in flat-topped clusters, much larger than *A. minus*, 1–1½in (3–4.5cm), on long petioles. Lower leaves have solid petioles with upper-surface groove. Roadsides, waste areas. Widespread in chiefly calcareous soil.

A. tomentosum Miller   Woolly burdock. Burs on long, hollow stems. Differs from *A. lappa* in having fine-hair webbing on prickly bracts. Waste areas. Sparingly established, N.H. to D.C., sometimes inland.

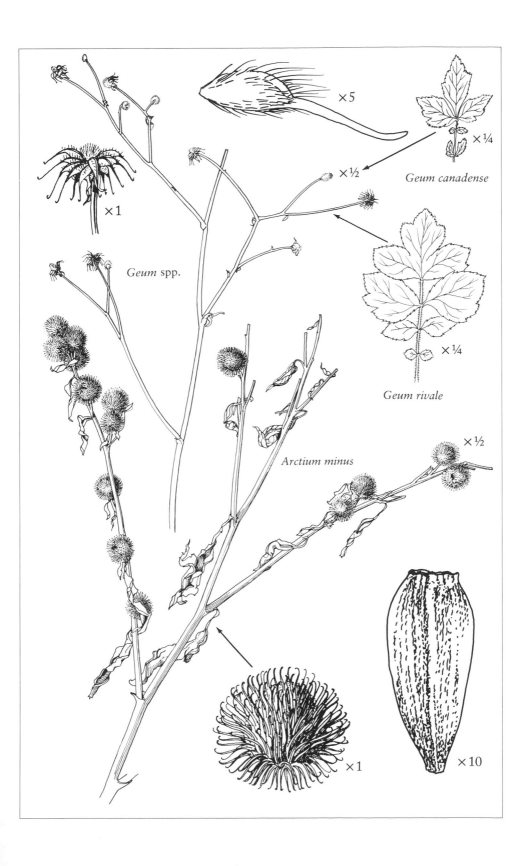

×5

×¼

Geum canadense

×½

×1

Geum spp.

×¼

Geum rivale

×½

Arctium minus

×1

×10

Sanicula marilandica L.

Black snakeroot

Carrot Family (Apiaceae)

KEY IMPRESSIONS   Grows 1–2ft (30–60cm). Fruits terminal, densely covered with hooked bristles. Inflorescence an irregular umbel with branches of uneven length.

FRUIT   Nearly sessile, 4–6mm, ovoid, slightly flattened, densely covered with hooked bristles sometimes arranged in definite rows. Bristles shorter toward base. Styles recurved, exceeding bristles.

LEAVES   Alternate, long-stemmed, palmately divided into 5 leaflets (lower 2 leaflets cleft).

STEM   Erect, branched at upper ends.

BIENNIAL OR PERENNIAL   From cluster of fibrous roots.

HABITAT   Moist or dry woods.

RANGE   Most of region.

SIMILAR SPECIES

S. trifoliata E. Bickn.   Beaked sanicle. Fruit ovoid to oblong, with comparatively fewer bristles than *S. marilandica;* sepals exceed bristles, forming conspicuous beak. Leaves 3-parted. Biennial. Moist or dry woods. Vt. to Mich., south to N.C. and Tenn.

Hackelia virginiana (L.) I. M. Johnston

Stickseed, beggar's lice

Borage Family (Boraginaceae)

KEY IMPRESSIONS   Stem to 3ft (1m). Woodland plant, freely branched above, bearing numerous racemes with oval nutlets covered with prickles.

FRUIT   Nutlets; dorsal side 2–3mm, warty, bearing 10–25 erect prickles as well as marginal ones.

LEAVES   Lower leaves oblong, narrowing to stem; upper leaves stemless.

STEM   Erect, hairy, branching toward terminal end.

BIENNIAL

HABITAT   Upland woods.

RANGE   S. Que. to N.Dak., south to Ga., La., and Tex.

Xanthium L. spp.

Cocklebur, clotbur

Daisy Family (Asteraceae)

KEY IMPRESSIONS   Grows 8in–6ft (.2–2m). Bur 1–1½in (3–4.5cm), brown, cylindric, with stiff hooked spines. *X. strumarium* L. has pair of longer incurved horns at apex. *X. spinosum* L. has either no horns at end or 1 short beak. Burs borne in branch axils. (Do not confuse with *Arctium minus*, which has round, not oval, burs at branch tips.) Hooked spines are former bracts of involucre, which completely enclosed 2 flowers. Bur is divided into 2 sections, each containing 1 achene.

FRUIT   2 enclosed achenes, brown to black, broadly ovate, ridged. No pappus.

LEAVES   Alternate. *X. spinosum*, lanceolate. *X. strumarium*, broad.

STEM   Erect, branching.

ANNUAL   From short taproot.

HABITAT   Fields, flood plains, beaches, waste areas.

RANGE   Throughout region.

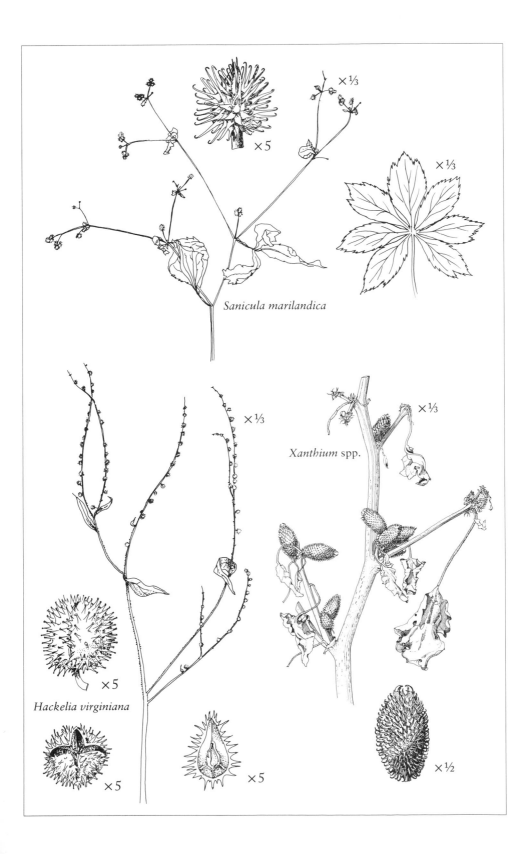

×5

×⅓

×⅓

Sanicula marilandica

×⅓

Xanthium spp.

×⅓

Hackelia virginiana

×5

×5

×5

×½

Bidens L. spp.

Beggar-ticks

Daisy Family (Asteraceae)

KEY IMPRESSIONS   Grows 1–4ft (.3–1.3m). Branching plant headed by numerous achenes that attach themselves to passersby by means of barbed teeth, or awns.

FRUIT   Achenes flat, topped by pappus of 1–8 but usually 2–4 teeth, or awns, often retrosely barbed. Achenes rest on flat receptacle subtended by involucral bracts of 2 types. Outer bracts large, leafy; inner bracts thin, membranous. (In *B. aristosa* outer bracts are shorter than inner.)

LEAVES   Opposite, toothed. Simple, *B. laevis, B. cernua, B. comosa, B. connata*. Tripartite, *B. tripartita*. Once to thrice pinnatifid, *B. frondosa, B. bipinnata, B. coronata, B. aristosa, B. polylepis*

STEM   Smooth, branched.

ANNUAL OR PERENNIAL   From narrow rhizomes with fibrous roots.

HABITAT   Swamps, wet meadows, low wet areas, waste areas.

RANGE   Throughout region.

Desmodium Desv. spp.

Tick-trefoil, tick-clover

Pea or Bean Family (Fabaceae)

KEY IMPRESSIONS   Species numerous, sometimes difficult to distinguish. Fruits called loments, are segmented into sections and covered with hooked hairs that stick to passersby. Inflorescences are elongated axillary or terminal racemes.

FRUIT   Pods, or loments, composed of transversely segmented sections that separate into 1-seeded indehiscent joints. Loments usually covered with hooked hairs and elevated on stipe above persistent calyx. 1 lima bean–shaped seed per section.

LEAVES   Alternate, with stems, pinnate with 3 leaflets.

STEM   Erect, branched.

PERENNIAL

HABITAT   Dry sandy woods, meadows, thickets.

SPECIES

a. *D. canadense* (L.) DC.   Canadian tick-trefoil, showy tick-trefoil. Grows 2–6ft (.6–2m). Racemes terminal, densely fruited. Seedpods hairy, 3–5-jointed. Leaves have 3 oblong leaflets. Open woods, wood edges. Sask., N.S., south to Mo., Ill., Ohio, and Md.

b. *D. canescens* (L.) DC.   Hoary tick-trefoil. Grows 3–5ft (1–1.5m). Much branched. Often sticky. Racemes branch from upper leaf axils. Seedpods usually 4–6-jointed, hairy, semi-rhomboidal. Leaflets ovate. Woods, sandy soil. Sw. Ont. to w. Mass., and south.

c. *D. ciliare* (Muhl.) DC.   Small-leaved tick-trefoil. Grows 1–3ft (.3–1m). Terminal panicle of elongate racemes. Seedpods 1–3-jointed, hairy, obliquely ovate. Leaflets ovate-oblong, very blunt. Stem and petioles pubescent. (Similar species, *D. marilandicum,* is smooth.) Dry or sandy soil. Okla., Mich., Ind., N.Y., Mass., and south.

d. *D. cuspidatum* (Muhl.) Loudon.   Large-bracted tick-trefoil. Grows 1–4ft (.3–1.3m). Inflorescence a simple raceme. Seedpods 3–7-jointed, rhomboidal, hairy. Terminal leaflets ovate; lateral leaflets oval to lance-shaped. Dry upland woods, thickets. S. Wis., Mich., to Vt., N.H., and south.

e. *D. glutinosum* (Muhl.) Wood.   Pointed-leaved tick-trefoil. Grows 1–4ft (.3–1.3m). Leaves in whorl at tip of short stem from which slender racemes of fruit stalks arise. Seedpods seldom more than 3-jointed, hairy. Terminal leaflets round-ovate; lateral leaflets asymmetrically ovate. Rich woods. Minn., sw. Que., Maine, and south.

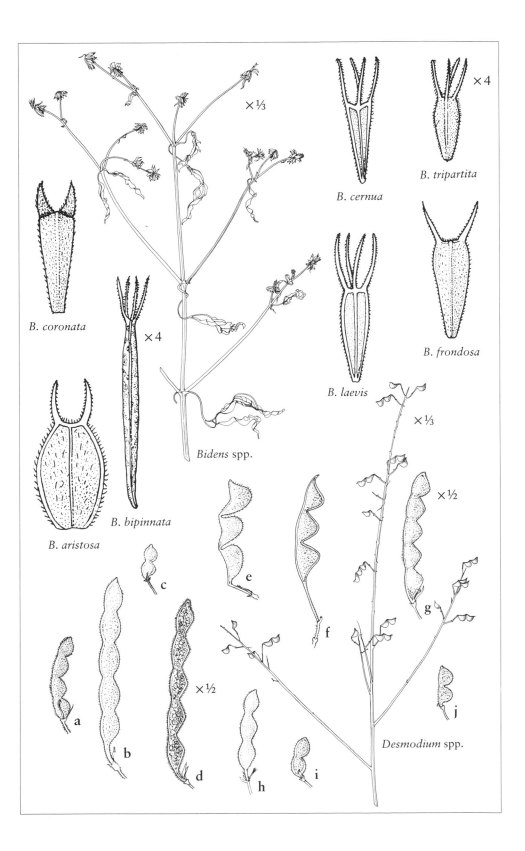

×⅓

B. cernua

×4

B. tripartita

B. coronata

×4

B. laevis

B. frondosa

B. bipinnata

B. aristosa

Bidens spp.

×⅓

×½

c

e

f

g

a

b

d

×½

h

i

j

Desmodium spp.

f. *D. nudiflorum* (L.) DC.   Naked-flowered tick-trefoil. Fruiting stalk leafless, 18–36in (45–90cm). Leaves in whorl at top of shorter (6–8in) separate stalk. Seedpods 2–4-jointed, semi-oval. Terminal leaflet elliptic; lateral leaflets ovate-oblong. Rich woods. Minn. to Que., s. Maine, and south.

g. *D. paniculatum* (L.) DC.   Panicled tick-trefoil. Grows 1–4ft (.3–1.3m). Large, much-branched terminal panicle. Seedpods 3–6-jointed, triangular in outline. Leaflets linear on long stems. Dry woods, clearings. Mich., Ont., s. Maine, and south.

h. *D. rotundifolium* DC.   Prostrate tick-trefoil. Plant prostrate, trailing. Racemes very loose, open. Seedpods 2–5-jointed, pubescent. Leaflets rotund, broadly oval. Dry woods, barrens. Mich., s. Ont., N.Y., c. New Eng., and south.

i. *D. sessilifolium* (Torr.) T. & G.   Sessile tick-trefoil. Grows 1–5ft (.3–1.5m). Panicle large, of several ascending branches. Seedpods 1–3-jointed, convex above, rounded below, hairy. Leaflets oblong to linear oblong. Dry or sterile soil. Ill., Mich., s. Ont., se. Mass., and south.

j. *D. strictum* (Pursh.) DC.   Stiff tick-trefoil. Erect, grows to 4ft (1.3m). Panicle with several ascending branches. Seedpods 1–2-jointed, rarely 3-jointed, rounded on lower margin, flat or slightly concave on upper. Coastal pine barrens. N.J. and south.

Plants Having Stems with Spines, Bristles, or Prickles

See also *Salsola kali* p. 14, *Solanum carolinense* p. 104, *Cirsium* spp. p. 204, *Carduus nutans* p. 204

Echium vulgare L.
Viper's bugloss, blue-weed
Borage Family (Boraginaceae)

KEY IMPRESSIONS   Grows to 3ft (1m), with curved snakelike branches. Bristly hairs cover plant. Long, pointed bracts along 1 side of each branch. Branches coil at first but straighten with age.
FRUIT   4 separating 3-angled basal nutlets fixed on flat receptacle. Nutlet coating roughened, wrinkled.
LEAVES   Alternate, linear to lance-shaped, toothless.
STEM   Covered with bristly hairs that feel prickly.
BIENNIAL   From taproot.
HABITAT   Waste areas, roadsides, meadows.
RANGE   Native to Europe; throughout region.

Dipsacus sylvestris Hudson
Common teasel, wild teasel
Teasel Family (Dipsacaceae)
See pl. 11b

KEY IMPRESSIONS   Grows 2–6ft (.6–3m). Prickly involucral bracts under dense heads that taper into long, flexible bristles with a straight point surpassing the head. Heads ¾–4in (3–10cm), cylindric, dense, terminating long, naked stems.
FRUIT   1-chambered with 1 ovule.

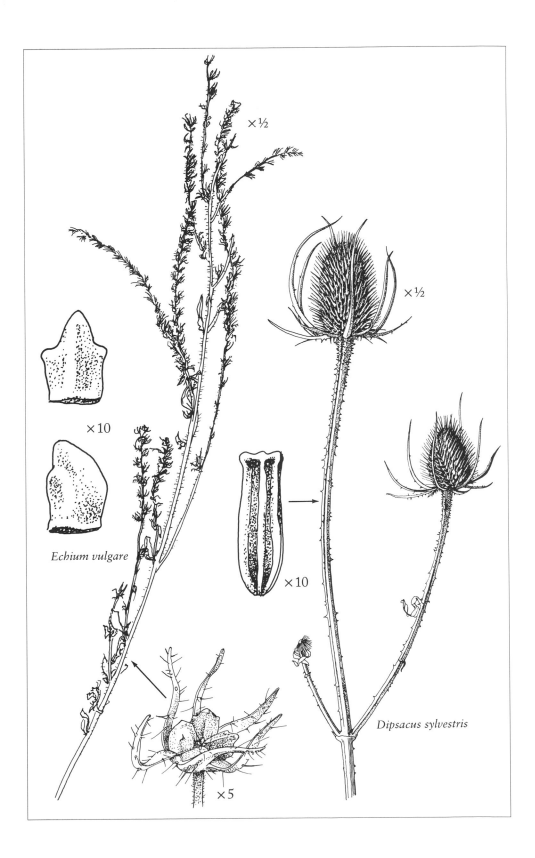

×½

×10

Echium vulgare

×10

×½

Dipsacus sylvestris

×5

LEAVES Opposite, entire, embracing stem, prickly on midvein beneath.
STEM Stout, erect, prickly.
BIENNIAL OR PERENNIAL
HABITAT Roadsides, waste areas.
RANGE Native to Europe; naturalized from Mich. and Ont. to w. New Eng. and south.
SIMILAR SPECIES

> *D. laciniatus* L. Similar to *D. sylvestris* but leaves coarsely lobed, bases forming cup around stem. Waste areas. Mich. to Mass.

Polygonum sagittatum L.
Arrow-leaved tearthumb
Smartweed Family (Polygonaceae)

KEY IMPRESSIONS Grows 3–6ft (1–2m). Plant of wet areas. Erect when young, reclining on other plants when older. Stems 4-angled with reflexed prickles along them.
FRUIT Achenes 3mm, 3-angled.
LEAVES Arrow-shaped, toothless.
STEM Mostly reclining, with reflexed prickles.
ANNUAL
HABITAT Marshes, wet meadows, pond banks.
RANGE Nfld. and Que., south to Ga. and Tex.
SIMILAR SPECIES

> *P. arifolium* L. Halberd-leaved tearthumb. Similar to *P. sagittatum* but even spinier. Leaves wider, with flaring basal lobes. Achenes lens-shaped. Marshes, swamps, wet meadows. N.B. to Minn., south to Ga. and Mo.

Opuntia humifusa (Raf.) Raf.
Eastern prickly pear
Cactus Family (Cactaceae)

KEY IMPRESSIONS Prostrate or spreading, forming large mats. Plant body consists of enlarged succulent stems; leaves scarcely developed. Oblong stems branched, jointed, and flattened. Stem surface contains areoles (clear round areas) 10–25mm apart. Areoles mostly spineless; occasionally 1 or rarely 2 spines.
FRUIT Red or purple pulpy berry. Seeds disk-shaped, with wavy, regular margin.
PERENNIAL From mostly fibrous roots.
HABITAT Rocks, shores, sand dunes, sandy prairies.
RANGE E. Mass. to s. Ont. and s. Minn., south to Fla. and Tex.
SIMILAR SPECIES

> *O. macrorhiza* Engelm. Plains prickly pear. Very similar to *O. humifusa* in habit and structure, differing in production of tuberous-thickened roots. Areole usually not spined but sometimes bearing as many as 3. Seeds disk-shaped, with irregular, corky margins. Prairies, plains. S.Dak. to Ariz. and Tex. and occasionally east.
>
> *O. fragilis* (Nutt.) Haw. Little prickly pear. Lower-growing than *O. humifusa* and *O. macrorhiza*. Areoles crowded, usually coarsely white-woolly, nearly all armed with 3–7 strongly barbed spines. Dry prairies, plains. Ill., Wis., and n. Mich. to B.C., n. Tex., and Ariz.

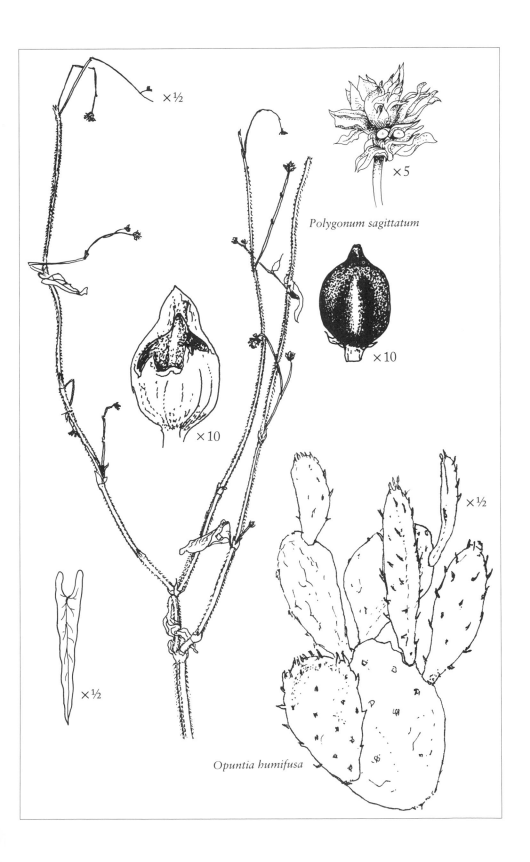

×½

Polygonum sagittatum

×5

×10

×10

×½

×½

Opuntia humifusa

Plants with Small and Delicate Remnants

See also *Hypericum gentianoides* p. 94, *Agalinis tenuifolia* p. 72

Linaria canadensis (L.) Dum.-Cours.

Blue toadflax, old field toadflax, annual toadflax

Figwort Family (Scrophulariaceae)

KEY IMPRESSIONS   Grows to 18in (45.5cm). Slender, delicate plant. Erect, single stem has small fruit capsules along terminal end.

FRUIT   Capsules 3–4mm diameter, 2-chambered, round. Seeds tiny, .5mm, black, ribbed, wedge-shaped, with bumps on apex and along sides.

LEAVES   Linear, alternate.

STEM   Erect, single.

ANNUAL   From short taproot.

HABITAT   Mostly in sandy soil.

RANGE   Mass. and Que. to Minn., south to Fla. and Mexico.

Polygonella articulata (L.) Meissner

Jointweed

Smartweed Family (Polygonaceae)

KEY IMPRESSIONS   Grows to 2ft (61cm). Slender, wiry, reddish brown, freely branching. Branches appear articulated on terminal ends owing to fine remnants of square-shaped bracts that had subtended flowers. Long ocrea tips appear serrated.

FRUIT   Achenes 2–2.5mm, shiny brown, 3-angled, usually dispersed early.

LEAVES   Narrow, rolled under.

STEM   Erect, freely branching, wiry, reddish brown, alternate.

ANNUAL

HABITAT   Dry, acid, sandy soil, heathlike areas.

RANGE   Maine and s. Que. to N.C. Found mostly on coastal plain, Great Lakes shores, and inland dunes.

Lechea L. spp.

Pinweed

Rock-rose Family (Cistaceae)

See pl. 15c

KEY IMPRESSIONS   Grows 4in–1½ft (10–46cm). Capsules tiny, 3-parted, terminating many branches, looking like pinheads from a distance, hence "pinweed."

FRUIT   Capsules 3-valved, mostly enclosed by persistent calyx. 1–6 boat-shaped seeds.

LEAVES   Numerous, tiny, linear. Basal leaves shiny, leathery.

STEM   Single basal stem, much branched above.

PERENNIAL

HABITAT   Dry sandy soil.

RANGE   Throughout region.

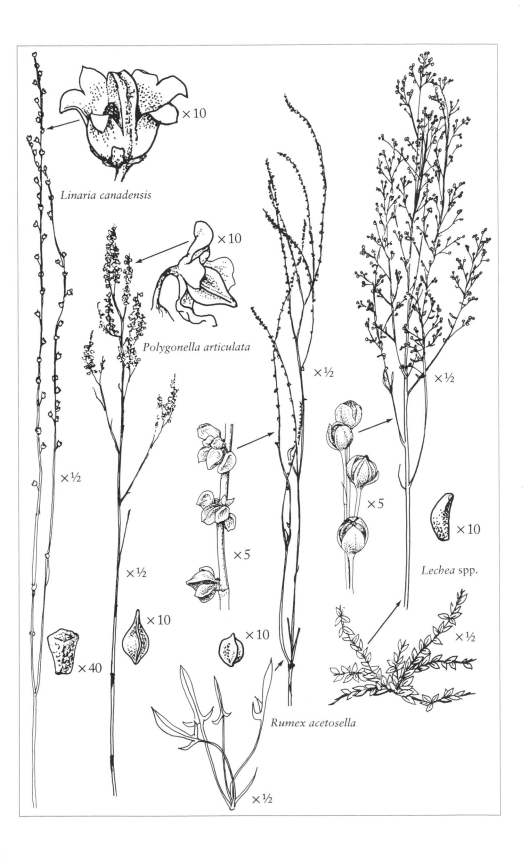

Linaria canadensis ×10

Polygonella articulata ×10

Lechea spp. ×10

Rumex acetosella

Rumex acetosella L.

Red sorrel, sheep sorrel

Smartweed Family (Polygonaceae)

KEY IMPRESSIONS Grows 4–12in (10–30cm). Dioecious; flower and fruit remnants may be half the length of shoot. Fruits turn from green to dark red-brown, growing in erect panicles. Plant grows prostrate, producing stolons.

FRUIT Male and female plants (dioecious). Achenes minute, 1–1.3mm, golden brown, glossy, oval with pointed apex, 3-angled in cross-section. Calyx at first attaches to achene but is soon diverted.

LEAVES Alternate, arrow-shaped, with spreading basal lobes (hastate).

STEM Erect.

PERENNIAL From slender creeping roots.

HABITAT Roadsides, fields, acid soil.

RANGE Native to Eurasia; throughout region.

Mint Family (Lamiaceae)

The Mint Family (Lamiaceae) has a number of easily identifiable characters even in winter. The branching is opposite, the stems are generally square, and the calyx remains on the stem after the petals have fallen. The calyx is tubular and lobed. The calyxes of the species included in these pages are depicted below.

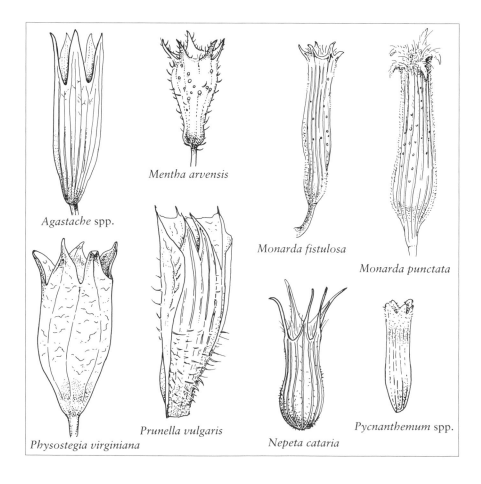

Agastache spp.

Mentha arvensis

Monarda fistulosa

Monarda punctata

Physostegia virginiana

Prunella vulgaris

Nepeta cataria

Pycnanthemum spp.

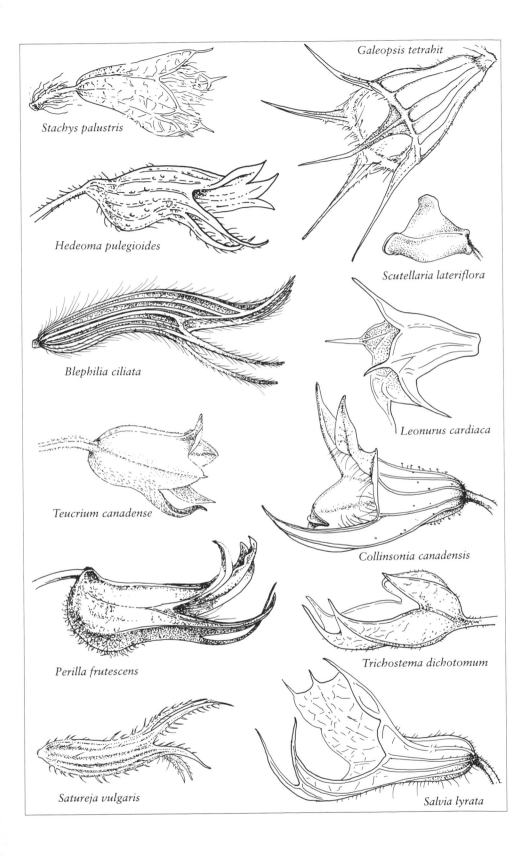

Galeopsis tetrahit

Stachys palustris

Hedeoma pulegioides

Scutellaria lateriflora

Blephilia ciliata

Leonurus cardiaca

Teucrium canadense

Collinsonia canadensis

Perilla frutescens

Trichostema dichotomum

Satureja vulgaris

Salvia lyrata

Plants with Opposite Branches and Leaves, Square Stems, and Flower and Fruit Remnants in Terminal Clusters, Spikes, or Panicles

See also *Silphium perfoliatum* p. 202, *Lysimachia terrestris* p. 96

Agastache Clayton spp.
Giant hyssop
Mint Family (Lamiaceae)

KEY IMPRESSIONS Grows 2–5 ft (.61–1.5m). Crowded clusters of flower remnants form many terminal continuous spikes (*A. nepetoides* [L.] Kuntze, catnip giant-hyssop, and *A. scrophulariifolia* [Willd.] Kuntze, purple giant-hyssop) or interrupted spikes (*A. foeniculum* [Pursh.] Kuntze, lavender giant-hyssop). Calyx nearly regular, cylindric, 15-nerved, tube slightly longer on upper side, 3-nerved lobes similar in size and shape. *A. nepetoides,* calyx lobes oval. *A. scrophulariifolia,* calyx lobes triangular to lance-shaped.
FRUIT Nutlets minutely hairy at apical end.
LEAVES Oval, acute, coarsely toothed, stemmed.
STEM Erect, branched.
PERENNIAL
HABITAT AND RANGE *A. nepetoides,* thickets, wood edges; Vt. to s. Ont., Wis., and Nebr., south to Ga. and Ark. *A. scrophuliariifolia,* upland woods; Vt. and N.Y. to Wis. and S.Dak., south to N.C., Ky., and Mo. *A. foeniculum,* dry upland woods, prairies; prairie states, locally eastward.

Monarda fistulosa L.
Monarda didyma L.
Bee-balm, Oswego-tea, wild bergamot
Mint Family (Lamiaceae)

KEY IMPRESSIONS Grow to 4½ft (1.4m). Dried calyx tubes are crowded into dense, rounded heads usually at top of stalk. Calyx tube regular, tubular, 13–15-nerved; 5 lobes alike or nearly so. Crushed heads are odorous.
FRUIT Nutlets, oblong, smooth.
LEAVES Lance-shaped to oval, toothed, larger on stems.
STEM Erect, simple or branched.
ANNUAL OR PERENNIAL Forming expanding patches and clumps.
HABITAT Varied; old fields, moist woods, thickets, prairies.
RANGE *M. didyma,* Maine to Mich., south to N.J., W.Va., and Ohio. *M. fistulosa,* Que. to Man., south to Ga., La., Tex., and Ariz.

Nepeta cataria L.
Catnip, catmint
Mint Family (Lamiaceae)

KEY IMPRESSIONS Grows to 3ft (1m). Stems much branched; branches decussate. Flower remnants tightly clustered, either continuous or interrupted along terminal stems. Calyx 15-nerved, tubular, weakly 2-lipped.
FRUIT Small nutlets, dark reddish brown, oval, with 2 white spots at base of 1 face.
LEAVES Deltoid, toothed, stemmed. Basal rosette in winter.

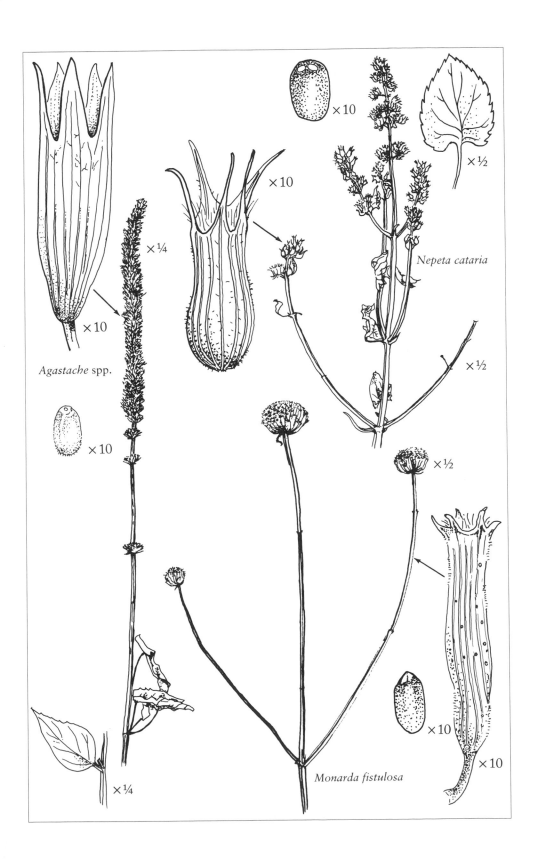

×10

×10

×½

Agastache spp.

×¼

×10

×10

Nepeta cataria

×½

×½

Monarda fistulosa

×10

×10

×¼

STEM   Erect, much branched.

PERENNIAL

HABITAT   Waste areas, roadsides.

RANGE   Native to Eurasia; found throughout region.

Scutellaria lateriflora L.
Mad-dog skullcap
Mint Family (Lamiaceae)

KEY IMPRESSIONS   Grows 1–2ft (30–60cm). Often branched with long racemes. Dried calyx has 2 distinct equal-sized halves, with smooth, not toothed, edges. Upper half has a little hump and falls off easily; bottom half remains, looking like a little scoop. Calyx lobes triangular, about equal in size. Calyxes are found in pairs along stalk.

FRUIT   4 pitted nutlets elevated above flower base.

LEAVES   Opposite, oval, toothed, stemmed.

STEM   Erect, square, branched.

PERENNIAL   From slender underground stems and stolons.

HABITAT   Wet thickets, meadows, wet woods.

RANGE   Que. to B.C., south to Fla., La., and Ariz.

SIMILAR SPECIES

There are many species of *Scutellaria*. Leaf shape and whether flowers are in racemes or solitary in leaf axils vary, but all species have the distinctive calyx remnant described for *S. laterifolia*.

Stachys palustris L.
Hedge-nettle, woundwort
Mint Family (Lamiaceae)

KEY IMPRESSIONS   Grows 2–3ft (.6–1m). Flower remnants in interrupted whorls along upper stem. Calyx tube densely downy, bell-shaped, nearly regular, 5–10-nerved. Calyx lobes nearly triangular, tapering to stiff pointed tip. Stem downy.

LEAVES   Oblong to oval, sharply toothed, stemless, downy on both sides.

STEM   Erect, downy, rarely branched.

PERENNIAL

HABITAT   Ditches, wet ground, low meadows, shores.

RANGE   Canada and n. U.S.

SIMILAR SPECIES

S. tenuifolia Willd.   Smooth hedge-nettle. Grows 2–4ft (.6–1.2m). Flower remnants similar to those of *S. palustris*. Calyx tube smooth. Leaves usually on stems. Stem bristly only on angles. Moist shaded soil, low woods, shores. N.Y. to Mich. and Minn., south to S.C., Ala., La., and Tex.

Collinsonia canadensis L.
Horse-balm, stone-root, knob-root
Mint Family (Lamiaceae)

KEY IMPRESSIONS   Grows to 3½ft (1.2m). Large plant with calyxes on terminal panicled branches. Calyx 15-nerved, borne on short stalk, with 5 teeth. 3 upper teeth short and

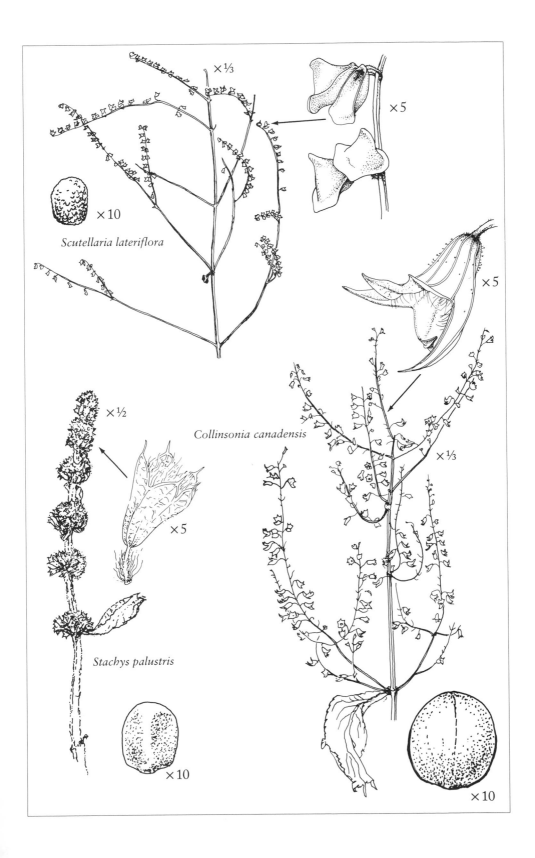

×⅓

×5

×10

Scutellaria lateriflora

×5

Collinsonia canadensis

×⅓

×½

×5

Stachys palustris

×10

×10

pointed; 2 lower teeth long, almost crossing each other. Stem vaguely square, may appear round.

FRUIT Nutlet usually solitary, round, smooth.

LEAVES Opposite, large, oval, toothed, stemmed.

STEM Vaguely square, not sharp-cornered, branched.

PERENNIAL From large, knobby, hard underground stem, hence the names "stone-root" and "knob-root."

HABITAT Rich woods.

RANGE Que. and Ont. to Mich., south to Fla.

Prunella vulgaris L.
Self-heal, heal-all
Mint Family (Lamiaceae)

See pl. 1c

KEY IMPRESSIONS Usually grows to several inches but can reach 2ft (60cm). Calyxes hairy, in spike at stem tip. Calyx an irregular tube, deeply 2-lipped, upper tip about equaling the tube and barely 3-lobed. Midveins excurrent as 3 short awns. Lower lip divided into 2 triangular lobes. Hairy, overlapping oval bracts contain 3 flower remnants in bract axils.

FRUIT Nutlets dark brown, oval, with noticeable flat ridge.

LEAVES Toothless, lance-shaped to oval, stemmed.

STEM Simple, erect or creeping.

PERENNIAL

HABITAT Varied; roadsides, waste areas, grasslands.

RANGE Throughout region.

Pycnanthemum Michx. spp.
Mountain-mint
Mint Family (Lamiaceae)

KEY IMPRESSIONS There are many similar species of mountain-mint all characterized by dense whitish heads described here. Grows 1–3ft (.3–1m) with dense heads of small calyx tubes on ends of branched stalks. Calyx tubular, 10–13-nerved, regular- or more or less 2-lipped. Calyx lobes shorter than tube.

FRUIT Nutlets smooth or hairy at summit.

LEAVES Opposite, variable.

STEM Erect, simple or branched.

PERENNIAL From underground stems.

HABITAT Varied; woods, fields, prairies, thickets.

RANGE Throughout region.

Physostegia virginiana (L.) Benth.
False dragonhead, obedience plant
Mint Family (Lamiaceae)

KEY IMPRESSIONS Grows 1–4ft (.3–1.3m). Flower remnants form an elongate terminal spike. Calyx regular, bell-shaped or nearly tubular, 10-nerved. Calyx lobes triangular, acute.

FRUIT Nutlets elliptic, angled.

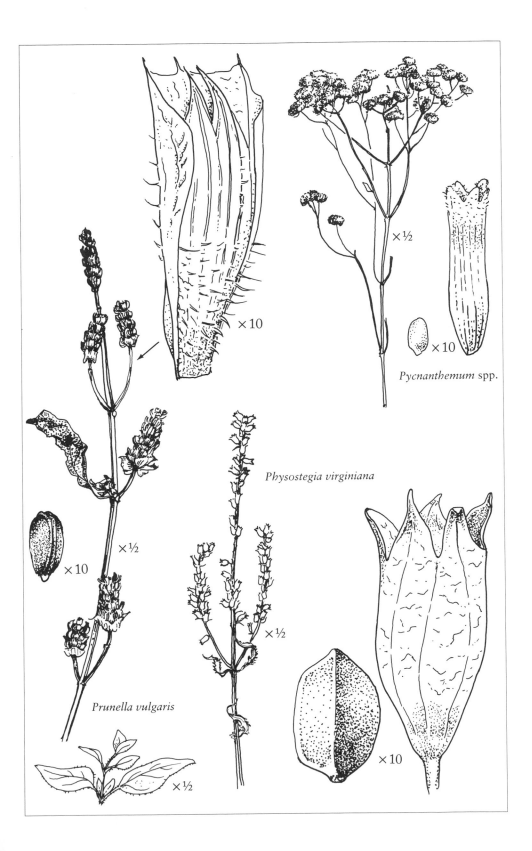

×10

×½

×10

Pycnanthemum spp.

Physostegia virginiana

×½

×10

×10

×½

×½

Prunella vulgaris

×½

×10

LEAVES   Lance-shaped, acute at apex, sharply toothed, stemless.
STEM   Erect, branched, stout.
PERENNIAL
HABITAT   Moist woods, riverbanks, thickets, prairies.
RANGE   Minn. and s. Que. to Mo. and N.C.

Trichostema dichotomum L.
Blue curls
Mint Family (Lamiaceae)

KEY IMPRESSIONS   Usually grows less than 8in (20cm) though it can reach 2½ft (75cm). Many upcurving decussate branches. Papery calyx with 5 teeth; 3 lower teeth are longer than 2 upper when fruiting, an inversion from flowering position. Branches and stems white.
FRUIT   Nutlets grayish, oval, sculptured with circular reticulations.
LEAVES   Narrow, toothless, stemless.
STEM   Much opposite branching; stiff white glandular hairs.
ANNUAL   From fibrous mats.
HABITAT   Poor sandy soil.
RANGE   Mich. to s. Maine and south.

Teucrium canadense L.
American germander, wood-sage
Mint Family (Lamiaceae)

KEY IMPRESSIONS   Grows 8–36in (20–90cm). Flower remnants grow as raceme at terminal end. Calyx downy, bell-shaped, 10-nerved, 2-lipped. 3 upper lobes wider and blunter than 2 lower.
FRUIT   Nutlets light to dark brown, oblong, covered with a network of veins, coarsely pitted.
LEAVES   Oval to lance-shaped, acute, rounded teeth, stemmed.
STEM   Square, rarely branched.
PERENNIAL   From slender underground stem.
HABITAT   Woods, moist thickets, marshes, shores.
RANGE   Throughout U.S.

Blephilia ciliata (L.) Benth.
Downy wood-mint
Mint Family (Lamiaceae)

KEY IMPRESSIONS   Grows 1–3ft (.3–1m). Inflorescence terminal in whorls separated by row of fringed bracts. Calyx tubular, 13-nerved, distinctly 2-lipped. Calyx lobes narrowly triangular, terminating in a point. Lower calyx lip extends beyond sinuses of upper lip.
FRUIT   4 nutlets.
LEAVES   Oval, toothless or with a few low teeth, mostly stemless.
STEM   Downy.
PERENNIAL
HABITAT   Dry woods, thickets.
RANGE   Mass. to s. Mich. and Wis., south to Ga., Miss., and Ark.

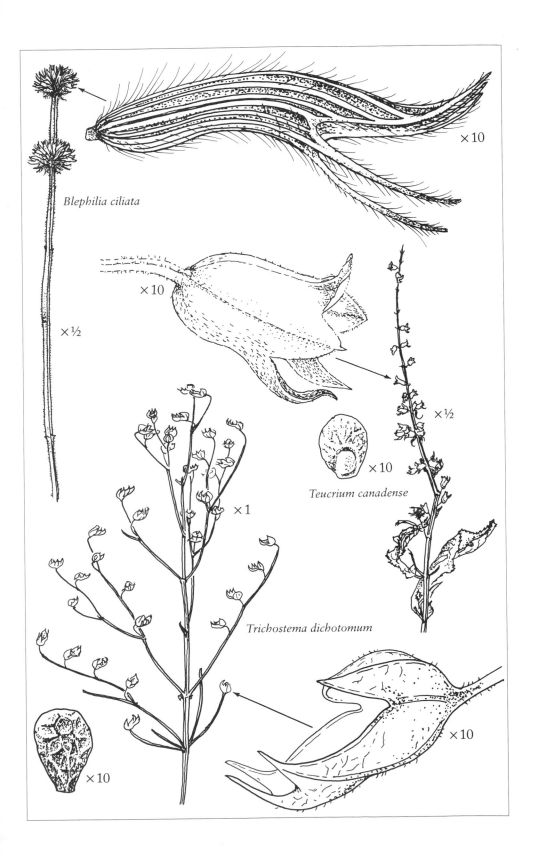

Blephilia ciliata

×10

×½

×10

Teucrium canadense

×10

×½

×1

Trichostema dichotomum

×10

×10

B. hirsuta (Pursh.) Benth. Hairy wood-mint. Similar to *B. ciliata* but with hairy stems. Lobes of lower calyx-lip do not reach sinuses of upper lip. Leaves have stems. Moist shade. Que. to Minn., south to N.C. and Ark.

Perilla frutescens (L.) Britton
Perilla-mint
Mint Family (Lamiaceae)

KEY IMPRESSIONS Grows 1–3ft (.3–1m). Plant erect, much branched, with terminal and axillary racemes that have many calyx remnants. Calyx enlarges when petals are gone, becoming distinctly 2-lipped. Upper lip 3-toothed, lower 2-cleft. Calyx sparsely hairy outside and hairy within.
FRUIT Rounded nutlets.
LEAVES Long-stemmed, broadly oval, coarsely toothed.
STEM Erect, much branched.
ANNUAL
HABITAT Native to India; garden escapee into waste areas, roadsides.
RANGE Mass. to Iowa and Kans., south to Fla. and Tex.

Chelone L. spp.
Turtlehead
Figwort Family (Scrophulariaceae)

KEY IMPRESSIONS Grows to 3½ft (1.2m). 2-chambered capsules cluster in spikes on upper branch parts.
FRUIT 2-parted white capsules look like turtle heads, as did flowers. Oval capsule splits along septum. Seeds numerous, compressed, orb-shaped, and winged.
LEAVES Opposite, oval to lance-shaped, with acute tips, toothed.
STEM Square, opposite, branched or simple.
PERENNIAL
HABITAT Damp areas.
RANGE Across s. Canada to Minn., south to Ga. and Ala.

Agalinis tenuifolia (M. Vahl) Raf. (*Gerardia tenuifolia*)
Slender gerardia
Figwort Family (Scrophulariaceae)

KEY IMPRESSIONS Grows 6–24in (15–60cm). Slight and fragile plant. Stems much branched. Leaves linear. Tiny rounded calyx remains. Calyx has 5 slight teeth.
FRUIT Tiny, fragile, 2-chambered, globose capsules.
LEAVES Opposite, linear, stemless.
STEM Much branched.
ANNUAL With fibrous roots.
HABITAT Dry woods, fields.
RANGE S. Mich. to Maine and south.
SIMILAR SPECIES
There are a number of similar *Agalinis* species. *A. purpurea,* purple gerardia, is a larger version and may reach 4ft (1.3m).

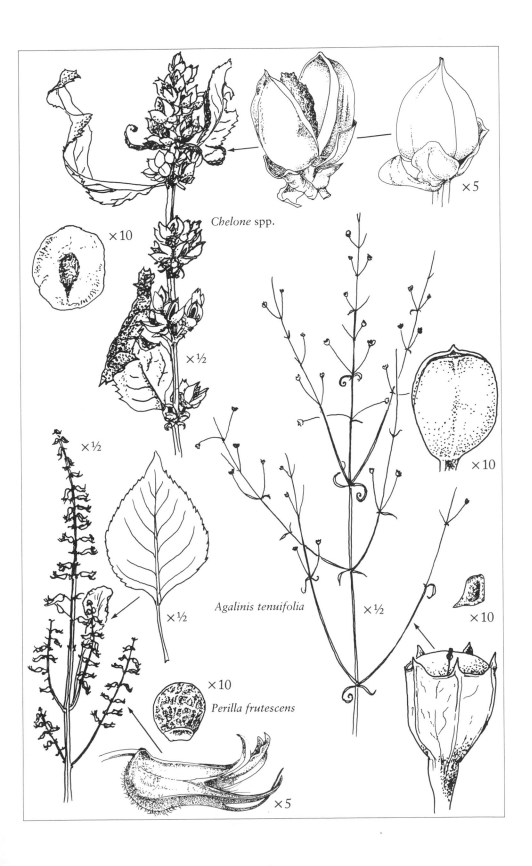

Chelone spp.

×10

×5

×½

×½

Agalinis tenuifolia

×10

×½

×½

×10

×10

Perilla frutescens

×5

Scrophularia lanceolata Pursh
Figwort
Figwort Family (Scrophulariaceae)

KEY IMPRESSIONS   Grows 3–6ft (1–2m). Oval 2-parted capsules on loose terminal branches. Apex of 2 sides of capsule extends upward to an acute point.

FRUIT   Capsules 2-parted, 6–9mm, dull brown, oval, sharply tipped, split along septum. Seeds angular, ridged.

LEAVES   Opposite, lance-shaped; stems with winged margins.

STEM   Square, opposite branched.

PERENNIAL   From underground stems, sometimes with fleshy knobs.

HABITAT   Wood edges, thickets, roadsides.

RANGE   Que. and N.S. to B.C., south to Va., Ind., Mo., Okla., and N.Mex.

Lythrum salicaria L.
Purple loosestrife
Loosestrife Family (Lythraceae)

KEY IMPRESSIONS   Grows 4–6ft (1.3–2m) with candelabra branching. Stems terminate in long fruited spikes (to 1½ft). Fruits enclosed in oblong covering open at apical end (hypanthium). Fruit visible only on dissection. Very invasive plant from Europe.

FRUIT   Small 2-chambered capsules split along septum, in whorls. Capsule enclosed by persistent hypanthium. Fruits disintegrate early, leaving stubs and stalks. About 100 seeds per capsule; up to 900 capsules per plant. Seeds orange, minute, and wind-transported.

LEAVES   Opposite, whorled or spiraled, all on same plant; stemless, lance-shaped, heart-shaped at base.

STEM   Stout, erect, candelabra branching, square.

PERENNIAL   From thick, woody taproot that sends up new stems near original plant. Small reddish buds found at base of flower stalk in winter become new flower stalks in spring.

HABITAT   Wet, open marshes and meadows.

RANGE   Native to Europe; Que. and New Eng. to Mich., south to Md.

SIMILAR SPECIES

L. alatum Pursh   Winged loosestrife. Grows 1–4ft (.3–1.3m). Fruits solitary in most upper axils. Leaves partly alternate. Stem 4-angled. Perennial. Moist or wet soil, especially on prairies. Maine to N.Dak. and se. Wyo., south to Fla. and Tex. and locally elsewhere.

L. hyssopifolia L.   Hyssop-leaved loosestrife, annual loosestrife. Grows 6–24in (16–60cm). Fruits solitary or paired in axils. Leaves linear, alternate. Stem 4-angled, simple or branched. Annual. Salt marshes. Coastal s. Maine to N.J., local in Ohio, Pa.

L. lineare L.   Narrow-leaved loosestrife. Similar to *L. hyssopifolia* but with leaves narrower, opposite. Perennial. Salt marshes. Coastal Long Island and south.

L. virgatum L.   Purple loosestrife. Similar to *L. salicaria* but smooth. Leaves more slender, narrowed to base. Perennial. Established locally in New Eng.

Rhexia virginica L.
Virginia meadow beauty, wing-stem meadow-pitcher
Melastome Family (Melastomaceae)

KEY IMPRESSIONS   Grows 8–24in (20–60cm). Flower remnants urn-shaped, topped by persistent sepals; terminal on numerous branches and also found in the nodes.

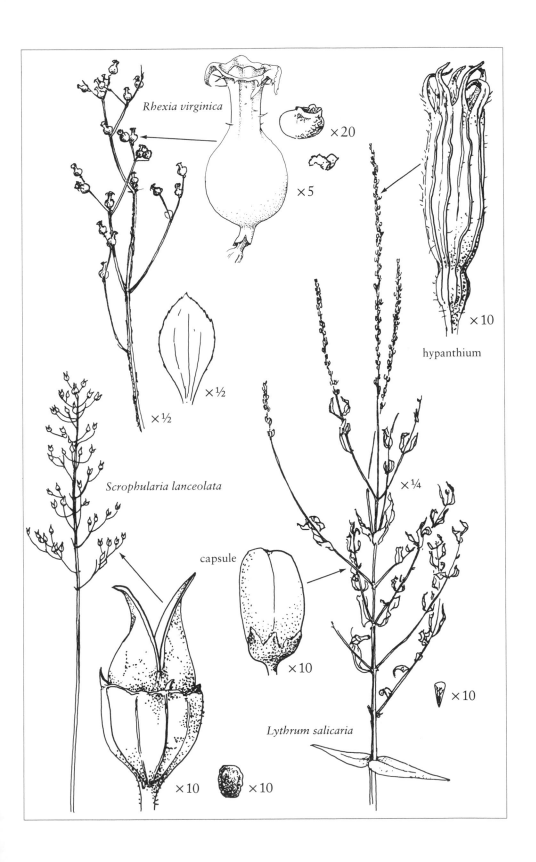

Rhexia virginica

×20

×5

hypanthium

×10

×½

×½

Scrophularia lanceolata

×¼

capsule

×10

×10

Lythrum salicaria

×10

×10

×10

FRUIT Urn-shaped cup surrounds capsule. Basal part is distended by capsule; terminal part is a tubular neck topped by persistent sepals. Seeds coiled, with small peglike projections on surfaces.

LEAVES Opposite, oval, finely toothed, rounded at stemless base.

STEM Subequally quadrangular, faces almost flat, branched; slightly winged.

PERENNIAL From roots that are often thickened.

HABITAT Moist, sandy meadows.

RANGE S. Ont., N.S., and south.

SIMILAR SPECIES

R. mariana L. Maryland meadow-beauty, dull meadow-pitcher. Differs from *R. virginica* in stem shape. Stems unequally quadrangular—one pair of opposing faces broad and convex, the other much narrower, concave. Moist open areas, often in disturbed habitats. Mass. to Fla., west to s. Ind., s. Mo., and Tex.

Verbena urticifolia L.
White vervain
Vervain Family (Verbenaceae)

KEY IMPRESSIONS Grows to 4ft (1.3m). Very slender, long, stiffly ascending spikes form branches at terminal stem ends. Spikes more slender than in *V. hastata*. Fruit remnants not contiguous—separated rather than overlapping.

FRUIT Nutlets 2mm, reddish brown, oblong, partly surrounded by dry calyxes.

LEAVES Nettlelike, stemmed, oblong to lance-shaped, opposite, coarsely toothed.

STEM Square, somewhat hairy, branched at terminal end.

ANNUAL OR PERENNIAL

HABITAT Rich thickets, wood edges, fields, meadows, waste areas.

RANGE Que. and Ont. to Nebr., south to Fla. and west to Okla. and Tex.

Verbena hastata L.
Common vervain, blue vervain
Vervain Family (Verbenaceae)

KEY IMPRESSIONS Grows 1–5ft (.3–1.5m). Fruits on tall erect spikes on branches at terminal stem ends. Spikes usually numerous, short and compact. Branching mostly opposite, sometimes alternate.

FRUITS Groups of 4 linear nutlets, tiny (2mm), enclosed in dry 4-toothed calyx.

LEAVES Opposite, lance-shaped, sharply pointed, coarsely toothed, stemmed.

STEM Square, grooved, hairy, mostly opposite branching, sometimes alternate.

PERENNIAL Grows in patches.

HABITAT Swamps, moist fields, meadows, prairies.

RANGE N.S. to B.C., south to Fla., Nebr., and Ariz.

SIMILAR SPECIES

V. officinalis L. European vervain. Spikes very slender, in branches, 3s or solitary. Lower leaves deeply lobed. Annual. Roadsides, waste areas. Mass and N.Y. south.

V. simplex Lehm. Narrow-leaved vervain. Spikes slender, solitary at stem apex, crowded. Leaves linear, toothed. Perennial. Dry soil; woods, fields, rocky areas, roadsides. Minn., Ont., s. Que., Mass., and south.

V. stricta Vent. Hoary vervain. Spikes solitary or several, long, thick, densely compact. Leaves oval, stemless, toothed. Perennial. Prairies, fields, roadsides. Midwest; introduced in East from Mass. to Del. and W.Va.

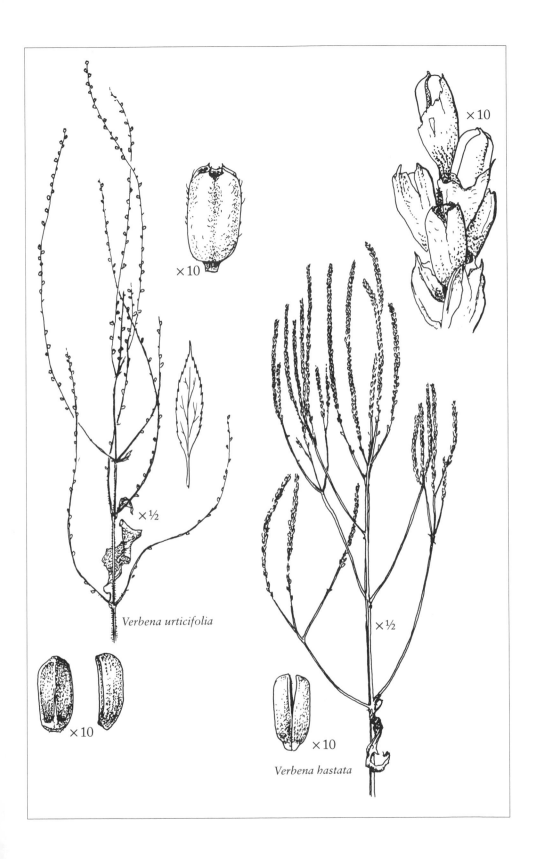

×10

×10

×½

Verbena urticifolia

×10

×½

×10

Verbena hastata

Plants with Opposite Branches and Leaves, Square Stems, and Flower and Fruit Remnants Opposite, Whorled, or in Leaf Axil Clusters along Length of Stem

See also *Scutellaria* spp. p. 66, *Lysimachia quadrifolia* p. 96

Mimulus ringens L.
Allegheny monkey-flower, square-stemmed monkey-flower
Figwort Family (Scrophulariaceae)

KEY IMPRESSIONS Grows to 3ft (1m). There are many fruits on opposite, upcurving stalks. Branching is decussate.

FRUIT Often covered by ribbed calyx that is easily torn, giving ragged appearance. Capsules flattened, 2-parted, with 2 notches at top, found on long, opposite stalks in leaf axils. Capsule walls curve upward at top. Capsules split along midline of chambers. Seeds numerous, cylindric.

LEAVES Opposite, lance-shaped, acute, stemless.

STEM Ridged, grooved on 2 sides, giving square appearance.

PERENNIAL From stoloniferous underground stems.

HABITAT Swamps, wet areas.

RANGE Que. and N.S. to Sask., south to Ga., La., and Okla.

SIMILAR SPECIES

M. alatus Aiton Sharpwing monkey-flower. Fruit capsules on short stalks in leaf axils. Stems square, with thin wings along angles.

Galeopsis tetrahit L.
Hemp-nettle
Mint Family (Lamiaceae)

KEY IMPRESSIONS Grows 1–2ft (30–60cm). Flower remnants in dense clusters in upper leaf axils. Calyx tubes broadly tubular to bell-shaped with 10 conspicuous ribs and usually 10 intermediate ones. Calyx lobes equal and narrowly triangular. Midvein extends out as prominent spine. Swollen area below joints on bristly stem.

FRUITS 4 nutlets, 3–4mm, broadly egg-shaped, smooth.

LEAVES Oval, stemmed, toothed.

STEM Swollen at nodes, bristly, branching.

ANNUAL

HABITAT Roadsides, waste areas, sometimes forests.

RANGE Native to Eurasia; found in Nfld. and Que., south to N.C., W.Va., Ohio, Wis., and Minn.

Hedeoma pulegioides (L.) Pers.
Pennyroyal
Mint Family (Lamiaceae)

KEY IMPRESSIONS Usually grows less than 1ft (30cm). Strong mint smell when crushed. Calyxes in whorls around stems, 5-toothed. 2 lower teeth longer, narrower than upper 3, and slightly hairy. Calyx tubular, 3-ribbed, with resin dots and throat filled with hairs.

FRUIT 4 nutlets, brownish black, smooth, egg-shaped.

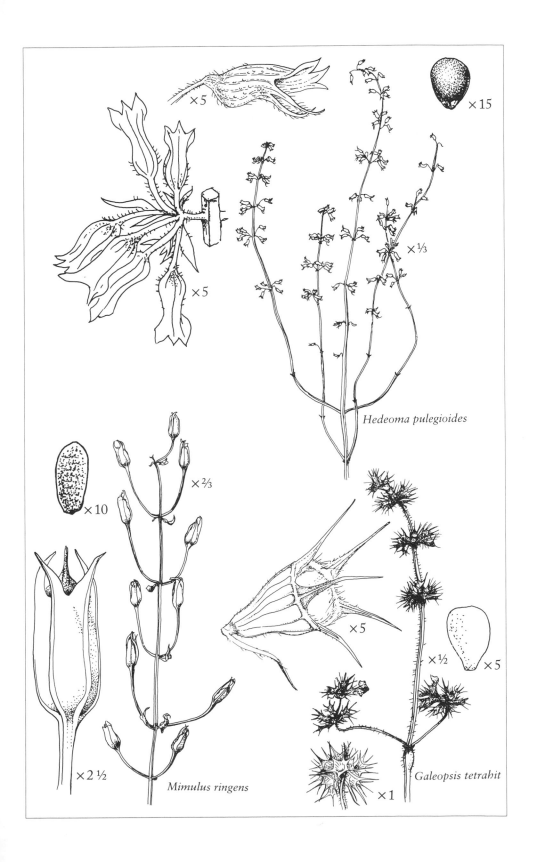

×5

×15

×5

×⅓

Hedeoma pulegioides

×⅔

×10

×5

×½ ×5

×2½

Mimulus ringens

×1

Galeopsis tetrahit

LEAVES Opposite, elliptic, toothless or slightly toothed; principal leaves stemmed.
STEM Erect, branched.
ANNUAL From fibrous roots.
HABITAT Poor dry soil, crushed rock.
RANGE Que. and N.S. to Mich. and S.Dak., south to Ala. and Ark.

Leonurus cardiaca L.
Motherwort
Mint Family (Lamiaceae)

See pl. 9b

KEY IMPRESSIONS Grows to 4½ft (1.3m). Branches erect. Tubular calyxes, 5–10-nerved, in whorls around square stem. Calyxes not hairy, unlike in most mints. 5-angled calyx conspicuous in winter, each lobe drawn out into a very sharp point, with lower 2 points often slightly deflexed.
FRUIT 4 nutlets, dark to reddish brown, pyramidal, 3–4-angled, truncate, hairy at summit, with roughened surfaces.
LEAVES Opposite, long-stemmed. Lower leaves larger, palmately lobed, sharply toothed; upper leaves progressively smaller. Basal rosette overwinters.
STEM Stout, erect, branched.
PERENNIAL
HABITAT Waste areas, clearings, roadsides.
RANGE Native to Asia, formerly cultivated; N.S. to Mont., south to N.C., Tenn., and Tex.

Lycopus virginicus L.
Bugle-weed, Virginia water-horehound
Mint Family (Lamiaceae)

KEY IMPRESSIONS Grows to 3½ft (1.2m). Erect, usually nonbranching. Flower remnants in leaf axils. Dried calyxes look like tufts encircling stem. Calyx bell-shaped and regular. Calyx lobes ovate, erect or somewhat spreading. 4 nutlets protrude beyond calyx base.
FRUIT 4 nutlets, tan, almost flat across summit, with rough, short, hard points, triangular, with 2 inner surfaces covered with gold bumps.
LEAVES Opposite, lance-shaped, toothed, abruptly narrowed to stemlike base.
STEM Erect, square.
PERENNIAL From a few short stolons without tubers.
HABITAT Low grounds, wet shores, western prairies, ditches.
RANGE Nfld. and Que. to B.C., south to Fla., Tex., and s. Calif.
SIMILAR SPECIES
  L. americanus Muhl. Cut-leaved water-horehound, American water-horehound. Grows to 2ft (60cm). Center of set of nutlets depressed because interior angle of nutlet is distinctly shorter than outer angle. Leaves strongly toothed, lobed. Wet soil. N.S. to Que. to Minn., south to Ga., Ark., Ala., and Okla.

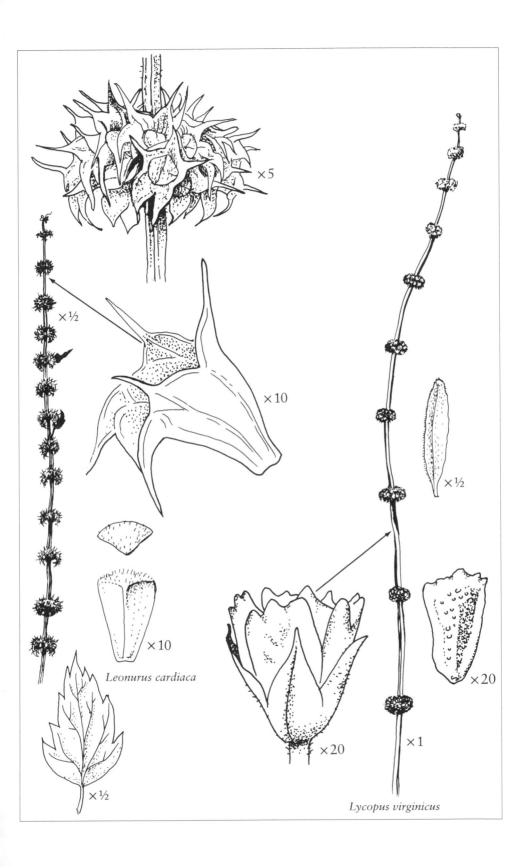

×5

×½

×10

×½

×10

Leonurus cardiaca

×20

×20

×1

×½

×½

Lycopus virginicus

Mentha arvensis L.

Field mint, wild mint

Mint Family (Lamiaceae)

KEY IMPRESSIONS   Grows 6–24in (15–60cm). Floral remnants clustered in leaf axils. Calyx 2–3mm, with short, soft hairs. Calyx lobes narrowly to broadly triangular.

FRUIT   4 egg-shaped nutlets.

LEAVES   Egg-shaped, toothed, stemmed.

STEM   Ascending or erect.

PERENNIAL   From underground stems.

HABITAT   Damp soil, shores.

RANGE   Lab. to Alaska, south to Va. Ky., and Mo., west to Calif.

Monarda punctata L.

Dotted monarda, horse-mint

Mint Family (Lamiaceae)

KEY IMPRESSIONS   Grows 12–40in (.3–1m). Erect, with simple or branched stems. Only *Monarda* with flower remnants both terminal and axillary on stems. Dried tubular calyxes crowded into dense, rounded heads after flowering. Calyxes 6–9mm, with short, narrowly triangular lobes and resin dots. Calyx lobes 1–1.5mm. 4-sectioned receptacle at base of calyx tube.

FRUIT   4 smooth, oblong nutlets within calyx tube.

LEAVES   Opposite, lance-shaped, toothed, stemmed.

STEM   Square, simple or branched.

PERENNIAL   From persistent underground tufted base.

HABITAT   Dry sandy soils on or near coastal plain.

RANGE   N.J. to Fla. and Tex.

Satureja vulgaris (L.) Fritsch.

Wild basil

Mint Family (Lamiaceae)

KEY IMPRESSIONS   Grows to 2ft (60cm). Small plant, all parts hairy. Basal stem creeps as stolon on ground and sends out roots. Runners remain green, usually hidden under dead leaves and grass. Calyxes in dense headlike clusters around stem. Calyx tube prominently 10–13-nerved, lined with hairs, with 5 pointed teeth and 2 distinct lips. Hairy tubes mingle with hairy bracts.

FRUIT   4 nutlets hidden at base of 2-lipped calyx tube.

LEAVES   Basal leaves remain green throughout winter. Look for them under grass and leaves. Leaves elliptic, toothless, stemless or on short stems.

STEM   Ascending, simple or branching, covered with hairs.

PERENNIAL   From short stolons.

HABITAT   Fields, roadsides.

RANGE   Que. to Nfld., south to N.C., Tenn., and Kans.

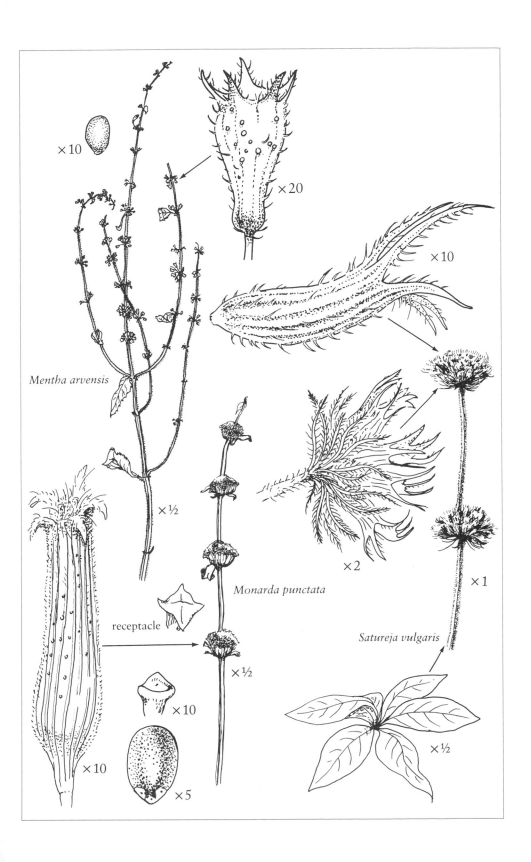

×10

×20

Mentha arvensis

×½

×10

×10

×2

Monarda punctata

×1

receptacle

×½

Satureja vulgaris

×10

×10

×5

×½

Salvia lyrata L.
Lyre-leaved sage
Mint Family (Lamiaceae)

KEY IMPRESSIONS Grows 1–2ft (30–60cm). Calyxes in whorls along length of upper stem. Calyx 10–15-nerved, 2-lipped, with 3 toothed upper lobes and 2 deeply lobed lower lobes.
FRUIT 4 oval nutlets with white dot at base.
LEAVES Principal leaves in basal rosette. Leaves deeply lobed into roundéd segments.
STEM Erect, square.
PERENNIAL
HABITAT Upland woods, thickets.
RANGE Conn. to Pa., s. Ohio, Ill., and Mo., south to Fla. and Tex.

Boehmeria cylindrica (L.) Swartz
False nettle
Nettle Family (Urticaceae)

KEY IMPRESSIONS Grows 1–3ft (.3–1m) in damp soil. Flower remnants minute, in small headlike clusters along upper stems, forming interrupted or continuous spikes.
FRUIT Tiny, oval, minutely winged.
LEAVES Opposite on long stems, egg-shaped, with acute tips, toothed.
STEM Erect, grooved, giving square appearance, unbranched.
PERENNIAL
HABITAT Moist or wet soil, flood plains, relatively rich sites.
RANGE Que. and Ont. to Minn., south to Fla., Tex., and N.Mex.

Plants with Opposite Branching, Round Stems, and Swollen Nodes: Pink Family (Caryophyllaceae)

These plants typically have opposite branching with conspicuous bulges in the stems at the nodes. The leaves have smooth margins. The fruit is a capsule dehiscent at least at the apex by valves or teeth of the same number or twice the number of styles. Capsules have 1–3 chambers with seeds attached to either the base of or the central column. Many pinks have a toothed or notched calyx that dries and often completely surrounds the fruit. The calyx frequently has prominent veins. Most of the genera have kidney-shaped seeds decorated with concentric bumps.
See also *Galeopsis tetrahit* p. 78, which also has swollen nodes.

Dianthus armeria L.
Deptford-pink
Pink Family (Caryophyllaceae)

KEY IMPRESSIONS Grows to 2ft (60cm). Stiff, forked appearance; may fork several times. Topped by branched flower remnants subtended by narrow bracts.
FRUIT Slender capsules with 4 recurved teeth at opening, surrounded by fine-toothed calyx and many bracts. Calyx has long, thin, strongly curved lobes. Seeds black, compressed, usually convex and ventrally concave.
LEAVES Opposite; basal leaves numerous. 5–10 pairs of stem leaves, linear to lance-shaped.

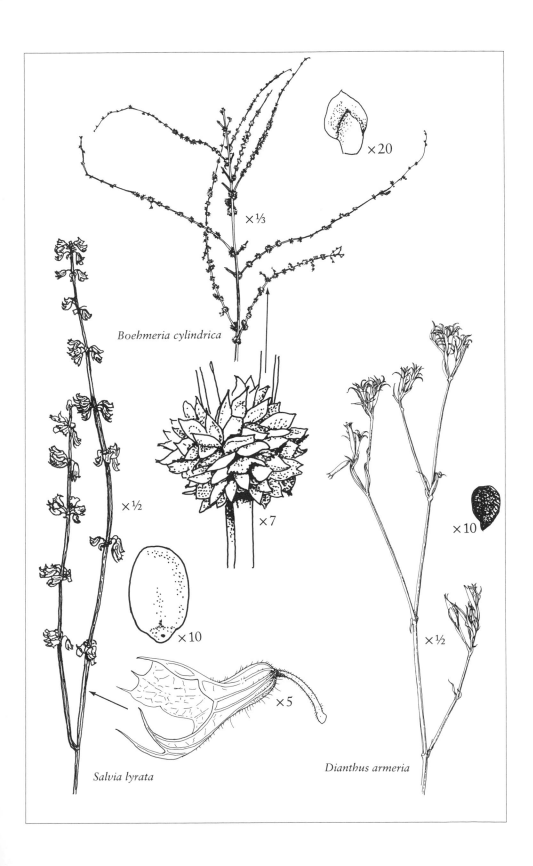

×20

×⅓

Boehmeria cylindrica

×½

×7

×10

×10

Salvia lyrata

×5

×½

Dianthus armeria

STEM   Opposite, branching, with swollen nodes.
BIENNIAL   From small taproot.
HABITAT   Roadsides, dry fields.
RANGE   Native to Europe; established as weed in e. U.S. and Canada.

Silene latifolia Poiret (*Lychnis alba*)
White campion, evening lychnis
Pink Family (Caryophyllaceae)

KEY IMPRESSIONS   May grow to 4ft (1.3m) but usually sprawls. All parts but capsule hairy. Flower remnants branch. Basal leaf rosettes in winter.
FRUIT   Calyx inflates and covers maturing fruit before disintegrating in winter. Capsule dehiscent, shiny, smooth, oval, 1-chambered, with many seeds attached to central column. Capsule opening surrounded by 8–10 (rarely 6) spreading teeth. Seeds 1.3–1.5mm, grayish brown, kidney-shaped, densely covered with short, blunt tubercles.
LEAVES   Opposite, entire.
STEM   Opposite branching, with swollen nodes.
BIENNIAL OR PERENNIAL   From stout rhizomes; dioecious.
HABITAT   Fields, waste areas.
RANGE   Native to Europe; established as common weed throughout much of N. Am.

Saponaria officinalis L.
Bouncing Bet, soapwort
Pink Family (Caryophyllaceae)

KEY IMPRESSIONS   Grows 1–2ft (30–60cm). Topped by congested branches.
FRUIT   Capsules dehiscent, 4-toothed, 1-chambered, elliptic to oblong, surrounded by rugged calyx. Seeds 1.5–2mm, black, kidney-shaped, covered with short, blunt tubercles in rows.
LEAVES   Opposite, oval-lanceolate.
STEM   Stout, square, with bulges at nodes.
PERENNIAL   From horizontal underground stems, forming large colonies.
HABITAT   Waste areas, disturbed areas, roadsides, railroad banks.
RANGE   Native to Old World; established as weed throughout most of temperate N. Am.

Silene antirrhina L.
Sleepy catchfly
Pink Family (Caryophyllaceae)

KEY IMPRESSIONS   Grows 8in–2½ft (20–76cm). Erect or ascending. Inflorescence branching.
FRUIT   Capsules 2–13mm, 3-chambered, oval; opening surrounded by 6 teeth. Capsule surrounded by closely adherent calyx 4–10mm, 10-nerved. Seeds .5–.7mm, lead gray to black, kidney-shaped, covered with short, blunt tubercles.
LEAVES   Opposite, linear, entire.
STEMS   Sticky, opposite branching, with swollen nodes.
ANNUAL OR BIENNIAL   From branching or substoloniferous caudex.
HABITAT   Dry sandy soil, dry or rocky open woods, fields, waste areas.
RANGE   Apparently native; throughout U.S. and s. Canada.

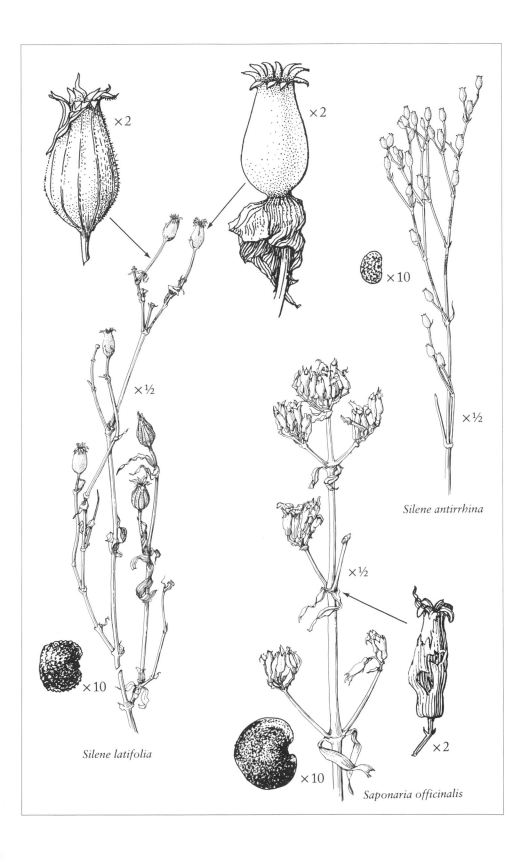

×2

×2

×10

×½

Silene antirrhina

×½

×½

×10

Silene latifolia

×10

×2

Saponaria officinalis

Stellaria media (L.) Villars
Common chickweed
Pink Family (Caryophyllaceae)

See pl. 16a

KEY IMPRESSIONS Grows to 16in (40cm). Stems sprawling, branched, with opposite oval leaves that remain green in winter. Flowers may bloom from March to November and into December. Flower white, with 5 deeply cleft petals that look like 10 narrow petals.

FRUIT Capsules oval, papery, with numerous seeds.

LEAVES Oval, toothless, smooth. Upper leaves stemless; lower leaves progressively longer-stemmed.

STEMS Sprawling, branched.

ANNUAL

HABITAT Variable weed of waste areas, cultivated areas, meadows, woodlands.

RANGE Throughout region.

SIMILAR SPECIES

Cerastium arvense L.   Mouse-ear chickweed, field-chickweed. Leaves hairy in winter.

Silene vulgaris (Moench) Garcke (*S. cucubulus*)
Bladder-campion
Pink Family (Caryophyllaceae)

KEY IMPRESSIONS Grows to 2½ft (76cm). Sprawling, often decumbent. Inflorescence cymose.

FRUIT Capsules small, 3-chambered, with 6 teeth paired around triangular opening. Surrounding calyx papery, inflated, 5-toothed, about 10mm, smooth, 10-nerved. Seeds 1–1.7mm, gray to gray-black, kidney-shaped, covered with pointed tubercles in concentric arrangement.

LEAVES Opposite, pointed, entire, ovate to lance-shaped.

STEMS Mostly smooth, opposite branching.

PERENNIAL From creeping underground stem.

HABITAT Grass, disturbed areas, fields, roadsides.

RANGE Native to Europe; occasionally found as weed throughout temperate N. Am.

Silene stellata (L.) Aiton f.
Starry campion
Pink Family (Caryophyllaceae)

KEY IMPRESSIONS Grows 1–3ft (.3–1m). Branches at upper end. Capsules round, open at top, with 6 teeth. Leaves whorled.

FRUIT Round capsules with 6 teeth at opening.

LEAVES Whorled, oval to lance-shaped, toothless.

STEM Round, smooth, erect, branched at top.

PERENNIAL

HABITAT Woodlands.

RANGE Conn. to Ohio and Nebr., south to Ga. and Tex.

SIMILAR SPECIES

Calyx inflated:

S. nivea (Nutt.) Otth.   Snowy campion, white campion. Calyx about 15mm, tubular–bell-shaped. Leaves opposite. Perennial. Woods.

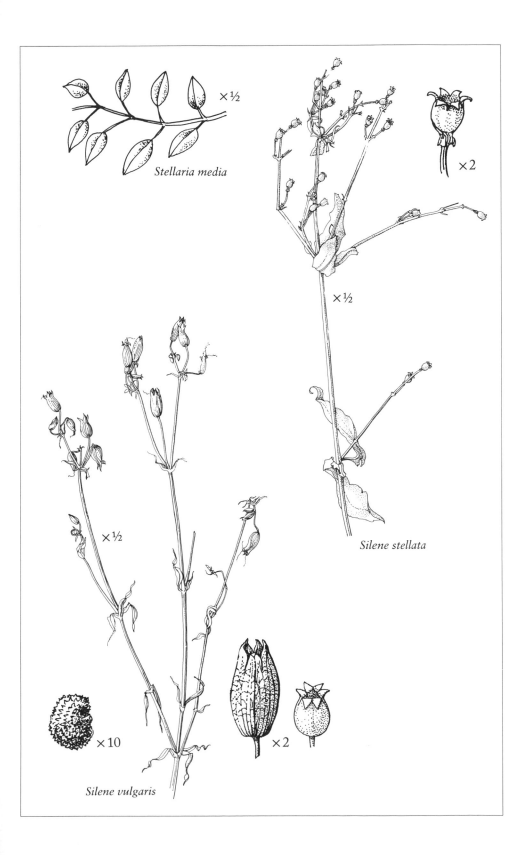

Stellaria media ×½

×2

×½

Silene stellata

×½

×10

×2

Silene vulgaris

S. noctiflora L.   Night-flowering catchfly, sticky cockle, catchfly. Hairy, sticky. Calyx 1–2in (2.5–5cm), oval–bell-shaped, 10-nerved, prominent (*S. latifolia* is 20-nerved). Capsule 3-chambered, 6-toothed. Annual. Waste areas.

Calyx not inflated, tight over capsule:

S. armeria L.   Sweet William catchfly. Calyx 13–17mm, tubular-split, 10-nerved. Annual. Roadsides.

S. caroliniana Walter   Wild pink. Calyx 15–22mm, narrowly tubular. Perennial from stout taproot. Dry or rocky woods, clearings.

S. dichotoma Ehrh.   Forking catchfly. Calyx 10–15mm, narrowly tubular, 10 nerves stiffly hairy. Annual. Waste areas.

S. regia Sims.   Royal catchfly, wild pink. Calyx 18–25mm, sticky, tubular. Perennial from fleshy taproot. Dry woods, prairies.

S. rotundifolia Nutt.   Roundleaf catchfly. Calyx ¾–1in (2–2.5cm), broadly tubular. Stem weak, decumbent. Perennial from stout, fleshy taproot. Rocky places, cliffs.

S. virginica L.   Fire-pink. Calyx 18–22mm, broadly cylindric-tubular. Stems ascending or erect. Perennial. Open woods, rocky slopes.

Plants with Opposite or Whorled Branches and Leaves, Non-swollen Nodes, and Round Stems

See also *Apocynum* p. 116, *Asclepias* p. 118, *Bidens* p. 55, *Circaea* p. 48, *Epilobium* p. 140, *Veronica* p. 122, Asteraceae—section on opposite branching, pp. 196–203

Aureolaria virginica (L.) Pennell (*Gerardia virginica*)
Downy false foxglove
Figwort Family (Scrophulariaceae)

KEY IMPRESSIONS   Grows to 5ft (1.5m). Branches opposite, upswept, with 2-parted, beaked capsules on short stalks in leaf axils. Found only in oak woods; thought to be parasitic on roots of oak trees.

FRUIT   Capsules ½–¾in (1.2–1.5cm), oval, 2-parted, with curved beak at each section tip. Capsules green at first, soon turning black, splitting open along midline of chambers. Seeds numerous, flattish, moon-shaped, with several wings.

LEAVES   Opposite, oval to lance-shaped. 1–2 pairs of lobes below middle of lower leaves.

STEMS   Ascending branches.

PERENNIAL

HABITAT   Oak woods.

RANGE   Mass. to Ont. and Mich., south to Fla. and Ala.

SIMILAR SPECIES

A. laevigata (Raf.) Raf.   Smooth false foxglove. Grows 2–6ft (.6–2m). Leaves shorter-stemmed, less lobed. Open woods, mainly in mountains. Pa. to s. Ohio, south to Ga.

A. pedicularia (L.) Raf.   Fern-leaved false foxglove. Grows 1–4ft (.3–1.3m). Leaves lacy, fernlike. Bushy branching. Dry oak woods, uplands. Maine to Ont. and Minn., south to Ill., Ohio, Pa., and Ga. mountains.

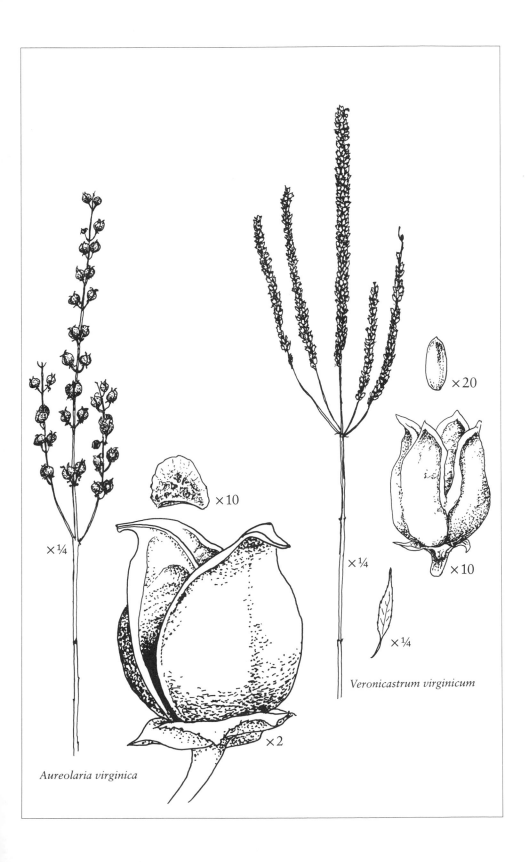

×¼

×10

×2

Aureolaria virginica

×20

×10

×¼

×¼

Veronicastrum virginicum

Veronicastrum virginicum (L.) Farw.

Culver's root

Figwort Family (Scrophulariaceae)

KEY IMPRESSIONS Grows 2–6ft (.6–1m). Plant elongated, stems unbranched except near top, where they give rise to whorls of erect spikes.

FRUIT Capsules 4–5mm, 2-chambered, elliptical, opening by means of 4 short terminal slits and containing many seeds. Seeds cylindrical, covered with minute networks of ridges.

LEAVES Whorls of 3–7 lance-shaped, finely toothed leaves.

STEMS Single round stem, unbranched except near top.

PERENNIAL

HABITAT Moist or dry upland woods and meadows, prairies.

RANGE Vt. to Ont. and Man., south to Ga. and La.

Penstemon Schmidel spp.

Beard-tongue

Figwort Family (Scrophulariaceae)

KEY IMPRESSIONS Numerous species of *Penstemon* look similar in winter. Plants grow to 4ft (1.3m), appearing straight because branches almost parallel main stem. Branches terminate in racemes or panicles of capsules.

FRUIT Capsules ¼–½in (.6–1.3cm), warm brown, oval, 2-parted, splitting along septum, in bracts. Each half has notched tip. Seeds numerous, .7–1mm.

LEAVES Opposite, lance-shaped to oblong, stemless. Fallen leaves leave small bulge on stem. Basal rosette of stemmed leaves in winter.

PERENNIAL

HABITAT Meadows, open woods, fields. *P. digitalis* is the most widespread beard-tongue.

RANGE Throughout N. Am.

Gentiana andrewsii Griseb.

Closed-gentian, bottle-gentian

Gentian Family (Gentianaceae)

KEY IMPRESSIONS Grows 1–2ft (30–60cm). Leaves toothless, opposite, stemless. Uppermost leaves form a 4–6-leaved base surrounding elliptical capsules. 2–5 capsules in terminal cluster, some often in upper axils.

FRUIT Capsules elliptical, 2-valved, splitting along 2 septa, on stalks. Seeds numerous, nearly covering inner capsule face, 2–3mm, whitish brown, shiny, oblong, broadly winged.

LEAVES Simple, opposite, toothless, stemless.

STEM Erect, 1–2ft (30–60cm).

PERENNIAL From stout, woody underground stem with coarse, long roots.

HABITAT Wet woods, meadows, shores, damp prairies.

RANGE Man., s. Ont., sw. Que., Vt., and south.

SIMILAR SPECIES

G. crinita (Froelich) Ma. Fringed gentian. Grows 1–2ft (30–60cm). Elliptical capsule, flared at terminal end. Leaves lance-shaped to ovate, stemless. Stem often branched. Annual or biennial from taproot. Low woods, wet meadows, brook banks. Maine to Md., west to Man., S.Dak., and Iowa.

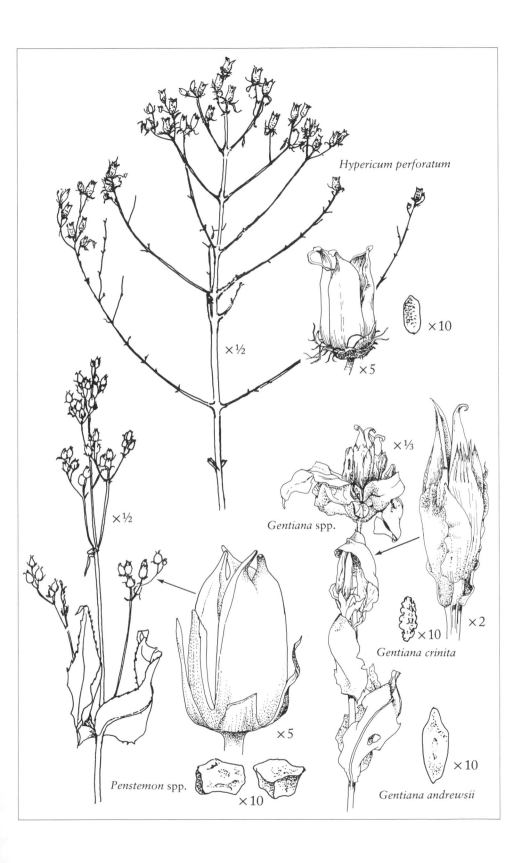

Hypericum perforatum

×½

×10

×5

×⅓

Gentiana spp.

×2

×10

Gentiana crinita

×½

×5

Penstemon spp.

×10

×10

Gentiana andrewsii

Hypericum perforatum L.

Common St. John's-wort

Mangosteen Family (Clusiaceae)

See pl. 15a

KEY IMPRESSIONS   Grows 1–3ft (.3–1m). Numerous opposite upward-curving branches, many small 3-parted capsules. Leaves dotted with resin on surfaces.

FRUIT   Capsules elongated, oval, 3-chambered, splitting along septa, red at first, drying to dark brown. Seeds numerous, 1–1.3mm, brown to black, oblong, rounded at tips, glossy from resin, with coarsely netted surfaces.

LEAVES   Opposite, linear to oblong, with numerous resin dots.

STEM   Erect, with numerous opposite branches. Mass of leafy shoots at stem base.

PERENNIAL   From underground stems.

HABITAT   Fields, meadows, roadsides.

RANGE   Native to Europe; abundant as weed throughout much of U.S. and s. Canada.

SIMILAR SPECIES

H. punctatum Lam.   Spotted St. John's-wort. Grows 1–3ft (.3–1m). Capsules cylindrical. Conspicuously dotted leaves. Thickets, damp places. Minn., s. Ont., s. Que., and south.

H. pyrimidatum Aiton   Great St. John's-wort. Grows 2–6ft (.6–2m). Leaves large, elliptic. Wet places. Man., Que., and Maine, south to Kans., Ind., and Pa.

Hypericum canadense L.

Canadian St. John's-wort

Mangosteen Family (Clusiaceae)

KEY IMPRESSIONS   Grows 6–20in (15–50cm). Small, 3-parted dark capsules on branched stems. Leaves narrow and linear.

FRUIT   Capsules 5–6mm, 3-parted, oval to cylindrical, somewhat pointed.

LEAVES   Linear, toothless, stemless.

STEM   Slender, erect, branched at upper end.

ANNUAL   Becoming perennial by short stolons.

HABITAT   Sandy or muddy shores, wet meadows.

RANGE   Man., Nfld., and south.

Hypericum gentianoides (L.) BSP.

Orange-grass, pineweed

Mangosteen Family (Clusiaceae)

KEY IMPRESSIONS   Usually grows no more than 6in (15cm). Many wiry, opposite branches. Leaves scalelike. Fruits 3-parted capsules, tiny, hard to see. Found mostly in sandy soil.

FRUIT   Capsules 5–7mm, 3-parted, slenderly cone-shaped.

LEAVES   Scalelike.

STEM   Repeatedly branched into numerous fine, erect branches.

ANNUAL

HABITAT   Sterile, sandy soil, crushed rock, quarries.

RANGE   Maine to Ont. and Minn., south to Fla. and Tex.

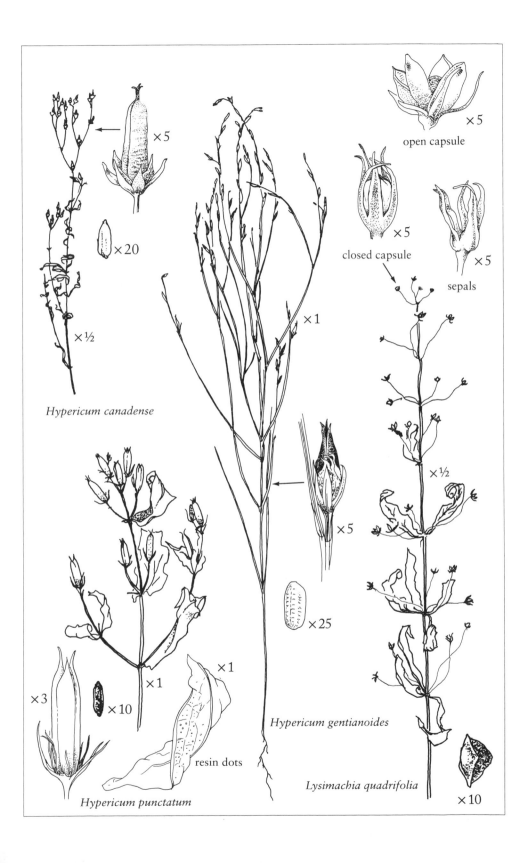

×5

open capsule

×5

closed capsule

×5

sepals

Hypericum canadense

×5

×20

×½

×1

×5

×25

Hypericum gentianoides

×½

×1

×3

×10

×1

resin dots

Hypericum punctatum

Lysimachia quadrifolia

×10

Lysimachia quadrifolia L.
Whorled loosestrife
Primrose Family (Primulaceae)

KEY IMPRESSIONS Grows 1–3½ft (.3–1.2m). Fruit stalks in axils (if leaves are gone, scars will be seen). Leaves and fruit stalks found in whorls of usually 4 but sometimes 3 or 5.
FRUIT Capsules small, round, with few to many seeds, splitting by longitudinal valves. Capsule often falls off, leaving 5–6 pointed sepals.
LEAVES Whorled, usually in 4s and 5s (or 3s), toothless, lance-shaped. Maroon basal leaf rosettes in winter.
STEM Erect, delicate, rarely branched. May appear slightly square in dry state.
PERENNIAL
HABITAT Woods, thickets, roadsides.
RANGE Maine to Wis., south to S.C., Ala., Ky., and Ill.

Lysimachia terrestris (L.) BSP.
Yellow loosestrife, swamp loosestrife, swamp-candle
Primrose Family (Primulaceae)

KEY IMPRESSIONS Grows to 3ft (1m). Fruit stalks in raceme at terminal end of main stem, overtopping side branches. Raceme grows to 12in (30cm). Reddish, vegetative bulblets sometimes found in leaf axils. Found in swamps.
FRUIT Similar to that of *L. quadrifolia*.
LEAVES Opposite, lance-shaped.
STEM Often branched. May appear square in dry state.
PERENNIAL From long stoloniferous underground stems.
HABITAT Open swamps, wet soil.
RANGE Que. and Nfld. to Man., south to Va., N.C., Ky., and Ill.
SIMILAR SPECIES

    L. ciliata L. Fringed loosestrife. Fruit remnants solitary in upper stem axils. Leaves, if present, distinct, with fringed (ciliate) leaf stems. Stems branched, firmer than in *L. quadrifolia*. Moist or wet ground. Throughout region.

Phryma leptostachya L.
Lopseed
Vervain Family (Verbenaceae)

KEY IMPRESSIONS Grows 1–3ft (.3–1m). 2–5 branches from main stem. Spikelike racemes terminate stems and grow from several upper axils. Fruits enclosed in calyxes, reflexed downward.
FRUIT Black achenes found within persistently closed calyxes. Calyx 10mm, 2-lipped, strongly ribbed, closely reflexed against axis. Long, slender teeth hooked at tip.
LEAVES Opposite, oval, toothed, with sharp tip.
STEM Erect, branching.
PERENNIAL
HABITAT Woods, thickets.
RANGE Que. to Man., south to Fla., Tenn., and Okla.

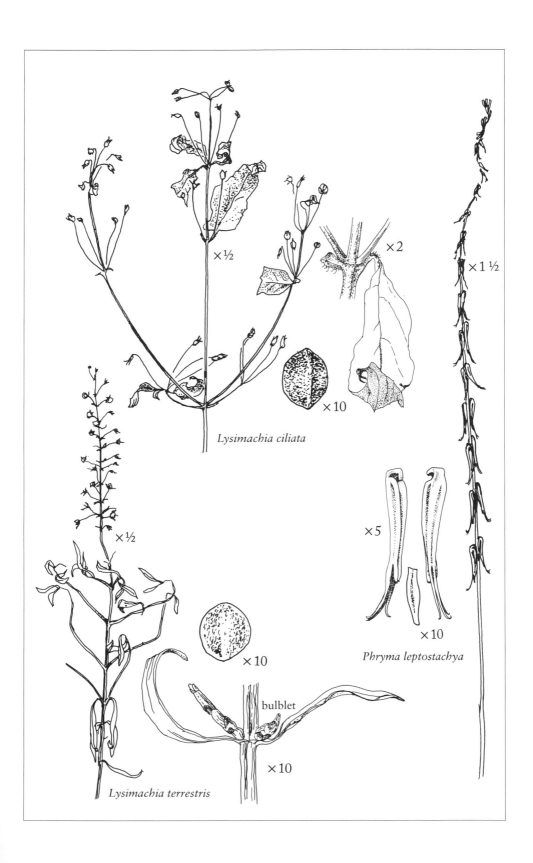

×½

×2

×1½

×10

Lysimachia ciliata

×5

×10

×½

Phryma leptostachya

×10

bulblet

×10

Lysimachia terrestris

Potentilla recta L.
Rough-fruited cinquefoil
Rose Family (Rosaceae)

KEY IMPRESSIONS   Grows to 2½ft (75cm). Flower remnants on opposite branching stalks and at each node. Remnants look like round capsules but are only hairy bracts that remain after small fruits (achenes) have been dispersed.

FRUIT   Small achenes with low, curved ridges on surfaces and winged margins.

LEAVES   Lower leaves divided into 5 "fingers," stemmed; upper leaves stemless, with 3 "fingers."

STEM   Frequent opposite branching.

PERENNIAL   From short underground stem hidden by thick tangle of roots.

HABITAT   Old fields, roadsides.

RANGE   Native to Europe; found as weed throughout region.

SIMILAR SPECIES

P. arguta Pursh.   Tall cinquefoil. Grows 1–3ft (.3–1m). Flower remnants fewer, bigger, less rounded. Branches closer to main stem. Leaves have 7–11 leaflets. Achenes have fine lines on the surfaces and lack winged margins. Perennial from stout underground stem. Dry woods, prairies. Throughout region.

P. norvegica L.   Rough cinquefoil, strawberry-weed. Achenes 1mm, pale brown, flattened, marked with curved ridges. Leaves divided into 3 "fingers." Clearings, thickets, roadsides. Throughout region.

Ruellia caroliniensis (Walter) Steudel
Hairy ruellia
Acanthus Family (Acanthaceae)

KEY IMPRESSIONS   Grows 1–2½ft (30–75cm). Covered with small soft hairs. Calyx lobes extend into long, hairy bristles. Calyxes stalkless, clustered around central stem at axils.

LEAVES   Oval, toothless.

STEM   Round, downy.

PERENNIAL

HABITAT   Moist or dry woods, clearings.

RANGE   N.J. to s. Ohio and s. Ind., south to Fla. and Tex.

SIMILAR SPECIES

R. strepens L.   Smooth ruellia. Flower remnants on stalks; plant essentially smooth.

Triadenum virginicum (L.) Raf.
Marsh St. John's-wort
Mangosteen Family (Clusiaceae)

KEY IMPRESSIONS   Grows 1–2ft (30–60cm). 3-chambered capsules arise on stems from axils of stemless glandular dotted leaves. Stem branches at terminal end. Wet areas.

FRUIT   Capsules 8–12mm, 3-chambered, cylindric, gradually tapering to styles, 2–3mm.

LEAVES   Opposite, simple, dotted with translucent glands, toothless, stemless.

STEM   Erect, branching at upper end.

PERENNIAL   From underground stems.

HABITAT   Bogs, marshes, wet shores.

RANGE   N.S. to Fla. and Miss., near coast and locally inland to Great Lakes.

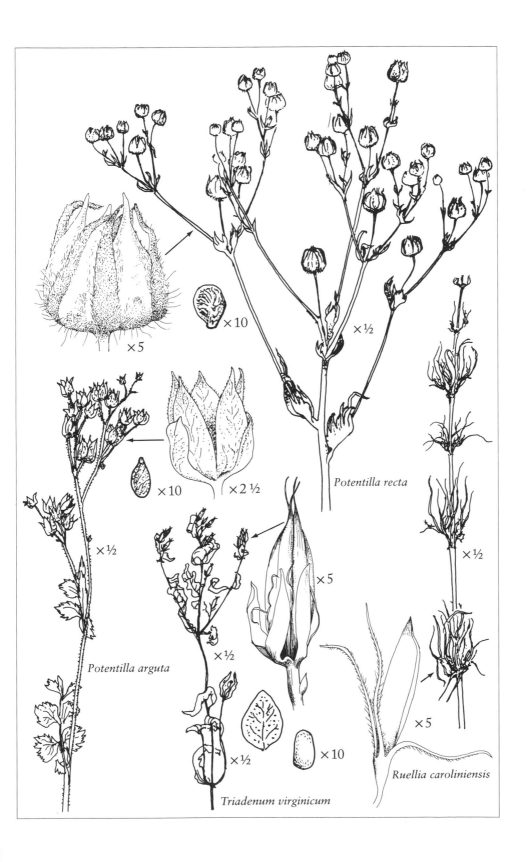

×10

×5

×½

Potentilla recta

×½

×10

×2½

Potentilla arguta

×5

×½

×½

×10

Triadenum virginicum

×5

Ruellia caroliniensis

Plants Bearing Fruits Appearing as Strings of Beads

See also *Amsonia tabernaemontana* p. 118, *Cakile edentula* p. 16

Raphanus raphanistrum L.
Jointed charlock, wild radish
Mustard Family (Brassicaceae)

KEY IMPRESSIONS Grows 1–2½ft (30–75cm). Fruits constricted between seeds, giving beaded appearance.

FRUIT Siliques become prominently several-ribbed and constricted between 4–10 seeds. Silique body ¾–1½in (2–4cm), beak ½–1in (1–3cm). Fruit appears beaded.

LEAVES Lobed, with large rounded lobe at terminal end.

STEM Erect.

ANNUAL From stout taproot.

HABITAT Fields, roadsides, waste areas.

RANGE Native to Eurasia; established as weed throughout most of U.S. and s. Canada.

Coronilla varia L.
Crown-vetch
Pea or Bean Family (Fabaceae)

KEY IMPRESSIONS Grows 12–30in (30–75cm). Loosely ascending plant. Narrow, jointed pods grouped in umbels. Leaves have numerous leaflets.

FRUIT Pods ¾–2½in (2–6cm), linear, 4-angled, with 3–7 joints, appearing beaded.

LEAVES 11–25 leaflets per leaf, stemless.

STEM Ascending or reclining.

PERENNIAL

HABITAT Widely planted along highways, roadsides.

RANGE Native to Mediterranean area; established throughout region.

Plants Bearing Berrylike Fruits or Seeds

See also *Smilax herbacea* p. 30, *Allium tricoccum* p. 152, *Gaultheria procumbens* p. 36, *Mitchella repens* p. 36

Caulophyllum thalictroides (L.) Michx.
Blue cohosh
Barberry Family (Berberidaceae)

KEY IMPRESSIONS Grows to 3½ft (1.2m). Simple naked stems terminate in racemes or panicles. Seeds appear as blue "berries." Stem bulges at nodes.

FRUIT 2 enlarging seeds, 6mm diameter, rupture ovary and appear as blue "drupes" (they are actually seeds on thick seed stalks). Seed coverings turn blue.

LEAVES Doubly compound; leaflets resemble those of tall meadow rue.

STEM Single, simple, shiny tan, bulging at nodes.

PERENNIAL From matted, tangled, knotty underground stems.

HABITAT Rich, moist woods.

RANGE N.B. to Ont. and Man., south to S.C., Ala., and Mo.

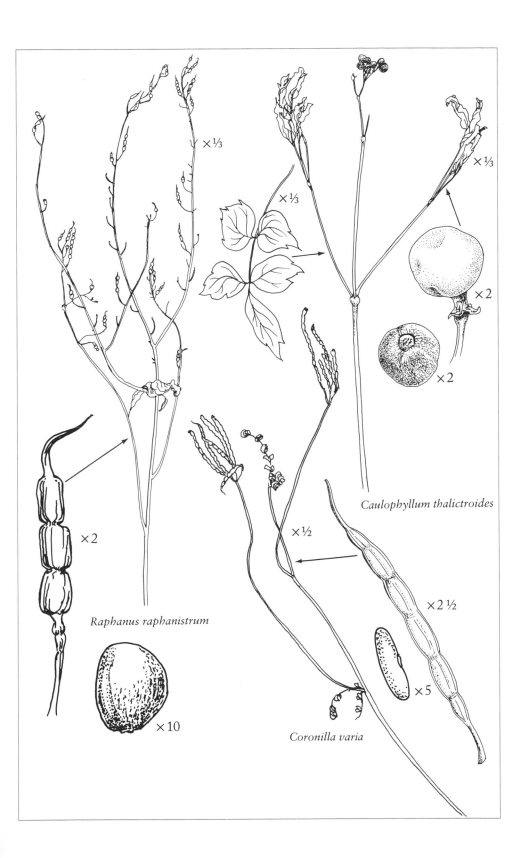

$\times \frac{1}{3}$

$\times \frac{1}{3}$

$\times \frac{1}{3}$

$\times 2$

$\times 2$

Caulophyllum thalictroides

$\times 2$

$\times \frac{1}{2}$

$\times 2\frac{1}{2}$

Raphanus raphanistrum

$\times 5$

$\times 10$

Coronilla varia

Maianthemum canadense Desf.

Canada mayflower, wild lily-of-the-valley

Lily Family (Liliaceae)

KEY IMPRESSIONS Grows 1–6in (3–15cm). Stem terminates with raceme of 10–15 red fruits. Grows in large colonies on forest floor.

FRUIT Berries 5mm, ruby red, round, fleshy. Seeds white, round, 1–2 per fruit.

LEAVES Oval to oblong, usually heart-shaped at base, stemless or short-stemmed.

STEM Erect.

PERENNIAL From thin, white underground, extensively creeping stems. Numerous tan roots at nodes. Occasional small elliptical tubes at root ends. Preformed white shoot (next year's preformed bud) inside leaf attachment to roots.

HABITAT Moist woods.

RANGE Lab. and Nfld., south to Md. and S.Dak., in mountains to Ky. and N.C.

Medeola virginiana L.

Indian cucumber-root

Lily Family (Liliaceae)

KEY IMPRESSIONS Grows to 1ft (30cm). 2 leaf whorls on central erect stem. Stem terminates with umbel of dark purple fruits.

FRUIT Berries, dark purple or black, round, few-seeded.

LEAVES Upper leaves 3 in a whorl, oval; lower leaves 5–11 in a whorl, oblong, toothless.

STEM Erect, unbranched.

PERENNIAL From thick, tuberlike horizontal underground stems. Cucumber-flavored.

HABITAT Rich woods.

RANGE N.S. and Que. to Mich. and se. Wis., south to Va. and n. Mo., in mountains to Ga. and Ala.

Phytolacca americana L.

Pokeweed, pokeberry

Pokeweed Family (Phytolaccaceae)

KEY IMPRESSIONS Grows 6–9ft (2–3m). Large, much branched. Skeletons of racemes of raspberry-colored stems remain after dark purple berries have gone. Pith in stem has white waferlike partitions.

FRUIT Berries ½in (1cm) diameter, dark purple, 5–15-chambered, arranged in racemes up to 8in (20cm) long. 1 seed per chamber.

LEAVES Alternate, toothless, oblong to lance-shaped, with large stems.

STEM Alternate branching. Thick, gray, with thin white "wafer" partitions in hollow pith.

PERENNIAL From large fleshy, thick, poisonous taproot.

HABITAT Fields, damp woods.

RANGE Maine to Minn., south to Gulf of Mexico.

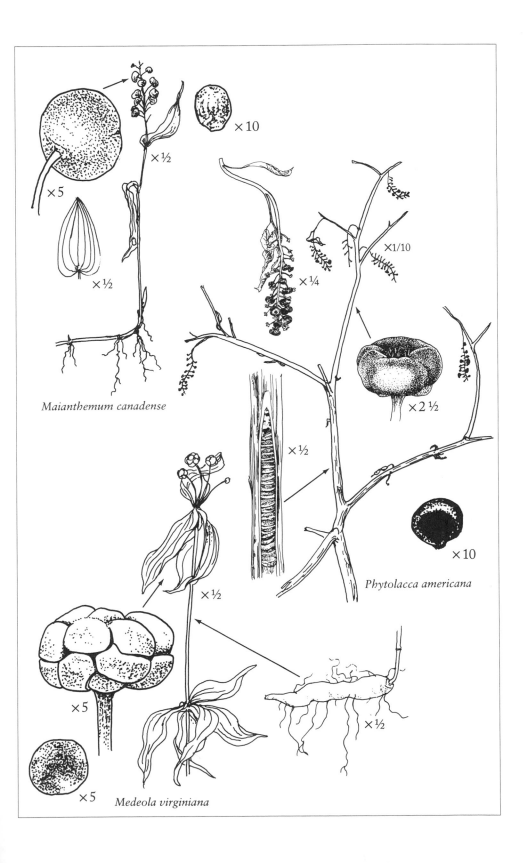

×10

×½

×5

×½

Maianthemum canadense

×¼

×1/10

×2½

×½

Phytolacca americana

×10

×½

×5

×½

×5

Medeola virginiana

Polygonatum biflorum (Walter) Elliott
Solomon's seal
Lily Family (Liliaceae)

KEY IMPRESSIONS   Grows 1–2ft (30–60cm). Single arching stem with blue-black fruits hanging from leaf axils all along stem length.

FRUIT   Berries blue-black, round, 3-chambered, with 1–2 seeds per chamber. 1–2 fruits per axil. Seeds 2.7–3.5mm, pale brown, roundish.

LEAVES   Oval, parallel-veined, alternate, stemless. Often gone when berries are ripe.

STEM   Single, curved, arched.

PERENNIAL   From creeping, horizontal, knotty, whitish underground stems.

HABITAT   Moist woods, thickets, roadsides.

RANGE   Mass. and s. N.H. to Minn., Man., and N.Dak., south to Fla.

SIMILAR SPECIES

   P. pubescens (Willd.) Pursh   Hairy Solomon's seal. Similar to *P. biflorum* but with hairs along veins beneath leaves. Leaves have 3–9 prominent veins (7–19 in *P. biflorum*).

Smilacina racemosa (L.) Desf.
False Solomon's seal
Lily Family (Liliaceae)

KEY IMPRESSIONS   Grows 1–2ft (30–60cm). Single arching stem with panicle of red fruit on terminal end.

FRUIT   Berries red, round, 3-chambered. 1–2 seeds per chamber. Berries are greenish at first, later turning red.

LEAVES   5–12, alternate, elliptic, parallel-veined, stemless.

STEM   Single, arched.

PERENNIAL   From creeping thickish underground stems that are fleshy, brownish, knotty, and elongated.

HABITAT   Rich woods.

RANGE   N.S. to B.C., south to Ga. and Ariz.

Solanum carolinense L.
Horse-nettle
Nightshade Family (Solanaceae)

KEY IMPRESSIONS   Grows 1–3ft (.3–1m). Spiny branched or forking stems. Fruits yellow round berries lateral to stems.

FRUIT   Berries 12mm diameter, yellow, round, smooth, 2-chambered. Calyx persistent at base. Seeds numerous, oval, flattened.

LEAVES   Alternate, elliptic to oval, with large teeth or shallow lobes, spiny along principal veins.

STEM   Forking, spiny.

PERENNIAL   From creeping, narrow, deep underground stems.

HABITAT   Sandy soil, fields, waste areas.

RANGE   Established throughout region.

Berrylike Fruits or Seeds

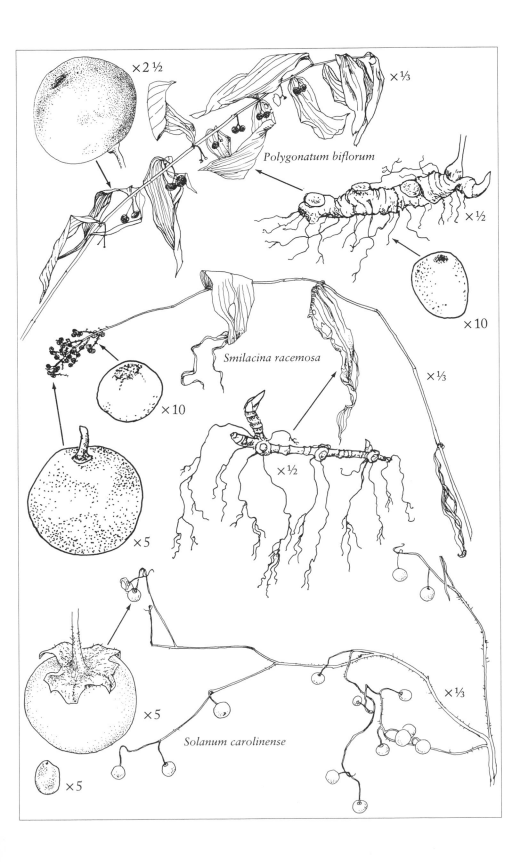

×2½

×⅓

Polygonatum biflorum

×½

×10

Smilacina racemosa

×10

×⅓

×½

×5

×⅓

×5

Solanum carolinense

×5

Arisaema triphyllum (L.) Schott.

Jack-in-the-pulpit, Indian turnip

Arum Family (Araceae)

KEY IMPRESSIONS   Grows 1–2½ft (30–75cm). Cluster of bright red berries terminates single stalk.

FRUIT   Berries bright red, round, with 1–3 seeds.

LEAVES   1–2, long, 3-parted, stemmed.

STEM   Single, erect.

PERENNIAL   From acrid corm.

HABITAT   *A. triphyllum*, rich, moist woods; var. *stewardsonii* and var. *pusillum,* mostly in boggy areas, wet woods.

RANGE   Throughout region.

Actaea alba (L.) Miller (*A. pachypoda*)

White baneberry, doll's eyes

Buttercup Family (Ranunculaceae)

KEY IMPRESSIONS   Grows 1–2½ft (30–75cm). Raceme of white berries terminates stem. Each berry has a thick red stalk. Fruits found more in fall than in winter. Poisonous.

FRUIT   White berries with a black dot, hence the name "doll's eyes."

LEAVES   Divided and subdivided into sharply toothed leaflets.

STEM   Erect.

PERENNIAL

HABITAT   Rich woods.

RANGE   Que. to Ont. and Minn., south to Ga., La., and Okla.

SIMILAR SPECIES

   A. rubra (Aiton) Willd.   Red baneberry. Much like *A. alba* except the plants have bright red berries on thinner stalks. Rich woods. Lab. and Nfld. to Alaska, south to Conn., n. N.J., n. Ind., Iowa, and Ariz.

Aralia racemosa L.

Spikenard

Ginseng Family (Araliaceae)

KEY IMPRESSIONS   Grows 3–6ft (1–2m). Large, sprawling plant. Dark purple drupes arranged on large panicles with numerous umbels.

FRUIT   Berrylike drupe, dark purple.

LEAVES   Widely spreading, toothed, the 3 primary divisions pinnately compound.

STEM   Branching, sprawling.

PERENNIAL

HABITAT   Rich woods.

RANGE   Que. and N.B. to Minn. and S.Dak., south to N.C.

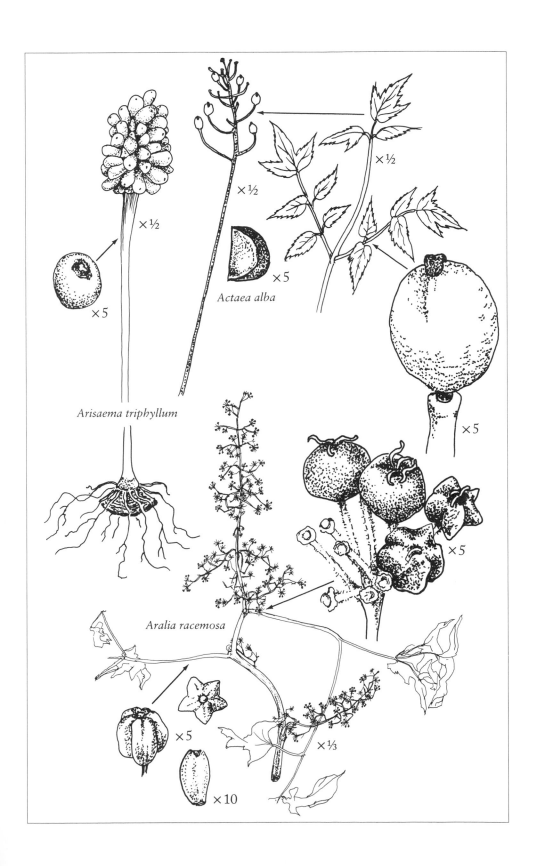

×½

×5

Actaea alba

×½

×5

Arisaema triphyllum

×5

×5

Aralia racemosa

×5

×⅓

×10

Clintonia borealis (Aiton) Raf.
Bead-lily, corn-lily
Lily Family (Liliaceae)

KEY IMPRESSIONS Grows to 1ft (30cm). Single stem, leafless, with blue berries at terminal end. Leaves basal.
FRUIT Berry blue, with 1 to several seeds.
LEAVES Basal, oblong to elliptic, toothless.
STEM Erect, single, leafless.
PERENNIAL From underground stems.
HABITAT Moist woods, wooded bogs.
RANGE Lab. and Nfld. to Man. and Minn., south to N.J., Pa., and n. Ind., in mountains to N.C. and Tenn.

Plants with 1-chambered Fruits (Pods) That Split on 2 Sides, and Hairless Seeds

See also *Lathyrus latifolius* p. 34

Baptisia australis (L.) R. Br.
Blue false indigo
Pea or Bean Family (Fabaceae)

KEY IMPRESSIONS Grows to 4ft (1.3m), with ascending branches that bear 1 to few terminal racemes. Pods black, oval-elliptic, ascending or divergent.
FRUIT Pods 1–1½in (3–4cm), black, oval-elliptic, narrowed below to thick stem and above to curved beak 8–20mm long. Stem slightly exceeds calyx. Seeds numerous.
LEAVES Alternate, each with 3 leaflets that blacken on drying.
STEM Smooth, branching.
PERENNIAL From thick underground stem.
HABITAT Moist, usually rocky or gravelly soil, woods, prairies.
RANGE S. Ind., W.Va., and Pa. south; introduced northward.
SIMILAR SPECIES

B. bracteata Elliott Large white wild indigo. Grows 3–6ft (1–2m). Widely branched. Pods drooping, 1–1¾in (3–5cm), elliptic, long, downy, abruptly narrowed to short beak, on stem that is long-stalked in calyx. Prairies, open upland woods. Ohio and Mich. to Minn. and Nebr., south to Miss. and Tex.

Baptisia tinctoria (L.) R. Br.
Wild indigo, yellow wild indigo, rattleweed, horsefly
Pea or Bean Family (Fabaceae)

KEY IMPRESSIONS Grows to 3ft (1m). Scraggly, tends to fall over, bushy branched. Pods numerous in terminal racemes and rattle when shaken.
FRUIT Pods oval, 8–15mm × 6–8mm, oval, round at base, with beaked summits. Pods fall off, leaving calyx behind. Seeds numerous.
LEAVES Alternate, with 3 leaflets, turning black when dry.
STEM Much branched. Tends to break from ground and act as "tumbleweed."

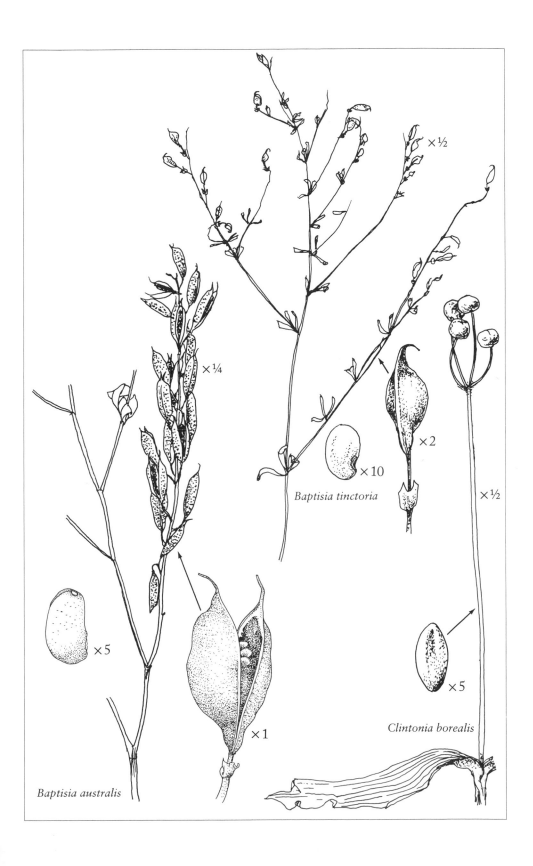

×½

×¼

Baptisia tinctoria

×2

×10

×5

×1

×½

×5

Clintonia borealis

Baptisia australis

PERENNIAL   From shallow woody root, thick underground stem.
HABITAT   Dry sandy soil.
RANGE   S. Maine to Ga. and Tenn., west to Mich., Ind., and Ill.

Senna hebecarpa (Fern.) Irwin & Barneby
Northern wild senna
Caesalpinia Family (Caesalpiniaceae)

KEY IMPRESSIONS   Grows 3–6ft (1–2m). Fruit pods in racemes, forming terminal panicle. Stem erect.
FRUIT   Pods 2¾–4¾in (7–12cm), joints nearly square. Seeds nearly as wide as long, flat, with depressed center.
LEAVES   Alternate, 6–10 pairs of toothless leaflets.
STEM   Erect.
PERENNIAL
HABITAT   Moist, open woods, roadsides, streambanks.
RANGE   Wis. to New Eng. and south.

Chamaecrista nictitans (L.) Moench (*Cassia nictitans*)
Wild sensitive plant
Caesalpinia Family (Caesalpiniaceae)

KEY IMPRESSIONS   Grows to 1½ft (45cm). Solitary pods that twist into spirals when open.
FRUIT   Pods 1–2in (2.5–5cm), brown, flat, oblong, on very short stalks near stem. Seeds 3–4mm, dark brown, glossy, flattened, with winged margins, marked with a row of pits.
LEAVES   9–29 pairs of toothless leaflets.
STEM   Erect, branching.
ANNUAL   From fibrous roots.
HABITAT   Dry sandy soil.
RANGE   Kans., Ill., Ind., Ohio, N.Y., and Mass. south.
SIMILAR SPECIES
   C. *fasciculata* (Michx.) Greene   Partridge pea, locust weed. Grows to 2½ft (75cm). Pods 1–2in (2.5–5cm). Fruit stalk upcurving, about 1in (2.5cm) long, in contrast to short fruit stalk of C. *nictitans*. Dry sandy soil. More widely distributed than C. *nictitans*. Minn., s. Ont., Mass., and south.

Crotalaria sagittalis L.
Rattlebox
Pea or Bean Family (Fabaceae)

KEY IMPRESSIONS   Grows 12–16in (30–40cm). Small, hairy plant. Seeds rattle in black pods when dry.
FRUIT   ½–1in (2–3cm), pods black, oblong, much inflated, nearly stemless in calyx.
LEAVES   Lance-shaped, almost stemless. Arrowhead-shaped stipules point down toward stem.
STEM   Simple or branched above.
ANNUAL
HABITAT   Dry open soil, waste areas.
RANGE   Minn., Wis., s. Mich., Ohio, s. N.Y., Mass., and south.

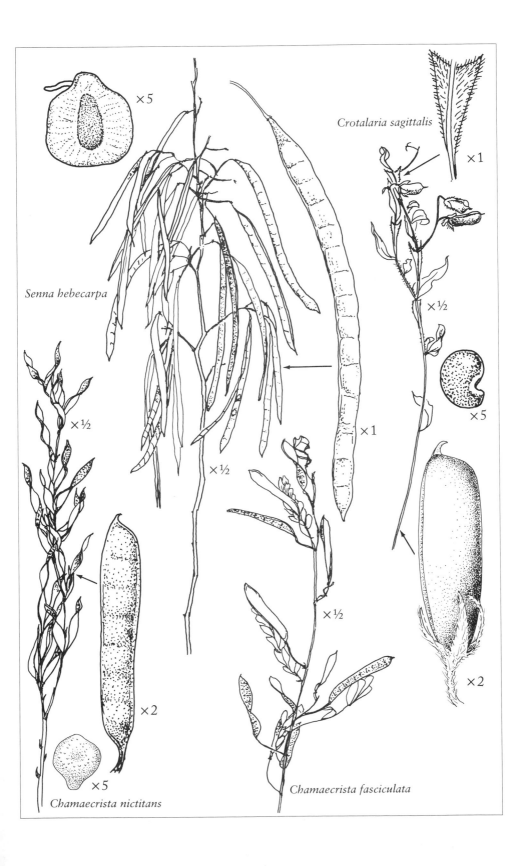

×5

Crotalaria sagittalis

×1

Senna hebecarpa

×½

×½

×1

×½

×5

×2

×2

×5

Chamaecrista nictitans

Chamaecrista fasciculata

Lupinus perennis L.
Wild lupine
Pea or Bean Family (Fabaceae)
See pl. 18a

KEY IMPRESSIONS Grows to 2ft (60cm). Racemes of fuzzy pods that twist into spirals after opening.
FRUIT Fuzzy pods constricted between seeds.
LEAVES Composed of leaflets arising from center point on the stem (palm-shaped).
STEM Several, erect.
PERENNIAL From creeping underground stems.
HABITAT Dry or moist sandy soil, dry open woods, clearings; uncommon in Northeast.
RANGE Maine to s. Ont. and Minn., south to Fla. and La.

Lathyrus maritimus (L.) Bigelow (*L. japonicus*)
Beach-pea
Pea or Bean Family (Fabaceae)

KEY IMPRESSIONS Grows to 3ft (1m). Low-growing along ground. Found on sandy shores of coastal areas and large inland lakes.
FRUIT Pod 1½–3in (4–8cm), oblong, veined, stemless.
LEAVES 3–6 pairs of oval, somewhat fleshy leaflets. Large arrowhead-shaped stipules at base of leaf stalks.
STEM Usually reclining along ground, sometimes upright.
PERENNIAL From stout rhizome.
HABITAT Sea beaches, lakeshores.
RANGE Coastal areas south to N.J.; shores of Great Lakes, Oneida Lake, and Lake Champlain.

Thermopsis villosa (Walter) Fern. & Schubert
Blue-Ridge buckbean, false lupine
Pea or Bean Family (Fabaceae)

KEY IMPRESSIONS Grows 1–3½ft (.3–1.2m). Erect stems terminate in racemes of erect or strongly ascending pods.
FRUIT Pods grayish, linear, flat, hairy, with several seeds.
LEAVES 3 elliptic leaflets.
STEM Erect.
PERENNIAL From underground stems.
HABITAT Woods, fields.
RANGE N.C., Tenn., and n. Ga., and locally escaped northward.

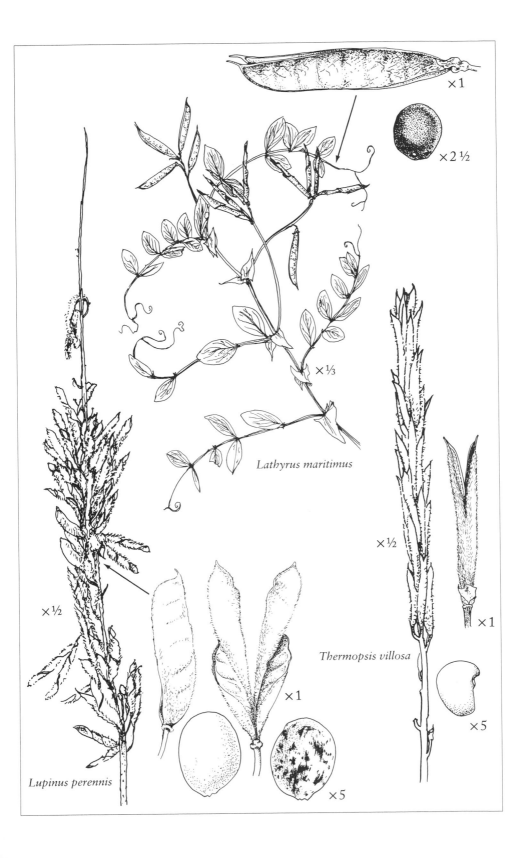

×1

×2½

×⅓

Lathyrus maritimus

×½

Thermopsis villosa

×1

×½

×1

Lupinus perennis

×5

×5

Plants with 1-chambered Fruits with Side Slits:
Orchid Family (Orchidaceae)

See also *Goodyera* spp. p. 38

Cypripedium acaule Aiton
Pink lady-slipper, moccasin-flower
Orchid Family (Orchidaceae)

KEY IMPRESSIONS   Grows to 1ft (30cm). 1 capsule terminal to naked stem. Curved bract at base of capsule. Capsule often fails to develop, so only bract may be present atop flower stem.

FRUIT   Capsule first topped by shriveled flower remains. Capsule 1–2in (2.5–5cm), with 6 lengthwise ribs, opening along 6 slits. Seeds very numerous, minute.

LEAVES   1 pair, basal, oblong, disappearing in winter.

STEM   Naked, erect.

PERENNIAL   From central underground stem with radiating, twisting, tufted fibrous roots.

HABITAT   Acid soils; swamps, bogs, mossy or dry woods, sand dunes; in north, bogs, mossy or wet woods.

RANGE   Nfld. to Man., south to n. U.S., locally in mountains to Ga.

Pogonia ophioglossoides (L.) Ker Gawler
Rose pogonia, snake-mouth
Orchid Family (Orchidaceae)

KEY IMPRESSIONS   Plants grow in wetlands 4–20in (10–50cm). Single capsule at the terminal end of the stem.

FRUIT   Capsule, ½–1in (1.5–2.5cm), oval, opening along 6 side slits.

LEAVES   1 basal, 1 stem, both disappearing in winter.

STEM   Single, erect.

PERENNIAL   From short underground stem with cluster of fibrous roots.

HABITAT   Open, wet meadows, sphagnum bogs.

RANGE   Nfld. to Minn., south to Fla. and Tex.

Habenaria Willd. spp.
Rein-orchid
Orchid Family (Orchidaceae)

KEY IMPRESSIONS   Grows ½–3ft (.15–1m), depending on species. Single stem terminates in spike or raceme.

FRUIT   6–13mm, globular, opening along 3 side slits.

LEAVES   Mostly basal, disappearing in winter.

STEM   Single, erect.

PERENNIAL   From bunch of fleshy roots.

HABITAT   Bogs, wet woods, pine barrens.

RANGE   Throughout region.

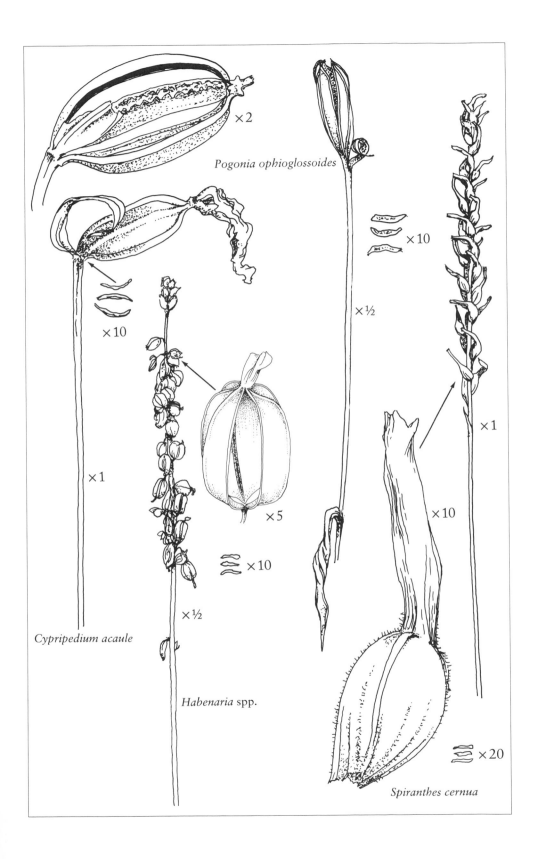

×2

Pogonia ophioglossoides

×10

×½

×10

×1

×1

×1

×5

×10

×10

×½

Cypripedium acaule

Habenaria spp.

×20

Spiranthes cernua

Spiranthes cernua (L.) Rich.
Nodding ladies'-tresses
Orchid Family (Orchidaceae)

KEY IMPRESSIONS Grows 6–18in (15–45cm). Single stem with terminal raceme, 1½–6in (4–15cm), arising from basal leaves. Fruits arranged in double spiral. Stem leaves scalelike.
FRUIT Capsules arranged in double spiral, terminating in extended pointed bracts, 1-chambered, containing minute seeds.
LEAVES Basal, narrowly lance-shaped. Along stem, reduced to overlapping scales.
STEM Single, erect.
PERENNIAL From fleshy roots with tuberous thickenings, descending 1–3in (2.5–7cm).
HABITAT Bogs, meadows.
RANGE Nfld. and Que. to Minn. and S.Dak., south to Fla. and Tex.
SIMILAR SPECIES

S. lacera (Raf.) Raf. Slender ladies'-tresses. Grows 4–16in (10–40cm). Slender. Raceme a single spiral. Dry soil, upland woods, barrens. N.S. to Minn. and south.
S. lucida (H. Eaton) Ames Shining ladies'-tresses. Grows 2–12in (5–30cm). Fruits in double spiral. Damp woods, marshes, wet shores. Maine and N.S. to Wis. and south.
S. romanzoffiana Cham. Hooded ladies'-tresses. Strongly resembles *S. cernua*. Racemes double-spiraled but denser. Meadows. Lab. and Nfld. to Alaska, south to Pa., Mich., Iowa, S.Dak., Colo., and Calif.

Plants with 1-chambered Fruits (Follicles) That Split on 1 Side and with or without Silky-haired Seeds

Note: Seeds may be gone, leaving only papery fruit remnants.

Apocynum androsaemifolium L.
Spreading dogbane
Dogbane Family (Apocynaceae)

KEY IMPRESSIONS Grows 1–4ft (.3–1m). Fruits 2 elongate pendulous follicles. Numerous seeds with tufts of silky hairs. Stems often inclined rather than upright, either simple or, when branched, lacking central axis.
FRUIT 2 long, 2–6in (5–15cm), brown, narrow follicles split open on 1 side. Seeds 2.5–3mm, brown, narrow, with silky hairs at apex.
LEAVES Opposite, oblong to oval, toothless, stemmed.
STEM Simple or branched, lacking central axis, inclined.
PERENNIAL From deep horizontal underground stems.
HABITAT Fields, thickets, woods.
RANGE Throughout region.
SIMILAR SPECIES

A. cannabinum L. Indian hemp, hemp-dogbane. Grows 1–4ft (.3–1m). Erect, with well-developed main axis. Fruit 4–6in (10–15cm). Leaves narrower than in *A. androsaemifolium*. Open places. Abundant from N.Y. to N.Dak., south to Fla. and Tex. Local in e. Canada and n. New Eng.

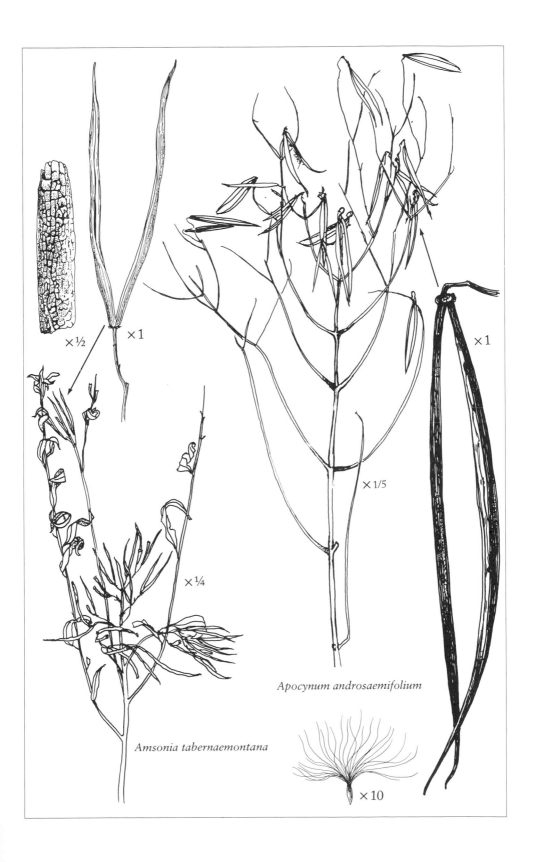

×½

×1

×¼

×1/5

×1

×10

Amsonia tabernaemontana

Apocynum androsaemifolium

Amsonia tabernaemontana Walter

Common bluestar, blue dogbane, willow amsonia

Dogbane Family (Apocynaceae)

KEY IMPRESSIONS Grows to 3ft (1m). Paired cylindric follicles grouped at terminal end.

FRUIT Paired follicles, 3–4¾in (8–12cm), narrow, cylindrical, slightly twisted, constricted at regular intervals, giving slightly beadlike appearance, many seeded. Seeds cylindrical, with no hairs attached, abrupt at both ends, packed in a row.

LEAVES Alternate, 3–6in (8–15cm), toothless, lance-shaped to elliptic.

STEM Erect, clustered.

PERENNIAL

HABITAT Moist or wet woods.

RANGE Coastal plain from N.J. south; interior, north to s. Ind., c. Ill., and Kans.; more widespread in s. U.S. than in n. U.S.

Asclepias syriaca L.

Common milkweed

Milkweed Family (Asclepiadaceae)

KEY IMPRESSIONS Grows to 6ft (2m). Warty follicles round at bottom and pointed at top, erect on deflexed stems. Follicles open down middle, often shiny yellow inside. Flowers grow in terminal or upper axil umbels, but only 1 flower in each umbel develops into a follicle. Flower stalks leave knob of scars.

FRUIT Follicles 2¾–4¾in (7–12cm), warty, hairy, round at bottom, pointed at top. Seeds 8–10mm, brown, flat-margined, with hairs at apex.

LEAVES Opposite, oblong to oval to elliptic.

STEM Tall, stout, hairy.

PERENNIAL From horizontal, creeping underground stems, white, massive, with storage side shoots, traveling long distances underground and creating large networks indicated aboveground by colonies. Roots fibrous.

HABITAT Fields, meadows, roadsides.

RANGE Throughout region.

Asclepias incarnata L.

Swamp-milkweed

Milkweed Family (Asclepiadaceae)

KEY IMPRESSIONS Grows 1–5ft (.3–1.5m). Branched at top. Follicles papery, wrinkled, usually in pairs, and terminal on stem. Found in wet places.

FRUIT Follicles 2–4in (5–10cm), long, narrow, on ascending stems. Seeds flat, margined, with tuft of silky hairs.

LEAVES Opposite, oblong to lance-shaped.

STEM Smooth, shreddy.

PERENNIAL From deep underground stems.

HABITAT Wet places, swamps, ditches, wet prairies.

RANGE Throughout region.

1-chambered Fruits (Follicles) That Split on 1 Side

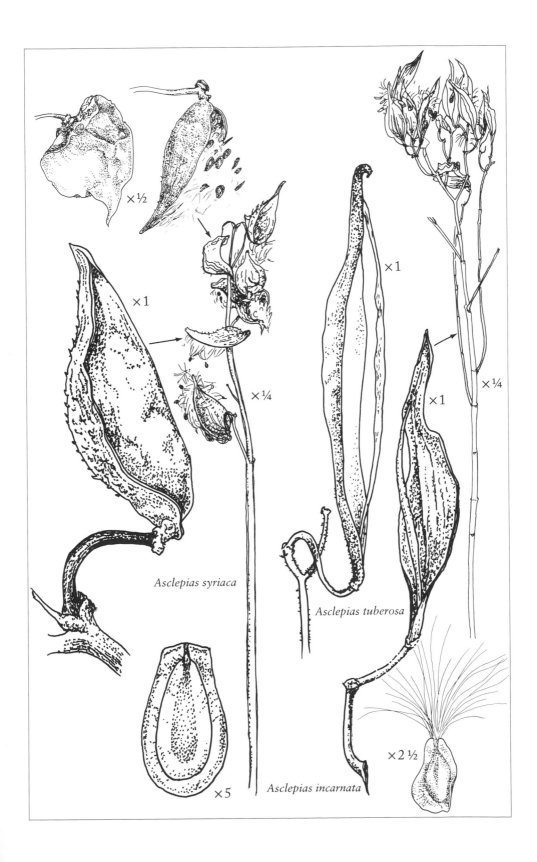

×½

×1

×1

×¼

×1

×1

×¼

Asclepias syriaca

Asclepias tuberosa

×5

Asclepias incarnata

×2½

Asclepias tuberosa L.
Butterfly-weed, pleurisy-root
Milkweed Family (Asclepiadaceae)

KEY IMPRESSIONS Grows to 2½ft (75cm). Rough, hairy plant. Follicles terminal or along upper branches.

FRUIT Follicles 3–5in (8–13cm), rough, hairy, narrow, erect atop deflexed stems. Seeds flat, with silky hairs at apex.

LEAVES Irregularly alternate, linear to oblong-ovate, stemless or with slight stem.

STEM Erect, hairy.

PERENNIAL From deeply penetrating thick taproot that acts as storage reservoir so plant can survive in harsh, dry soil.

HABITAT Dry fields, prairies, upland woods, especially in sandy soil.

RANGE S. N.H. to Fla., west to Minn., S.Dak., and Ariz.

SIMILAR SPECIES

A. amplexicaulis J. E. Smith Clasping milkweed, blunt-leaved milkweed. Follicles longer, more slender than in *A. syriaca*, 4–5in (10–13cm), on strongly deflexed stems. Leaves wavy, with deeply clasping bases. Dry soil, open areas, sandy soil. Throughout region.

A. exaltata L. Poke milkweed, tall milkweed. Follicles erect on strongly deflexed stems, about 6in (15cm) long. Leaves broadly elliptic, pointed at both ends. Moist upland woods. S. Maine to Va. and in mountains to Ga., west to Minn., Iowa, Ill., and Tenn.

A. purpurascens L. Purple milkweed. Similar to *A. syriaca,* but follicles downy, not warty. Dry soil. S. N.H. to Va., west to Wis., Iowa, and Kans.

A. quadrifolia Jacq. Four-leaved milkweed. Follicles 3¼–4¾in (8–12cm), very slender, erect on erect stems. Leaves in whorls of 4. Dry upland woods. Vt. to Va., in mountains to n. Ga., west to s. Ont., Ill., s. Iowa, and Okla.

A. variegata L. White milkweed. Follicles slender, ⅓–¾in (1–2cm) thick, erect on deflexed stems. Leaves 3¼–4¾in (8–12cm), broadly oval. Upland woods, thickets. Conn. and s. N.Y. to n. Fla., west to Ohio, s. Ill., se. Mo., and Tex.

A. verticillata L. Whorled milkweed. Follicles 1½–2in (4–5cm), slender, erect on erect stems. Leaves linear, numerous. Roots fibrous. Fields, roadsides, upland woods, prairies. Mass. to Fla., west to Kans. and Ariz.

Vincetoxicum nigrum (L.) Moench (*Cynanchum nigrum*)
Black swallow-wort
Milkweed Family (Asclepiadaceae)

KEY IMPRESSIONS Grows to 3ft (1m). Climbing, twining, nearly smooth plant. Follicles grow in leaf axils.

FRUIT Follicles 2in (5cm), smooth, linear, papery. Seeds small, flat, with silky hairs.

LEAVES Opposite, oblong to oval, sharply tipped.

STEM Twining, smooth.

PERENNIAL Spreading aggressively by underground stems.

HABITAT Woods, thickets, roadsides.

RANGE Native to s. Europe; escaped from cultivation and locally established throughout region.

1-chambered Fruits (Follicles) That Split on 1 Side

×1

×½

Vincetoxicum nigrum

×5

×1

Plants with 2-chambered Heart-shaped Capsules

Capsella bursa-pastoris (L.) Medikus
Shepherd's purse
Mustard Family (Brassicaceae)

See pl. 14b

KEY IMPRESSIONS Grows 6–20in (15–50cm). 1 to several branches terminated by elongated racemes. Fruits heart-shaped at first; 1 septum remains after sides fall away.
FRUIT Heart-shaped, stemmed. Seeds .9–1.2mm, reddish brown, oval, flattened, each face with longitudinal groove.
LEAVES Basal rosette lobed, overwintering; stem leaves few, linear, toothless.
STEM Sparingly branched.
ANNUAL OR BIENNIAL
HABITAT Open waste areas, roadsides.
RANGE Probably native to s. Europe; common throughout region.

Veronica L. spp.
Speedwell
Figwort Family (Scrophulariaceae)

See pl. 15b

KEY IMPRESSIONS There are many species of *Veronica* in the region. Most are crawlers, but a few are upright. All have similar heart-shaped fruits.
FRUIT Capsules 2-parted, heart-shaped, almost flat.
LEAVES Opposite, tending to remain throughout winter.
PERENNIAL
HABITAT *V. officinalis*, woods, dry fields; *V. serpyllifolia*, *V. persica*, *V. arvensis*, *V. agrestis*, lawns.
RANGE Native to Eurasia; established throughout region.

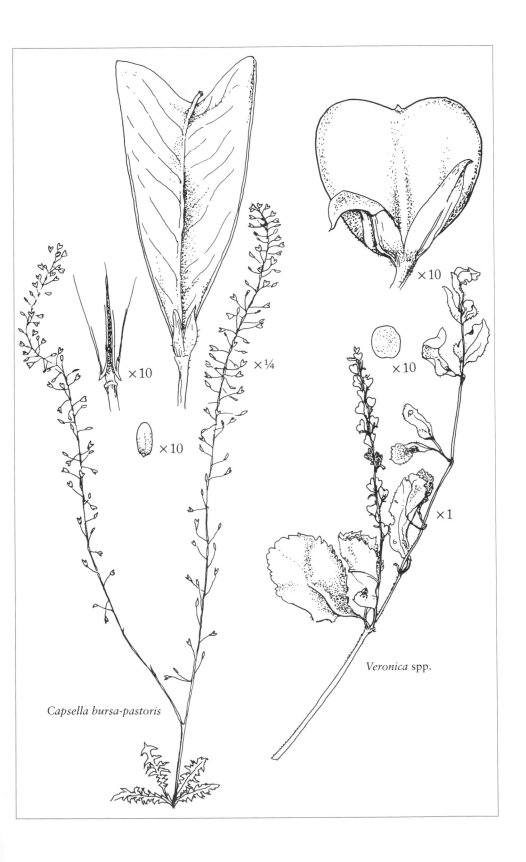

×10

×¼

×10

×10

×10

×1

Veronica spp.

Capsella bursa-pastoris

Plants with 2-chambered Capsules

See also *Epifagus* p. 186, *Aureolaria* p. 90, *Chelone* p. 72, *Agalinis* p. 72, *Mimulus* p. 78, *Penstemon* p. 92, *Scrophularia* p. 74, *Veronicastrum* p. 92, *Verbascum thapsus* p. 168, Mustard Family (Brassicaceae) p. 156

Linaria vulgaris Miller
Butter-and-eggs
Figwort Family (Scrophulariaceae)

KEY IMPRESSIONS   May grow to 3ft (1m), but usually reaches 1ft (30cm). Capsules climb stem as raceme. Leaves linear.

FRUIT   Capsules 8–12mm, oval to globose, divided by thin wall, toothed at top of each half, disintegrating easily. Seeds 1.2–2.5mm, brown to black, flattened, circular, with many winged margins.

LEAVES   Numerous, narrow, linear.

STEMS   Alternate branching.

PERENNIAL   From underground stems that spread to form colonies.

HABITAT   Fields, roadsides, waste areas.

RANGE   Throughout N. Am.

Pedicularis canadensis L.
Lousewort, woody-betony
Figwort Family (Scrophulariaceae)

See pl. 13a

KEY IMPRESSIONS   Grows 1–1½ft (30–45cm). Single stem. 2-parted capsules in raceme at terminal stem end.

FRUIT   Sturdy, woodlike capsules 15mm, oval, dark, with lighter, curled-up underlip, compressed on sides. Capsules split between 2 chambers, opening most deeply along upper median line. Seeds numerous, not winged.

LEAVES   Basal rosette, deeply lobed, pinnate.

STEM   Erect, single.

PERENNIAL   From short underground stems, forming large clumps.

HABITAT   Upland woods, prairies.

RANGE   Que. and Maine to Man., south to Fla. and Tex.

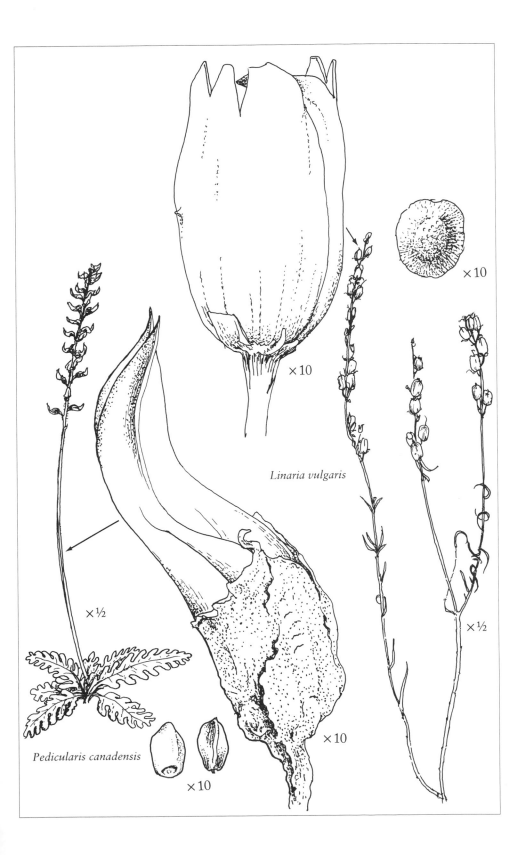

×10

×10

Linaria vulgaris

×½

×½

×10

Pedicularis canadensis

×10

Rhinanthus crista-galli L.

Yellow rattle

Figwort Family (Scrophulariaceae)

KEY IMPRESSIONS   Grows 8–20in (20–50cm). Fruits in upper leaf axils, forming raceme. Capsule surrounded by inflated round to oval calyx. Seeds rattle in capsule.

FRUIT   Capsule orb-shaped, flattened. Seeds winged.

LEAVES   Opposite, toothed, narrowly oblong.

STEM   Single or becoming loosely branched.

ANNUAL

HABITAT   Fields, thickets.

RANGE   Circumboreal; south in U.S. to N.Y., Colo., and Oreg. Lowland *Rhinanthus* species introduced from Europe, alpine species native.

Verbascum blattaria L.

Moth-mullein

Figwort Family (Scrophulariaceae)

KEY IMPRESSIONS   Grows 3–5ft (1–1.5m). Sometimes branched. Capsules line up alternately along straight stem, each on short, upcurved stalk, forming loose raceme.

FRUIT   Capsules round, splitting in 2 along septum. Seeds longitudinally ridged.

LEAVES   Alternate, stemless but not decurrent.

STEM   Smooth, not downy like *V. thapsus*. Basal rosette in first year (biennial).

BIENNIAL

HABITAT   Fields, waste areas, roadsides.

RANGE   Native to Europe; established as weed in disturbed sites throughout region.

Lobelia siphilitica L.

Great lobelia

Lobelia cardinalis L.

Cardinal-flower

Bellflower Family (Campanulaceae)

KEY IMPRESSIONS   These 2 species are very similar in winter appearance. Both grow 20–60in (.5–1.5m). Hairy single stem. Fruit remnants on dense terminal raceme.

FRUIT   Capsule 2-chambered, opening at top. Seeds numerous, fragile, wrinkled, resembling tiny sponges.

LEAVES   Lance-shaped to oval, finely toothed, acutely tipped. *L. siphilitica* leaves stemless; *L. cardinalis* lower leaves stemmed, upper leaves stemless.

STEM   Single, erect, hairy.

PERENNIAL   From basal offshoots.

HABITAT   *L. siphilitica,* rich low woods, swamps, wet ground; *L. cardinalis,* wet areas, shores, meadows, swamps.

RANGE   Throughout region.

2-chambered Capsules

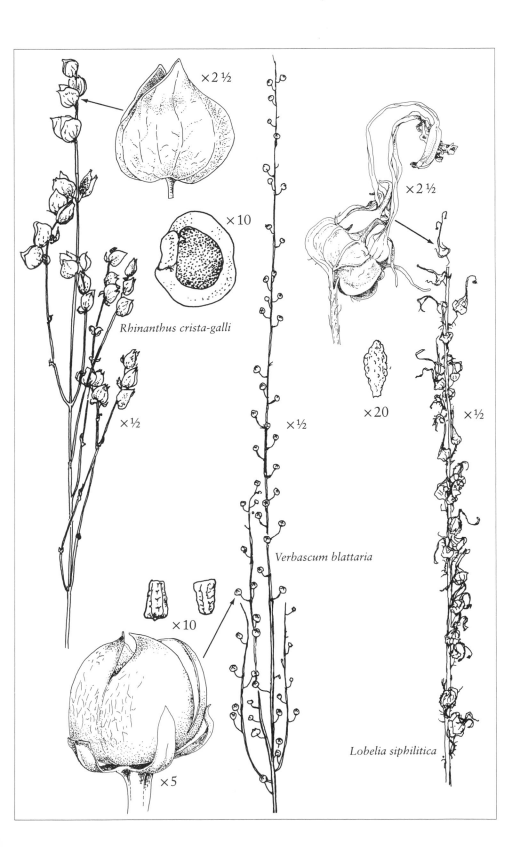

×2 ½

Rhinanthus crista-galli

×10

×½

Verbascum blattaria

×10

×5

×2 ½

×20

×½

Lobelia siphilitica

Plants with 3-chambered Capsules, 1–3in (2.5–7.5cm)

Lilium canadense L.
Canada lily, wild yellow lily
Lily Family (Liliaceae)

KEY IMPRESSIONS Grows to 6ft (2m). Stem pattern varies; sometimes 1 stem, but usually candelabra-type branching.

FRUIT Capsules erect, 3-chambered, 3-angled, oblong, splitting along midline of chamber wall. Seeds flat, papery, densely packed in 2 rows in each locule.

LEAVES Lance-shaped to linear, yielding whorled leaf scars. (Compare to *Iris* spp., which have wraparound leaf scars.)

STEM Sometimes single but more likely candelabra-branched.

PERENNIAL From scaly bulb.

HABITAT Moist woods, meadows, thickets, clearings.

RANGE Que. and Maine to Minn., south to Ala., Ohio, and Ind.

SIMILAR SPECIES

L. superbum L. Turk's-cap lily. Very similar to *L. canadense* in winter appearance, when flowers and leaves unavailable. Leaves, if remaining, appear smooth, whereas leaves of *L. canadense* are rough on veins.

L. lancifolium Thunb. (*L. tigrinum*) Tiger-lily. Leaves alternate, upper with bulblets in axils. Native to Asia; frequent escapee from cultivation, found on roadsides, around dwellings.

Yucca filamentosa L.
Spanish bayonet, Adam's needle
Agave Family (Agavaceae)

KEY IMPRESSIONS Grows 4–9ft (1.3–3m). Fruit remnants in branched racemes raised far above leaves on tall stem. Individual fruit stems covered with short spiny spurs. Basal leaves arise from short, stout underground stem and remain through winter. Leaves thick, rigid, spreading, and ascending, with loose twisting threads on margins.

FRUIT Capsule ½–2in (1.5–4.5cm), cylindric, oval, often constricted near middle, 3-chambered, splitting along midline of capsule wall. Seeds numerous, lustrous black, semi-orbicular.

LEAVES Numerous, stiff, in a tussock, to 32in (81cm), prolonged at summit into a short, stout spine. Somewhat folded at midrib, with fibrous threads along margins.

PERENNIAL From stout, short underground stem.

HABITAT Dry sands of beaches, dunes, old fields, pinelands; mostly near coast.

RANGE Md. to Ga., escapee northward.

Iris versicolor L.
Blue flag, wild iris
Iris Family (Iridaceae)

KEY IMPRESSIONS Grows 2–3ft (.6–1m). Linear, basal leaves wrap around stem. Capsules 3-chambered. Found in wet areas.

FRUIT 3-chambered capsule 1½–2in (3.5–5cm), cylindric, beaked, fragile, appearing 3-angled. Closed through part of winter before flying open along midline of chamber wall.

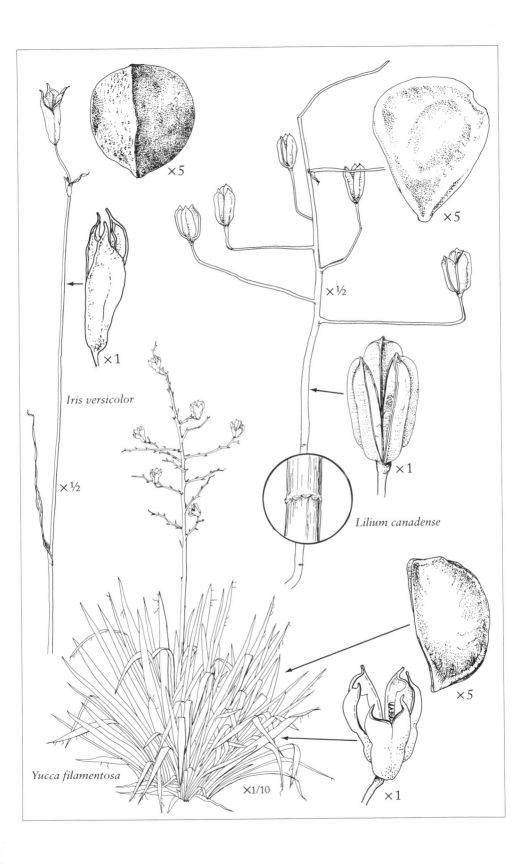

×5

×½

×5

×1

Iris versicolor

×½

×1

Lilium canadense

×5

Yucca filamentosa

×1/10

×1

Inner surface looks varnished. Seeds brown, 3-sided, stacked in 1 row within capsule, with pebbled, firm coat.

LEAVES Erect, sword-shaped, wrapped around stem; when broken off, leave wraparound scars.

STEM Unbranched, stiffly erect, or 1–2 branches from upper part of stem.

PERENNIAL From spreading, stout underground stem.

HABITAT Wet areas, lakeshores, wet meadows.

RANGE Nfld. to Man., south to Minn. and Va.

Xerophyllum asphodeloides (L.) Nutt.
Turkey-beard
Lily Family (Liliaceae)

KEY IMPRESSIONS Large basal tuft of leaves appears grasslike until central stem elongates 2–5ft (.6–1.8m) to produce inflorescence, a dense terminal raceme usually not lasting into winter.

FRUIT 3-lobed capsule splitting between septa.

LEAVES Dense basal cluster, long, slender, persistent, sharp-tipped. Tall stem with similar but smaller leaves.

STEM 2–5ft (.6–1.8m), with small leaves.

PERENNIAL From thick underground stems.

HABITAT Pine barrens.

RANGE N.J., south occasionally to N.C.; mountain woods from Va. to Tenn. and Ga.

Plants with 3-chambered Capsules 1in (2.5cm) or Less

See also *Drosera* spp. p. 26, *Rhexia* spp. p. 74, *Hypericum* spp. p. 94,
Decodon verticillatus p. 24, *Triadenum virginicum* p. 98

Sisyrinchium L. spp.
Blue-eyed grass
Iris Family (Iridaceae)

KEY IMPRESSIONS Grows to 1ft (30cm). Tiny plant, with capsules clustered at terminal end of stem.

FRUIT Capsules less than 8mm across, globular, 3-angled, opening on midline of chambers into 3 main sections. Seeds 2–4mm, black, globular, with pitted surface.

LEAVES Linear to lance-shaped, clasping lower stem, parallel-veined.

STEM Appears flat but is actually round, with 2 wings running up sides.

PERENNIAL From fibrous roots.

HABITAT Grass meadows, clearings, fields.

RANGE Throughout region.

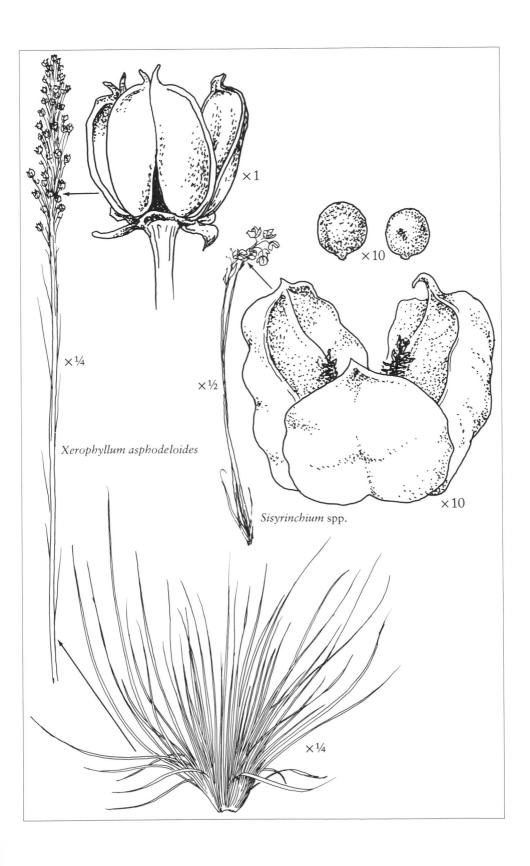

×1

×10

×¼

×½

Xerophyllum asphodeloides

×10

Sisyrinchium spp.

×¼

Euphorbia corollata L.

Flowering spurge

Spurge Family (Euphorbiaceae)

KEY IMPRESSIONS Grows to 3 ft (1 m). Stem simple below, branched above.

FRUIT Capsules 3-lobed, 3-seeded. Seeds 2–2.5 mm long, oval, with dull, pitted surface.

LEAVES Alternate, oval-linear, stemless.

STEM Branching in upper part.

PERENNIAL From deep root with long, stout rootstocks.

HABITAT Dry open woods, clearings, fields, prairies.

RANGE Mass. to Minn., south to Fla. and Tex.

Plants with 4-chambered Capsules

See also *Epilobium* spp. p. 140, *Datura stramonium* p. 48

Ludwigia alternifolia L.

Seedbox, square-pod water-primrose

Evening-primrose Family (Onagraceae)

KEY IMPRESSIONS Grows 1–3 ft (.3–1 m). Fruit capsules are square boxes. Found in wetlands.

FRUIT Capsules 4–5 mm, cube-shaped, 4-chambered, rounded at base, opening by terminal pores. Cube wing-angled. Sepals persistent on capsules.

LEAVES Alternate, lance-shaped, acute at each end, stemmed.

STEM Erect, branched.

PERENNIAL From spindle-shaped roots in bundles.

HABITAT Wet fields, swamps.

RANGE Mass. and s. Ont. to Iowa, south to Fla. and Tex.

Oenothera biennis L.

Common evening-primrose

Evening-primrose Family (Onagraceae)

See pl. 2a

KEY IMPRESSIONS Grows 3–6 ft (1–2 m). Capsules on racemes at terminal ends of branching stems.

FRUIT Capsules 4-chambered, cylindrical, splitting along midline of chambers. Seeds numerous, 1.5 mm, reddish brown, dull, wrinkled, with winged margins, in 2 or more rows.

LEAVES Basal rosette leaves long, smooth, toothed, tinged with spots of red throughout first year. Stem leaves alternate, lance-shaped to oblong, in second year.

STEM Simple or branching.

BIENNIAL From large yellow taproot, edible in first year.

HABITAT Fields, waste areas, roadsides.

RANGE Throughout region.

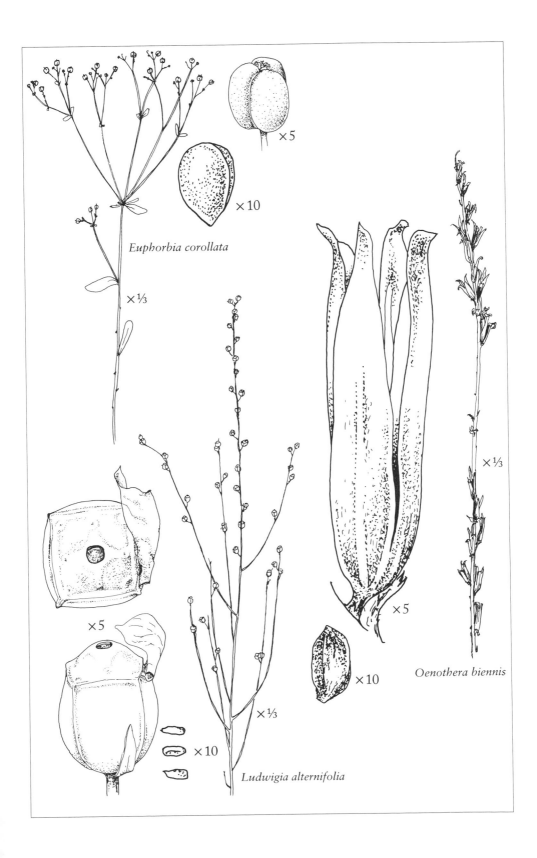

Euphorbia corollata ×⅓ ×5 ×10

Ludwigia alternifolia ×⅓ ×5 ×10

Oenothera biennis ×⅓ ×5 ×10

O. *humifusa* Nutt. Spreading evening-primrose, seabeach evening-primrose. Small, stems rather woody. Capsules few, not forming distinct spike, linear, curved. Seeds dark brown, oval, obscurely pitted. Perennial. Woods, beaches. N.J. to La.

O. *laciniata* Hill. Cut-leaf evening-primrose. Capsules few, stemless, not forming distinct spike, linear, straight or curved. Seeds pale brown, elliptical, conspicuously pitted. Perennial. Dry sandy soil. S.Dak., Ill., Pa., N.J., and south.

O. *parviflora* L. Small-flowered evening-primrose. Smaller than O. *biennis,* usually unbranched. Capsules only slightly tapering. Gravelly shores, sands, dry clearings. Canada and n. U.S.

Plants with Capsules or Follicles Having 5 or More Chambers

See also *Althaea officinalis* p. 18, *Monotropa uniflora* p. 184, *Monotropa hypopithys* p. 186

Abutilon theophrasti Medikus
Velvet-leaf, pie marker
Mallow Family (Malvaceae)

KEY IMPRESSIONS   Grows 2–5ft (.6–1.5m). Stout, branching plant. Fruit many-sectioned, arranged around central "spool."

FRUIT   Fruit 1in (2.5cm) or more diameter; 12–15 chambers around central "spool." Capsule densely hairy, opening at apex. Each chamber has a horizontally spreading beak. Seeds 3–3.6mm, brownish, velvety, kidney-shaped, 3–9 per chamber.

LEAVES   Alternate, velvety, with heart-shaped base and acute tips.

STEM   Stout, branched, downy.

ANNUAL

HABITAT   Cultivated fields, vacant lots.

RANGE   Native to s. Asia; established as weed nearly throughout region but more abundant southward.

Hibiscus moscheutos L.
Rose-mallow
Mallow Family (Malvaceae)

KEY IMPRESSIONS   Grows 3–6ft (1–2m). Upward branches few, terminating in 5-parted capsules.

FRUIT   Capsules 5-chambered, rounded at summit, sometimes with short beak. Velvety sepals if present subtend capsules. Several seeds per chamber.

LEAVES   Stem leaves alternate, broadly oval, sometimes 3-lobed, 1½ times as long as wide.

STEM   Several upward, downy above.

PERENNIAL

HABITAT   Coastal and inland marshes.

RANGE   Mass. and N.Y. to Ohio, s. Wis., and Mo., south to Gulf of Mexico.

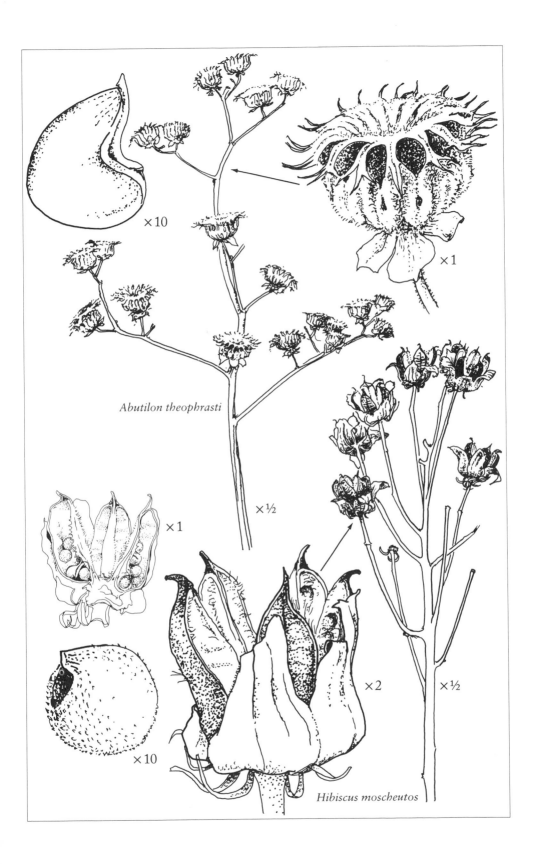

×10

×1

Abutilon theophrasti

×½

×1

×10

×2

×½

Hibiscus moscheutos

Malva neglecta Wallr.
Common mallow, cheeses
Mallow Family (Malvaceae)

See pl. 8b

KEY IMPRESSIONS Small creeping plant. Capsules round, flat, composed of about 15 chambers. The name "cheeses" reflects fruits' appearance.
FRUIT Capsule composed of about 15 chambers. Depressed central portion of head about ⅓ as wide as head. Chambers rounded on back, not wrinkled, usually finely hairy. Seeds reddish brown, kidney-shaped, with finely roughened surfaces; may appear as notched circle.
LEAVES Round, with heart-shaped base, very long stemmed, only obscurely lobed.
STEM Prostrate, trailing to ascending to 3ft (1m).
BIENNIAL From deep root.
HABITAT Waste areas, gardens.
RANGE Native to Eurasia and n. Africa; abundant as weed throughout region.

Aquilegia canadensis L.
Canada-columbine
Buttercup Family (Ranunculaceae)

KEY IMPRESSIONS Grows to 3ft (1m). Fruits erect at branch tips. The fruit has 5 sections.
FRUIT 5 follicles, parallel, ascending, attached, with outcurving summits tipped by persistent styles. Follicles erect, veined in herringbone pattern. Seeds numerous, small, shiny black, cylindrical.
LEAVES Compound, with lobed leaflets.
STEM Erect, branching.
PERENNIAL From stout underground stem.
HABITAT Dry woods, rocky cliffs, rarely swamps.
RANGE Canada, south to Fla. and Tex.

Porteranthus trifoliatus (L.) Britton (*Gillenia trifoliatus*)
Bowman's root, mountain Indian-physic
Rose Family (Rosaceae)

KEY IMPRESSIONS Grows 20–40in (.5–1.1m). Branching, with terminal fruits, each consisting of 5 grouped follicles.
FRUIT 5 follicles, small, 5.5–8mm, downy, rupturing through receptacle. Follicles open completely on ventral side and partially on dorsal side. 2–4 seeds per follicle. Seeds large, flattened.
LEAVES Alternate, with 3 sharply and irregularly finely toothed leaflets, almost stemless.
STEM Branching.
PERENNIAL From underground stems.
HABITAT Dry or moist upland woods, chiefly in mountains.
RANGE S. Ont. to Del., N.C., and Ga., west to e. Ohio, Ky., and Ala.

Capsules or Follicles Having 5 or More Chambers

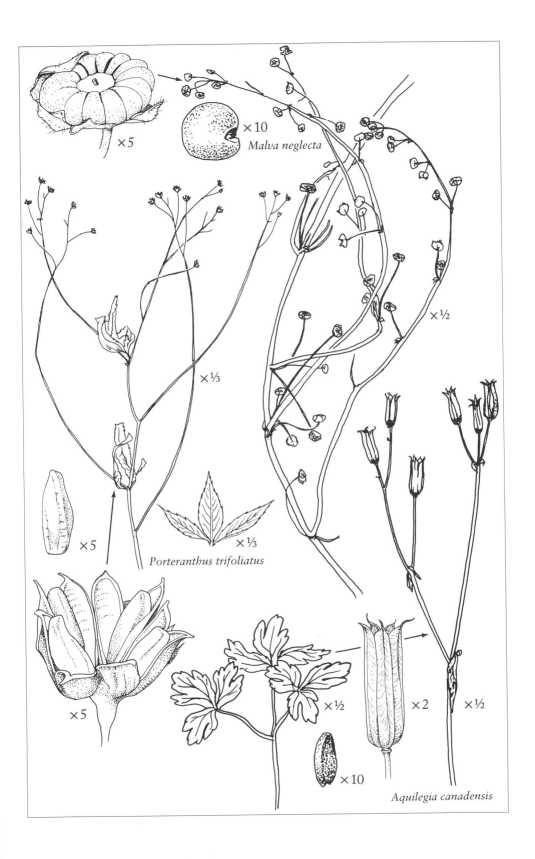

×5

×10

Malva neglecta

×½

×⅓

×⅓

×5

Porteranthus trifoliatus

×5

×½

×2

×½

×10

Aquilegia canadensis

Penthorum sedoides L.

Ditch-stonecrop

Saxifrage Family (Saxifragaceae)

KEY IMPRESSIONS   Grows 1–3ft (.3–1m). 2–4 branches arch out from terminal stem end.

FRUIT   5 follicles, reddish brown, lie on flat, starlike dried calyx. Fruits less than ¼in (1cm) diameter, many-seeded. Seeds tiny, teardrop-shaped, covered with numerous minute white projections at each end.

LEAVES   Alternate, elliptic.

STEM   Simple or branched above.

PERENNIAL   From underground stems.

HABITAT   Open wet areas, marshes, muddy soil.

RANGE   Maine to Ont. and Minn., south to Fla. and Tex.

Dodecatheon meadia L.

Eastern shooting star

Primrose Family (Primulaceae)

KEY IMPRESSIONS   Grows to 2ft (60cm). Stem leafless, with terminal umbels.

FRUIT   Capsules 10.5–18mm, reddish brown, oblong or cylindric, with 5–6 valves and firm, woody walls, on erect terminal umbels. Seeds numerous.

LEAVES   Basal leaf rosette. Bases of leaves sometimes marked with red. Leaves elliptic to oblong, tapering to stem, with blunt or rounded apex.

STEM   Erect, leafless.

PERENNIAL   From stout underground stem with fibrous roots.

HABITAT   Moist or dry woods or prairies.

RANGE   Wis., w. Pa., D.C., and south.

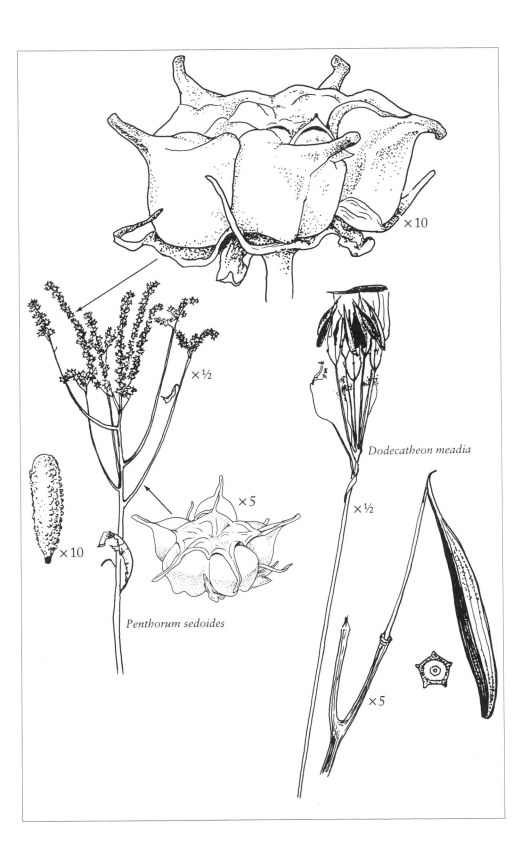

×10

×½

×10

×5

Penthorum sedoides

Dodecatheon meadia

×½

×5

Plants Bearing Fruits or Seeds with Silky, Woolly, or Bristly Hairs Attached

See also *Asclepias* spp. p. 118, *Apocynum* spp. p. 116, *Vincetoxicum nigrum* p. 120, *Clematis* spp. p. 32, Daisy Family (Asteraceae) pp. 204–224

Anemone virginiana L.
Tall anemone, thimbleweed
Anemone cylindrica A. Gray
Long-headed anemone, thimbleweed
Buttercup Family (Ranunculaceae)

KEY IMPRESSIONS These 2 species are hard to distinguish. Plants grow 1–4ft (.3–1.3m). Long, slender stems bulge at nodes with terminal cylindrical receptacles. After fruits have blown away, remaining receptacles form densely woolly heads, ½–¾in (1.2–1.5cm) thick, resembling thimbles.
FRUIT Achenes flattened, topped by persistent hooked style and with spiral of fuzzy hairs attached. Cylindrical receptacles remain after achenes have blown away.
LEAVES Opposite, toothed, palmately compound, sometimes attached in winter, found drooping from stem. Several divided basal leaves.
STEM Erect, slender, with bulges at nodes.
PERENNIAL From stout, branching underground stems.
HABITAT Dry open woods.
RANGE Que. to N.Dak., south to Ga., Ala., and Ark.

Epilobium L. spp.
Willow-herb, fireweed
Evening-primrose Family (Onagraceae)

KEY IMPRESSIONS Some species, such as *E. angustifolium* (see below), grow to 6ft (2m); others grow 1–2ft (.3–.6m). All species have linear, 4-valved fruit and seeds with tufts of hairs.
FRUIT Capsules linear, elongate, 4-valved. Seeds numerous, small, linear, with terminal tuft of hairs. Capsules curl up after seeds have blown away.
LEAVES Alternate to opposite, linear to oval, toothless, stemless.
STEM Erect or ascending.
PERENNIAL
HABITAT Varied; many species found in swampy, boggy, wet areas.
RANGE Throughout region.

Epilobium angustifolium L.
Fireweed, great willow-herb
Evening-primrose Family (Onagraceae)

KEY IMPRESSIONS Grows to 6ft (2m). Silky seeds attached to fruit capsules eventually blow away, leaving capsules all curled up. Fruits on elongate racemes.
FRUIT Capsules long, narrow, 4-sided, 4-chambered, splitting between septa. When open, look like curly spikes. Seeds numerous, small, bearing terminal tuft of white silky hairs.
LEAVES Numerous, mostly alternate, toothless.
STEM Solitary or few, erect, smooth.

Fruits or Seeds with Silky, Woolly, or Bristly Hairs Attached

×5

×½

Anemone virginiana

×⅓

Epilobium angustifolium

×3

×1

×⅓

Epilobium spp.

×10

×5

PERENNIAL From coarse running roots.

HABITAT Varied, especially moist soils, recent clearings, burned woodlands, damp ravines; often found after a fire.

RANGE Cirumboreal; south to N.J., Ohio, n. Ill., Nebr., and N.Mex.

Plants with Flower Remnants Nearly Stemless (Sessile) along Main Stem

Triodanis perfoliata (L.) Nieuwl.

Venus looking-glass, round-leaved triodanis

Bellflower Family (Campanulaceae)

KEY IMPRESSIONS Grows 4in–3ft (.1–1m). Single stem or several long branches. Flower remnants stemless along middle to upper main stem, subtended by bracts that clasp stem.

FRUIT Capsules ¼in (1cm), oblong, opening by pores below fruit tip. Seeds numerous.

LEAVES Alternate, oval, clasping main stem, usually toothless, stemless.

STEM Erect, single or with several long branches.

ANNUAL

HABITAT Varied; often in disturbed sites.

RANGE Throughout region.

Cichorium intybus L.

Chicory

Daisy Family (Asteraceae)

See pl. 6b

KEY IMPRESSIONS Grows 1–3ft (.3–1m). Very common roadside plant. Heads borne 1–3 together, stemless, at leaf axils (leaves have disappeared) along main stems. Bracts of heads are only remnants.

FRUIT Achenes light brown, roughly peg-shaped (triangular in cross-section), ridged, with crown of bristlelike, often minute scales.

LEAVES Basal and small alternate stem leaves usually not seen in winter.

STEM Branching.

PERENNIAL From large, deep, long taproot.

HABITAT Fields, roadsides, waste areas.

RANGE Native to Europe; found as weed throughout region.

Acalypha virginica L.

Three-seeded mercury, Virginia copperleaf

Spurge Family (Euphorbiaceae)

KEY IMPRESSIONS Grows 8in–2ft (20–60cm). Stemless, lobed bracts in leaf axils.

FRUIT Capsules with 1–3 chambers.

LEAVES Lance-shaped to oval, alternate.

STEM Erect, often branched.

ANNUAL

HABITAT Dry or moist open woods, fields, roadsides.

RANGE Maine to Ind. and se. S.Dak. to Fla. and Tex.

Flower Remnants Nearly Stemless (Sessile) along Main Stem

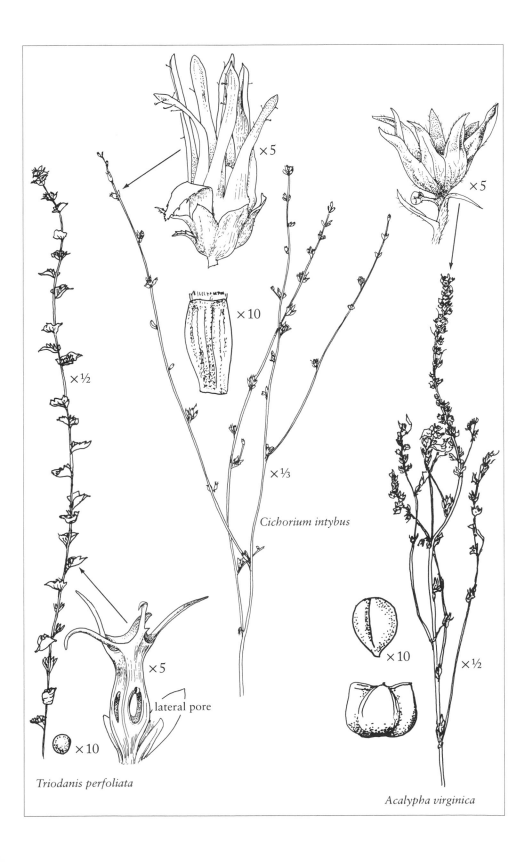

×5

×10

Cichorium intybus

×½

×5

lateral pore

×10

Triodanis perfoliata

×5

×10

×½

Acalypha virginica

×⅓

Plants with Fruit Remnants on Branches Resembling Inverted Umbrellas and Emanating from 1 Point

Although species from several families are represented in this grouping, most members of the Carrot Family (Apiaceae) fit this description. The floral remnants are characterized by inverted umbrella shapes known as "umbels." Because the remnants of many Apiaceae appear quite similar in their winter state, it is helpful to find fruits still clinging to the umbels and to identify the species from these. The fruits, called "schizocarps," are composed of 2 adhering parts. When ripe, they separate upward from the base. At the summit, they are connected by a slender attachment. Each of the 2 portions is marked lengthwise with 5 primary ribs and often 4 intermediate ones.

Oil tubes, longitudinal canals containing aromatic oil, are found in the intervals.

(These are best seen in cross-section cuts of the fruits.)

The leaves are chiefly alternate or basal. They are frequently compound or divided or deeply lobed. The stems of the leaves are dilated to a sheathing base, forming a bulge. The bulges and wrap-around leaf scars remain in winter. The stems are usually hollow and are often grooved.

See also *Medeola virginiana* p. 102, *Dodecatheon meadia* p. 138, *Coptis trifolia* p. 42

Key to Carrot Family (Apiaceae)

1a Plants of wetlands 2
1b Plants of fields, waste areas, and woods 5
   2a Fruits with lateral wings 3
   2b Fruits without lateral wings 4
3a Large, many-branched umbels: Purplestem-angelica (*Angelica atropurpurea*) p. 144
3b Few, loosely branched umbels: Cowbane (*Oxypolis rigidior*) p. 150
   4a Fruit with pale brown ribs: Common water-hemlock (*Cicuta maculata*) p. 146
   4b Fruit with prominent ribs: Water-parsnip (*Sium suave*) p. 152
5a Plants of woods and wood edges 6
5b Plants of fields, meadows, and waste areas 7
   6a Bases of fruits prolonged into bristly tails: Bland sweet cicely (*Osmorhiza claytonii*) p. 150
   6b Umbel branches of differing lengths: Honewort (*Cryptotaenia canadensis*) p. 148
7a Fruits with lateral wings 8
7b Fruits without lateral wings 9
   8a Fruits heart-shaped: Cow-parsnip (*Heracleum lanatum*) p. 148
   8b Fruits with a shallow notch at the top: Parsnip (*Pastinaca sativa*) p. 150
9a Fruits with barbed spines: Queen Anne's lace (*Daucus carota*) p. 148
9b Fruits without barbed spines 10
   10a Fruits with slightly flared apex: Poison hemlock (*Conium maculatum*) p. 146
   10b Fruit apex not flared 11
11a Fruits broadly oval: Fool's parsley (*Aethusa cynapium*) p. 146
11b Fruits oblong: Common golden alexander (*Zizia aurea*) p. 152

Angelica atropurpurea L.
Purplestem-angelica
Carrot Family (Apiaceae)

KEY IMPRESSIONS   Grows 4–6ft (1.3–2m). Large compound umbels, 4–8in (10–20cm) diameter. No subtending bracts. 20–45 primary rays. Found in wetlands.

FRUIT   Broadly oblong to elliptic, ⅓–½in (1–1.3cm), flattened dorsally. Dorsal and intermediate ribs prominent, lateral ribs extending into broad, distinct wings. Oil tubes numer-

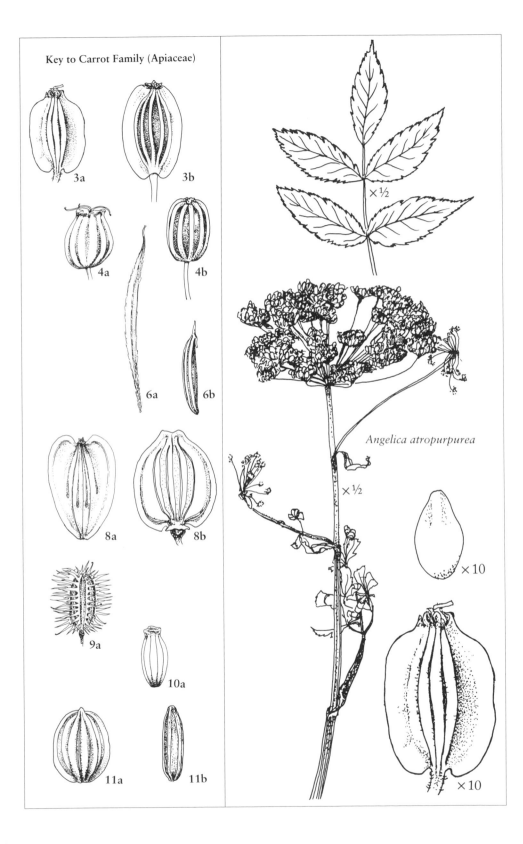

Key to Carrot Family (Apiaceae)

3a

3b

4a

4b

6a

6b

8a

8b

9a

10a

11a

11b

×½

Angelica atropurpurea

×½

×10

×10

ous, 25–30, in cross-section. Seeds loosen from covering, ripening in late fall; spicy and pungent in taste.

LEAVES   Alternate, pinnately compound, long-stemmed.

STEM   Stout, usually hollow, purple or purple-stained.

PERENNIAL OR DELAYED BIENNIAL   With seeds in the third year, from thick, aromatic taproot.

HABITAT   Swamps, wetlands, moist ground.

RANGE   Lab. to Minn., south to Del., W.Va., and Ind.

Aethusa cynapium L.
Fool's parsley
Carrot Family (Apiaceae)

KEY IMPRESSIONS   Grows 1–2½ft (30–76cm). Flower remnant umbels 1¾–2in (2–5cm) wide. No subtending bracts. Leaves dissected. Poisonous.

FRUIT   Broadly oval, ribs corky, very prominent, much wider than intervals. Oil tubes solitary in intervals.

LEAVES   Dissected.

STEM   Freely branched.

ANNUAL

HABITAT   Waste areas, fields.

RANGE   Native to Eurasia; established sparsely as weed from N.S. and Maine to Pa. and Ohio.

Cicuta maculata L.
Common water-hemlock
Carrot Family (Apiaceae)

KEY IMPRESSIONS   Grows to 6ft (2m). Stout branched stems. Numerous loose umbels. Poisonous. Found in swamps, marshes, and other wet areas.

FRUIT   2–4mm, oval, with prominent, rounded, pale brown ribs separated by dark brown intervals. Seam runs down middle of each face, indicating where 2 sides split away.

LEAVES   Broadly oval or triangular, coarsely toothed; principal leaves 2–3 times pinnately compound.

STEM   Stout, branched.

PERENNIAL   From tuberous roots.

HABITAT   Swamps, marshes, ditches, other wet areas.

RANGE   Que. to Minn. and Wyo., south to Fla. and Tex.

Conium maculatum L.
Poison hemlock
Carrot Family (Apiaceae)

KEY IMPRESSIONS   Grows 2–5ft (.6–1.5m). Large leaf scars at nodes of spotted stems. Numerous compound umbels, mostly terminal, to 3in (8cm) diameter. Numerous primary rays. Poisonous.

FRUIT   3mm, oval to circular, with slightly flared apex and longitudinal seam indicating where fruit splits in 2. 5 prominent ribs on each part. Oil tubes small.

LEAVES   Alternate, 3–4 times pinnately compound. Leaflets oval, toothed.

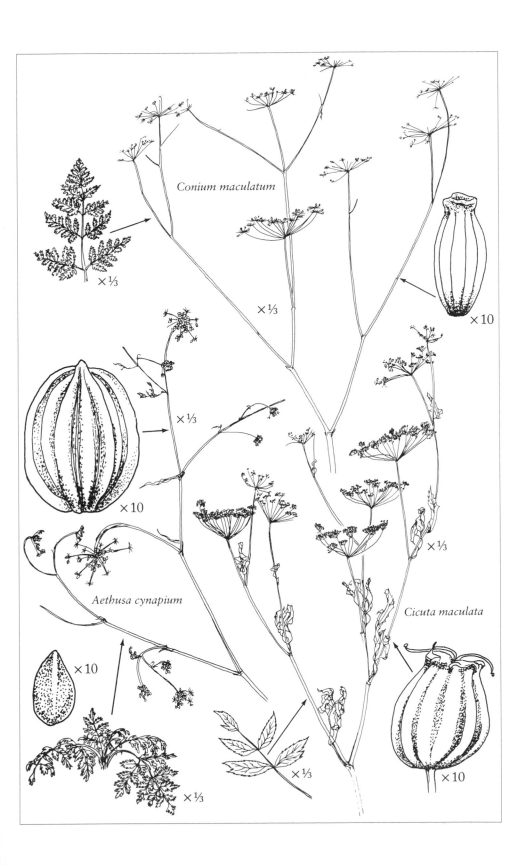

Conium maculatum

×⅓

×⅓

×10

×⅓

×10

Aethusa cynapium

×10

×⅓

×⅓

Cicuta maculata

×⅓

×10

BIENNIAL From large taproot.
HABITAT Waste areas.
RANGE Native to Eurasia; established as weed from Que. to Fla. and west to Pa.

Cryptotaenia canadensis (L.) DC.
Honewort
Carrot Family (Apiaceae)

KEY IMPRESSIONS Grows 1–3ft (.3–1m). Compound umbels irregular and unequally few rayed, 2–7. Fruit stems unequal. Umbels grow terminally from upper axils.
FRUIT 4–6mm, dark, linear to oblong, beaked, ribbed, often curved. 1–4 oil tubes in intervals and beneath each rib.
LEAVES Alternate, compound with 3 leaflets. Lower leaves long-stemmed, upper ones short-stemmed.
STEM Single.
PERENNIAL From fibrous roots.
HABITAT Rich woods, thickets.
RANGE S. Canada south to Ga., Ala., and Tex.

Daucus carota L.
Wild carrot, Queen Anne's lace
Carrot Family (Apiaceae)
See pl. 19a

KEY IMPRESSIONS Basal rosette of dissected leaves in first year. Grows to 3ft (1m) in second year. Many-rayed compound umbels, 2–6in (5–15cm) diameter, terminal on stems. Umbels close up like bird's nests and then reopen, dispersing fruits. Dissected bracts beneath umbels. Fruits have barbed spines.
FRUIT 2.5–3.4mm, oval, with 5 primary and 4 secondary ribs, all with barbed spines. 1 oil tube under each secondary rib.
LEAVES Alternate, dissected. Overwinters as basal rosette of dissected leaves in first year.
STEM Grooved, often hairy.
BIENNIAL From large white taproot with carrot odor.
HABITAT Fields, roadsides, waste areas.
RANGE Native to Eurasia; established as weed throughout U.S.

Heracleum lanatum Michx. (*H. maximum*)
Cow-parsnip
Carrot Family (Apiaceae)

KEY IMPRESSIONS Grows 3–9ft (1–3m). Terminal, compound umbels 4–8in (10–20cm) diameter. No bracts.
FRUIT Heart-shaped, strongly flattened dorsally. 4 dark lines (oil tubes) extend from summit about halfway to base. Lateral ribs broad-winged, each with conspicuous nerve. Oil tubes solitary in intervals.
LEAVES Large, compound, rotund in general outline. Leaflets broadly oval, heart-shaped at base.

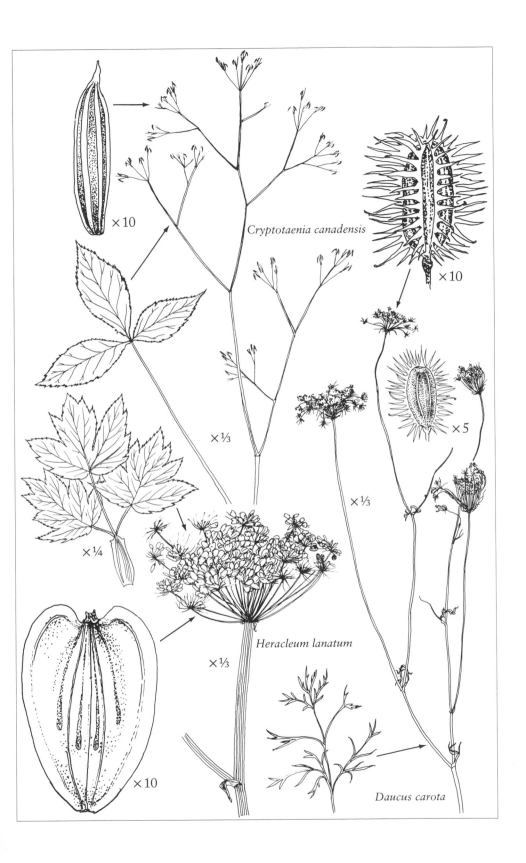

×10

Cryptotaenia canadensis

×10

×1/3

×5

×1/3

×1/4

×1/3

Heracleum lanatum

×1/3

×10

Daucus carota

STEM Stout, downy, grooved, hollow.
PERENNIAL
HABITAT Rich, damp soil.
RANGE Lab. to Alaska, south to Ga. and Ariz.

Osmorhiza claytonii (Michx.) C. B. Clarke
Bland sweet cicely
Carrot Family (Apiaceae)

KEY IMPRESSIONS Grows 16–30in (40–76cm). Irregular umbels have few branches and no bracts beneath. Plants fragile, found broken down to the ground. Long, hooked fruits with upcurved hairs along ribs stick to passersby.
FRUIT Linear, slightly flattened laterally, bristly. Base prolonged into bristly tails. Oil tubes obscure or lacking.
LEAVES Twice compound. Lower leaves stemmed, upper leaves stemless. Leaflets toothed, often much cleft.
STEM Slender.
PERENNIAL From fibrous, rank-tasting roots.
HABITAT Moist woods.
RANGE Canada, south to N.C., Ala., and Mo.

Oxypolis rigidior (L.) Raf.
Cowbane, common water-dropwort
Carrot Family (Apiaceae)

KEY IMPRESSIONS Grows 2–6ft (.6–2m). Few leaves or branches. Few, loose compound umbels grow to 6in (15cm) diameter. No bracts under umbel.
FRUIT 4.5–6mm, elliptic or oblong, strongly flattened dorsally, rounded at both ends. Lateral ribs expand into wings and bear a longitudinal nerve near margins. Oil tubes are solitary in intervals, 2–6 in commissures.
LEAVES Alternate, once pinnately compound. 5–9 stemless leaflets, varying from narrowly linear to elliptic.
STEM Erect, smooth.
PERENNIAL From tuberous roots.
HABITAT Marshes, swamps, wet woods, wet prairies.
RANGE Long Island to s. Ont. and Minn., south to Fla. and Tex.

Pastinaca sativa L.
Parsnip
Carrot Family (Apiaceae)

KEY IMPRESSIONS Grows to 5ft (1.6m). Large compound umbels 4–8in (10–20cm) diameter. No bracts subtend umbels.
FRUIT 5–7mm, broadly elliptic, flattened dorsally, with broad, shallow notch at apex. Lateral ribs extend into broad wings with distinct nerve near margins. Central rib flanked by dark brown stripes on ventral side; 3 fine ribs alternating with 4 brown stripes on dorsal side.
LEAVES Alternate, compound. Lower leaves long-stemmed, upper leaves short-stemmed. Leaflets oblong, toothed or lobed. Basal rosette in first winter.

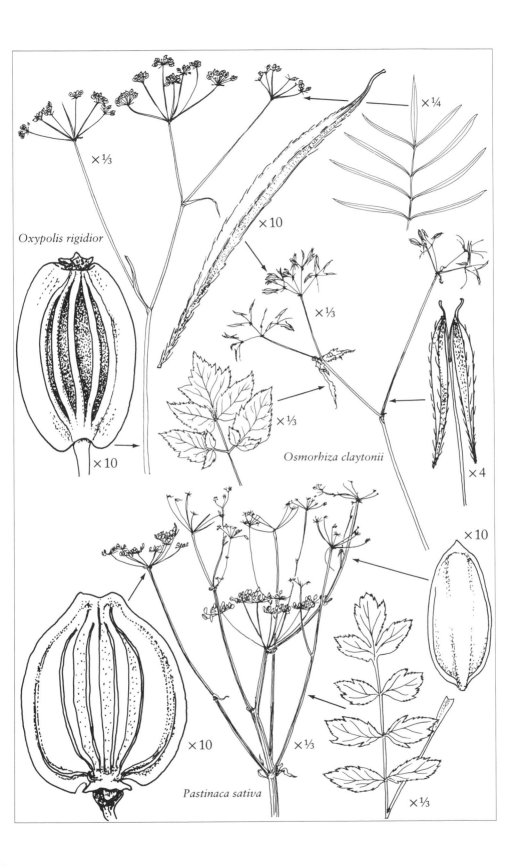

×¼

×⅓

Oxypolis rigidior

×10

×10

×⅓

×⅓

Osmorhiza claytonii

×4

×10

×10

×⅓

Pastinaca sativa

×⅓

STEM Stout, grooved.
BIENNIAL From taproot.
HABITAT Waste areas, roadsides.
RANGE Native to Eurasia; established as weed throughout most of N. Am.

Sium suave Walter
Water-parsnip
Carrot Family (Apiaceae)

KEY IMPRESSIONS Grows 2–6ft (.6–2m). Compound umbels 1¼–4¾in (3–12cm) wide. 2 to several bracts under umbels. Stem solitary.
FRUIT 2–3mm, oval, flattened laterally, ribs very prominent.
LEAVES Compound, alternate. 5 to many leaflets, elongate, toothed.
STEM Stout, strongly ridged.
PERENNIAL From short, erect underground stem with fibrous roots.
HABITAT Swamps, wet meadows, muddy waters.
RANGE Canada, south to Fla., La., and Calif.

Zizia aurea (L.) Koch
Common golden alexander
Carrot Family (Apiaceae)

KEY IMPRESSIONS Grows 1–2½ft (30–76cm). Compound umbels with 10–18 primary rays, stiffly ascending at maturity of fruit. No bracts subtend umbels.
FRUIT Oblong, flattened laterally, with 5 ribs in each of 2 sections and no wings.
LEAVES Lower leaves are twice compound, upper leaves once compound with 3 leaflets. Leaflets oval, finely toothed.
STEM Erect, branched.
PERENNIAL From cluster of thickened roots.
HABITAT Moist fields, meadows.
RANGE Que. and Maine to Sask., south to Fla. and Tex.

Allium tricoccum Aiton
Wild leek, ramps
Lily Family (Liliaceae)

KEY IMPRESSIONS Grows 6–12in (15–30cm). Leaves appear in spring, then disappear, followed by appearance of flower and fruit. Underground bulb has strong onion odor. Leafless stem terminated by 1 umbel bearing capsules and seeds.
FRUIT Capsules 3-lobed, oval, carried on umbel branches, splitting between septa. Seeds 1 per chamber, black, large, globular, smooth, contained inside 3-parted capsules, developing late in fall. Capsule walls open downward under seeds.
LEAVES Basal leaves wither before flowers appear.
STEM Erect, leafless.
PERENNIAL From 3–4 bulbs with fleshy coats that cluster, forming crown on underground stem.
HABITAT Rich woods.
RANGE S. Que. and New Eng. to Minn., south to N.C., Tenn., and Va.

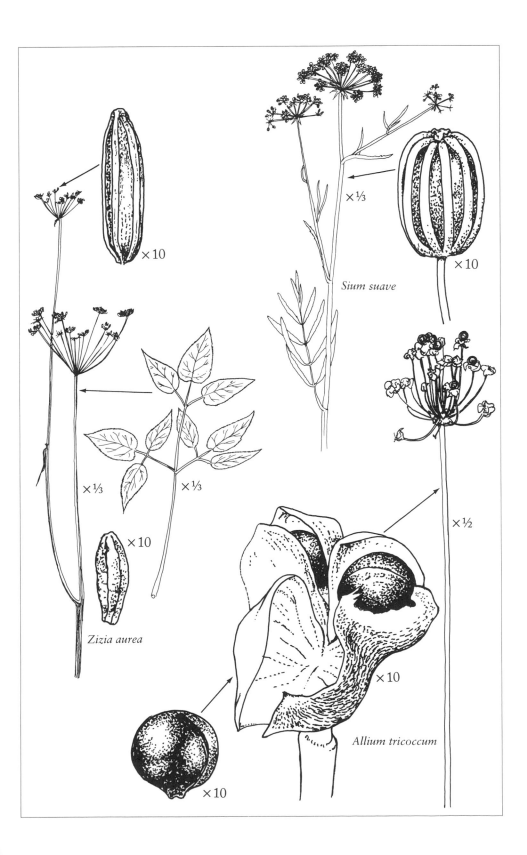

×10

×⅓

Sium suave

×10

×⅓

×⅓

×⅓

×10

×½

Zizia aurea

×10

×10

Allium tricoccum

×10

Allium vineale L.
Field-garlic, scallions
Lily Family (Liliaceae)

KEY IMPRESSIONS   Grows 1–2½ft (30–75cm). Terminal umbel projects from bracts that fall early. Numerous oval bulblets tipped by curving tail.

FRUIT   Usually umbels of bulblets with curving tails, but some develop into 3-parted capsules.

LEAVES   Grow halfway up stem, hollow. Basal leaves overwinter.

STEM   Erect, hollow, round, stiff.

BIENNIAL   From small, round bulbs crowded on short rootstocks. Outer bulb coats membranous. Older bulbs form dense mats.

HABITAT   Fields, meadows.

RANGE   Native to Europe; established as pervasive weed from New Eng. to Va., Tenn., and Kans.

Aralia nudicaulis L.
Wild sarsaparilla
Ginseng Family (Araliaceae)

KEY IMPRESSIONS   Grows 1.5–3ft (.5–1m). Stem terminated by round umbel of blue-black drupes, separate from leaf stem. Umbel of empty receptacles remains after drupes have gone.

FRUIT   Drupes blue-black, round, grooved, topped by persistent styles.

LEAVES   Alternate, rising from base on erect petioles, twice compound. Absent in winter.

STEM   Leaves and fruits on separate stems; fruit stem remains after leaf stem has blown away.

PERENNIAL   From long, horizontal, aromatic, ropelike underground stems, often in the form of runners, sending up several individual plants.

HABITAT   Dry woods, sandy soil.

RANGE   Canada, south to D.C., Ind., Nebr., and Colo.; in mountains to Ga.

SIMILAR SPECIES

  A. hispida Vent.   Bristly sarsaparilla. Compound leaves on same stem with terminal umbels. Stem has soft spines. Dry open woods. Nfld. and Que. to Minn., south to N.J., W.Va., and n. Ind.

Plants with Exploded Fruits Resembling Non-inverted Umbrellas

The Geranium Family (Geraniaceae) is characterized by having 5 parts to the ovary, each attached to a persistent style. The 5 styles are elongated in a central column. When ripe, the 5 parts of the fruit separate elastically from the elongated axis, roll up on the style, and discharge their seeds.

Geranium maculatum L.
Wild geranium
Geranium Family (Geraniaceae)

KEY IMPRESSIONS   Grows 1–2ft (30–60cm). Basal leaves, 1 pair of stem leaves. Basal rosettes overwinter. Look for umbrellalike fruit remnants.

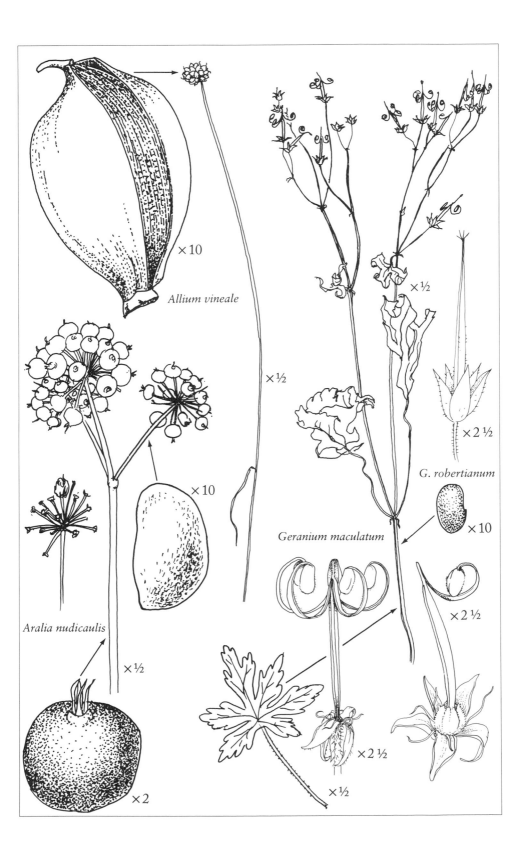

×10

Allium vineale

×½

×½

×½

×½

×2½

×2½

G. robertianum

×10

Geranium maculatum

×10

×2½

Aralia nudicaulis

×2

×½

×2½

FRUIT Does not last into winter. Vertical beak, the style, ¾–1¼in (2–3cm), extends upward from 5-parted ovary. Long beak attached to length of style on each part. When fruit ripens, beaks kick off and curl upward from style, remaining attached at tip. Seeds dark brown, oval, covered with network of light-colored veins. 1 seed per part.
LEAVES Basal leaves long-stemmed, lobed like palm of hand. 1 pair of opposite stem leaves.
STEM Forking.
PERENNIAL From branching, stout underground stems.
HABITAT Woodlands, thickets, meadows.
RANGE Maine to S.C., west to Man., Nebr., and ne. Okla.
SIMILAR SPECIES
> A number of *Geranium* species differ in leaf shape but are alike in conformation of fruit remnants, closely resembling the "umbrella" arrangement found in *G. maculatum*.
> *G. robertianum* L. Herb-Robert. Stems grow to 2ft (60cm). Low-growing, much branched, spreading. 5 parts of ovary detach entirely from stylar beak when ripe, unlike in *G. maculatum*; fruit remnant therefore lacks "umbrella" appearance. Leaves finely divided, pinnately lobed, triangular in outline. Annual or winter annual from slender taproot. Damp, rich woods, talus slopes. Native to Eurasia; widely naturalized throughout region.

Plants Having Spikes and Racemes with Translucent Partitions of Fruits (Septa) Remaining Attached to the Stem, Often Having Evergreen Basal Leaf Rosettes: Mustard Family (Brassicaceae)

See also *Capsella bursa-pastoris* p. 122, *Raphanus raphanistrum* p. 100
The Mustard Family (Brassicaceae) is characterized by 2-chambered fruit capsules separated by a central septum. The septum usually remains after the 2 sides of the capsule have fallen away. There are 2 types of these capsules, siliques (long, narrow) and silicles (short, round).

Key to Mustard Family (Brassicaceae)

1a Fruits siliques, narrow, elongate 2
1b Fruits silicles, short, oval 6
    2a Fruits 2–5½in (5–13cm) 3
    2b Fruits 1½–2¾in (3.5–7cm) 4
3a Fruits 3½–5½in (8–13cm), hanging strongly downward on stem: Rock-cress (*Arabis* spp.) p. 158
3b Fruits 2–4in (5–10cm) long, projecting perpendicularly from stem: Dame's rocket (*Hesperis matronalis*) p. 160
    4a Fruits 1½–2¾in (4–7cm), pointing outward and upward: Garlic-mustard (*Alliaria petiolata*) p. 158
    4b Fruits 1¼–2in (3–5cm), pointing strongly upward 5
5a Septa and fruits crowded on stem: Yellow rocket (*Barbarea vulgaris*) p. 158
5b Septa and fruits not crowded on stem: Mustard (*Brassica* spp.) p. 160
    6a Fruits and septa 1½–2in (3.5–5cm), broad and flat: Honesty (*Lunaria annua*) p. 164
    6b Fruits smaller than above 7

Key to Mustard Family (Brassicaceae)

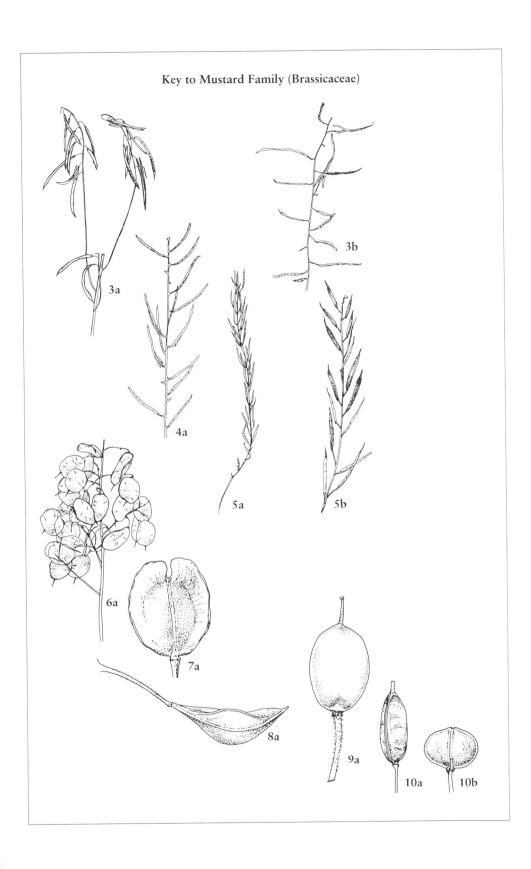

7a Fruits with distinct notch at top: Field penny-cress (*Thlaspi arvense*) p. 164
7b Fruits without distinct notch at top **8**
  8a Fruits distinctly spoon-shaped: Field-cress (*Lepidium campestre*) p. 162
  8b Fruits round to oval and not spoon-shaped **9**
9a Fruits 5.5–8mm, plump, downy, oblong: Hoary alyssum (*Berteroa incana*) p. 160
9b Fruits flat, elliptic **10**
  10a Fruits 2.5–9mm, topped by persistent style: Common yellow-cress (*Rorippa palustris*) p. 164
  10b Fruits 2.5–4mm, style not persistent: Poor-man's pepper (*Lepidium virginicum*) p. 162

Arabis L. spp.
Rock-cress
Mustard Family (Brassicaceae)

KEY IMPRESSIONS   Grows to 3ft (1m). Stems erect, unbranched. Fruits typically elongated, slender, extending outward and downward.
FRUIT   Siliques narrow, slender, 3–5in (8–13cm) long, 1–2mm wide. Seeds flattened, often with marginal wing.
LEAVES   Basal leaves stemmed. Stem leaves usually smaller, stemless.
STEM   Erect, unbranched.
ANNUAL, BIENNIAL, OR PERENNIAL
HABITAT   Moist or dry soil in varied habitats.
RANGE   Widely distributed in northern temperate zone.

Alliaria petiolata (Bieb.) Cavara & Grande (*A. officinalis*)
Garlic-mustard
Mustard Family (Brassicaceae)
See pl. 8c

KEY IMPRESSIONS   Grows to 4ft (1.3m). Few branches, terminal racemes. Silvery septa project out perpendicular to stem in winter. Look for green basal rosette that gives off a garlic odor when crushed.
FRUIT   Silique 1½–2½in (4–7cm), 4-angled, falling apart easily along septum. Seeds 3mm, black, oblong, striate.
LEAVES   Alternate. Lower leaves kidney-shaped, upper leaves triangular or oval. Green winter leaf rosette scalloped, kidney-shaped.
STEM   Somewhat branched.
BIENNIAL OR PERENNIAL
HABITAT   Roadsides, open woods.
RANGE   Native to Europe; pervasive weed throughout region.

Barbarea vulgaris R. Br.
Yellow rocket, winter-cress
Mustard Family (Brassicaceae)
See pl. 12a

KEY IMPRESSIONS   Grows to 3ft (1m). Bushy branched, with many fruits in terminal racemes. Winter leaf rosette continues to produce some leaves. Fruits point upward.

Arabis spp.

×½
×2
×½
×10

Alliaria petiolata

×2
×10
×⅓

×⅓

×2
×⅓
×⅓
Barbarea vulgaris
×10

FRUIT   Siliques 1 in (2.5 cm), thin. Beak at tip 1.5–3 mm. Silvery septa project upward when fruit opens in winter. Seeds 1.5–1.9 mm, grayish, oval, in 1 row, finely pitted.

LEAVES   Alternate. Green winter leaf rosette. Lower leaves lyre-shaped; terminal lobe largest, smaller lobes narrow, in 1–4 pairs. Upper leaves rounded, coarsely toothed.

STEM   Much branched.

BIENNIAL OR PERENNIAL   From underground stems.

HABITAT   Wet meadows, damp soil of fields, roadsides, gardens.

RANGE   Widespread.

Berteroa incana (L.) DC.
Hoary alyssum
Mustard Family (Brassicaceae)

KEY IMPRESSIONS   Grows 1–2 ft (30–60 cm). Branching above, with terminal racemes of oblong silicles. After silicles have opened, remaining central septa are small translucent ovals with pointed tips.

FRUIT   Silicles 5–8 mm long, 2.5–3.5 mm thick, plump, downy, oblong, with short, pointed tips. Seeds 1.5–1.9 mm, reddish brown, circular, grooved, slightly winged. 2–6 seeds per cell.

LEAVES   Alternate, toothless.

STEM   Branching above, stiffly erect.

ANNUAL

HABITAT   Roadsides, disturbed areas.

RANGE   Native to Europe; established as weed throughout region, especially northward.

Brassica L. spp.
Mustard
Mustard Family (Brassicaceae)

KEY IMPRESSIONS   Grows 1–3 ft (.3–1 m). Stems erect, not branching. Fruits elongate and cylindrical, terminated by a beak.

FRUIT   Siliques ¼–1½ in (1–4 cm), cylindrical, round to angled, terminated by round to angular beak. Beak either nerveless or 1-nerved on each side. Capsule sides have 1 prominent mid-nerve. Seeds in 1 row on each side, round, globose.

LEAVES   Lower leaves more or less deeply cut and lobed.

STEM   Erect, not branched.

ANNUAL OR BIENNIAL

HABITAT   Fields, waste areas.

RANGE   Native to Eurasia; established as weed throughout region.

SIMILAR SPECIES

   Sinapsis spp. L.   Charlock, white mustard. 3–5 prominent veins on capsule valves, beak 3-nerved on each side, often flattened, 2-edged, with 1–3 seeds.

Hesperis matronalis L.
Dame's rocket
Mustard Family (Brassicaceae)

KEY IMPRESSIONS   Grows to 3 ft (1 m). Simple or branched above. Racemes terminal, with slender siliques.

FRUIT   Siliques 2–4 in (5–10 cm), slender, linear, somewhat constricted between seeds.

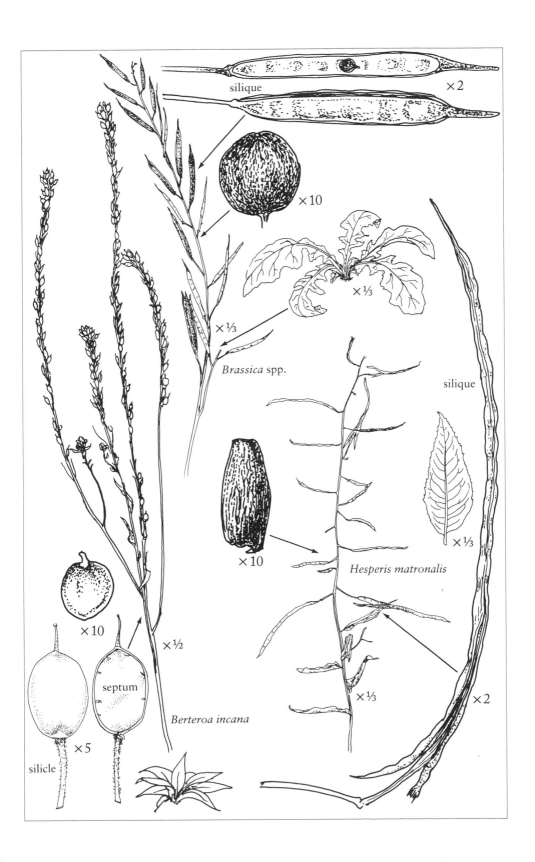

silique ×2

×10

×1/3

Brassica spp.

×1/3

silique

×1/3

×10

Hesperis matronalis

×10

×1/2

septum

×5

silicle

Berteroa incana

×1/3

×2

Fruits widely spreading on stout stems, scarcely opening, with persistent stigma. Seeds numerous, large (3–4mm), in 1 row.

LEAVES Lance-shaped to oblong, terminating in acute point.

STEM Erect, simple or branched above.

PERENNIAL

HABITAT Formerly cultivated as garden plant; frequent escapee along roads, fencerows.

RANGE Que. and N.S. to Mich. and Iowa, south to Ga. and Ky.

Lepidium campestre (L.) R. Br.
Field-cress, cow-cress
Mustard Family (Brassicaceae)

KEY IMPRESSIONS Grows to 2ft (60cm). Simple to branched, with numerous racemes. Silicle spoon-shaped, broadly winged.

FRUIT Silicle 5–6mm, deeper (spoon-shaped) and more oblong than in *L. virginicum* (below), broadly winged, with barely extending short style. Seeds 2–2.5mm, dark to reddish brown, oval, with dull, granular surface. 1 seed per chamber.

LEAVES Arrowhead-shaped, clasping stem with acute wings. Basal rosette leaves elongated, toothless or shallowly lobed.

STEM Simple to branched.

ANNUAL OR BIENNIAL

HABITAT Waste areas, roadsides, fields.

RANGE Native to Europe; established as weed throughout region.

Lepidium virginicum L.
Poor-man's pepper
Mustard Family (Brassicaceae)

KEY IMPRESSIONS Grows to 3ft (1m). Single stalk or bushy branching, numerous and persistent fruit septa.

FRUIT Silicle 2.5–4mm, flat, 2-chambered, elliptic to orb-shaped, narrowly winged across tip, style included in notch. Silvery central septum remaining on stem after chambers open. Seeds 1.1–1.5mm, orange to yellow, oval. 1 seed per chamber.

LEAVES Winter basal rosette sharply toothed, alternate. Linear leaves on stem incised or toothless.

STEM Single or bushy branched.

ANNUAL OR BIENNIAL Depending on when seeds germinate; from narrow, deep taproot.

HABITAT Roadsides, fields, waste areas.

RANGE Nfld. to Fla.

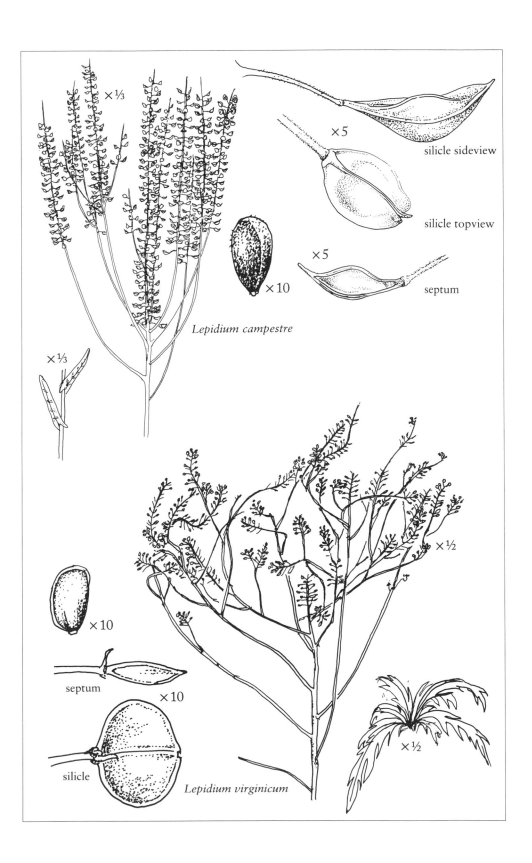

×⅓

×5

silicle sideview

silicle topview

×5

septum

×10

Lepidium campestre

×⅓

×½

×10

septum

×10

silicle

×½

Lepidium virginicum

Lunaria annua L.
Honesty, silver-dollar-plant, money-plant
Mustard Family (Brassicaceae)
KEY IMPRESSIONS   Grows to 3ft (1m). Distinctive large, round fruits.
FRUIT   Silicles 1½–2in (3.5–5cm) long and ⅔ as wide, very broad, flat, net-veined. Silvery septum persists in winter. Seeds blackish, flat, kidney-shaped.
LEAVES   Heart-shaped, coarsely toothed.
STEM   Erect, branched.
ANNUAL OR BIENNIAL
HABITAT   Roadsides, waste ground.
RANGE   Native to se. Europe; garden escapee.

Rorippa palustris (L.) Besser
Common yellow-cress
Mustard Family (Brassicaceae)
KEY IMPRESSIONS   Grows to 3ft (1m). Taller plants usually much branched.
FRUIT   Siliques short, 2.5–9mm, up to twice as long as their stems, topped by short, persistent style. Seeds minute, numerous, in 2 rows in each chamber.
LEAVES   Mostly sharply lobed.
STEM   Erect, unbranched.
ANNUAL OR BIENNIAL   From taproot.
HABITAT   Wet areas, shores.
RANGE   Throughout region.

Thlaspi arvense L.
Field penny-cress
Mustard Family (Brassicaceae)
KEY IMPRESSIONS   Grows 4in–3ft (.1–1m). Fruits round, flattened, winged, notched at tip. Flat, pointed silvery membranes remain in winter.
FRUIT   Silicles round to broadly elliptical, entirely winged, deeply notched at tip, flattened contrary to septum. Seeds numerous in each chamber, flattened, oval with concentric ridges.
LEAVES   Lance-shaped, clasping stem at base with 2 acute wings.
STEM   Erect, sometimes single, sometimes branched.
ANNUAL OR WINTER-ANNUAL
HABITAT   Common in waste areas.
RANGE   Native to Europe; commonly established throughout N. Am.

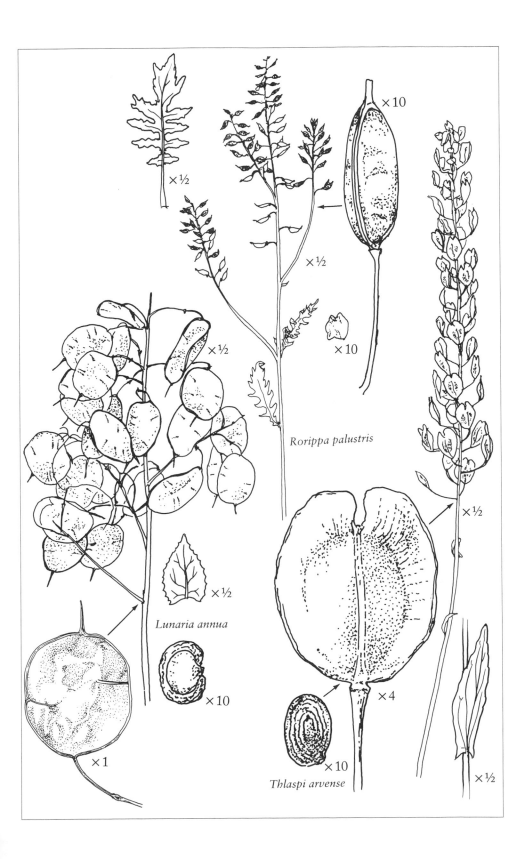

×½

×½

×10

×½

×½

×10

Rorippa palustris

×½

×½

Lunaria annua

×10

×4

×1

×10

Thlaspi arvense

×½

Plants with Fruit Remnants in Spikes and Racemes, 6–18in (15–45cm)

See also *Verbena urticifolia* p. 76, *V. hastata* p. 76, *Lysimachia terrestris* p. 96,
Phryma leptostachya p. 96, *Veronicastrum virginicum* p. 92, *Lespedeza* spp. p. 174,
Verbascum blattaria p. 126, *Liatris* spp. pp. 214–216, *Lobelia inflata* p. 184,
Phytolacca americana p. 102, *Aralia racemosa* p. 106, *Anemone* spp. p. 140

Campanula americana L.
Tall bellflower
Bellflower Family (Campanulaceae)

KEY IMPRESSIONS   Grows 1½–5ft (.5–1.5m), erect and freely branched. Capsules stemless in groups along stem. Spikes 1ft (30cm) or more.

FRUIT   Capsules 7–12mm, strongly ribbed, opening by 3–5 lateral pores, with 5 sepals at terminal end. Seeds 1.3mm, oval.

LEAVES   Lance-shaped to oval, alternate, stemmed, toothed.

STEM   Erect, branched, round.

ANNUAL OR BIENNIAL

HABITAT   Moist borders, open woods.

RANGE   Minn. to s. Ont., N.Y., and south.

Cimicifuga racemosa (L.) Nutt.
Black snakeroot, black cohosh
Buttercup Family (Ranunculaceae)

KEY IMPRESSIONS   Grows 3–8ft (1–1.6m). Erect, elongate, many-fruited racemes 1–3ft (.3–1m), branching at terminal stem end. Fruits small follicles.

FRUIT   Follicles 6–9mm, oval, on short stems, firm-walled, tipped with persistent style that becomes recurved. Seeds 2.2 × 1.6mm, obliquely elliptic, rough on sides, lying horizontally in double row. Several seeds per fruit.

LEAVES   Compound, toothed.

STEM   Tall, erect, round.

PERENNIAL   From knotty underground stem.

HABITAT   Moist or dry woods.

RANGE   Mass. to N.Y., Ohio, Ind., and Mo., south to S.C., Va., and Tenn.

Sanguisorba canadensis L.
American burnet
Rose Family (Rosaceae)

KEY IMPRESSIONS   Grows 1–6ft (.3–2m). Spikes 6–10in (15–25cm), erect on long stems. Receptacle tubes persistent, 4-angled, dry and thickish, constricted at throat, enclosing achene.

lateral pore

×5

×10

×½

seed

×10

capsule

×5

×½

Campanula americana

Cimicifuga racemosa

×¼

FRUIT Achene 2mm, oval.
LEAVES Compound with 7–15 sharply toothed leaflets, stemmed.
STEM Erect, simple below, branched above.
PERENNIAL From thick underground stem.
HABITAT Marshes, wet meadows, damp prairies.
RANGE Lab. and Nfld. to Man., south to N.J., Pa., Ohio, and Ind.; in mountains to N.C.
SIMILAR SPECIES

> *S. officinalis* L. European great burnet. Resembles *S. canadensis* in habit and foliage. Spikes smaller, ⅓–1⅓in (1–3cm). Damp, grassy areas, low fields. Native to Eurasia; cultivated, rare escapee.

Verbascum thapsus L.
Common mullein
Figwort Family (Scrophulariaceae)

See pl. 3a

KEY IMPRESSIONS Grows to 6ft (2m). Hairy and woolly throughout. Capsules crowded on prolonged spikelike raceme. Leaves flannel-like, stemless, and decurrent along stem, forming wings.
FRUIT Capsules round, 2-parted, splitting along septum, with 2 sides more or less cleft. Seeds numerous, .6–.9mm, brown, with trapezoidal outline and roughened longitudinal ridges on surface.
LEAVES Flannel-like, alternate, toothless. Lower leaves oblong, to 1ft (30cm), stemmed; upper leaves progressively smaller, stemless, decurrent along stem.
STEM Stout, straight, single; tough, woolly, and winged owing to decurrent leaf bases.
BIENNIAL From deep taproot. Basal rosette of large hairy, woolly light green leaves in first year.
HABITAT Roadsides, waste areas, wherever soil is dry and rocky.
RANGE Native to Eurasia; established throughout most of temperate N. Am.

Polygonum virginianum L.
Jumpseed
Smartweed Family (Polygonaceae)

KEY IMPRESSIONS Grows 20–40in (.5–1m). Racemes grow to 16in (41cm), elongated, terminal, slender, and much interrupted. Small, ripe fruits (achenes) spring off when touched, hence the name "jumpseed." Found in woodlands.
FRUIT Achenes 4mm, oval, often with persistent styles bent and hooked at tip.
LEAVES Oval to lance-shaped, acute at tip, toothless.
STEM Erect, with sheaths (ocrea) at nodes.
PERENNIAL From underground stems.
HABITAT Moist woods.
RANGE N.H. to Minn. and Nebr., south to Fla. and Tex.

Fruit Remnants in Spikes and Racemes, 6–18in (15–45cm)

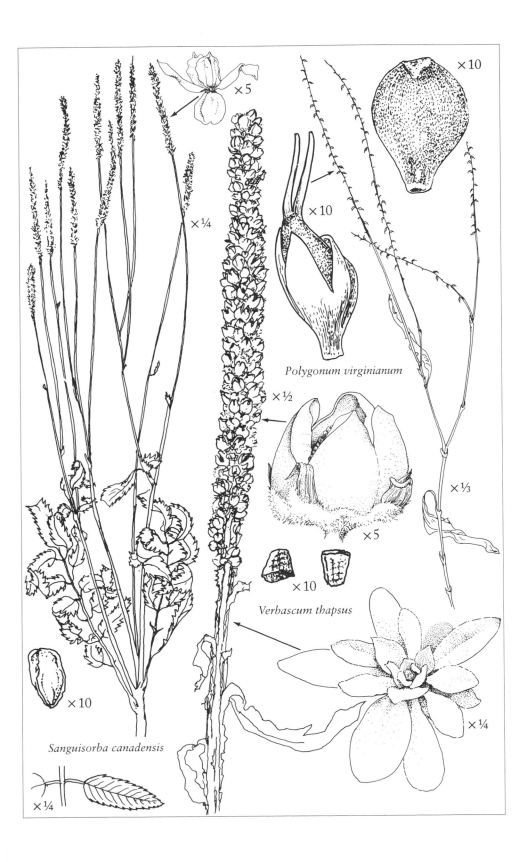

×5

×¼

×10

×10

×½

Polygonum virginianum

×5

×⅓

×10

Verbascum thapsus

×10

×¼

Sanguisorba canadensis

×¼

Plants with Panicled Clusters

Spiraea alba Duroi. (*S. latifolia*)
Meadowsweet
Rose Family (Rosaceae)

KEY IMPRESSIONS Grows to 6ft (2m) in fields. Woody shrub. Buds along stem produce new leaves and shoots in spring. All parts smooth and brown. Branches more widely spread than in *S. tomentosa*. Brown fruits on terminal panicles. Found in fields.

FRUIT Smooth follicles, opening along suture, arranged in groups of 5–8, not inflated, with few to several seeds. Seeds linear, with thin, loose coat.

LEAVES Simple, alternate, oval, coarsely toothed.

STEM Branches red or purplish brown.

PERENNIAL

HABITAT Old fields, meadows.

RANGE Nfld. and Que., south to N.C.

Spiraea tomentosa L.
Steeplebush, hardhack
Rose Family (Rosaceae)

KEY IMPRESSIONS Grows 4–6ft (1.3–2m). Branches shorter, more closely spaced than in *S. latifolia;* plant looks narrower, steeplelike, with fruits in close panicles. All parts fuzzy (tomentose).

FRUIT Similar to *S. alba*, but follicle slightly hairy.

LEAVES Alternate, irregularly toothed, oval to lance-shaped, very woolly. Underside whitish.

STEM Branched, close panicles.

PERENNIAL

HABITAT Swamps, wet meadows.

RANGE N.S. and N.B. to Que. and Minn., south to N.C., Tenn. and Ark.

Thalictrum pubescens Pursh
Tall meadow-rue
Buttercup Family (Ranunculaceae)

KEY IMPRESSIONS Grows to 8ft (2.5m). Fruit panicles with rounded to flattish tops.

FRUIT Achenes less than 7mm, black, flattened, beaked, ribbed on surface, falling early.

LEAVES Alternate, tri-compound. Leaflets roundish to oblong with small, abrupt tips.

STEM Smooth, shiny, tan.

PERENNIAL

HABITAT Wet meadows, low thickets, swamps.

RANGE Lab. to Que. and Ont., south to N.C., Ind., and Tenn.

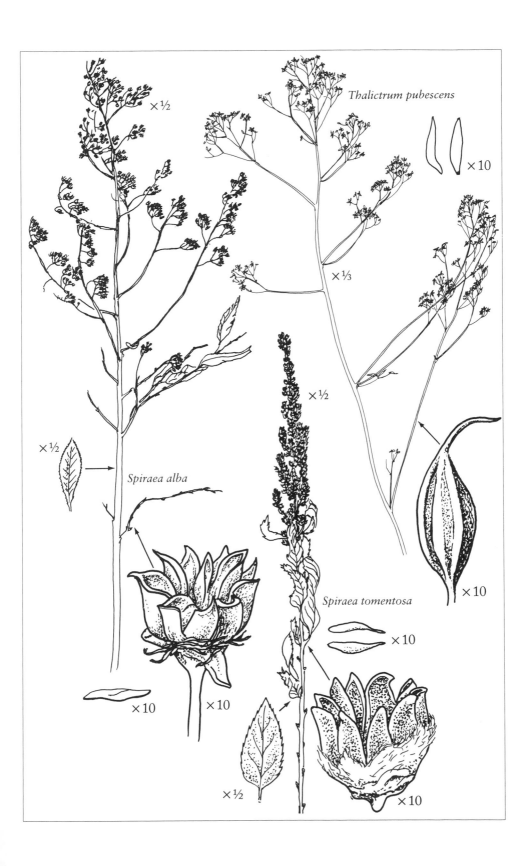

×½

Thalictrum pubescens

×10

×⅓

×½

×½

×½

Spiraea alba

×10

×10

×10

×½

Spiraea tomentosa

×10

×10

×½

×10

Heuchera L. spp.

Alum-root

Saxifrage Family (Saxifragaceae)

KEY IMPRESSIONS   Grows to 2ft (60cm). The basal leaves surround slender stems with capsules in sets of 2 and 3. Panicle narrow and cylindric.

FRUIT   Capsules elliptic, 1-chambered, 2-beaked, with an opening between beaks. Seeds numerous, oval, with rough coat.

LEAVES   Basal leaves mostly round, heart-shaped, long-stemmed, palmately lobed. Stem leaves alternate, if remaining.

STEM   Erect, hairy, usually leafless.

PERENNIAL   From stout, short underground stem.

HABITAT   Dry woods, prairies.

RANGE   New Eng. and west to Midwest.

Chenopodium album L.

Lamb's-quarters, pigweed

Goosefoot Family (Chenopodiaceae)

KEY IMPRESSIONS   Grows to 3ft (1m). Variable branching. Branches terminated by dense spikes grouped into panicles. Common weed, scraggly and hard to distinguish.

FRUIT   Small, bladdery (utricle). Fruit may be enclosed in grayish covering contained within 5-parted calyx. Seeds 1.3–1.5mm broad, black, lens-shaped.

LEAVES   Alternate, oval to lance-shaped, larger ones toothed.

STEM   Much branched.

ANNUAL

HABITAT   Common in waste areas, roadsides.

RANGE   Native to Europe; established throughout N. Am.

Amaranthus retroflexus L.

Redroot, rough pigweed

Amaranth Family (Amaranthaceae)

KEY IMPRESSIONS   Grows to 5ft (1.5m). Flower remnants grow as elongated terminal panicle of bracted spikes and smaller axillary panicles. 3 bracts, twice as long as calyx.

FRUIT   Utricle (soft 1-seeded bladder) shorter than sepals, opening around middle. Seeds tiny, 1mm, red-black, shiny, lens-shaped, with slightly ridged margin.

LEAVES   Alternate, toothless.

STEM   Erect, rough.

ANNUAL   From long, red taproot.

HABITAT   Cultivated areas, waste areas.

RANGE   Native to tropical Am.; common weed throughout most of U.S.

SIMILAR SPECIES

A. *hybridus* L.   Smooth pigweed. Grows 2–6ft (.6–2m). Similar to A. *retroflexus* but taller, with more slender, supple fruiting spikes. Waste ground, roadsides. Throughout region.

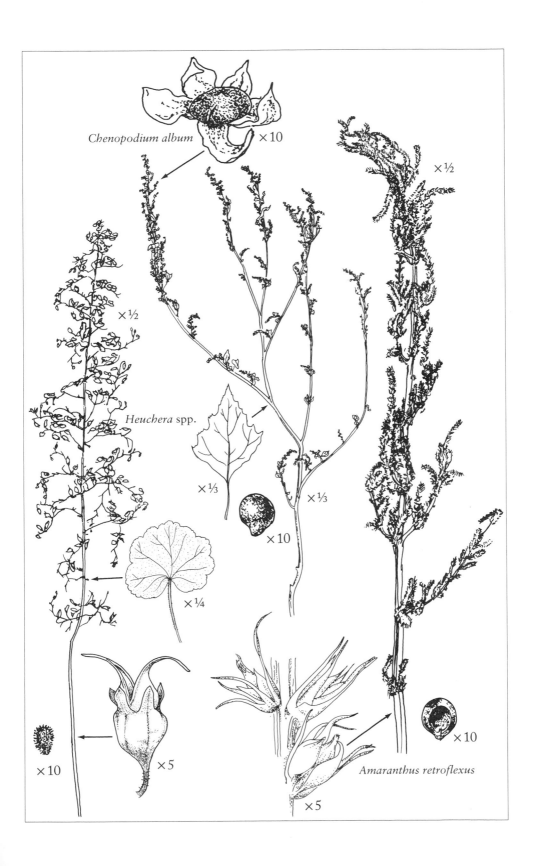

Chenopodium album ×10

Heuchera spp.

×½

×⅓

×⅓

×10

×¼

×10

×5

×5

Amaranthus retroflexus

×10

×½

Plants Having Dried Bracts or Calyxes with Round or Oval Heads

See also related group of Daisy Family (Asteraceae) p. 224

Lespedeza capitata Michx.

Round-headed bush-clover

Pea or Bean Family (Fabaceae)

KEY IMPRESSIONS Grows 2–5ft (.6–1.5m). Terminated by fuzzy, brown, oval heads of dried calyxes. Upper part with several erect branches.

FRUIT Pods oval to elliptic, 1-seeded, indehiscent, conspicuously shorter than persistent 5-cleft calyx. Calyxes densely crowded on rounded spike.

LEAVES Composed of 3 oblong to linear leaflets.

STEM Erect, stiff, single or with several upright branches.

ANNUAL TO PERENNIAL

HABITAT Open dry woods, fields, dunes, prairies.

RANGE Maine and s. Que. to Minn. and Nebr., south to Fla. and Tex.

SIMILAR SPECIES

L. hirta (L.) Hornem Hairy bush-clover. Grows 2–3ft (.6–1m). Heads of calyxes cylindric. Calyx lobes densely fuzzy. Pods elliptic, pointed at both ends. Leaflets oval to round. Stems fuzzy. Dry open soil, roadsides. Maine to Mich. and Mo., south to Fla. and Tex.

L. intermedia (S. Wats.) Britton Wandlike bush-clover. Grows 1–3ft (.3–1m). Flower remnants in short racemes from leaf axils. Leaflets elliptic. Wandlike appearance. Dry upland woods. Vt. to Mich. and Okla., south to Fla. and Tex. *L. stuevii* Nutt. (velvety bush-clover) similar but downy.

L. procumbens Michx. Trailing bush-clover. Trailing or decumbent. Flower remnants in loose racemes terminating long, upright stem. Leaflets oval. Plant downy. Dry upland woods. N.H. to Wis., south to Fla., Okla., and Tex.

L. repens (L.) Barton Creeping bush-clover. Closely resembles *L. procumbens* but more slender and smooth. Dry woods, fields. Conn. to Wis. and Kans., south to Fla. and Tex.

L. violacea (L.) Pers. Violet bush-clover. Grows 1–3ft (30–90cm). Tall, upright, much branched. Racemes loose, few-fruited. Leaflets elliptic. Leaves long-stemmed. Dry woods, clearings. Mass. and Vt. to Mich. and Wis., south to Fla. and Tex.

Trifolium arvense L.

Rabbit-foot clover

Pea and Bean Family (Fabaceae)

KEY IMPRESSIONS Grows 6–18in (15–45cm). Heads to 1in (2.5cm), gray, densely flowered, oval to cylindric. Hairy calyxes remain on heads.

FRUIT Pods short, straight, enclosed in persistent calyx that is densely hairy with gray hairs. Seeds tiny, yellowish, smooth, wrapped in "cottony" material.

LEAVES 3 leaflets, broadest above middle, tapering to base.

STEM Erect, freely branched, alternate.

ANNUAL From fibrous roots.

HABITAT Fields, roadsides.

RANGE Native to Eurasia and n. Africa; established as weed throughout most of U.S. and s. Canada.

Dried Bracts or Calyxes with Round or Oval Heads

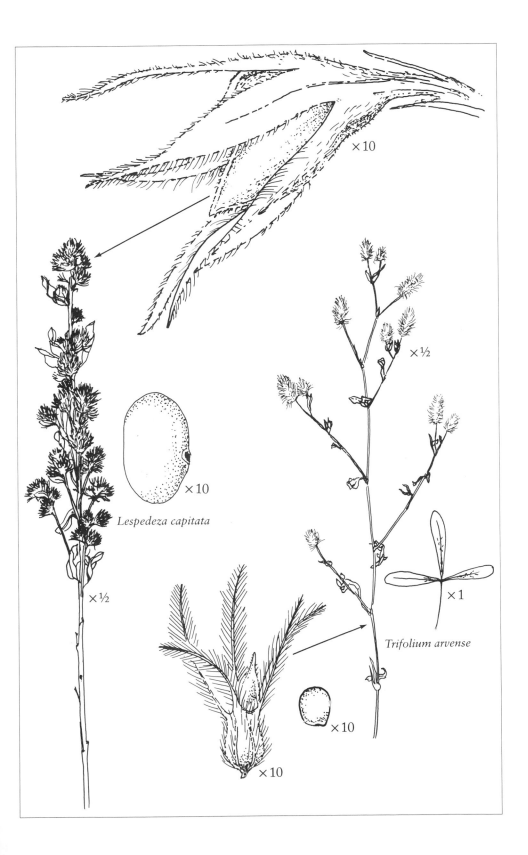

×10

×½

Lespedeza capitata ×10

×½

×½

×1

Trifolium arvense

×10 ×10

Trifolium pratense L.
Red clover
Pea and Bean Family (Fabaceae)
See pl. 17b

KEY IMPRESSIONS   Grows to 2½ft (75cm). Heads blackish, round, stemless or on short stems subtended by a pair of leaves. Overwinters as basal rosette.

FRUIT   Pods short, straight, opening by a lid and enclosed in calyx lobes.

LEAVES   3 leaflets; 2 lower long-stemmed, upper 1 either stemless or short-stemmed. Leaves alternate on flower stem, with opposite pair subtending head. Surface marked with white chevron.

STEM   Erect to decumbent to ascending.

ANNUAL OR PERENNIAL   From fibrous roots nodular with bacteria.

HABITAT   Fields, roadsides.

RANGE   Native to Europe; widely cultivated, common escapee throughout temperate N. Am.

SIMILAR SPECIES

T. repens L.   White clover. Almost round heads not subtended by leaf pair as in *T. pratense*. Stems creeping, sending up long-stemmed leaves and long-stemmed heads. Perennial. Fields, roadsides. Throughout temperate N. Am.

Trifolium aureum Pollich
Palmate hop-clover
Pea and Bean Family (Fabaceae)

KEY IMPRESSIONS   Grows to 20in (51cm). Stems terminated by compact, short, cylindric rusty orange heads made up of persistent calyxes.

FRUIT   Pods short, straight, in persistent calyxes.

LEAVES   3 leaflets.

STEM   Mostly erect.

ANNUAL OR BIENNIAL

HABITAT   Roadsides, waste areas, fields.

RANGE   Native to Eurasia; established as weed from Nfld. to B.C. to S.C. and Ark.

Dried Bracts or Calyxes with Round or Oval Heads

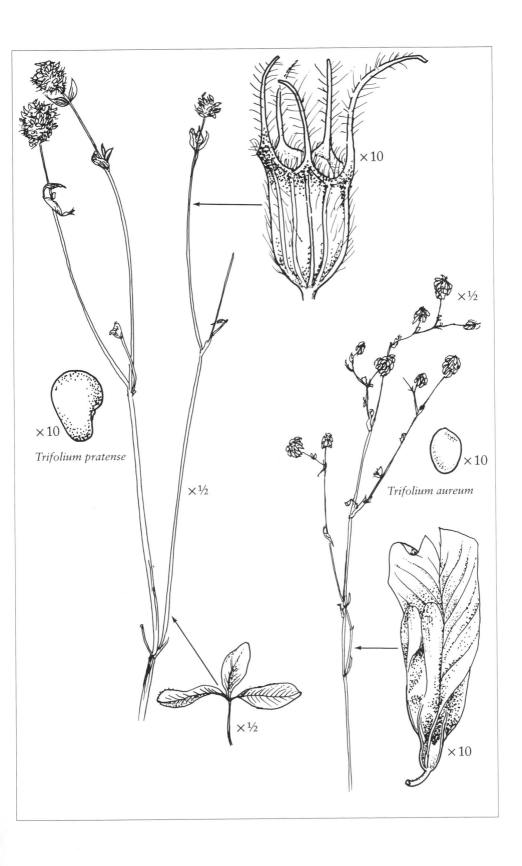

×10

Trifolium pratense

×½

×½

×½

×10

×10

Trifolium aureum

×10

Eryngium yuccifolium Michx.

Rattlesnake-master

Carrot Family (Apiaceae)

KEY IMPRESSIONS Grows 3–4ft (1–1.3m). Stiffly erect, unbranched except for fruiting portion. Heads dense, almost round, terminal on branches. Bracts under heads, bractlets under fruits. Bractlets smooth, with 1 terminal spine.

FRUIT ⅓–¾in (1–2cm), oval, covered with scales or small projections, ribless, usually with 5 slender oil tubes in each of 2 fruit chambers.

LEAVES Toothless, linear, with parallel veins and spiny margins.

STEM Erect, grooved.

PERENNIAL

HABITAT Dry or moist open woods, thickets, prairies.

RANGE Minn., Wis., Mich., Ohio, N.J., and south.

SIMILAR SPECIES

E. aquaticum L. Marsh-eryngo. Bractlets 3-lobed, each lobe ending in a spine. Coastal marshes and bogs. N.J. to ne. Fla.

Polygala L. spp.

Milkwort

Milkwort Family (Polygalaceae)

KEY IMPRESSIONS Grows to 1ft (30cm) or slightly more. Usually single-stemmed, branching at upper end. Branches terminated by very short, compact racemes of fruit remnants.

FRUIT Capsules splitting between septa. Seeds often hairy.

LEAVES Simple, toothless, generally alternate.

STEM Erect, single, branching at terminal end.

PERENNIAL, BIENNIAL, OR ANNUAL

HABITAT Sandy soil, open fields, prairies, pine barrens.

RANGE Throughout region.

Dried Bracts or Calyxes with Round or Oval Heads

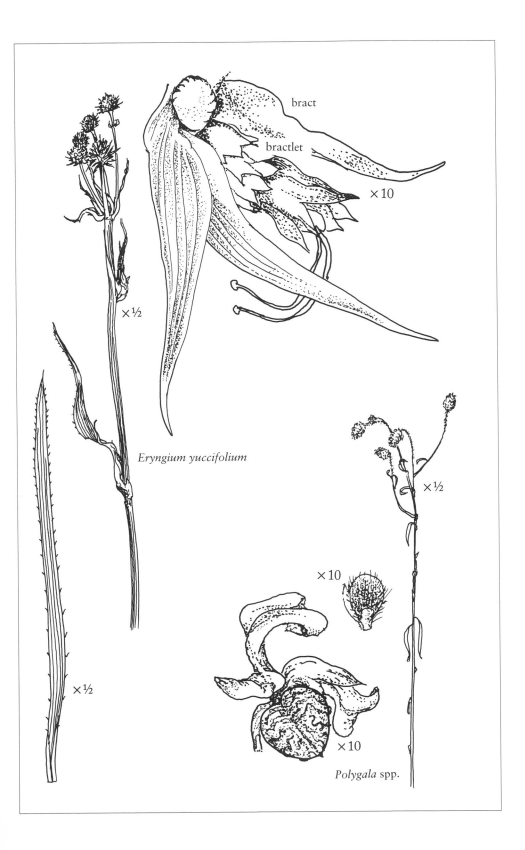

bract

bractlet

×10

×½

×½

Eryngium yuccifolium

×½

×10

×10

Polygala spp.

Plants Having Stems with Wraparound Leaf Scars and Lens-shaped or 3-angled Fruits: Smartweed Family (Polygonaceae)

Smartweeds are easily recognized by the swelling and sheath, or ocrea, at each leaf joint on the stem. Some species have a fringed sheath, whereas others do not. Fruits are either lens-shaped or 3-angled and wholly or partly enclosed in the persistent calyx.

See also *Dioscorea villosa* p. 30, *Rumex acetosella* p. 62, *Polygonum scandens* p. 32, *Polygonum virginianum* p. 168

Polygonum cuspidatum Sieb. & Zucc.
Japanese knotwood, Mexican bamboo
Smartweed Family (Polygonaceae)

KEY IMPRESSIONS Grows to 9ft (3m). Very large, usually in dense clumps. Stems arch out, while fruit stalks zigzag upward. Fruits fall early, leaving small stems attached to racemes. Has the woody appearance of a shrub. Stems grooved and hollow, with wraparound leaf scars. Highly invasive.

FRUIT Achenes 4mm, triangular, 3-angled, with 3 wings that originate from 3 sepals and extend beyond tip along stem to joint.

LEAVES Large, approximately 3 × 5in (7–12cm), alternate, entire. Leaf stem encircles stem, leaving a wraparound leaf scar.

STEM Erect, arched, grooved, hollow except at nodes, often mottled, widely bushy-branched, turning reddish brown in winter.

PERENNIAL From stout, rapidly spreading underground stems and offshoots.

HABITAT Rapidly spreading in waste areas, roadsides, wet or dry areas.

RANGE Native to Japan; escaped from cultivation and well established throughout region.

Polygonum pensylvanicum L.
Pennsylvania smartweed
Smartweed Family (Polygonaceae)

KEY IMPRESSIONS Grows to 3ft (1m). Flower and fruit remnants in terminal and axillary racemes. Stems ascending to erect, with unfringed sheaths at leaf joint. Glandular hairs may remain on stem in winter.

FRUIT Achenes 2.6–3.4mm, black, glossy, smooth, lens-shaped, circular to oval with short pointed tip, concave on both sides, enclosed in 3-winged persistent calyx.

LEAVES Lance-shaped, toothless, alternate, sheathing stem.

STEM Swollen nodes with unfringed wraparound sheaths. Glandular hairs may be visible.

ANNUAL From fibrous roots.

HABITAT Common in disturbed areas, fields, thickets.

RANGE N.S. and Que. to Minn. and S.Dak., south to Fla. and Tex.

SIMILAR SPECIES

Some species that have *unfringed* sheaths:

P. lapathifolium L. Dock-leaved smartweed. Achenes lens-shaped. Floral spikes long, narrow, drooping. Calyx veins uniquely forked.

P. hydropiper L. Water-pepper. Achenes dull, 3-angled or lens-shaped. Punctate glands on sepals. Racemes continuous. Shallow water.

P. amphibium L. Water smartweed. Achenes lens-shaped. Mostly found in shallow water.

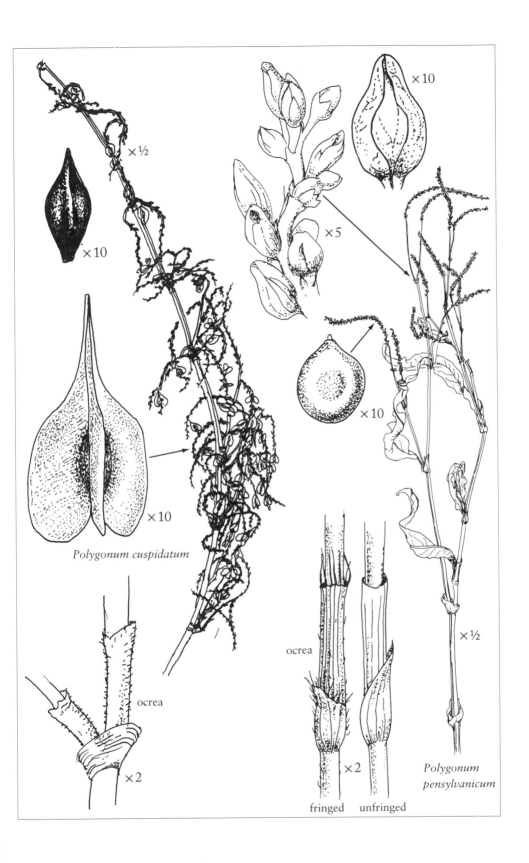

×½

×10

×10

×5

×10

Polygonum cuspidatum

×10

×10

ocrea

ocrea

×2

fringed   unfringed

×2

Polygonum
pensylvanicum

×½

P. punctatum Elliott   Dotted smartweed. Achenes 3-angled or lens-shaped. Punctate glands on sepals. Racemes much interrupted.

Some species with *fringed* sheaths:

P. persicaria L.   Lady's thumb. Achenes lens-shaped, rarely 3-angled.

P. cespitosum Blume   Achenes 3-angled.

P. hydropiperoides Michx.   False water-pepper. Achenes 3-angled. Shallow water.

P. orientale L.   Prince's feather. Grows to 7ft (2.3m). Achenes lens-shaped.

Rumex crispus L.
Curly dock, sour dock
Smartweed Family (Polygonaceae)
See pl. 7b

KEY IMPRESSIONS   Grows 2–4ft (.6–1.3m). Straight brown stalks. Dense clusters of dried 3-winged, smooth-edged, heart-shaped sepals hang from stems. 1 shiny, 3-angled fruit between each sepal wing. Leaves curly-edged.

FRUIT   Achene dark brown, shiny, 3-angled.

LEAVES   Lance-shaped, acute at tip, with wavy, curled margins. Large basal rosette.

STEM   Ribbed, with wraparound leaf scars.

PERENNIAL   From stout, long, orange-brown taproot.

HABITAT   Old fields, roadsides, waste areas.

RANGE   Native to Europe; established as weed throughout region.

Rumex obtusifolius L.
Broad dock, bitter dock
Smartweed Family (Polygonaceae)
See pl. 7a

KEY IMPRESSIONS   Grows 1–4ft (.3–1.3m). Differs from *R. crispus* (above) in its prominently toothed sepal wings surrounding 3 achenes. Small grainlike projection on 1 sepal wing; slightly thickened midrib on other 2. Leaves broadly oblong, not curly along edges.

FRUIT   Achene, 3-angled.

LEAVES   Lower leaves heart-shaped at base, broadly oblong to oval, to 6in (15cm) wide, much wider than in *R. crispus*.

STEM   Stout, usually simple up to freely branching inflorescence.

PERENNIAL   From large tap- or branched root.

HABITAT   Fields, waste areas, roadsides.

RANGE   Native to Europe; naturalized throughout region.

SIMILAR SPECIES

R. orbiculatus A. Gray   Great-water-dock. Grows 8ft (2.5m). Large, water-loving. Fruits large; sepal wings round-oval, toothless. 3 grains between sepal wings, half as long as wing, their base above wing base. Leaves long-stalked, leathery, to 2ft (60cm). Swamps, shores. S. Canada, south to Iowa, Ill., Ind., Ohio, Pa., and N.J.

R. pallidus Bigelow   Seabeach-dock. Grows 1–2ft (30–60cm). Sepal wings broad, oval, toothless, tips only slightly exceeding conspicuous large, whitish, oval fruits. Leaves narrowly lance-shaped. Coastal marshes, beaches. Long Island and north.

R. patienta L.   Patience-dock. Closely resembles *R. crispus* but with not very wavy leaves. Sepal wings broadly oval, toothless, with heart-shaped bases, 1 bearing small grainlike projection. Waste areas, roadsides. Found in region.

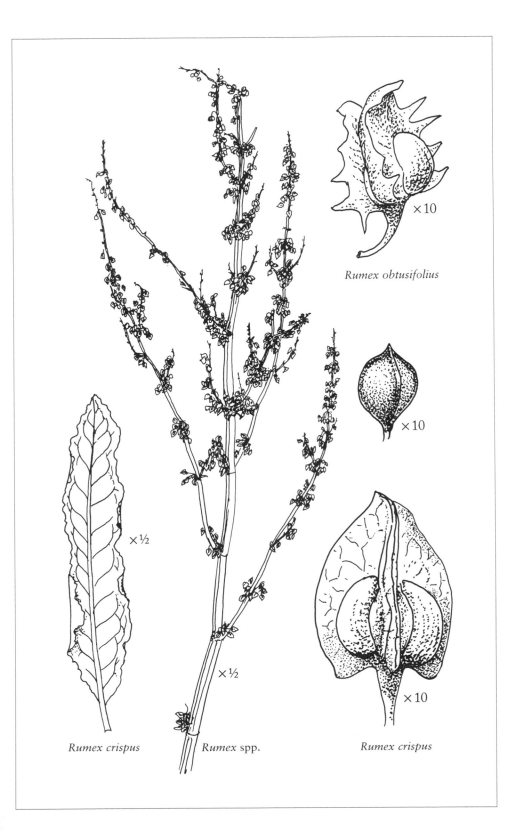

Rumex obtusifolius ×10

×10

Rumex crispus ×½

Rumex spp. ×½

Rumex crispus ×10

Plants Bearing Fruits Enclosed in Inflated Papery Calyxes

See also *Rhinanthus crista-galli* p. 126

Lobelia inflata L.
Indian tobacco
Bellflower Family (Campanulaceae)

KEY IMPRESSIONS   Grows 8–36in (.2–1m). Terminal racemes. Fruit remnant appears inflated. Usually grows singly rather than in large patches. Poisonous.

FRUIT   2-chambered capsule enclosed within persistent inflated papery calyx, opening at top. Seeds numerous, .6mm, cylindric.

LEAVES   Alternate, stemless, oval.

STEM   Upward branched.

ANNUAL   From fibrous roots.

HABITAT   Open woods, sometimes garden weed.

RANGE   Common throughout region.

Physalis L. spp.
Ground-cherry
Nightshade Family (Solanaceae)

KEY IMPRESSIONS   Grows to 3ft (1m). Branching stems, fruit solitary at nodes. Berries resemble small yellow tomatoes, loosely enclosed in an inflated, 5-angled calyx that opens at mouth.

FRUIT   2-chambered berry, reddish purple or yellow, pulpy, many-seeded, within calyx, which enlarges after flowering and is filled with the berry. Calyx 5-angled, often 10-ribbed, covered with network of veins and open at mouth. Seeds 2–2.5mm, deep yellow, kidney-shaped, flattened, with wavy veins on surface.

LEAVES   Vary by species, but always simple, alternate.

STEM   Soft; not long-lasting.

PERENNIAL   From fleshy, stout horizontal underground stem.

HABITAT   Shores, meadows, dry soil in open woods, disturbed areas.

RANGE   Throughout region.

Short, Leafless Plants of Forest Floors, Sometimes Parasitic on Tree Roots or Living on Decayed Plant Matter

Monotropa uniflora L.
Indian pipe, corpse-plant
Indian Pipe Family (Monotropaceae)

KEY IMPRESSIONS   Grows to 8in (20cm). Forms dense clumps. 1 fruit that turns black. Either saprophytic, or perhaps parasitic on fungi, without chlorophyll. White in flower, but turning black as it goes to fruit, hence the common name "corpse-plant."

FRUIT   Capsule ½–1in (1–2.5cm) diameter, 4–5-chambered, woody, almost round, erect (flowers nodded), with 8–10 grooves, splitting between septa. Seeds numerous, minute.

LEAVES   Mere scales on stem with no chlorophyll.

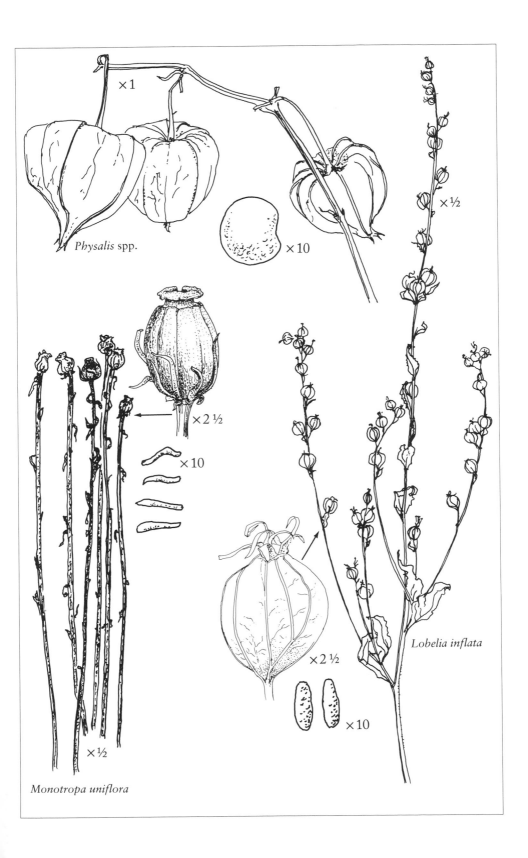

×1

Physalis spp.

×10

×½

×2½

×10

×2½

×10

×½

Monotropa uniflora

Lobelia inflata

STEM Solitary, erect.
PERENNIAL From strongly mycorrhizal roots (having a fungal association).
HABITAT In leaf mold on densely shaded floor of rich woods.
RANGE Nfld. to B.C., south to Fla.

Monotropa hypopithys L.
Pinesap
Indian Pipe Family (Monotropaceae)

KEY IMPRESSIONS Grows 4–12in (10–30cm). Single, erect stem covered with scalelike leaves. Flower remnants in dense, terminal raceme, nodding when in flower but erect when in fruit.
FRUIT Capsule 4–5-chambered, oval to round, splitting between septa. Seeds numerous, minute.
LEAVES Scalelike.
STEM Erect, single.
PERENNIAL From matted, fibrous rootlets.
HABITAT Humus of moist or dry woods, usually in acid soil.
RANGE Throughout region.

Epifagus virginiana (L.) Barton
Beech-drops
Broom-Rape Family (Orobanchaceae)

KEY IMPRESSIONS Grows to 1–1½ft (30–45cm). Branches small, brown, panicled, with scattered, stemless capsules. Found only under or near beeches; probably parasitic. Upper flowers male, lower flowers female, containing seeds.
FRUIT Capsule 5mm, 2-valved, opening across tip. Seeds numerous, minute.
LEAVES Scales.
STEM Brown, with somewhat arched branches.
PERENNIAL From short, woody roots that extend from little knobs.
HABITAT Parasitic or saprophytic in ground underneath or near beeches.
RANGE Que. and N.S. to Wis., south to Fla. and La.

Conopholis americana (L.) Wallr.
Squaw-root, cancer-root
Broom-Rape Family (Orobanchaceae)

KEY IMPRESSIONS Stout, erect, 2–8in (5–20cm). Suggests an upright, black pinecone on forest floor. Parasitic on several species of oaks. Stem mostly concealed by overlapping leaf scales that become dry and hard.
FRUIT Capsule oval, tipped with persistent style and stigma. Seeds numerous, minute.
LEAVES Oval scales.
STEM Erect.
PERENNIAL From roots parasitic on trees.
HABITAT Rich woods, beneath oaks.
RANGE N.S. to Fla., west to n. Mich., Wis., Ill., and Ala.

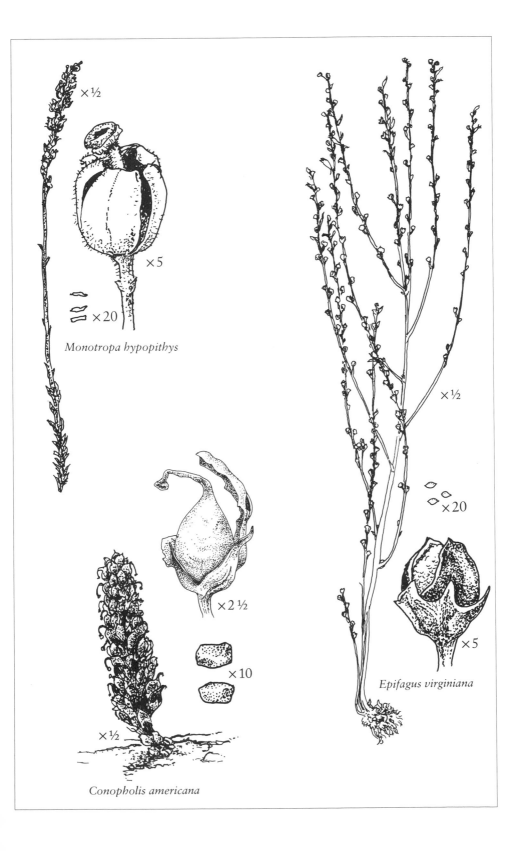

×½

×5

×20

Monotropa hypopithys

×½

×2½

×10

×½

Conopholis americana

×20

×5

Epifagus virginiana

Daisy Family (Asteraceae): Introduction

The Daisy Family (Asteraceae, formerly Compositae) is one of the largest and most widely distributed of the flowering plant families. Amateur naturalists are often deceived by its flowers, however, because what looks like 1 flower is actually many small individual flowers (florets) grouped in 1 head. This "composite" head of many flowers performs the biological function of a single flower, giving the family its former name.

The florets are attached to a receptacle and surrounded by protective bracts, or involucre. The receptacle and often the bracts dry up and remain throughout winter after the fruits have dispersed. The florets or fruits are sometimes individually subtended by small bracts called "chaff." If these bracts are present, the receptacle is termed "chaffy." If absent, it is termed "naked."

Asteraceae fruits are achenes. These are often mistaken for seeds because they are small and dry, containing just 1 seed, and do not open when ripe. Achenes often have a modified calyx, or pappus, attached to their apex. This is made up of hairs, scales, bristles, or awns that help distribute the fruits. Some species lack pappi. Knowing the pappus type will aid in identification (see the visual key below), but since the fruits are usually dispersed quickly with the help of the pappi, this is a more useful tool for identification in autumn than in winter. In winter, if all the achenes have disappeared, one must recognize the receptacle and dried bracts.

See also *Bidens* spp. p. 54, *Cichorium intybus* p. 142, *Mikania scandens* p. 34, *Arctium* spp. p. 50, *Xanthium* spp. p. 52

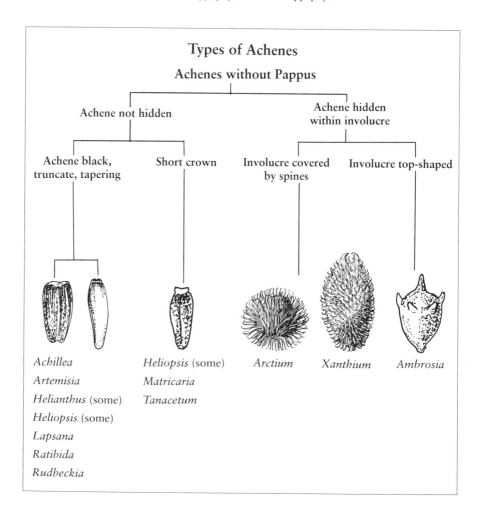

Types of Achenes

Achenes without Pappus

Achene not hidden

Achene hidden within involucre

Achene black, truncate, tapering

Short crown

Involucre covered by spines

Involucre top-shaped

Achillea
Artemisia
Helianthus (some)
Heliopsis (some)
Lapsana
Ratibida
Rudbeckia

Heliopsis (some)
Matricaria
Tanacetum

Arctium

Xanthium

Ambrosia

Achenes with Pappus

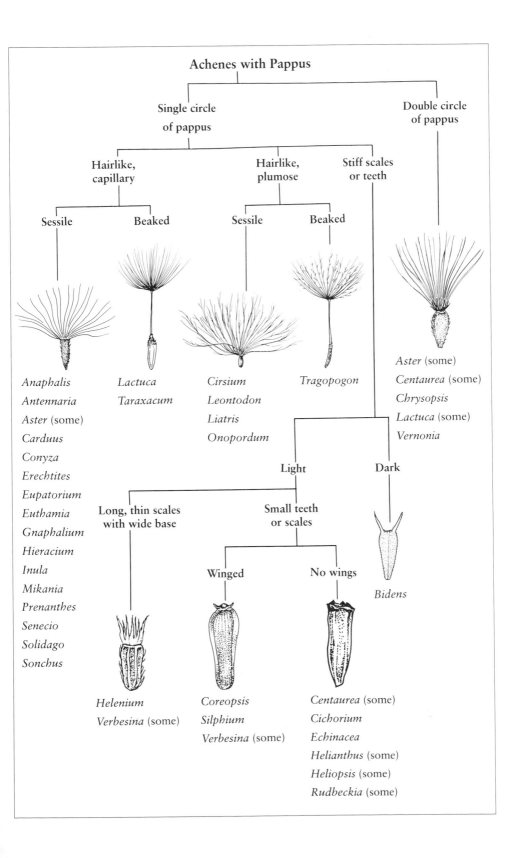

Single circle of pappus

Double circle of pappus

Hairlike, capillary

Hairlike, plumose

Stiff scales or teeth

Sessile

Beaked

Sessile

Beaked

Anaphalis
Antennaria
Aster (some)
Carduus
Conyza
Erechtites
Eupatorium
Euthamia
Gnaphalium
Hieracium
Inula
Mikania
Prenanthes
Senecio
Solidago
Sonchus

Lactuca
Taraxacum

Cirsium
Leontodon
Liatris
Onopordum

Tragopogon

Aster (some)
Centaurea (some)
Chrysopsis
Lactuca (some)
Vernonia

Light

Dark

Long, thin scales with wide base

Small teeth or scales

Winged

No wings

Bidens

Helenium
Verbesina (some)

Coreopsis
Silphium
Verbesina (some)

Centaurea (some)
Cichorium
Echinacea
Helianthus (some)
Heliopsis (some)
Rudbeckia (some)

Plants Showing Aromatic Inflorescence, with Aromatic and Lobed or Dissected Leaves, White or Silver Underneath

See also *Artemisia stelleriana* p. 16

Artemisia vulgaris L.
Mugwort
Daisy Family (Asteraceae)

KEY IMPRESSIONS Grows 1–3½ft (.3–1m). Aromatic, with terminal panicles of small heads of achenes. Alternate leaves persist in winter; white, downy underneath, deeply lobed. Found in waste areas.

FRUIT Achenes elongate, smooth, elliptical, grouped into numerous heads subtended by hairy, layered bracts. No pappus.

LEAVES Alternate, aromatic, persistent in winter, cleft nearly to midrib with further cleft segments, white and downy underneath.

STEM Smooth, erect, much branched.

PERENNIAL From stout, horizontal, forking underground stems.

HABITAT Waste areas, roadsides, fields.

RANGE Native to Eurasia; established as invasive weed throughout region.

SIMILAR SPECIES

The *Artemisias* as a group have leaves that persist in winter, are deeply lobed, and are silvery underneath. More than 12 species occur in this range; 4 are listed here:

A. campestris L. Tall wormwood. Grows 2–5ft (.6–1.5m). Leaves with deeply cut lobes, narrowly linear, little odor. Biennial or perennial. Open areas, often in sandy soil. Throughout region, south to Fla. and Ariz.

A. absinthium L. Absinthe wormwood, common wormwood. Grows 1–3ft (.3–1m). More aromatic than *A. vulgaris*. Leaves silvery and silky on both sides, with blunter lobes. Perennial. Fields, waste areas. Throughout region.

A. annua L. Annual wormwood. Grows 1–3ft (.3–1m). Leaves finely cut, fernlike, sweet-scented. Annual. Fields, waste areas. Throughout region.

A. biennis Willd. Biennial wormwood. Grows 1–3ft (.3–1m). Leaves linear, forked, almost odorless, liberally interspersed among fruit clusters that hug stem. Annual or biennial. Waste areas, streambanks, sandy soil. Native to nw. U.S. but widely distributed throughout region.

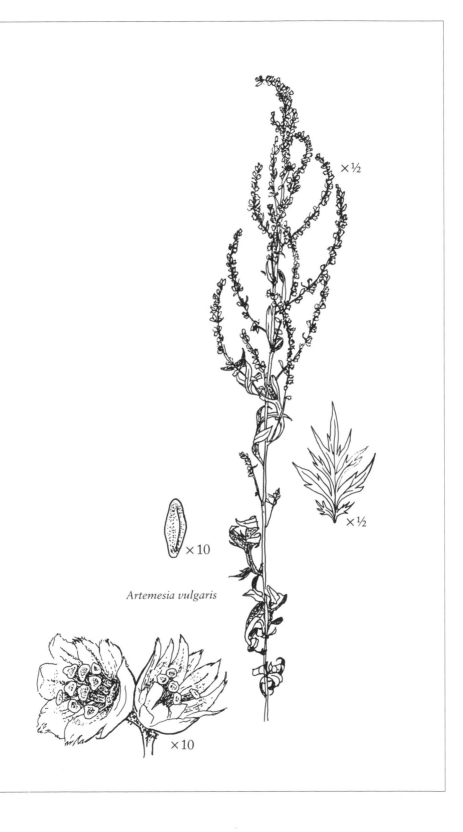

×½

×10

Artemesia vulgaris

×½

×10

Plants with Extended, Needlelike Receptacles on Terminal Ends and Top-shaped Fruits

Ambrosia artemisifolia L.
Common ragweed
Daisy Family (Asteraceae)

KEY IMPRESSIONS Grows to 3½ft (1.1m). Upswept branches, ragged appearance. Flower remnants on long terminal racemes in autumn, but male flowers fall off in winter, leaving needlelike white receptacle 2¾–4in (7–10cm) pointing upward. Lower branches gray-black. Fruit, if remaining, found at needle base, where female flowers were located. Fruit toplike, crowned with knobby protuberances.

FRUIT Achene not visible. No pappus. Achene 3–4mm, yellowish brown, enclosed in ribbed, top-shaped bract (involucre), crowned by beak surrounded by 4–7 spines.

LEAVES Alternate above, opposite below; deeply lobed.

STEM Smooth, branched. Upper branches alternate; lower branches opposite.

ANNUAL From long, thin white roots.

HABITAT Waste areas, roadsides, cultivated areas.

RANGE Throughout region.

Ambrosia trifida L.
Great ragweed, giant ragweed
Daisy Family (Asteraceae)

KEY IMPRESSIONS Grows 3–17ft (1–5.5m). Very large, with opposite leaves and coarse, bristly texture. Leaves much larger than in *A. artemisifolia,* but fruits and needlelike receptacles are similar.

FRUIT Achene similar to that of *A. artemisifolia* but larger, 6–12mm, grayish to yellowish brown.

LEAVES Opposite, palmately cleft into 3 parts.

STEM Hairy, branched, sandpapery above, smooth below.

ANNUAL From long taproot with long, fibrous roots.

HABITAT Waste areas, roadsides.

RANGE Throughout region.

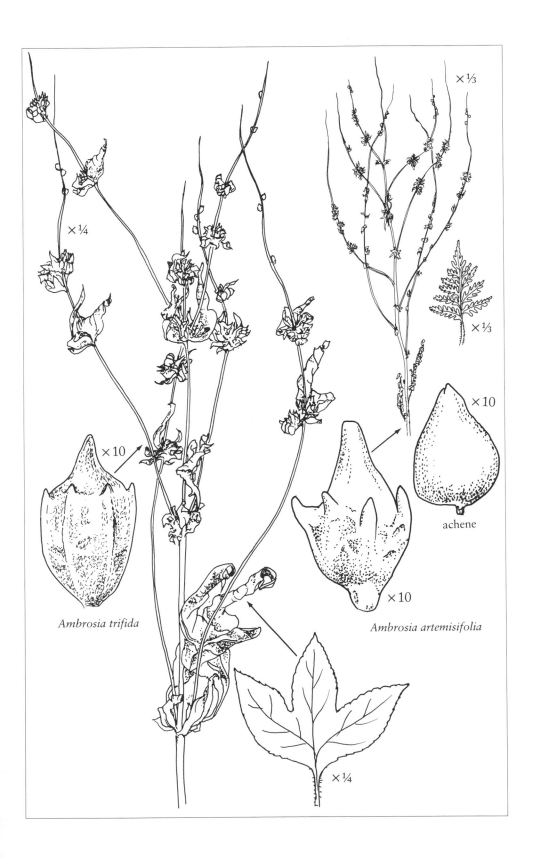

×¼

×⅓

×⅓

×10

×10

achene

×10

Ambrosia trifida

Ambrosia artemisifolia

×¼

Plants with Flower and Fruit Remnants in Flat-topped Clusters on Branches That Alternate Slightly

See also *Eupatorium* spp. pp. 196–198

Achillea millefolium L.
Common yarrow
Daisy Family (Asteraceae)

See pl. 18b

KEY IMPRESSIONS   Grows 1–2ft (30–60cm). Dissected fernlike, aromatic leaves persist in winter as basal rosettes with some leaves clinging to stem. Stem terminated by flat-topped branches of flower and fruit remnants made up of small heads of tan, layered bracts.

FRUIT   Achenes 1.7–2.5mm, oblong, tapered, slightly compressed, papery thin with winged margins. No pappus.

LEAVES   Alternate, dissected, fernlike, with overwintering basals; aromatic when crushed.

STEM   Erect, round.

PERENNIAL   From horizontal underground stems that may form large colonies.

HABITAT   Varied, especially disturbed sites.

RANGE   Throughout region.

Euthamia graminifolia (L.) Nutt. (*Solidago graminifolia*)
Common flat-topped goldenrod, lance-leaved goldenrod
Daisy Family (Asteraceae)

KEY IMPRESSIONS   Grows 1–5ft (.3–1.5m). Flower and fruit remnants on flat-topped branches. Receptacles star-shaped, with fuzzy, tan bracts. Leaves linear, 3-nerved.

FRUIT   Achenes short, hairy. Pappus of tan, capillary bristles.

LEAVES   Alternate, linear to lance-shaped, 3-nerved.

STEM   Smooth to downy.

PERENNIAL   From creeping underground stems.

HABITAT   Open, usually moist ground.

RANGE   Throughout region.

SIMILAR SPECIES

E. tenuifolia (Pursh) Nutt. (*Solidago tenuifolia*)   Coastal-plain flat-topped goldenrod, slender goldenrod, fragrant goldenrod. Grows 1–3ft (.3–1m). Similar to *E. graminifolia* but leaves more finely cut. Leaves usually 1-veined. Open sandy soil, especially near coast. N.S. to Fla. and La.

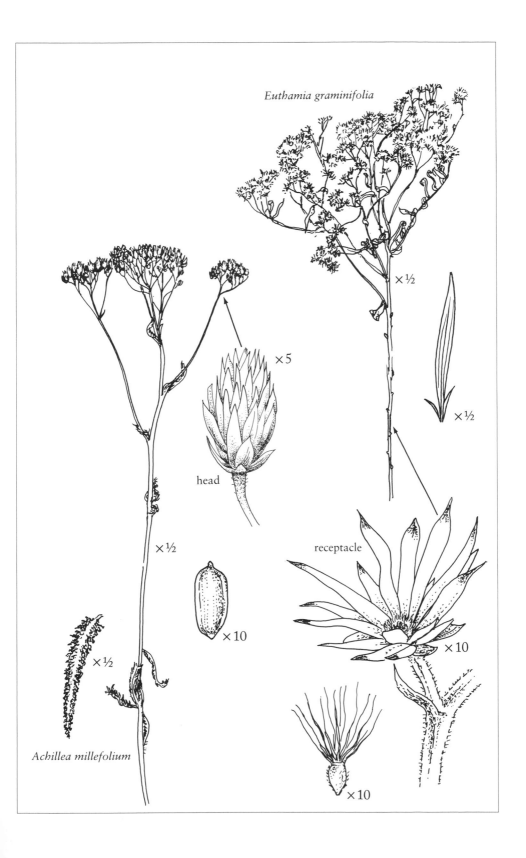

Euthamia graminifolia

×½

×½

head ×5

receptacle

×10

×10

×10

Achillea millefolium

×½

×½

Tanacetum vulgare L.
Common tansy
Daisy Family (Asteraceae)
See pl. 19b

KEY IMPRESSIONS Grows 1–3ft (.3–1m). Flat, round fruit heads found on flat-topped branched cluster. Heads may release aromatic scent when crushed. Dissected, aromatic leaves.

FRUIT Achenes 1.3–1.7mm, grayish brown, elongated, broadest near apex, with prominently rimmed base. Pappus of short, toothed collar on crown.

LEAVES Alternate, fernlike, dissected, aromatic. Basal rosettes overwinter.

STEM Erect, smooth, terminated by fruit remnants.

PERENNIAL From stout underground stems.

HABITAT Roadsides, fields, waste areas.

RANGE Native to Old World; established throughout most of U.S. and adjacent Canada.

Plants with Opposite Leaves and Branches and Bristle-haired Fruits

Eupatorium maculatum L.
Spotted joe-pye weed
Daisy Family (Asteraceae)

KEY IMPRESSIONS Grows to 4ft (1.3m). Flower clusters flat-topped to domed. Flower stalks topped by tiny white button receptacles after fruits have gone, sometimes with dried, layered bracts. Found in damp or wet areas.

FRUIT Achenes 5-angled, smooth, flat-topped, with yellowish glandular dots on surface. Pappus of 1 series of numerous bristly hairs.

LEAVES Whorled in 4s and 5s, lance-shaped to oval, usually 1-veined.

STEM Erect, spotted purple.

PERENNIAL From short underground stems with long fibrous roots.

HABITAT Damp areas, wet thickets, shores, especially in rich calcareous soil.

RANGE Nfld. to B.C., south to Md., W.Va., Ill., Nebr.; in mountains to N.C. and Tenn.

SIMILAR SPECIES

E. purpureum L. Sweet joe-pye weed, purple-node joe-pye weed. Grows 3–6ft (1–2m). Tall, similar to *E. maculatum,* but with plain stem and flower clusters rounded or convex at summit. Leaves whorled in 3s and 4s, lance-shaped to elliptic. Stem greenish but purple at nodes (when fresh), solid. Perennial from fibrous roots. Thickets, open woods, often in drier habitats than are related species. S. N.H. to Va., west to Wis., Iowa, Okla., and w. Fla.

E. fistulosum Barratt Hollow-stemmed joe-pye weed. Grows to 3ft (1m). Similar to *E. purpureum,* but with hollow, purplish, plain stem. Inflorescence domed. Bottomlands, moist woods. S. Maine to Iowa, south to Fla. and Tex.

E. dubium Willd. Three-nerved joe-pye weed. Similar to *E. maculatum,* but leaves more oval, contracted abruptly into stem, with 3 main veins. Moist places, especially in sandy or gravelly acid soil. Near coast from N.S. and s. N.H. to S.C.

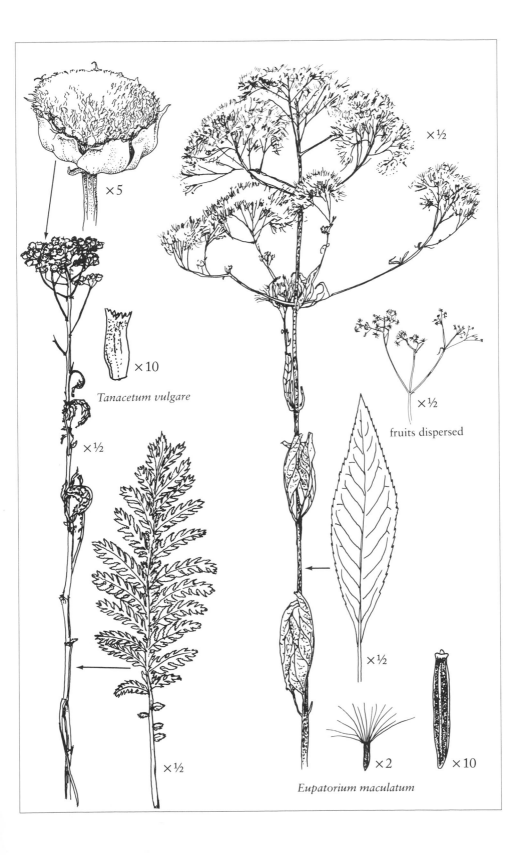

×5

×½

×10

Tanacetum vulgare

×½

×½

fruits dispersed

×½

×½

×2

×10

Eupatorium maculatum

Eupatorium perfoliatum L.

Boneset

Daisy Family (Asteraceae)

KEY IMPRESSIONS   Grows to 4ft (1.3m). Flower remnants flat-topped. Leaves perfoliate (surrounding stem on both sides). Stem hairy.

FRUIT   Achenes 5-angled, flat-topped. Pappus of numerous bristly, tan hairs.

LEAVES   Perfoliate, tapering gradually to sharp tip.

STEM   Erect, hairy.

PERENNIAL   From stout underground stems with fibrous roots.

HABITAT   Moist or wet low areas.

RANGE   N.S. and Que. to s. Fla., west to N.Dak., Nebr., Okla., and Tex.

Eupatorium rugosum Houttuyn.

White snakeroot

Daisy Family (Asteraceae)

KEY IMPRESSIONS   Grows to 3ft (1m). Open, loose branching. Leaves toothed and opposite on long stems. Flower remnants flat-topped.

FRUIT   See *E. maculatum.*

LEAVES   Opposite, long-stemmed, oval with sharp tip, toothed.

STEM   Erect, branched above.

PERENNIAL   From knotty, tough underground stems with fibrous roots.

HABITAT   Woodlands, thickets.

RANGE   N.S. to Sask., south to Ga. and Tex.

SIMILAR SPECIES

E. hyssopifolium L.   Hyssop-leaved thoroughwort. Leaves linear, grasslike, in whorls of 4s, with smaller leaves in axils. Sandy soil, clearings, fields. Coastal states, sometimes inland.

E. sessilifolium L.   Upland boneset. Leaves stemless, rounded at base, with 1 main vein. Woodlands, uplands, especially in sandy acidic soils.

E. serotinum Michx.   Late-flowering thoroughwort, late-flowering eupatorium. Leaves longer-stemmed, narrower than in *E. rugosum,* usually 3-veined. Mostly in bottomlands, moist woods.

E. pilosum Walter   Hairy thoroughwort. Leaves stemless, with relatively few blunt teeth. Chiefly in wet soil.

E. leucolepis (DC.) T. & G.   White-bracted thoroughwort. Leaves narrow, toothed; often smaller leaves in axils. Pine barrens, wet meadows, pond margins, especially in sandy soil.

E. rotundifolium L.   Round-leaved thoroughwort. Leaves stemless, almost as broad as long, with semiclasping bases. Woods, in dry or, rarely, wet soil.

Opposite Leaves and Branches, Bristle-haired Fruits

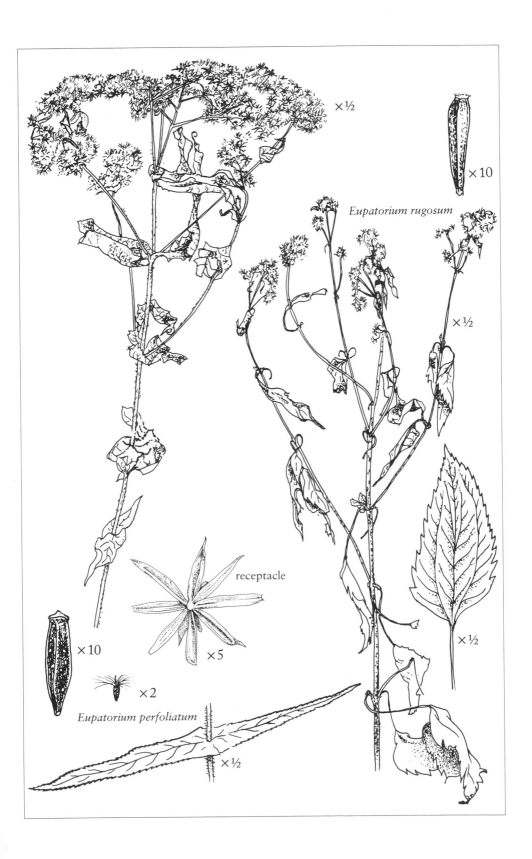

×½

×10

Eupatorium rugosum

×½

receptacle

×10

×5

×2

Eupatorium perfoliatum

×½

×½

Plants Having Heads of Dried Bracts, with Opposite Leaves and Branches and Hairless Fruits

See description of *Helianthus* p. 228
See also *Ambrosia trifida* p. 192, *Bidens* spp. p. 54, *Helianthus tuberosus* p. 230,
Helianthus decapetalus p. 228

Helianthus divaricatus L.
Woodland sunflower, divaricate sunflower
Daisy Family (Asteraceae)

KEY IMPRESSIONS Grows 2–6½ft (.6–2.5m). Heads with convex receptacles ⅓–½in (1–1.5cm) wide. Bracts acute at tip, fringed, rather loose, often with reflexed tips.

FRUIT Achenes 4-sided, smooth, laterally compressed. Pappus of 2 short scales that drop off early.

LEAVES Opposite, lance-shaped, shallowly toothed or toothless, rough, hairy, stemless or on short stems.

STEM Erect, smooth.

PERENNIAL From long underground stems and fibrous roots.

HABITAT Dry woods, open places.

RANGE Widespread in e. U.S. and adjacent Canada.

SIMILAR SPECIES

H. microcephalus T. & G. Small-headed sunflower. Grows 3–6ft (1–2m). Heads numerous, small, less than 1in (2.5cm) diameter. Bracts few, acute, fringed, not layered. Receptacles convex. Leaves resemble those of *H. divaricatus*. Perennial from short underground stem and fibrous roots. Woods, brushlands. N.J. to nw. Fla., west to Minn., Ark., and se. La.

H. mollis Lam. Hairy sunflower, ashy sunflower. Grows 2–3½ft (.6–1m). Bracts slightly layered, densely hairy. Receptacles convex. Leaves rough, heart-shaped, stemless, clasping stem. Perennial from stout underground stems, usually in colonies. Prairies, other dry areas. Ozarks, Midwest, occasionally introduced east to Atlantic.

Heliopsis helianthoides (L.) Sweet
Oxeye, everlasting sunflower
Daisy Family (Asteraceae)

KEY IMPRESSIONS Grows 1–3ft (.3–1m). Heads solitary, or several on long stem. Receptacles conic, sometimes narrowly so. Bracts in 3 rows, outermost leafy and spreading, innermost shorter than disk.

FRUIT Achenes 4-angled, smooth, thick, truncate. Pappus may be absent or present as short irregular crown or few teeth.

LEAVES Oval, toothed, acute, rounded at base.

STEM Erect, smooth.

PERENNIAL From fibrous roots.

HABITAT Rich to dry woods, prairies, waste areas.

RANGE Que. to B.C., south to Ga. and N.Mex.

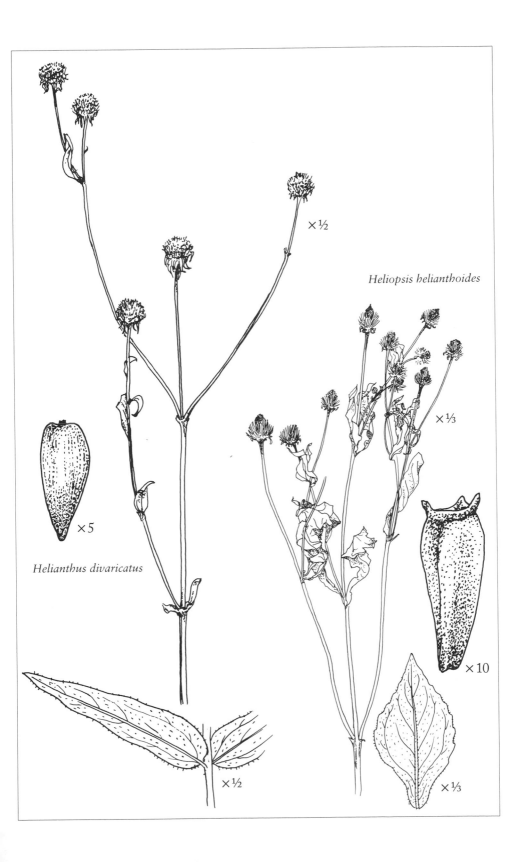

×½

Heliopsis helianthoides

×⅓

Helianthus divaricatus

×5

×10

×½

×⅓

Coreopsis lanceolata L.

Tickseed, lance-leaved coreopsis

Daisy Family (Asteraceae)

KEY IMPRESSIONS Grows to 2½ft (75cm). Heads few or 1 on long, naked stem. The dried bracts make a flat-bottomed cup around the dried receptacle. There are 2 rows of bracts, the outer shorter and leafier.

FRUIT Achenes 2.3–3mm, black, oblong, with broad, thin, flat wings. Pappus of 2 short teeth.

LEAVES Opposite, chiefly at lower stem end, linear or with 1–2 pairs of small lateral lobes.

STEM Upper branching opposite, if any.

PERENNIAL From short, woody underground stem.

HABITAT Dry, often sandy areas.

RANGE Mich. to Fla. and N.Mex. Cultivated and often escaped.

Coreopsis verticillata L.

Whorled coreopsis, threadleaf tickseed

Daisy Family (Asteraceae)

KEY IMPRESSIONS Grows 1–2ft (30–60cm). Leaves may be found in autumn, in whorls of 3-forked finely linear leaflets. Involucral bracts linear to oblong.

FRUIT Achenes 3–5mm, narrowly winged. No pappus.

LEAVES Stemless whorls of 3-forked finely linear leaflets.

STEM Erect, smooth.

PERENNIAL From underground stems.

HABITAT Open woods.

RANGE Md. and D.C. south, mainly on coastal plain but also inland to mountains; escapee elsewhere.

Silphium perfoliatum L.

Cup-plant

Daisy Family (Asteraceae)

KEY IMPRESSIONS Grows 4–8ft (1.3–2.5m). Tall, with stem branching above or sometimes simple stem with several heads. Receptacles surrounded by subequal broad bracts with loose, leafy summits. Center flowers sterile, so achenes develop from ray flowers on rim. Disk flat, ½–1in (1.5–2.5cm) wide.

FRUIT Achenes broad, dorsally compressed, surrounded by 2 wings, notched at apex. Pappus may be absent or present as 2 simple teeth.

LEAVES Opposite bases attached, creating perfoliate leaf that forms a cup around stem.

STEM Square, smooth.

PERENNIAL From short underground stems and fibrous roots.

HABITAT Woods, low ground.

RANGE S. Ont. to N.Dak., south to N.C., Miss., La., and Okla.; introduced into New Eng.

SIMILAR SPECIES

   S. integrifolium Michx. Prairie rosin-weed. Grows 2–6ft (.6–2m). Heads similar to those of *S. perfoliatum*. Leaves paired but not joined at base, stemless. Stem round. Perennial. Prairies, roadsides, less often open woods. S. Mich. to Nebr., south to Ala., Miss., and Tex.

Heads of Dried Bracts, Opposite Leaves and Branches, Hairless Fruits

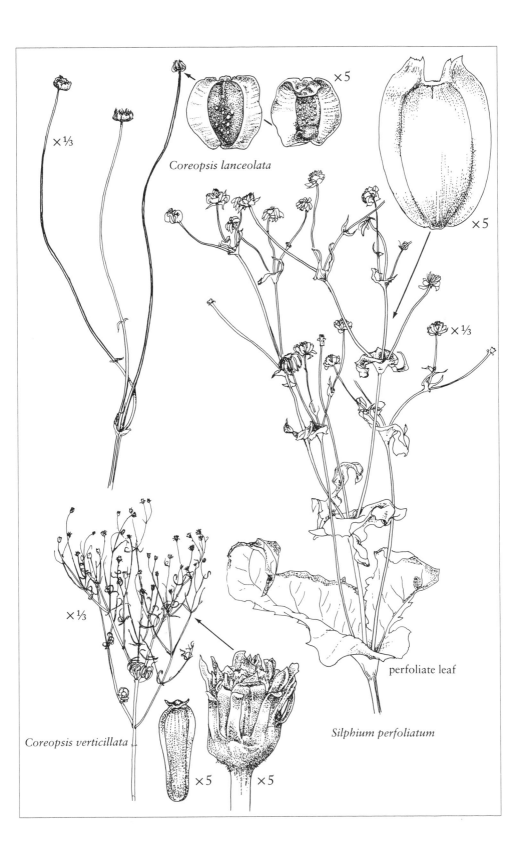

×⅓

×5

Coreopsis lanceolata

×5

×⅓

perfoliate leaf

×⅓

Silphium perfoliatum

Coreopsis verticillata

×5   ×5

S. laciniatum L.   Compass-plant. Grows 4–10ft (1.3–3.3m). Hairy. Leaves alternate, large, deeply lobed. Perennial from woody taproot. Prairies. Midwest; locally introduced east along railroad lines to N.Y.

S. terebinthinaceum Jacq. Prairie dock, basal-leaved rosin-weed. Grows 4–10ft (1.3–3.3m). Very tall. Leaves to 2ft (.6m), huge, oval, somewhat heart-shaped, found near plant base. Prairies. S. Ont. to Minn., south to Ga. and Miss.

S. trifoliatum L.   Whorled rosin-weed. Grows 3–9ft (1–3m). Leaves rough, in whorls of 3–4. Perennial. Open woods, prairies, disturbed open areas. Se. Pa. to Ohio and Ind., south to N.C., Ga., and Miss.

Plants Having Spiny Stems and Leaves, Fruits with Hairs Attached, and Heads with Pointed and Prickly Bracts

Cirsium vulgare (Savi) Tenore
Bull-thistle
Daisy Family (Asteraceae)
See pl. 11a

KEY IMPRESSIONS   Grows 2–6ft (.6–2m). Yellow-tipped spines on bracts of fruiting heads. Receptacles flat and densely bristly. Stems conspicuously spiny-winged from decurrent leaf bases. Leaves strongly spiny and deeply lobed.

FRUIT   Achenes 3.5–4mm, yellowish brown streaked with black, smooth, elongated. Pappus of numerous feathery (plumose) white hairs. Circular depression with center knob at large end of achene. Pappus attaches to collar that fits into this circular depression.

LEAVES   Alternate, spiny, lobed if still attached to stem. Basal rosette in first year.

STEM   Conspicuously spiny and winged from decurrent leaf bases.

BIENNIAL (as are most thistles)   From root that may reach 6ft (2m) deep.

HABITAT   Pastures, fields, roadsides, waste areas.

RANGE   Native to Eurasia; widely established in N. Am.

SIMILAR SPECIES

C. palustre (L.) Scop.   Marsh-thistle. Grows 2–6ft (.6–2m). Bracts appressed, not at all spine-tipped. Stem spiny-winged from decurrent leaf bases. Often invades woods. Ne. U.S. and se. Canada.

Onopordum acanthium L.   Scotch thistle. Grows to 6ft (2m). Coarsely branching, strongly spiny. Differs from *Cirsium* chiefly in receptacle, which is flat, fleshy, honeycombed, often with short bristle tips on partitions but not densely bristly. Pappus of barbed hairs, not feathery. Biennial. Roadsides, waste areas. Native to Eurasia; patchily naturalized over much of U.S. and s. Canada.

Carduus nutans L.
Nodding-thistle, musk-thistle
Daisy Family (Asteraceae)

KEY IMPRESSIONS   Grows 1–6ft (.3–2m). Heads large, 1¾–3¼in (4–8cm) diameter, mostly solitary, nodding at branch ends. Middle and outer bracts broad, with long spreading or reflexed spine-pointed tips. Inner bracts narrower and softer. Receptacles flat, densely bristly.

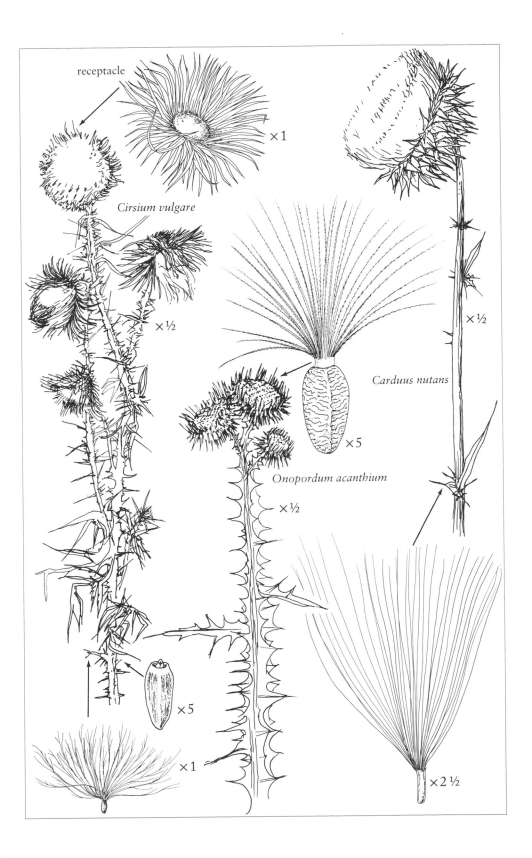

receptacle

Cirsium vulgare

×1

×½

Carduus nutans

×½

×5

Onopordum acanthium

×½

×5

×5

×1

×2½

Pappus of straight hairs, not feathery as in *Cirsium* (this is the main difference between the 2 genera).

FRUIT Achenes quadrangular or somewhat flattened. Pappus of straight hairs.

LEAVES Deeply lobed, spiny.

STEM Spiny, winged.

BIENNIAL OR RARELY ANNUAL

HABITAT Roadsides, waste areas.

RANGE Native to Europe; widely established in U.S. and Canada.

SIMILAR SPECIES

C. *crispus* L. Welted thistle. Grows 2–4ft (.6–1.3cm). Fruiting heads smaller than in C. *nutans*, erect in small clusters. Much branched. Biennial. Roadsides, waste areas. Sparingly introduced throughout region.

C. *acanthoides* L. Plumeless thistle. Heads *not* nodding. Involucral bracts *less* than 2mm diameter. Stem tough, strongly spiny. Biennial. Roadsides, pastures, waste areas. Native to Europe; widely but not heavily introduced throughout region.

Plants Having Spiny Leaves, Spineless Stems, Fruits with Hairs Attached, and Heads with Pointed and Prickly Bracts

See also *Sonchus asper* p. 218, *Sonchus oleraceus* p. 218, *Lactuca serriola* p. 222

Cirsium arvense (L.) Scop.
Canada-thistle
Daisy Family (Asteraceae)

KEY IMPRESSIONS Grows 1–5 ft (.3–1.5cm). Forms spreading colonies. Heads more or less numerous, clustered, small, ⅓–⅔ in (1–2cm) diameter. Involucral bracts appressed, pointed but not spiny. Invasive; difficult to control once introduced.

FRUIT Achenes elongated, broader above middle. Apex encircled by narrow, rimmed collar, usually bearing slender remnant of style. Pappus hairs feathery (plumose) rather than straight.

LEAVES Lobed, spiny.

STEM Smooth.

PERENNIAL From deep-seated underground roots that are widely creeping.

HABITAT Roadsides, pastures, fields.

RANGE Native to Eurasia; widely introduced in n. U.S. and s. Canada.

SIMILAR SPECIES

C. *discolor* (Muhl.) Sprengel Field-thistle. Grows 3–9ft (1–3m). Heads numerous, subtended by upper leaves. Involucral bracts end in long bristles. Leaves deeply lobed, spiny, with white wool on undersurface. Biennial. Fields, open woods, prairies, waste areas. Man., s. Que., sw. Maine, and south.

C. *altissimum* (L.) Sprengel Tall thistle. Grows 3–12ft (1–4m). Similar to C. *discolor* but leaves lance-shaped, tapered at each end and not deeply lobed. Perennial from fibrous roots. Woods, thickets, banks. Mass. to N.Dak., south to Fla. and Tex.

C. *horridulum* Michx. Yellow thistle. Grows 1–3ft (.3–1m). Heads large, 3in (8cm) diameter, supported by series of narrow, strongly spiny-toothed leaves. Involucral bracts have erect spine tips. Leaves deeply lobed, spiny. Biennial from thickened roots. Open

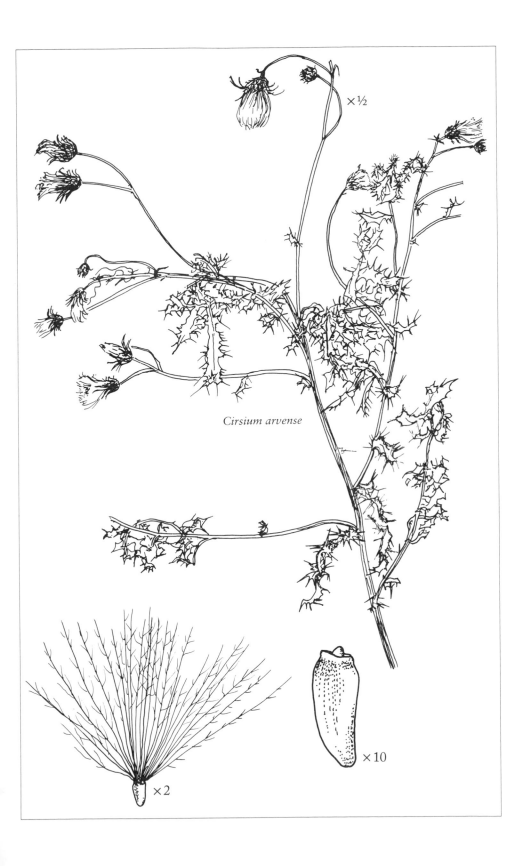

×½

Cirsium arvense

×2

×10

areas, especially in sandy soil or along salt or fresh marshes. Coastal states from Maine to Fla. and Tex.; also Pa.

C. muticum Michx. Swamp-thistle. Grows 2–10ft (.6–3.3m). Heads clustered. Involucral bracts *not* spine-tipped but sticky. Leaves deeply lobed but only weakly spiny. Stem hollow, rising from rosette of long-petioled leaves. Biennial from stout roots. Swamps, wet woods, thickets. Nfld. to Fla., west to Sask. and Tex.

C. pumilum (Nutt.) Sprengel Pasture-thistle. Grows 1–3ft (.3–1m). Largest head 2–3in (5–8cm) diameter, few to solitary. Involucral bracts spine-tipped. Leaves lobed with long spines. Stems hairy. Biennial from coarse, thickened roots. Pastures, old fields, open woods. Maine to Va. and W.Va.

C. virginianum (L.) Michx. Virginia-thistle. Grows 1–4ft (.3–1.3m). Heads several. Involucral bracts, some weakly spiny. Leaves narrow, lance-shaped, much reduced on upper stem, spine-tipped. Biennial from cluster of fleshy-fibrous roots. Bogs, wet pinelands. Coastal plain from s. N.J. to Fla.

Plants Having Heads with Bracts Neither Pointed Nor Spiny, Fruits with Non-beaked Bristly Hairs, and Alternate or Basal Leaves

The achenes in this grouping are easily windborne and are released early in winter owing to their fine hairy bristles. The receptacles and overlapping dried bracts remain and can be used for identification if the achenes are absent.
See also *Solidago* spp. pp. 232–240, *Aster* spp. pp. 242–252, *Lactuca floridana* p. 222, *Lactuca biennis* p. 222

Antennaria Gaertner spp.
Pussytoes
Daisy Family (Asteraceae)

See pl. 3b

KEY IMPRESSIONS Scaly stem grows to 1ft (30cm), rising from basal rosette of toothless, fuzzy green leaves. Group of flower receptacles tops stem, each receptacle surrounded by star-shaped bracts. A number of *Antennaria* species are quite similar in appearance.
FRUIT Achenes oblong, slightly compressed. Copious pappus of hairy bristles in 1 row, slightly united at base.
LEAVES Basal rosette of toothless, fuzzy green leaves often still alive in winter. Alternate scaly leaves on stem.
STEM Erect, scaly.
PERENNIAL From underground stems with fibrous roots that often form large mats; often spreads overground by stolons.
HABITAT Dry, open areas, meadows, open woods.
RANGE Widespread throughout region.

Chrysopsis mariana (L.) Elliott (*Pityopsis mariana*)
Maryland golden aster
Daisy Family (Asteraceae)

KEY IMPRESSIONS Grows 1–2ft (30–60cm). Heads numerous, crowded at branch tips. Receptacles flat or slightly convex. Involucral bracts layered. Found in dry, sandy places.

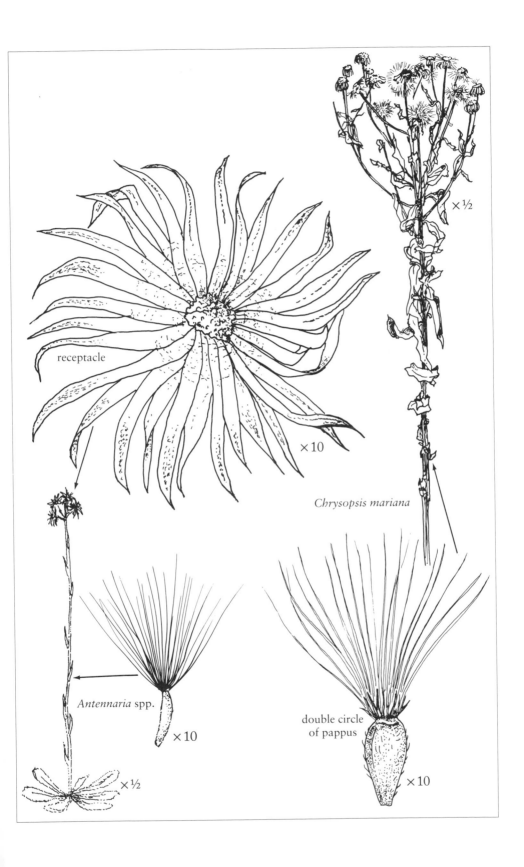

receptacle

×10

Chrysopsis mariana

×½

Antennaria spp.

×10

×½

double circle
of pappus

×10

FRUIT Achenes oval, compressed, attached at apex to double circle of tan pappus bristles. Inner circle consists of numerous rough, hairy bristles, outer of smaller or minute bristles.
LEAVES Toothless or slightly toothed. Upper oblong leaves ¾–1½in (2.5–5cm), stemless; lower, lance-shaped leaves narrow to stem.
STEM Single or slightly branched, becoming much branched at summit.
PERENNIAL From short, woody underground stem with fibrous roots.
HABITAT Pine woods, sandy areas.
RANGE S. N.Y. to s. Ohio and e. Ky., south to Fla. and La.
SIMILAR SPECIES

C. falcata (Pursh) Elliott Sickle-leaved golden aster, falcate golden aster. Grows 8–15in (20–40cm). Leaves stiff, crowded, linear, curved. Stems white, downy. Perennial. Pine barrens, sandy soil near coast. Mass. to N.J.

C. graminifolia (Michx.) Elliott Grass-leaved golden aster. Grows 1–3ft (.3–1m). Leaves linear, parallel-veined. Achenes linear. Perennial. Sandy, dry areas. Del. to s. Ohio, south to Fla.

Conyza canadensis (L.) Cronq. (Erigeron canadensis)
Horseweed
Daisy Family (Asteraceae)

KEY IMPRESSIONS Grows 3–5ft (1–1.6m). Flower remnants in large panicle much branched into vaguely overall diamond shape. Heads numerous, tiny. Involucral bracts layered. Common weed of waste areas.
FRUIT Achenes flattened. Pappus of numerous hairy bristles in 1 series.
LEAVES Numerous, lance-shaped to linear, toothed (especially the lower) or toothless.
STEM Erect, single, branched above.
ANNUAL OR WINTER-ANNUAL
HABITAT Waste areas, roadsides.
RANGE Throughout region.

Erechtites hieracifolia (L.) Raf.
Pilewort, fireweed
Daisy Family (Asteraceae)

KEY IMPRESSIONS Grows 1–9ft (.3–3m). Heads numerous in flat-topped or elongate panicle. Involucral bracts in 1 series, not layered, slightly dilated at base. Receptacles 5–8.5mm diameter, flat.
FRUIT Achenes 10–12-ribbed. Pappus copious, with white, slender bristles.
LEAVES Lance-shaped to elliptic, sharply toothed.
STEM Erect, grooved.
ANNUAL From fibrous roots.
HABITAT Varied, including dry woods, marshes, waste areas; often abundant after fires.
RANGE Throughout region.

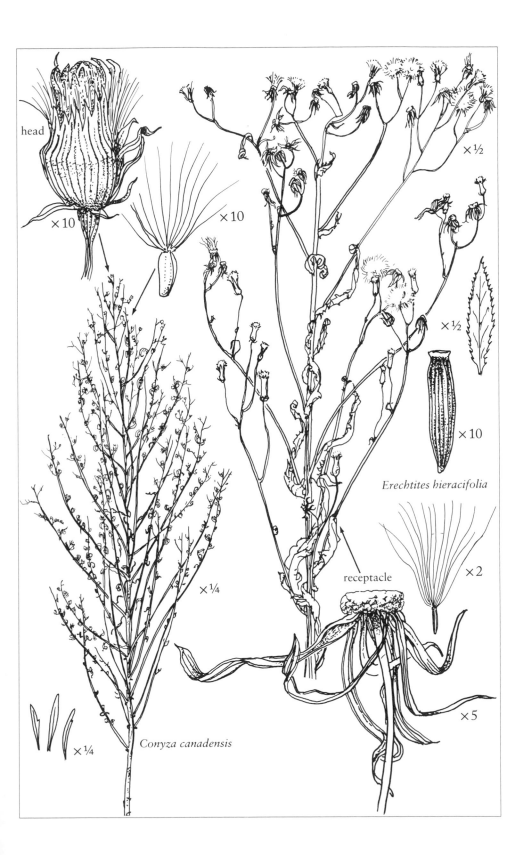

head

×10

×10

×½

×½

×10

Erechtites hieracifolia

receptacle

×2

×¼

×¼

×5

Conyza canadensis

Hieracium aurantiacum L.
Orange-red king-devil, orange hawkweed
Hieracium caespitosum Dumort (*H. pratense*)
Yellow king-devil, yellow hawkweed
Daisy Family (Asteraceae)
See pl. 4a

NOTE   In flower these two plants differ in color but otherwise look very much alike.
KEY IMPRESSIONS   Grows 6–20in (15–50cm). Single hairy stem with either 1 leaf or none. Stem topped with grouping of 5–25 heads. Involucral bracts hairy with blackish, gland-tipped hairs.
FRUIT   Achenes 1.5–2mm, dark brown to black, cut straight at apex (truncate), ribbed. Pappus of numerous whitish to brownish hairy bristles.
LEAVES   Basal rosette hairy, toothless, lance-shaped to elliptic, 5–12 times long as wide.
STEM   Hairy, erect, leafless or with 1 leaf.
PERENNIAL   From short or, more often, elongated underground stems with fibrous roots; slender stolons found along ground.
HABITAT   Fields, roadsides, disturbed areas.
RANGE   Native to Europe; now widespread as weeds throughout region.

Hieracium kalmii L. (*H. canadense*)
Canada hawkweed
Daisy Family (Asteraceae)

KEY IMPRESSIONS   Grows 2–5ft (.6–1.5m). Numerous stemless leaves on single erect stem. Heads on branches at terminal end.
FRUIT   Achenes black, ribbed, flat across apex. Pappus yellowish to tawny.
LEAVES   Stemless, somewhat clasping, oval to elliptic, toothed.
STEM   Single, erect, branched at terminal end.
PERENNIAL   From short, thick underground stem.
HABITAT   Woods, beaches, fields, especially in sandy soil.
RANGE   Nfld. and Lab. to N.J., west through Man. and Iowa to B.C. and Oreg.

Hieracium paniculatum L.
Panicled hawkweed
Daisy Family (Asteraceae)

KEY IMPRESSIONS   Grows 1–3ft (.3–1m). Single stem terminated by number of heads on branching panicle. Involucral bracts 5–9mm, layered, narrow. Found in woods.
FRUIT   Achenes straight across at apex (truncate). Pappus of numerous whitish hairy bristles.
LEAVES   Elliptic, slightly toothed, ascending stem.
STEM   Erect, single, smooth, branched at terminal end.
PERENNIAL   From short, woody underground stem.
HABITAT   Woods.
RANGE   N.S. and Que. to Minn., south to Va., Ohio, and, in mountains, n. Ga.

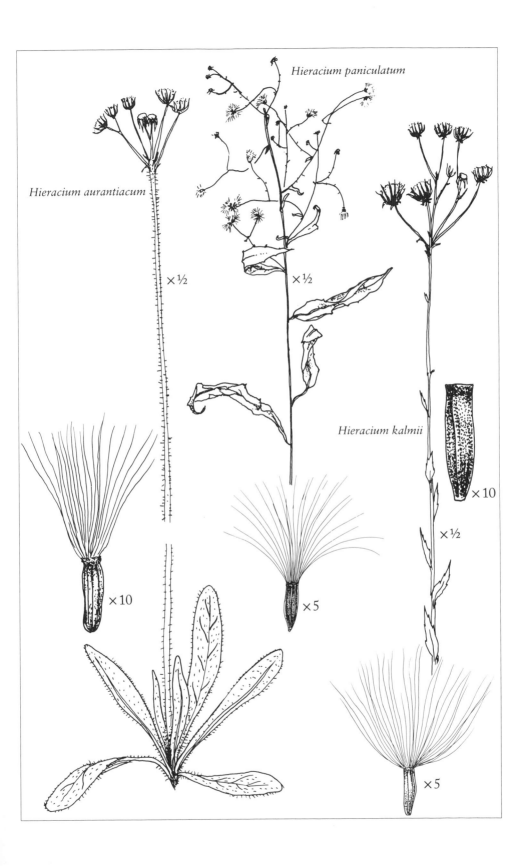

Hieracium paniculatum

Hieracium aurantiacum

×½

×½

Hieracium kalmii

×10

×½

×10

×5

×5

×5

Inula helenium L.
Elecampane
Daisy Family (Asteraceae)

KEY IMPRESSIONS   Grows 2–6ft (.6–2m). Simple or somewhat branched. Heads have flat receptacle with discs 1¼–2in (3–5cm) diameter, pockmarked by absent flowers. Receptacle surrounded by long, thin, shiny bracts and subtended by more round, overlapping leaflike bracts.
FRUIT   Achenes 4–5-ribbed, 4-angled. Pappus of hairy bristles. Achenes fall early and are hard to find in winter.
LEAVES   Broadly oval, slightly toothed, clasping stem.
STEM   Erect, coarse, hairy.
PERENNIAL   From large, thick underground stem.
HABITAT   Moist or wet disturbed areas.
RANGE   Native to Europe; cultivated, escaped, and occasionally naturalized.

Leontodon autumnalis L.
Fall-dandelion
Daisy Family (Asteraceae)

See pl. 13b

KEY IMPRESSIONS   Grows 4in–2ft (10–60cm). Heads solitary at ends of leafless stems. Involucral bracts narrow and layered, with long black hairs. Basal rosette leaves narrowly lobed. 3–7 stems arise from basal rosette. (The common dandelion has just 1 stem.)
FRUIT   Achenes columnar, weakly nerved. Pappus of feathery (plumose) bristles.
LEAVES   Basal rosette deeply, narrowly, distantly lobed.
STEM   Branched, leafless, ridged.
PERENNIAL   From stout, short, woody underground stem with fibrous roots.
HABITAT   Roadsides, pastures, fields, waste areas.
RANGE   Native to Eurasia; established from Greenland to Del., inland occasionally to Wis.

Liatris spicata (L.) Willd.
Dense blazing star, sessile blazing star
Daisy Family (Asteraceae)

NOTE   Numerous *Liatris* species are very similar in appearance (see below). All appear as crowded spikes with linear leaves and are distinguished by pappus type and involucral bract shape.
KEY IMPRESSIONS   Grows 1–5ft (.3–1.6m). Heads stemless, crowded into elongate, dense spike. Linear grasslike leaves on stem. Bracts layered, long, cylindric.
FRUIT   Achenes 10-ribbed, hairy. Pappus of hairy barbed bristles.
LEAVES   Linear, numerous.
STEM   Erect, single, covered by leaves and flower heads.
PERENNIAL   From thickened rootstock.
HABITAT   Wet meadows, other moist open areas.
RANGE   N.Y. to Mich. and se. Wis., south to Fla. and La.

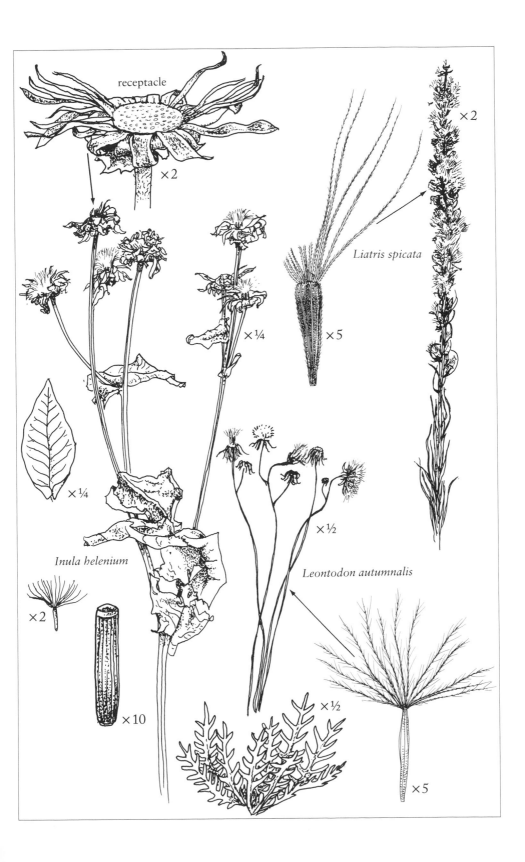

receptacle

×2

Liatris spicata

×2

×5

×¼

×¼

Inula helenium

×2

×10

×½

×½

Leontodon autumnalis

×5

SIMILAR SPECIES

L. aspera Michx.   Rough blazing star. Grows 1–4ft (.3–1.3m). Heads stemless or short-stemmed. Bracts flaring, broadly rounded, with curled margins. Pappus of barbed hairs. Dry, open areas, thin woods, especially in sandy soil. N.Dak. to Okla. and Tex., east to Mich. and Miss.

L. scariosa (L.) Willd.   Northern blazing star. Grows 1–3ft (.3–1m). Heads large, loose, stemmed. Bracts broadly rounded. Pappus hairs barbed. Prairies, open woods, other dry, open areas. Maine to Mich., south to Pa., Mo., Ark., and, in mountains, n. Ga.

L. cylindracea Michx.   Few-headed blazing star. Grows 8–24in (20–60cm). Heads few. Bracts in tight cylinder, sharp-pointed, flat. Pappus feathery (plumose). Dry, open areas. W. N.Y. and s. Ont. to s. Ohio, Ind., Mich., and Minn.

L. ligulistylis (A. Nels.) K. Schum.   Northern plains blazing star. Grows 8in–4ft (.2–1.3m). Heads not uniform; terminal head distinctly large. Bracts with broad, uneven borders. Pappus hairs barbed. Damp low places. Wis. to Alb., Colo., and N.Mex.

L. punctata Hook.   Dotted blazing star. Grows 3–4ft (1–1.3m). Heads several, stemless. Bracts pointed, flat, with hairy margins and glandular dots. Pappus feathery. Rootstock (unlike other species) elongated, pointed at base, like short, thickened taproot. Dry open places, especially in sandy soil. Mich. to Man., Alb., Ark., N.Mex.

L. pycnostachya Michx.   Prairie blazing star. Grows 2–5ft (.6–1.6m). Heads stemless. Bracts tapering to spreading, reflexed tip. Pappus hairs barbed. Moist or dry prairies or open woods. Ind. and Ky. to Minn., N.Dak., Tex., and Miss.; introduced east to N.J. and w. N.Y.

Prenanthes L. spp.
White lettuce, rattlesnake-root
Daisy Family (Asteraceae)

KEY IMPRESSIONS   Grows to 7ft (2.3m). Tall. Heads nodding downward in clusters. Receptacle small. 4–15 principal bracts and some reduced outer ones. Leaves highly variable in size and shape.

FRUIT   Achenes mostly reddish brown, elongate, cylindric, ribbed. Pappus of numerous hairy bristles.

LEAVES   Alternate, varying by species.

STEM   Tall, erect.

PERENNIAL   From thickened tuberous roots.

SPECIES

P. alba L.   White lettuce, rattlesnake-root. Grows 2–5ft (.6–1.6m). Pappus cinnamon-brown. 8 principal involucral bracts. Leaves triangular to deeply lobed. Woodlands, thickets. Maine to Man., south to N.C., W.Va., and Mo.

P. altissima L.   Tall white lettuce. Grows 2–7ft (.6–2.3m). Pappus whitish and bright yellow-brown. 5 principal involucral bracts. Leaves triangular to lobed. Woods. Throughout region.

P. serpentaria Pursh   Lion's foot. Grows 1½–4ft (.45–1.3m). Similar to *P. alba,* but pappus creamy and involucral bracts bristly, often sprinkled with fine black dots. Leaves more often distinctly pinnately lobed, broader above middle. Woods, especially in sandy soil. Mass. to n. Fla., west to Ky., Tenn., and Miss.

P. trifoliata (Cass.) Fern.   Gall-of-the-earth. Grows 1–5ft (.3–1.6m). Pappus pale brown. 8 involucral bracts. Leaves vary, lower ones long-stemmed; deep but few lobes. Woods, especially in sandy soil. Nfld. to Md. and Pa., south along coast and in mountains to N.C. and n. Ga.

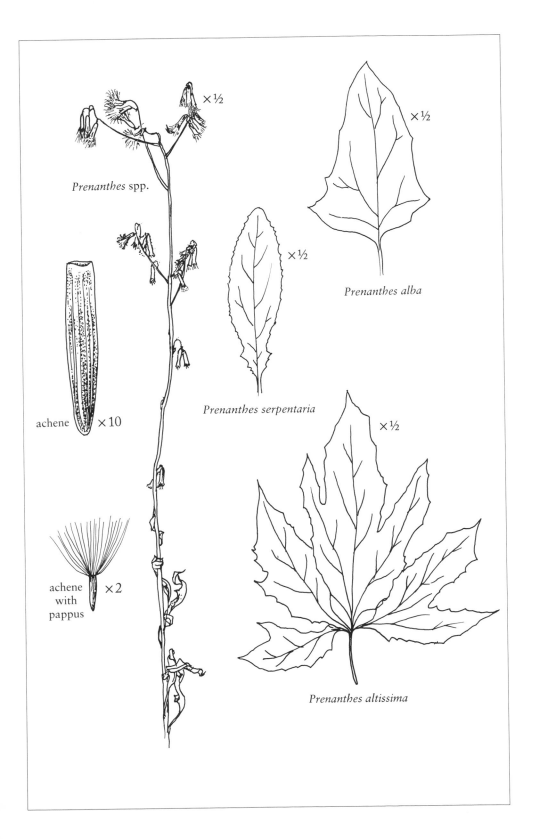

Prenanthes spp. ×½

achene ×10

achene
with
pappus ×2

Prenanthes serpentaria ×½

Prenanthes alba ×½

Prenanthes altissima ×½

Sonchus oleraceus L.

Common sow-thistle

Daisy Family (Asteraceae)

KEY IMPRESSIONS Grows 1–8ft (.3–2.6m). Heads several, small, on terminal branches. Involucral bracts layered. Leaves prominently lobed at base, with weakly spiny margins.

FRUIT Achenes wrinkled, 3–5-ribbed on each face, strongly tapered, flattened, with short style remnant. Pappus of numerous white, hairy bristles.

LEAVES Prominent, acute basal lobes, margins lobed to merely toothed, margins weakly or scarcely prickly.

STEM Smooth, angled.

ANNUAL From short taproot.

HABITAT Varied; common.

RANGE Native to Europe; throughout region.

SIMILAR SPECIES

S. arvensis L. Field sow-thistle, perennial sow-thistle. Grows 1½–4ft (.45–1.3m). Heads several, relatively large. Involucral bracts with spreading gland-tipped hairs. Achenes wrinkled, 5-ribbed or more on each face. Leaves prickly margined, lobed. Fields, waste areas, roadsides. Throughout region.

S. asper (L.) Hill. Spiny-leaved sow-thistle, prickly sow-thistle. Grows 1–5ft (.3–1.6m). Achenes smooth, 3–4-ribbed on each face. Leaves very spiny, curled, with rounded basal lobes clasping angled stem. Waste areas, roadsides. Throughout region.

Vernonia noveboracensis (L.) Michx.

New York ironweed

Daisy Family (Asteraceae)

KEY IMPRESSIONS Grows 3–6ft (1–2m). Tall. Single stem terminated by branches carrying numerous brownish heads. Involucral bracts oval at base, abruptly narrowing to hairlike tip, layered. Receptacle flat or convex.

FRUIT Achenes 4–4.5mm, hairy-ribbed. Pappus brownish purple to tawny, in 2 series, the outer of short bristles or scales, the inner of longer bristles.

LEAVES Lance-shaped, toothless to slightly toothed, stemless.

STEM 3–6ft (1–2m) high, branched at top.

PERENNIAL

HABITAT Low wet woods, marshes, especially along coast.

RANGE Mass. to Fla., inland to w. Pa., W.Va., e. Ky., Tenn., and Ala.

SIMILAR SPECIES

V. fasciculata Michx. Smooth ironweed. Heads smaller than in *V. noveboracensis*, flatter, more tightly clustered. Involucral bracts rounded, lacking hairlike tips. Achenes not hairy-ribbed. Pappus tawny to purple. Wet prairies, marshes. Minn. and Wis. to Ohio and south.

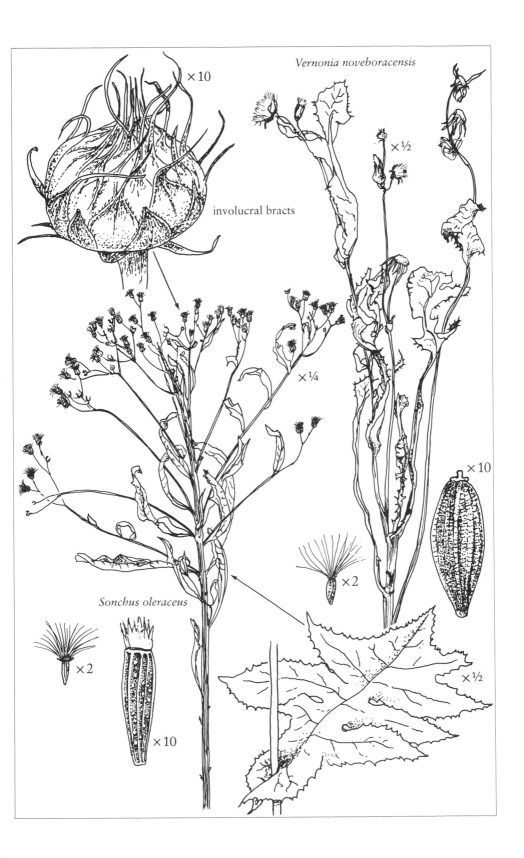

×10

Vernonia noveboracensis

involucral bracts

×½

×¼

×10

×2

Sonchus oleraceus

×2

×10

×½

Plants Bearing Round-headed Fruits with Bristly, Beaked Hairs

Taraxacum officinale Weber
Common dandelion
Daisy Family (Asteraceae)

See pl. 14a

KEY IMPRESSIONS   Overwinters aboveground with basal leaf rosette. In mild winters plants may even bloom and produce fruit in conspicuous round ball of achenes.

FRUIT   Achenes 3–4mm, brown. Pappus of numerous white hairy bristles on long beak. Beak 2.5–4 times as long as body. Mature achenes and pappus form a ball about 1in (2.5cm) diameter.

LEAVES   Basal rosette leaves smooth, lobed, terminal lobe tending to be larger.

STEM   2–18in (5–50cm), solitary, erect.

PERENNIAL   From taproot.

HABITAT   Lawns, disturbed areas.

RANGE   Native to Eurasia; established as weed throughout region.

Tragopogon pratensis L.
Showy goat's beard, meadow salsify
Daisy Family (Asteraceae)

KEY IMPRESSIONS   Grows 1–2ft (30–60cm). Large, globose heads of achenes, 3–4in (7.5–10cm) diameter, solitary at end of single stem. Not really a winter weed; short-lived. Fruit head looks like large dandelion head.

FRUIT   Achenes ½–1in (1.5–2.5cm), highly elongated, gradually tapering to long beak topped with pappus of 1 series of feathery (plumose) bristles, united at base, branches interwebbed; several bristles commonly longer than others. Achenes 5–10-nerved, 5-sided in cross-section, ribbed.

LEAVES   Alternate, linear, toothless, clasping, grasslike.

STEM   Erect, round.

BIENNIAL   From fleshy taproot.

HABITAT   Roadsides, fields, waste areas.

RANGE   Throughout region.

Lactuca L. spp.
Lettuce
Daisy Family (Asteraceae)

Plants of the genus *Lactuca* are tall and leafy, with loose panicles of many small flower remnants. There is much variation, and identification is often highly technical. Examples are given below.

Lactuca canadensis L.
Wild lettuce, tall lettuce
Daisy Family (Asteraceae)

KEY IMPRESSIONS   Grows 4–10ft (1.3–3.3m). Branched above into narrow, elongate panicle with numerous small heads. Involucral bracts generally layered.

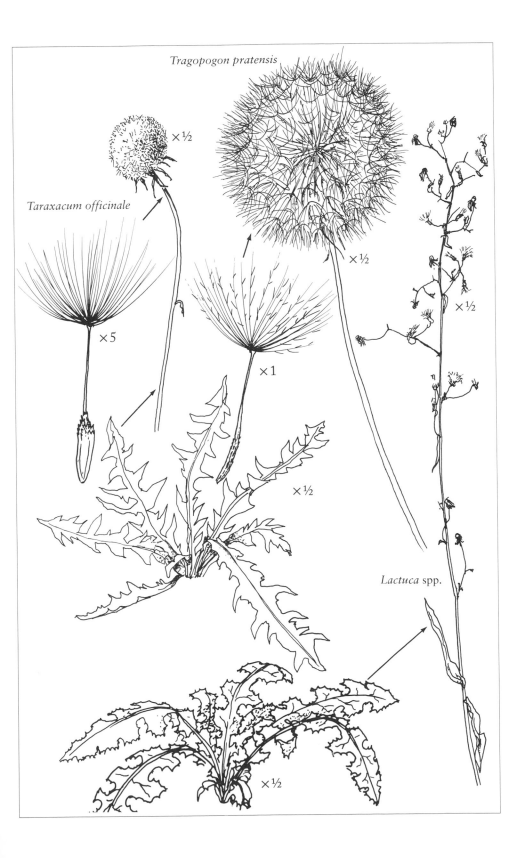

Tragopogon pratensis

×½

Taraxacum officinale

×5

×½

×1

×½

×½

Lactuca spp.

×½

FRUIT Achenes 4.5–6.5mm, blackish, oblong, highly flattened, with wrinkled surfaces and median nerve on each face. Apex bears a long, slender beak expanded at tip and bearing white bristles. Bristles detach easily, but beak remains.

LEAVES Basal rosette leaves often growing to 1 ft (30cm). Stem leaves usually lobed, though upper leaves sometimes unlobed.

STEM Erect, branched at upper end.

ANNUAL OR USUALLY BIENNIAL From taproot.

HABITAT Fields, waste areas, woods.

RANGE Que. to Sask., south to Fla. and Tex.

SIMILAR SPECIES

L. hirsuta Muhl. Hairy tall lettuce. Similar to *L. canadensis* but often hairier, heads larger. Leaves have broad, toothed lobes. Dry open woods, clearings. S. Ont. and w. N.Y., south to Va. and W.Va.

L. serriola L. Prickly lettuce. Grows 1–4ft (.3–1.3m). Achenes gray or yellowish gray, compressed, several-nerved on each face. Beak slender, same length as body. Leaves prickly on midrib underneath, finely prickly-toothed on margins, lobed or lobeless. Biennial or winter-annual. Fields, waste areas. Native to Europe; common throughout U.S.

L. floridana (L.) Gaertner Woodland lettuce. Grows 3–7ft (1–2.3m). Achenes narrowed upward, beakless or with stout beak sometimes ⅓ as long as body, several-nerved on each face. Pappus hairs white. Leaves deeply lobed, dandelionlike. Thickets, woods, moist open areas. N.Y. to Fla., west to Minn., Kans., and Tex.

L. biennis (Moench) Fern. Tall blue lettuce. Often taller than *L. canadensis;* grows to 15ft (5m). Crowded flower and fruit remnants. Achenes thin-edged, several-nerved on each face, tapering to beakless or short stout-beaked tip. Pappus brown. Very leafy. Leaves lobed or only toothed. Annual or biennial. Moist areas. Nfld. to B.C., south to N.C., Ill., Colo., and Calif.

L. pulchella (Pursh) DC. Blue lettuce. Grows 1–3½ft (.3–1.2m). Flower remnants larger than in all species mentioned above. Achenes several-nerved on each face, beak stout, often whitish, up to as long as body. Leaves toothless, lobeless or only lower leaves lobed. Meadows, thickets, prairies, other moist low areas. More common in West; Alaska to Calif., east to Minn. and Mo., occasionally introduced eastward.

Plants with Heads of White or Brown Papery Bracts, White and Woolly Stems, and Bristle-haired Fruits

Anaphalis margaritacea (L.) Benth. & Hook.

Pearly everlasting

Daisy Family (Asteraceae)

KEY IMPRESSIONS Grows 1–3ft (.3–1m). Woolly stem with alternate, narrow woolly leaves. Stem branched at summit, supporting numerous round heads of pure white, woolly, papery bracts with yellowish bracts in center.

FRUIT Achenes with pappus of hairy bristles. Plant either male or female, thus no achenes on male plant.

LEAVES Alternate, linear, downy above, woolly underneath.

STEM Erect, branched above.

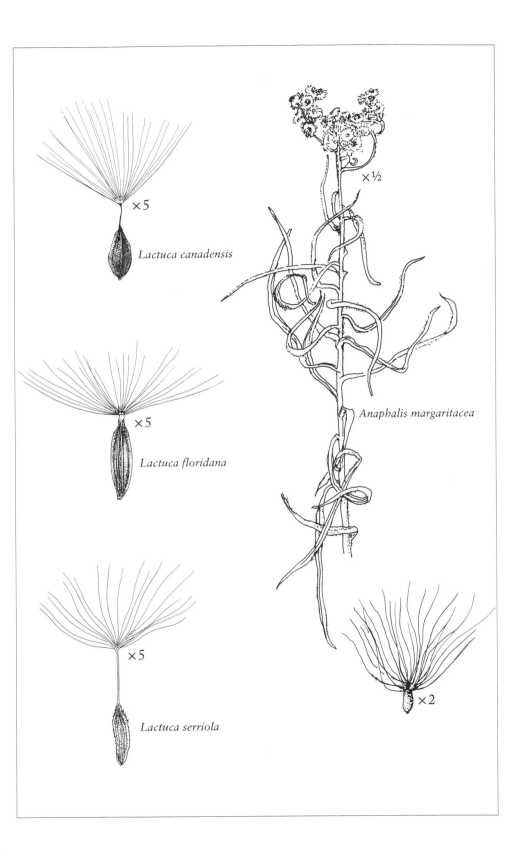

×5

Lactuca canadensis

×5

Lactuca floridana

×5

Lactuca serriola

×½

Anaphalis margaritacea

×2

PERENNIAL From long underground stems with fibrous roots.
HABITAT Chiefly dry open spaces.
RANGE Northern N. Am. south to Va., W.Va., Nebr., and Calif.

Gnaphalium obtusifolium L.
Sweet everlasting, fragrant cudweed, catfoot
Daisy Family (Asteraceae)

KEY IMPRESSIONS Grows 1–2ft (30–60cm). Alternate linear leaves tend to remain in winter. Stem branched at summit, with heads browner than in *Anaphalis margaritacea,* which it somewhat resembles. Dingy white bracts of varying lengths, outer ones rounded, inner ones narrower. Gives off odor of tobacco when crushed.
FRUIT Achenes small, smooth, with 1 series of rough hairy bristles that fall separately.
LEAVES Linear, alternate, woolly underneath. Rosette leaves hairy and spatulate in 1st year.
STEM Woolly, white.
ANNUAL OR WINTER-ANNUAL
HABITAT Dry soil, old fields, pastures.
RANGE Throughout region.

Plants Having Fruits and Bracts with Dense and Rounded or Cone-shaped Heads and Hairless Fruits
See also *Heliopsis helianthoides* p. 200

Verbesina alternifolia (L.) Britton
Wingstem
Daisy Family (Asteraceae)

KEY IMPRESSIONS Grows 3–8ft (1–2.5m). Leaves alternate, flowing into stem, forming decurrent wings. Receptacle convex, its bracts partly enfolding achenes, which spread loosely in all directions, forming rounded heads.
FRUIT Achenes more or less flattened at right angles to involucral bracts. Most broadly winged, some wingless. Pappus of 1–4 bristles.
LEAVES Alternate, simple, lance-shaped, toothed, flowing into stem to form wings on stem.
STEM Erect, winged, hairy.
PERENNIAL
HABITAT Thickets, woods, bottomlands.
RANGE N.Y. and s. Ont. to e. Nebr., south to Fla., La., and Okla.

Echinacea purpurea (L.) Moench
Purple coneflower
Daisy Family (Asteraceae)

KEY IMPRESSIONS Grows 2–4ft (.6–1.3m). 1 head, 1½in (3.5cm) diameter, terminates stem. Receptacle large, conic, surrounded by stiff, pointed bracts in 2–4 series.
FRUIT Achenes quadrangular. Pappus a short-toothed crown.

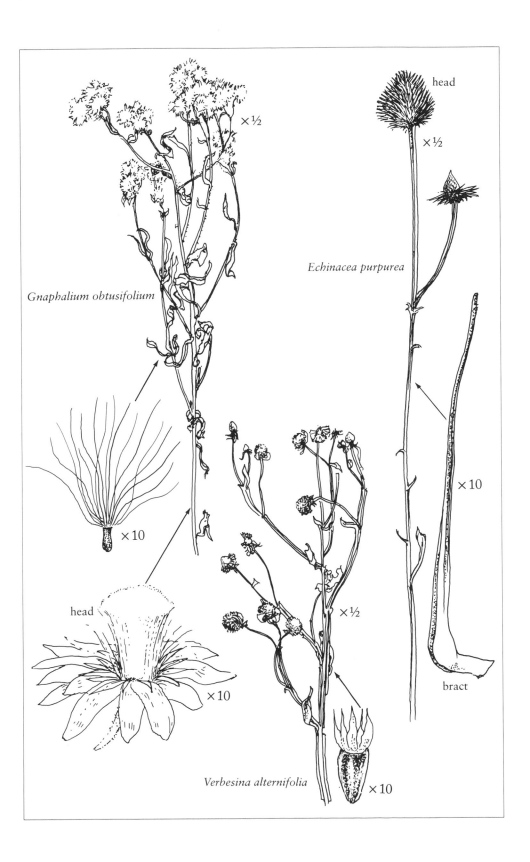

Gnaphalium obtusifolium

×½

×10

head

×10

Verbesina alternifolia

×10

Echinacea purpurea

head

×½

×10

bract

LEAVES Alternate, lance-shaped, hairy, toothed.

STEM Erect, 1 to few.

PERENNIAL From thickened, short, stout, black woody underground stem with fibrous roots.

HABITAT Woods, prairies.

RANGE Midwest, east irregularly to s. Mich., Ky., Tenn., and Ga.

Helenium autumnale L.
Common sneezeweed
Daisy Family (Asteraceae)

KEY IMPRESSIONS Grows 2–5ft (.6–1.6m). Round-headed dried bracts on convex receptacle. Involucral bracts narrow, soon deflexed. Stems rough and winged.

FRUIT Achenes top-shaped, 4–5-angled with intermediate ribs and small hairs on angles. Pappus of 5–8 ovate scales tapering to slender bristles, generally brownish.

LEAVES Alternate, rough, lance-shaped, tapering to stem and forming wings on stem.

STEM Erect, winged.

PERENNIAL From fibrous roots.

HABITAT Moist low ground.

RANGE Que. to Fla., west to Ariz.

SIMILAR SPECIES

H. amarum (Raf.) H. Rock. Narrow-leaved sneezeweed. Grows 1–2ft (30–60cm). Heads numerous. Pappus scaled, with midrib terminating in slender bristle nearly as long as body. Involucral bracts linear, soon deflexed. Leaves numerous, linear. Annual. Open woods, prairies, fields, waste areas, especially in sandy soil. Midwest; introduced east from Conn. to Ga.

H. flexuosum Raf. Purple-headed sneezeweed, Southern sneezeweed. Grows 1–3½ft (.3–1.1m). Heads numerous. Involucral bracts lance-shaped, soon deflexed. Pappus scales mostly oval, bristle-tipped. Leaves smaller, less numerous, more erect than in *H. autumnale*. Perennial from fibrous root. Moist ground, waste areas. Mass. and N.H. to Fla., west to Wis., Ill., Mo., and Tex.

Rudbeckia hirta L.
Black-eyed Susan
Daisy Family (Asteraceae)

See pl. 3c

KEY IMPRESSIONS Grows 2–3ft (.6–1m). Sparingly branched or single-stemmed, bearing 1 to few black cone-shaped heads. Stems, bracts, and leaves hairy.

FRUIT Achene black, 4-angled. No pappus.

LEAVES Alternate, hairy, lance-shaped to oval, toothless.

STEM Erect, hairy.

BIENNIAL OR SHORT-LIVED PERENNIAL From narrow underground stem.

HABITAT Fields, thickets, roadsides, disturbed areas.

RANGE Nfld. to Fla., west to B.C. and Mexico.

SIMILAR SPECIES

R. laciniata L. Green-headed coneflower. Grows 3–12ft (1–4m). Cone-shaped heads grayish rather than black, as in *R. hirta*. Achenes equally 4-angled. Pappus a short, 4-

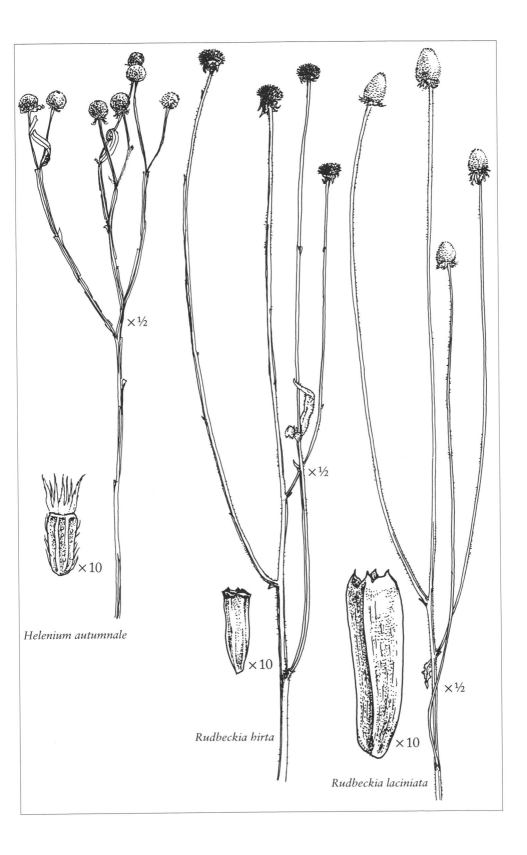

Helenium autumnale

×½

×10

Rudbeckia hirta

×½

×10

Rudbeckia laciniata

×½

×10

toothed crown. Involucral bracts spreading or reflexed. Leaves deeply lobed or coarsely toothed. Perennial from woody base. Moist places. Que. to Fla., west to Mont. and Ariz.

Ratibida pinnata (Vent.) Barnhart
Globular coneflower, gray-headed coneflower
Daisy Family (Asteraceae)

KEY IMPRESSIONS   Grows 3–5ft (1–1.5m). Heads several or occasionally solitary. Receptacle disk 12–20mm, cylindric.
FRUIT   Achenes smooth, compressed. No pappus.
LEAVES   Alternate, deeply lobed.
STEM   Erect.
PERENNIAL   From stout, woody underground stem.
HABITAT   Prairies, old fields, dry woods, often on limestone.
RANGE   S. Ont. to Minn. and S.Dak., south to Tenn., Ga., w. Fla., and La.; adventive east to Vt. and Mass.

Plants Having Heads of Dried Bracts and Alternate Leaves
See also *Cichorium intybus* p. 142, *Coreopsis* spp. p. 202, *Silphium* spp. p. 202

Helianthus L. spp.
Sunflower
Daisy Family (Asteraceae)

The many species of *Helianthus* have very similar heads of dried bracts in winter. They differ in leaf shape and distribution—some with opposite leaves, others with alternate leaves, and some with opposite lower leaves and alternate upper ones. Species described in this section have alternate leaves, but also see the section with opposite-leaved species.

Helianthus decapetalus L.
Forest sunflower, thin-leaved sunflower
Daisy Family (Asteraceae)

KEY IMPRESSIONS   Grows 1–5ft (.3–1.6m). Branched. Receptacle disks ⅓–½in (1–1.5cm) diameter, surrounded by enlarged, loose bracts. Outer bracts loosely leafy, with fringed, pointed tips, usually surpassing disk.
FRUIT   Achenes smooth. Pappus of 2 small scales that fall early.
LEAVES   Slightly hairy, oval to lance-shaped, sharply toothed, more or less abruptly contracted toward base. Upper usually alternate; lower sometimes opposite. Leaf stalks winged.
STEM   Smooth.
PERENNIAL   From well-developed underground stems with fibrous roots and usually without tubers.
HABITAT   Open woods, thickets.
RANGE   Maine and Que. to Wis. and Iowa, south to Ga. and Mo.

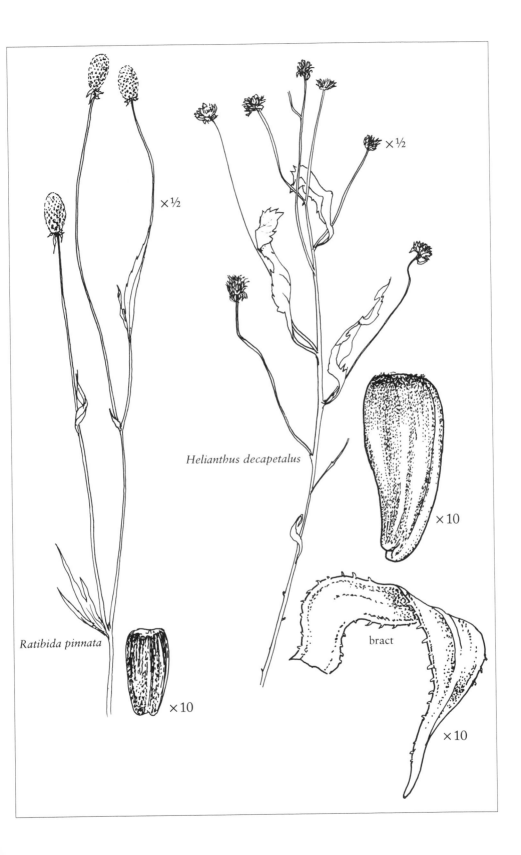

×½

×½

Helianthus decapetalus

×10

Ratibida pinnata

×10

bract

×10

SIMILAR SPECIES

H. annuus L.   Common sunflower. Grows 3–12ft (1–4m). Branched. Heads several, large. Receptacles 1½–2in (3–5cm) diameter. Bracts abruptly contracted above middle, coming to fringed point. Leaves long-stalked, oval, toothed. Lower leaves may be opposite. Annual from fibrous roots. Disturbed soil, especially moist, low ground. Throughout region.

H. giganteus L.   Swamp-sunflower, giant sunflower. Grows 4–10ft (1.3–3.3m). Bracts narrow, thin, often surpassing disk, strongly fringed. Disks ½–1in (1.5–2.5cm) diameter. Leaves lance-shaped, toothed, stemless or short-stemmed. Lower leaves may be opposite. Perennial from short underground stems and thickened fleshy roots. Swamps, other moist areas. Maine and N.B. to n. S.C. and Ga., west to Nebr.

H. grosseserratus Martens   Saw-toothed sunflower. Grows 4–10ft (1.3–3.3m). Bracts linear, loose, often surpassing disk, more or less fringed. Leaves hairy, lance-shaped, strongly toothed, tapering at base to often winged stem. Perennial from underground stems. Damp prairies, other moist areas. Maine to Minn., south to Ga. and Tex.; may be introduced east of Ohio.

H. tuberosus L.   Jerusalem-artichoke. Grows 6–10ft (2–3.3m). Branched. Heads numerous. Disks ½–1in (1.5–2.5cm) diameter, surrounded by darkish bracts. Achenes downy, 4-sided. Pappus of 2 thin scales that fall early. Leaves oval, toothed, tapering to winged stem. Lower leaves opposite. Stem rough. Perennial from fleshy, thickened, edible underground stems bearing tubers. Moist soil, waste areas. Throughout e. U.S. and adjacent Canada and west across Great Plains.

H. petiolaris Nutt.   Plains-sunflower, prairie-sunflower. Grows 1–3ft (.3–1m). Similar to *H. annuus* but smaller. Bracts tapering, scarcely fringed. Receptacle flat. Leaves oval, hairy, usually toothless. Annual. Prairies, plains, waste areas, in sandy soil. Great Plains, occasionally eastward.

Lapsana communis L.
Nipplewort
Daisy Family (Asteraceae)

KEY IMPRESSIONS   Grows 1–2ft (30–60cm). Heads several, small, 5–8mm, on branching stem. 8 bracts, erect, with 1 short outer series.
FRUIT   Achenes oblong, curved. No pappus.
LEAVES   Lower leaves oval, shallowly toothed, often with several lobes at the base.
STEM   Erect, branched.
ANNUAL
HABITAT   Woodlands, fields, waste areas.
RANGE   Native to Europe; found throughout region.

Centaurea maculosa Lam.
Spotted knapweed
Daisy Family (Asteraceae)

KEY IMPRESSIONS   Grows 2–3ft (.6–1m). Scraggly, much branched. Most common of knapweeds, which can be distinguished by different fringe patterns on bracts. In *C. maculosa* lower dried bracts have distinctive black triangular tips.
FRUIT   Achenes olive-green, with 4 yellow longitudinal lines, widest at apex and tapered at base, alternating with fine hairs on receptacle. Pappus of 2 rows of bristles, inner shorter than outer.

Heads of Dried Bracts, Alternate Leaves

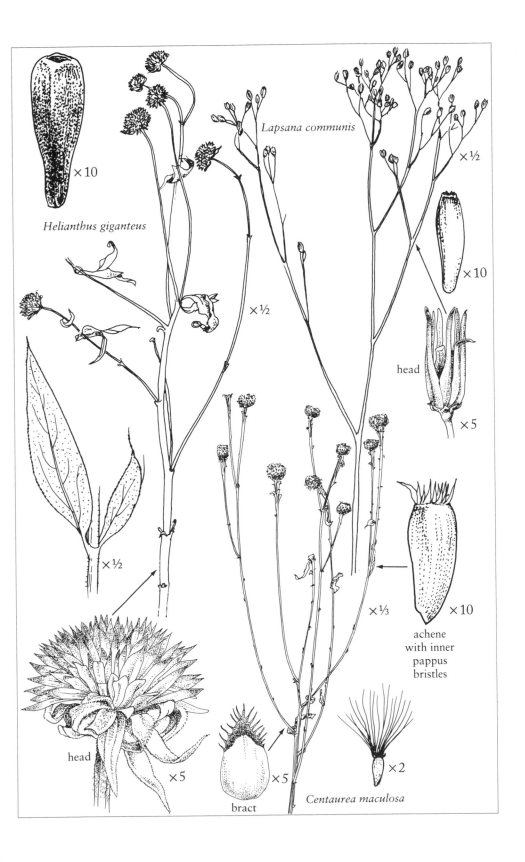

×10

Helianthus giganteus

Lapsana communis

×½

×½

×10

head

×5

×½

head

×5

achene
with inner
pappus
bristles

×10

head

×5

×⅓

bract ×5

×2

Centaurea maculosa

LEAVES Deeply, narrowly lobed.

STEM Many branched.

BIENNIAL

HABITAT Fields, roadsides, waste areas.

RANGE Native to Europe; common throughout region.

SIMILAR SPECIES

C. *jacea* L. Brown knapweed. Grows 1–3ft (.3–1m). Bracts scalelike, lacking long fringes of other species. No pappus. Lower leaves long-stemmed, often toothed; upper leaves toothless. Perennial. Fields, roadsides, waste areas. Throughout region.

C. *nigra* L. Black knapweed. Grows 1–3ft (.3–1m). Bracts dark, heavily fringed, giving black look to globular base of head. No pappus. Leaves lance-shaped, toothless. Perennial. Fields, roadsides, waste areas. Throughout region.

C. *scabiosa* L. Great knapweed, hard-heads. Grows 1–2ft (30–60cm). Heads much larger than in C. *maculosa* and at tip of long, grooved stem, swollen at summit. Pappus of bristles 3–6mm. Leaves deeply lobed. Perennial. Fields, waste areas. Northern part of region.

C. *dubia* Suter. Short-fringed knapweed. Grows 1–3ft (.3–1m). Similar to C. *nigra* but with dark fringed tips of bracts not concealing pale base, giving paler look to receptacle. Pappus mostly lacking. Fields, roadsides. Se. Canada and ne. U.S., south to Va.

Matricaria matricarioides (Less.) Porter
Pineapple weed
Daisy Family (Asteraceae)

See pl. 19c

KEY IMPRESSIONS Grows 3–18in (5–40cm). Much branched. Gives off pineapple scent when crushed. Inflorescence remnants sand-colored, shallow, cuplike heads with pointed cone centers (often called "Mexican sombreros").

FRUIT Achenes with 2 marginal and 1 or more ventral nerves. Pappus a short, obscure crown.

LEAVES Alternate, dissected, fernlike.

STEM Forms flat, branching mat.

ANNUAL From fibrous roots.

HABITAT Roadsides, paths, disturbed areas.

RANGE Introduced east to Atlantic; s. Canada, south to Mo., Ind., Ohio, Pa., and Del.

Plants 2–5ft (.6–1.6m), with Tiny Star-shaped Receptacles in Dense Clusters and Bristle-haired Fruits: Goldenrods (*Solidago* spp.)

See also *Euthamia* spp. p. 194

Introduction to Goldenrods

KEY IMPRESSIONS Goldenrods are easy to confuse with *Aster* species in their winter state but goldenrods tend to be taller and more stoutly branched, with numerous small heads in more compact groups along the branches.

FRUIT Achenes are several-nerved, frequently angled. Pappus bristles are usually white. A star-shaped receptacle remains after achenes have fallen.

Centaurea bracts

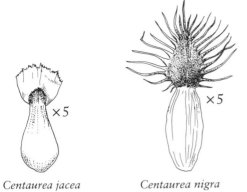

×5

Centaurea jacea

×5

Centaurea nigra

×5

Centaurea scabiosa

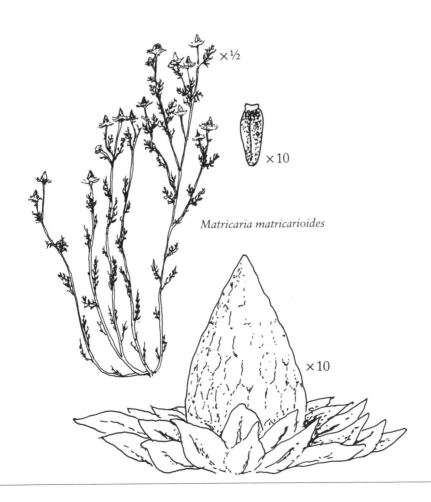

×½

×10

Matricaria matricarioides

×10

PERENNIAL   From underground stems with fibrous roots.

IDENTIFICATION   To identify goldenrods in winter, first observe the overall shape of the inflorescence and the distribution of the heads—not an easy task, given the many species of *Solidago*. Leaves can be of help if any still showing structures remain on the specimen. Unfortunately, leaves fall off early. Habitat is sometimes helpful in identification, and a number of goldenrods have galls, which also aid in identification (see p. 240). The most common *Solidagos* are described here. There are 4 general types of *Solidago* inflorescences:

A. Heads in axillary clusters p. 234

B. Heads in a terminal spike or club-shaped inflorescence, on all sides of the branch axis
   1. Slender wandlike inflorescence p. 234
   2. Full clublike inflorescence p. 236

C. Heads in terminal, usually large panicles, mostly on 1 side of the branch axis (secund)
   1. Parallel-veined leaves p. 238
   2. Net-veined leaves p. 238

D. Heads in flat-topped inflorescences: see *Euthamia* (formerly considered part of *Solidago*) p. 194

A. Heads in Axillary Clusters

Solidago caesia L.

Axillary goldenrod, blue-stemmed goldenrod

Daisy Family (Asteraceae)

KEY IMPRESSIONS   Grows 1–3½ft (.3–1.3m). Small heads in axillary clusters or racemes. Found in woodlands.

FRUIT   Achenes downy, many-ribbed, with white pappus bristles.

LEAVES   Alternate, oblong, net-veined, stemless.

STEM   Smooth.

PERENNIAL   From short, stout underground stem with abundant fibrous roots, sometimes with long, creeping underground stems.

HABITAT   Woods.

RANGE   N.S. and s. Que. to Wis., south to Fla. and Tex.

SIMILAR SPECIES

S. flexicaulis L.   Zigzag goldenrod, broad-leaved goldenrod. Grows 2–4½ft (.6–1.5m). Achenes downy. Leaves very broad. Note zigzag stem. Woods. N.S. and N.B. to N.Dak., south to Va., Ky., and Ark.; in mountains to Ga.

B. Heads in a Terminal Spike or Club-shaped Inflorescence, on All Sides of the Branch Axis

1. Slender wandlike inflorescence

Solidago bicolor L.

Silver-rod

Daisy Family (Asteraceae)

KEY IMPRESSIONS   Grows 6in–3ft (.15–1m). Small heads crowded both into terminal wandlike inflorescence and in upper axils.

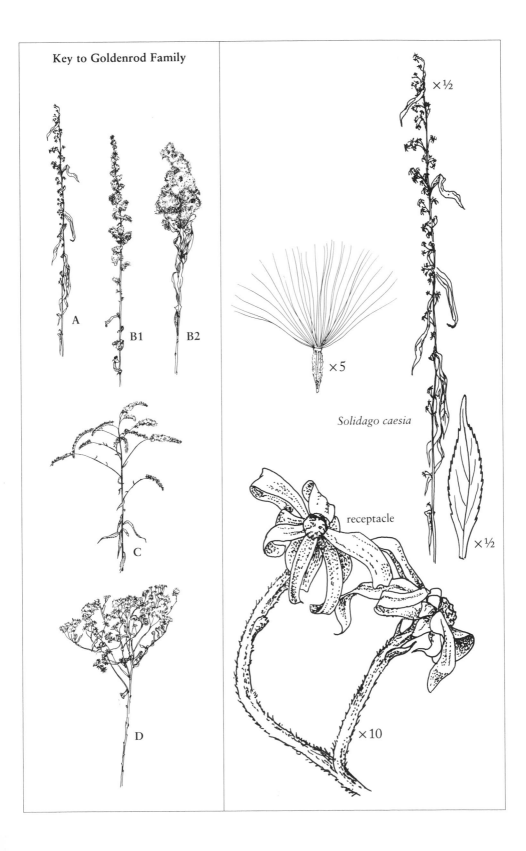

Key to Goldenrod Family

A

B1 B2

C

D

×½

×5

Solidago caesia

receptacle

×10

×½

FRUIT   Achenes smooth. Pappus of white bristles.

LEAVES   Alternate, oblong, downy, net-veined. Upper leaves toothless, stemless; lower leaves toothed, long-stemmed.

STEM   Downy to smooth.

PERENNIAL   From stout, short underground stem and fibrous roots.

HABITAT   Dry woods, open, often rocky places.

RANGE   N.S. and Que. to Wis., south to Ga. and La.

SIMILAR SPECIES

S. puberula Nutt.   Downy goldenrod, dusty goldenrod. Grows 1–3ft (.3–1m). Achenes fibrous. Pappus of white bristles. Leaves of stem oblong, toothless, stemless; leaves at base often sharply toothed, stemmed. Stem may retain minute spreading hairs. Sandy or rocky soil. N.S. and s. Que., south to Fla. and La.

S. hispida Muhl.   Hairy goldenrod. Grows 1–3ft (.3–1m). Achenes smooth. Upper leaves toothless, stemless; lower leaves toothed, stemmed. Stem very hairy, leaves sometimes remaining. Dry woods, open rocky places. Nfld. to Minn. and s. Ohio, south to Ga. and Ark.

S. erecta Pursh   Erect goldenrod, slender goldenrod. Grows 1–4ft (.3–1.3m). Very similar to S. hispida, but with stem and leaves smooth. Achenes smooth. Dry woods. Coastal Mass. and N.J. to s. Ohio and Ind., south to Ga. and Miss.

S. stricta Aiton   Wandlike goldenrod. Grows 2–7ft (.6–2.3m). Achenes mostly smooth. Leaves very small, bractlike, hugging stem. Moist sand, pine barrens, coastal marshes. N.J. coastal plain to Fla. and Tex.

2. Full clublike inflorescence

Solidago sempervirens L.

Seaside-goldenrod

Daisy Family (Asteraceae)

See pl. 2b

KEY IMPRESSIONS   Grows 1½–8ft (.5–2.6m). Inflorescence densely panicled. Leaves numerous, smooth, lance-shaped, and toothless. Found in coastal areas.

FRUIT   Achenes hairy.

LEAVES   Basally disposed, toothless, the largest ones lance-shaped, dense on stem.

STEM   Erect, smooth.

PERENNIAL   From short, compact underground stem.

HABITAT   Coastal salt marshes, dunes, beaches. Now spreading inland locally, especially along highways salted in winter.

RANGE   Gulf of St. Lawrence to tropical Am.

SIMILAR SPECIES

S. squarrosa Muhl.   Squarrose goldenrod. Grows 1½–5ft (.5–1.6m). Inflorescence sometimes 12in (30cm), often leafy. Achenes smooth, with pappus of white bristles. Basal leaves very large, toothed, often forming rosette. Perennial. Rocky woods. N.B. to Ont., south to Ohio and Ind.; in mountains to N.C.

S. speciosa Nutt.   Showy goldenrod. Grows 2–6ft (.6–2m). Similar to S. squarrosa, but lacking strong teeth on lower leaf margins. Achenes smooth. Open woods, prairies, plains. Mass. and s. N.H. to Minn. and Wyo., south to Ga., Ark., Tex., and N.Mex.

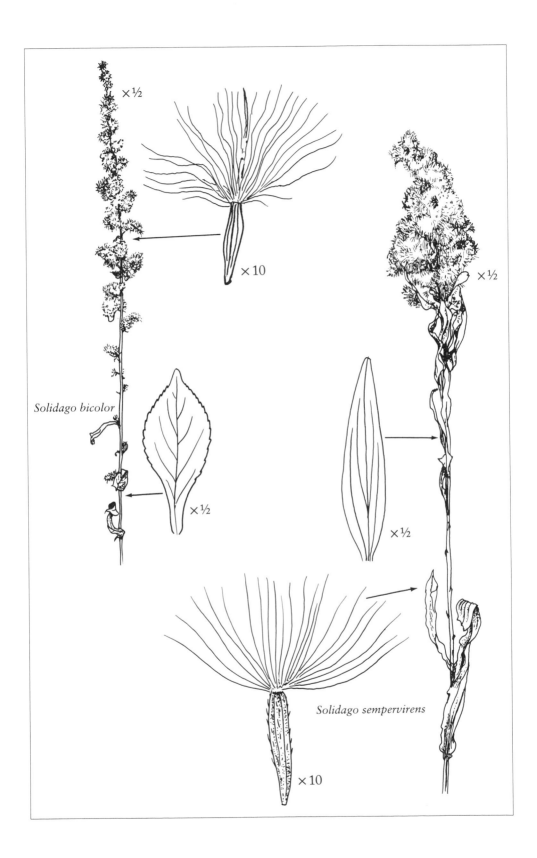

× ½

× 10

Solidago bicolor

× ½

× ½

× ½

Solidago sempervirens

× 10

S. macrophylla Pursh   Large-leaved goldenrod. Grows 1–4ft (.3–1.3m). Individual heads larger than in *S. speciosa*. Achenes smooth. All but uppermost leaves stemmed. Leaves rounded at stem (leaves of *S. speciosa* taper into leafstalk). Moist, cool, often shaded places. N.Y. Catskills and Mt. Greylock, Mass., to Nfld., Lab., and Hudson Bay.

C. Heads in Terminal, Usually Large Panicles, Mostly on 1 Side of the Branch Axis (Secund)

1. Parallel-veined leaves

Solidago canadensis L.

Canada goldenrod, common goldenrod

Daisy Family (Asteraceae)

KEY IMPRESSIONS   Grows 1–5ft (.3–1.6m). Small heads on secund racemes, forming over-all pyramidal panicle.

FRUIT   Achenes ribbed, nearly smooth, with white bristles.

LEAVES   Alternate, crowded along stem, toothed, with 3 parallel veins. No basal rosettes.

STEM   Smooth to downy above. Sometimes a globose stem gall is found. (See p. 240)

PERENNIAL   From creeping underground stems.

HABITAT   Open places, thin woods.

RANGE   Throughout most of U.S. and Canada.

SIMILAR SPECIES

S. odora Aiton   Sweet goldenrod, licorice goldenrod. Grows 1½–3ft (.5–1m). Achenes covered with short hairs. Leaves toothless. Fresh plant gives off licorice odor when crushed. Dry open woods, especially in sandy soil. Mass., N.H., and Vt. to s. Ohio and Mo., south to Fla. and Tex.

S. gigantea Aiton   Late goldenrod, smooth goldenrod. Grows 2–7ft (.6–2.3m). Achenes smooth. Leaves smooth, toothed. Stem smooth. Moist, open places. Throughout region.

2. Net-veined leaves

Solidago rugosa Miller

Rough-stemmed goldenrod, wrinkle-leaved goldenrod

Daisy Family (Asteraceae)

KEY IMPRESSIONS   Grows 1–7ft (.3–2.3m). Inflorescence in panicles with recurved branches. Leaves mainly on hairy stem, numerous, hairy, deeply toothed.

FRUIT   Achenes covered with short hairs. Pappus of white bristles.

LEAVES   Oval to elliptic, hairy, deeply toothed.

STEM   Hairy.

PERENNIAL   From long, creeping underground stems.

HABITAT   Varied; widespread.

RANGE   Nfld. to Fla., west to Mich., Mo., and Tex.

SIMILAR SPECIES

S. juncea Aiton   Early goldenrod. Grows 1–4ft (.3–1.3m). Terminal panicle about as broad as long, dense, with recurved branches. Achenes hairy, short, with white bristles. Basal leaves large, toothed, tapering to long leafstalk. Upper stem leaves smaller, tooth-less, with tiny leaflets in axils. Dry open spaces, open woods, especially in sandy soil. N.S. and N.B. to Minn., south to Va., Miss., and Mo.; in mountains to Ga. and Ala.

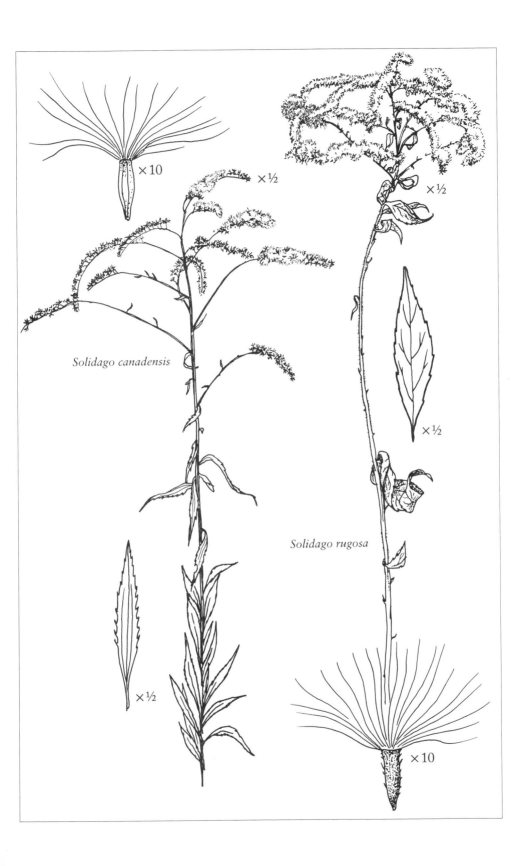

×10

×½

×½

Solidago canadensis

×½

Solidago rugosa

×½

×½

×10

S. arguta Aiton Sharp-leaved goldenrod, forest goldenrod. Grows 2–6ft (.6–2m). Achenes smooth. Leaves rough, broad, toothed. Open woods, clearings, dry meadows. Maine to Fla., west to Ky., Mo., and La.

S. nemoralis Aiton Gray goldenrod. Grows ½–2ft (15–60cm). Small. Plumes slender, 1-sided. Achenes appressed, tiny hairs on surface. Leaflets in axils. Leaves and stems hairy. Dry sandy soil, dry open woods. N.S. to Fla., west to Alb. and Tex.

S. uliginosa Nutt. Bog goldenrod. 2–5ft (.6–1.6m). Achenes smooth. Leaves and stems smooth. Lower leaves lance-shaped, long leafstalk clasping stem. Swamps, bogs, wet meadows. Nfld. and Que. to Minn., south to Md., Ohio, and Ind.; in mountains to N.C. and Tenn.

S. fistulosa Miller Hairy piney-woods goldenrod, pine-barren goldenrod. Grows 2½–6ft (.75–2m). Achenes downy. Leaves elliptical, crowded, slightly clasping stem. Moist sandy soil, pine barrens. Coastal plain and swamps, N.J. south to Fla. and La.

S. elliottii T. & G. Coastal swamp-goldenrod, Elliott's goldenrod. Grows 2–6ft (.6–2m). Achenes downy. Leaves elliptical, short-pointed, crowded on stem. Stem smooth. Fresh or brackish swamps near coast. N.S. and Mass. to Fla.

S. patula Muhl. Rough-leaved goldenrod. Grows 2–7ft (.6–2.3m). Inflorescence of spreading elmlike shape. Achenes minutely downy. Lower leaves very large, often longer than 12in (30cm), tapering to base. Leaves rough. Stem 4-angled, smooth. Swamps, bogs, wet meadows. Vt. to Wis., south to Ga., Miss., and Tex.

S. ulmifolia Muhl. Elm-leaved goldenrod. Grows 2–4½ft (.6–1.3m). Achenes minutely downy. Racemes of heads few and widely divergent, giving elmlike appearance. Leaves coarsely toothed. Woods. N.S. to Ga. and Fla., west to Minn., Kans., and Tex.

Goldenrod Galls

The goldenrods (*Solidago*) support a number of highly interesting insects that create galls on their leaves and stems. Galls are growths of abnormal plant tissue on roots, stems, leaves, flowers, and seeds caused by external sources—insects in the goldenrods, but also fungi, viruses, bacteria, and other agents in many other species.

Goldenrod galls are formed when the eggs laid by gall insects mature as larvae in the host plants. Gall insects and the other organisms that stimulate gall formation may be found wherever the host plants grow. Knowledge of galls and their host plants will aid in the identification of many goldenrods. Four galls are described here:

The goldenrod ball gall: This is a globular stem swelling, 1¼in (3cm) diameter, common to various *Solidago* species. Good-sized patches of goldenrods are sometimes hosts, and two galls are occasionally found on a single stem. Goldenrod ball galls often form at approximately the same height on all the stems in a patch. They are incited by the gall fly *Eurosta solidaginus* Fitch, a fairly large fly with brown marked wings.

The elliptical goldenrod gall: This elongate spindle-shaped stem gall is caused by the whitish caterpillar of the gall moth *Gnorimoschema gallaesolidaginus* Riley, and is found on *S. canadensis*. The caterpillar keeps the interior walls smooth and neat, and its castings can be found packed in the bottom of the cavity.

The goldenrod bunch gall: A number of gall midges affect the goldenrods. The common gall midge *Rhopalomyia solidaginus* Loew. attacks *S. canadensis* leaf buds, producing globular masses of deformed leaflets at the stem's apex to shelter its maggots.

The black blister gall: The gall midge *Asteromyia carbonifera* Felt (*A. euthamiae* Gagné) affects the leaves of *Euthamia graminifolia* (formerly *S. graminifolia*). Resulting black blister galls give the leaves the appearance of having been spattered with black oil.

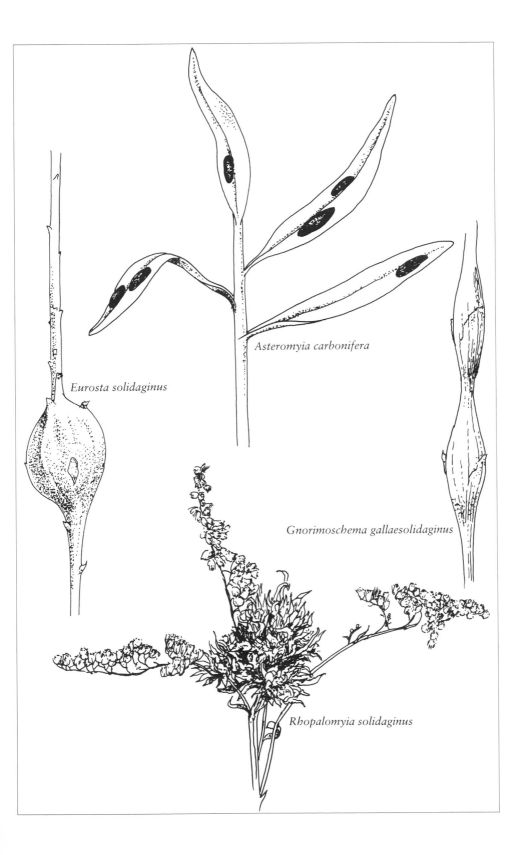

Eurosta solidaginus

Asteromyia carbonifera

Gnorimoschema gallaesolidaginus

Rhopalomyia solidaginus

Plants 1–4ft (.3–1.3m), with Star-shaped Receptacles Not Densely Clustered and Bristle-haired Fruits: Asters (*Aster* spp.)

Introduction to Asters

Aster L. spp.

Asters

Daisy Family (Asteraceae)

KEY IMPRESSIONS Asters are easily confused with goldenrods (*Solidago* spp.) in winter. Asters tend to be smaller and more thinly branched, with the numerous small heads spread out on branchlets rather than compacted. Most asters are perennial; a few are annual.

FRUIT Achenes with hairy bristles, varying in color according to species from tan or tawny to white. A star-shaped receptacle remains after the achenes have fallen.

IDENTIFICATION The numerous *Aster* species are very difficult to distinguish in winter. The approach used here to divide the large numbers into a manageable system is separation by habitat. Only the more common species are covered. Note that because of the overlapping of habitats this is not a foolproof method for identification of asters.

The following habitat divisions are used here:

A. Woods, dry open clearings, wood edges
    1. Leaves with stems p. 242
    2. Leaves without stems, clasping the stem p. 244
B. Fields, meadows, prairies, dry open areas
    1. Leaves not clasping the stem p. 246
    2. Leaves clasping the stem, p. 248
C. Damp open ground, wet meadows, shores p. 248
D. Swamps, wet woods, bogs p. 250
E. Sandy soil, pine barrens p. 250
F. Salt marshes p. 252

A. Woods, Dry Open Clearings, Wood Edges

1. Leaves with stems

Aster divaricatus L.

White wood aster

Daisy Family (Asteraceae)

KEY IMPRESSIONS Grows 1½–2½ft (45–75cm). Medium-sized woodland plant. Few small heads borne on rather flat-topped branches with heart-shaped basal leaves. Stems zigzag.

FRUIT Achenes with whitish hairy bristles.

LEAVES Basal leaves heart-shaped. Stem leaves not heart-shaped.

STEMS Zigzag, changing angle at each node.

PERENNIAL From creeping underground stems; may form colonies.

HABITAT Dry woodlands.

RANGE N.H. and Que., west to Ont., south to D.C. and Ohio.

SIMILAR SPECIES

A. acuminatus Michx. Whorled aster. Grows 1–3ft (.3–1m). Inflorescence flattish. Achenes very glandular, downy. Pappus nearly white, soft, fine. Leaves scattered on stem

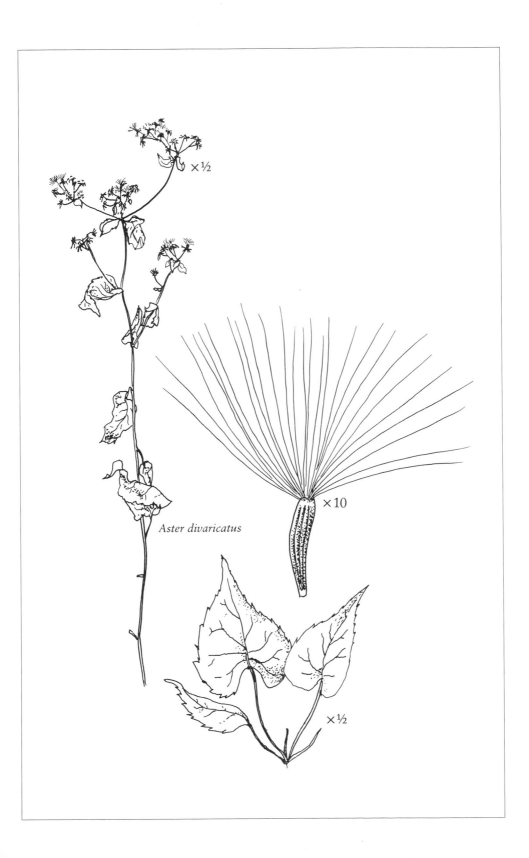

Aster divaricatus

×½

×10

×½

so as to appear whorled. Perennial from slender, creeping underground stems that are scaly and enlarged at apex. Woods. Nfld., Que., and Ont. to N.J., N.Y., and Pa.; in mountains to Ga.

A. lowrieanus T. C. Porter Lowrie's aster, smooth heart-leaved aster. Grows 1–4ft (.3–1.3m). Heads usually not numerous, loosely panicled. Stem of leaf winged. Woods. Ont. and Que., south through N.Y., N.J., and Pa.; in mountains to Ga.

A. schreberi Nees. Schreber's aster. Grows 1–4ft (.3–1.3m). Inflorescence flattish. Basal leaves very large, with broad, angular sinuses. Woods. N.H. and Maine to Del. and Va., west to Ohio and W.Va.

A. macrophyllus L. Large-leaved aster. Grows 2–3ft (.6–1m). Hard to distinguish from *A. schreberi* because of similar leaves. Inflorescence broadly branched. Long, creeping underground stems form colonies. Woods. E. Canada to Wis. and Minn., south to Pa.; in mountains to Ga.

A. cordifolius L. Heart-leaved aster. Grows 1–4ft (.3–1.3m). Inflorescence *not* flat-topped, as in *A. divaricatus*. Heads very numerous, whereas *A. divaricatus* has sparser heads. Leaves broadly heart-shaped, sharply toothed. Woods, clearings. S. Canada and n. U.S., south to Va., n. Ga., Ala., and Mo.

A. sagittifolius Willd. Arrow-leaved aster. Grows 2–5ft (.6–1.6m). Heads numerous, crowded, in racemes. Leaves arrow-shaped on flat-winged stalks. Perennial from short underground stems. Streambanks, woods, less often in open places. Vt. to Minn., south to Ga., Fla., Miss., and Mo.

A. undulatus L. Wavy-leaved aster. Grows 1–3ft (.3–1m). Heads numerous in racemes. Leaves wavy-edged. Leaf stems winged, dilated into lobes clasping stem. Dry open woods, clearings. Maine to Fla., west to Ohio, Ind., Tenn., Miss., and La.

2. Leaves clasping the stem

Aster patens Aiton
Late purple aster, clasping aster
Daisy Family (Asteraceae)

KEY IMPRESSIONS Grows 1–3ft (.3–1m). Heads usually single at ends of branchlets on open, branched inflorescence.

FRUIT Achenes several-nerved. Pappus tawny.

LEAVES Oval to oblong, toothless, with basal lobes nearly encircling hairy stem.

STEM Slender, loosely hairy.

PERENNIAL From short, stout underground stem and fibrous roots; sometimes from creeping underground stems.

HABITAT Woods, dry open places.

RANGE Mass. and s. N.H. to Mich. and Kans., south to Fla. and Tex.

SIMILAR SPECIES

A. laevis L. Smooth aster. Grows 1–3ft (.3–1m). Leaves mostly toothless, weakly clasping stem. Heads numerous. Achenes smooth. Pappus tawny or reddish. Perennial from short, stout underground stem, and sometimes slender, creeping red underground stems. Dry open places, wood edges. Maine to B.C., south to Ga., Ark., and N.Mex.

A. prenanthoides Muhl. Crooked-stemmed aster. Grows 1–3ft (.3–1m). Heads numerous. Achenes downy. Pappus tawny to yellowish. Leaves narrow, toothless below middle, clasping stem. Stem zigzag. Perennial and colonial from well-developed creeping

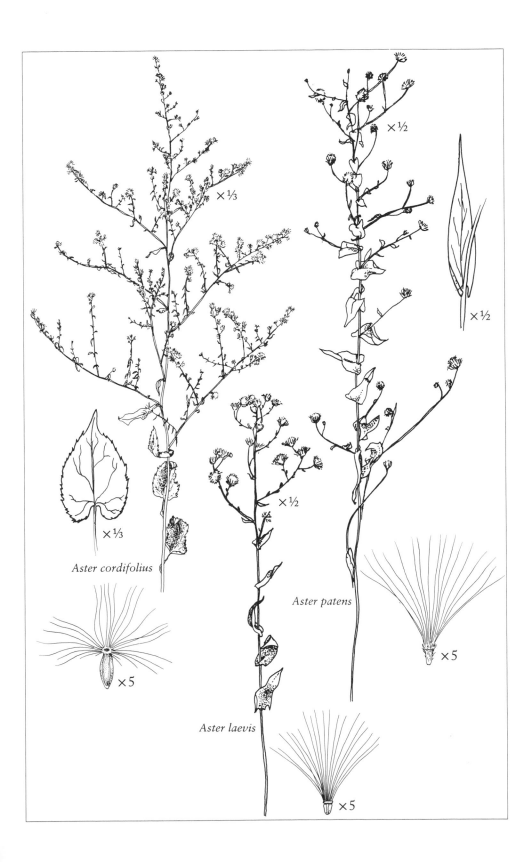

×⅓

×½

×½

Aster cordifolius

×⅓

×½

Aster patens

×5

Aster laevis

×5

×5

underground stems. Moist woods, meadows, streambanks. N.Y. to Minn., south to D.C., Ky., and Iowa; in mountains to N.C. and Tenn.

B. Fields, Meadows, Prairies, Dry Open Areas

1. Leaves not clasping the stem

Aster pilosus Willd.

Awl-aster

Daisy Family (Asteraceae)

KEY IMPRESSIONS   Grows 1–4ft (.3–1.3m). Small heads on often diffuse inflorescence, usually growing on 1 side of branch (secund). Involucral bracts marginally inrolled at tip.

FRUIT   Achenes slightly downy or smooth. Pappus of whitish bristles.

LEAVES   Linear, toothless, stemless.

STEM   Diffusely branched.

PERENNIAL   From short, stout underground stem.

HABITAT   Open, rather dry places, often sandy soil.

RANGE   Common throughout region.

SIMILAR SPECIES

A. ericoides L.   White heath aster, squarrose white aster. Grows 1–3ft (.3–1m). Heads very small, very numerous on bushy branches. Achenes finely downy; pappus white. Leaves rigid, numerous, linear, tiny, toothless, stemless. Perennial from long, creeping underground stems. Dry open areas. Maine to Man., south to Del., Va., Tenn., Ill., Ark., and Tex.

A. lateriflorus (L.) Britton   Calico aster, goblet-aster, starved aster. Grows 1–5ft (.3–1.6m). Heads numerous, crowded, but not as tiny as in *A. pilosus*. Achenes somewhat hairy. Pappus white. Stem leaves oblong, coarsely toothed. Perennial from short, stout underground stem. Dry open places, beaches. Common throughout region.

A. oblongifolius Nutt.   Aromatic aster. Grows 1–2ft (30–60cm). Heads much larger than in *A. ericoides*. Inflorescence branched. Achenes finely downy. Pappus light brown. Leaves oblong, stemless, rigid, entire. Stems widely branched. Perennial from underground stems. Prairies, dry open places, limestone banks. Pa. and D.C., south in mountains to N.C. and Ala., west to N.Dak., Wyo., and N.Mex.

A. turbinellus Lindl.   Prairie aster. Grows 2–3ft (.6–1m). Heads in open panicles, mostly solitary at ends of branchlets, which have many small bractlets. Achenes dotted, finely downy. Pappus tawny. Perennial from branched underground stems. Dry prairies, open woods. Ill. to La. and Kans.

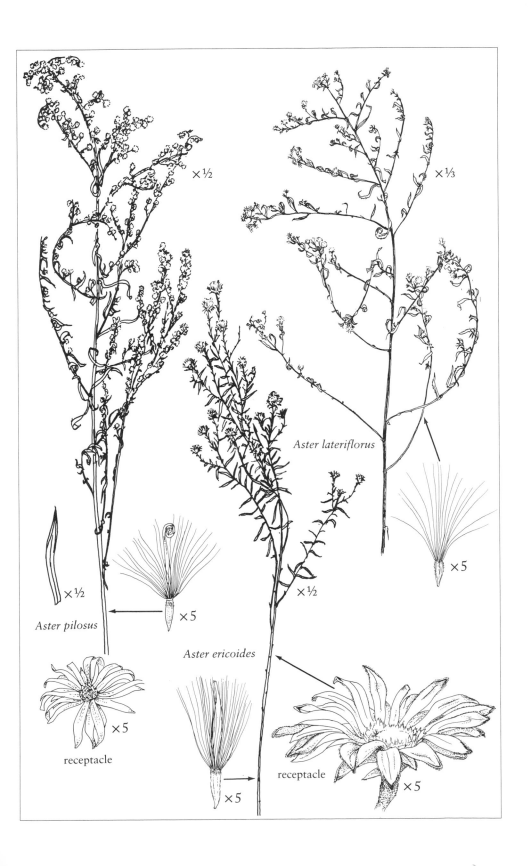

×½

×⅓

Aster lateriflorus

×½

×½

×5

Aster pilosus

×5

receptacle

Aster ericoides

×5

×5

receptacle

×5

2. Leaves clasping the stem

Aster novae-angliae L.
New England aster
Daisy Family (Asteraceae)

KEY IMPRESSIONS   Grows 2–8ft (.6–2.6m). Tall, hairy. Heads panicled. Leaves conspicuously clasping, alternate.
FRUIT   Achenes appressed, densely downy. Pappus reddish white to tawny.
LEAVES   Alternate, hairy, strongly clasping stem. Basal leaves not heart-shaped.
STEM   Hairy.
PERENNIAL   From short, stout underground stem and creeping underground stems and fibrous roots. Colonial.
HABITAT   Meadows, thickets, shores.
RANGE   Mass. and Vt. to N.Dak. and Wyo. South to D.C., Tenn., Ark., and N.Mex.; south in mountains.
SIMILAR SPECIES
See also *A. prenanthoides* p. 244.

C. Damp Open Ground, Wet Meadows, Shores

Aster novi-belgii L.
New York aster
Daisy Family (Asteraceae)

KEY IMPRESSIONS   Grows 1–4ft (.3–1.3m). Usually numerous heads on branched inflorescence.
FRUIT   Achenes smooth. Pappus whitish.
LEAVES   Lance-shaped, slightly toothed or toothless, not deeply clasping stem.
STEM   Erect, smooth, slightly to somewhat hairy.
PERENNIAL   From long, creeping underground stems.
HABITAT   Moist places, often salt marshes.
RANGE   Nfld. to S.C.; mainly near coast.
SIMILAR SPECIES
A. lanceolatus Willd.   Panicled aster, eastern lined aster. Grows 3–8ft (1–2.6m). Heads numerous on panicled branches. Achenes minutely downy. Pappus white. Leaves lance-shaped, narrowed to short-stalked or stemless base. Colonial by long underground stems. Moist low places. N.S. to N.C., west to N.Dak. and Tex.

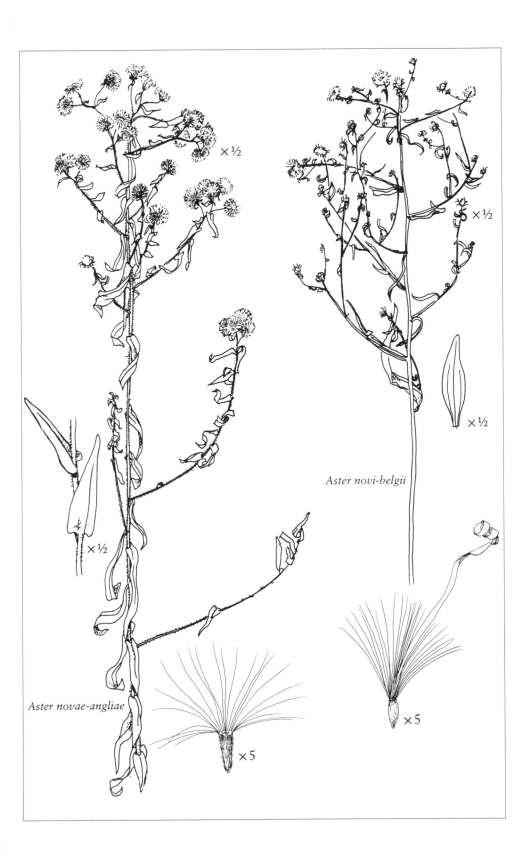

×½

×½

Aster novi-belgii

×½

×½

Aster novae-angliae

×5

×5

D. Swamps, Wet Woods, Bogs

Aster puniceus L.

Bristly aster, purple-stemmed aster

Daisy Family (Asteraceae)

KEY IMPRESSIONS Grows 2–7ft (.6–2.3m). Heads numerous on branching inflorescence. Stem purple.

FRUIT Achenes smooth, several-nerved. Pappus white.

LEAVES Toothed, clasping stem.

STEM Purple, bristly.

PERENNIAL From short, stout underground stem.

HABITAT Swamps, wet thickets.

RANGE Nfld. to Sask., south to Va., Ill., and Nebr.; in mountains to Ga. and Ala.

SIMILAR SPECIES

A. umbellatus Miller Tall flat-topped white aster. Grows 2–7ft (.6–2.3m). Inflorescence flat-topped. Heads numerous in terminal branches. Achenes nerved, slightly downy. Pappus nearly white. Leaves lance-shaped, toothless, stemless or short-stemmed. Moist, low places. Nfld. to Minn., south to Va., Ky., and Ill.; in mountains to Ga. and Ala.

A. borealis Prov. Northern bog aster. Grows 1–3ft (.3–1m). Heads distant, panicled. Achenes smooth, several-nerved. Pappus pale. Leaves linear, toothless, stemless, slightly clasping base. Cold bogs. N. N.J. to Que., west to Minn., Colo., and Alaska.

A. nemoralis Aiton Leafy bog-aster. Grows 6–24in (15–60cm). Head large, 1–1½in (2.5–4cm), 1 or several. Achenes glandular, downy, several-nerved. Pappus white. Leaves very numerous, lance-shaped, toothless, stemless. Stem either simple or branched above. Spreads by runners. Acid bogs, peat. Nfld. and Lab. to N.J., N.Y., and Mich.

A. radula Aiton Rough-leaved aster. Grows 1–3ft (.3–1m). Heads several to numerous on branches. Achenes smooth. Pappus nearly white. Leaves rough, toothed, stemless. Perennial from creeping underground stems. Bogs, streambanks, swamps. Lab. and Nfld. to Md., Va., W.Va., and Ky.

E. Sandy Soil, Pine Barrens

Aster dumosus L.

Long-stalked aster, bushy aster

Daisy Family (Asteraceae)

KEY IMPRESSIONS Grows 1–3ft (.3–1m). Heads numerous, terminating slender, paniculate branches and branchlets.

FRUIT Achenes slightly downy, few-nerved. Pappus white.

LEAVES Main leaves linear, spreading. Tiny bractlike leaves on inflorescence branches.

STEM Smooth, slightly to somewhat hairy, somewhat branched.

PERENNIAL From creeping underground stems or sometimes short stem.

HABITAT Sandy soil, mainly coastal but extending inland.

RANGE S. Maine to Fla., west to Mich., Ark., and La.

×⅓

×5

Aster dumosus

×5

×⅓

×⅓

×⅓

Aster puniceus

×5

Aster umbellatus

A. concolor L. Eastern silvery aster. Grows 1–2ft (30–60cm). Heads numerous on elongated narrow racemes. Achenes hairy. Pappus tawny. Leaves numerous, oblong, toothless, stemless. Stem slender. Perennial from short, stout, creeping underground stems. Sandy soil, pine barrens. Coastal Mass. to Fla., La., and Miss.; occasionally inland to Ky. and Tenn.

A. spectabilis Aiton Showy aster. Grows 1–2ft (30–60cm). Heads large, terminating branches. Achenes downy. Pappus whitish. Basal leaves lance-shaped, sparingly toothed, long-stemmed. Upper leaves toothless, stemless. Perennial from underground stems. Dry sandy soil, pine barrens. Mass. to S.C. and Ala. along coast.

A. linariifolius L. Stiff aster. Grows 6–20in (15–52cm). Heads large, terminating branches. Achenes copiously long, hairy. Pappus bristles in 2 series; inner bristles firm, tawny, long; outer ones much shorter. Leaves numerous, rigid, short, 1-nerved, toothless, linear. Stem stiff, tufted. Perennial from stout, short underground stems, rarely with creeping stems. Dry ground, especially in sandy soil; also ledges, rocky banks. Maine and Que. to Fla., west to Wis., Mo., Ark., and Tex.

F. Salt Marshes

Aster tenuifolius L.
Perennial salt-marsh aster
Daisy Family (Asteraceae)

KEY IMPRESSIONS Grows 1–2ft (30–60cm). Heads large, ½–1in (1.5–2.5cm) diameter. Heads few, terminating branches.
FRUIT Achenes downy, raised, 5-nerved. Pappus whitish to tawny.
LEAVES Few, linear.
STEM Single, often zigzag.
PERENNIAL From slender, creeping underground stems.
HABITAT Salt marshes.
RANGE Along coast from Mass. to Fla. and La.
SIMILAR SPECIES

A. subulatus Michx. Annual salt-marsh aster. Grows 6–30in (15–75cm). Heads smaller than *A. tenuifolius,* numerous on panicled branches. Achenes compressed, minutely downy, several-nerved. Pappus white, copious, fine. Leaves fleshy, linear, toothless, stemless, sparingly on stem (grasslike). Annual from short taproot. Coastal salt marshes. N.B., s. Maine, and N.H. to Fla. and Ala.

See also *A. novi-belgii* p. 248.

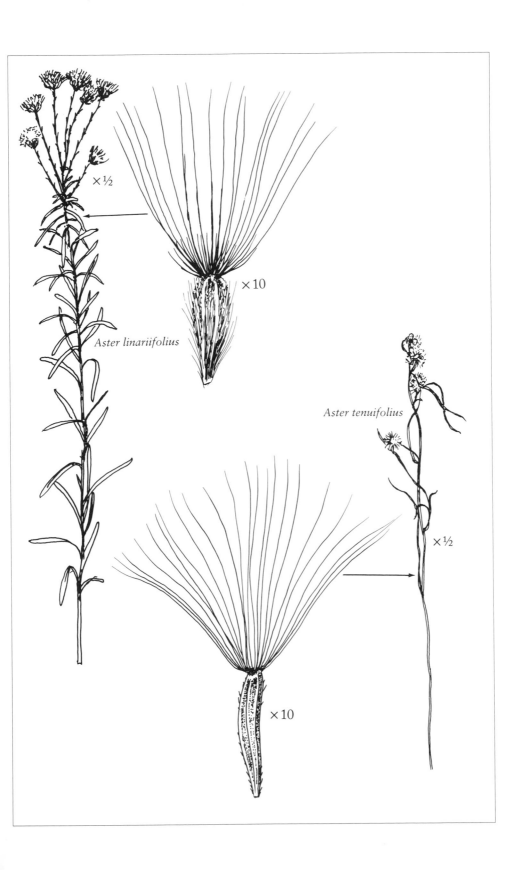

×½

Aster linariifolius

×10

Aster tenuifolius

×½

×10

Ferns

Most ferns disappear in winter, reappearing in the spring from underground stems, but a number of species are visible throughout winter. These appear in two forms: (1) 2 species—the sensitive fern and the ostrich-fern—are represented by dry, brown spore-bearing stalks though their leaves are not present; (2) several species have leaves that remain green in winter.

Ferns with Brown Spore Stalks but No Leaves in Winter

Matteuccia struthiopteris (L.) Todaro
Ostrich-fern
Sensitive Fern Family (Onocleaceae)

Grows 6–12in (15–30cm). Fertile spore stalk appears woody and brown, widest at terminal end and tapering downward (lyre-shaped). Segments tightly rolled to protect spore sacs (sori) within—spores released early in spring. Wooded river bottomlands, swamps, in neutral to alkaline muck. N. N. Am.

Onoclea sensibilis L.
Sensitive fern
Sensitive Fern Family (Onocleaceae)

Grows 10–16in (25–40cm). Fertile spore stalks appear woody and brown, widest at lower end and tapering to point at terminal end. Segments beadlike, tightly rolled to protect spore sacs (sori) within—spores released early in spring. Marshes, ditches, swamps, wooded or exposed areas. E. N. Am.

Ferns with Evergreen Leaves

Once-cut ferns: Species with leaves or fronds cut into numbers of simple leaflets
Twice-cut ferns: Species with more complicated leaflets; not only are fronds cut into numbers of leaflets but these leaflets are again cut into subleaflets
Thrice-cut ferns: Species with lacy leaflets; the fronds are cut into leaflets, the leaflets are cut into subleaflets, and the subleaflets are again cut into lobes

Dryopteris intermedia (Muhl. ex Willd.) A. Gray
Evergreen wood-fern
Spleenwort Family (Aspleniaceae)

Leaves (fronds) grow 1½–3ft (.3–1m), 6–10in (15–25cm) wide. Stem (stipe) ½–⅓ frond length. Frond thrice-cut, giving lacy or dissected appearance. Spore sacs (sori), if found, medial on leaflet backs. Moist shaded woods, rocky slopes. E. N. Am.

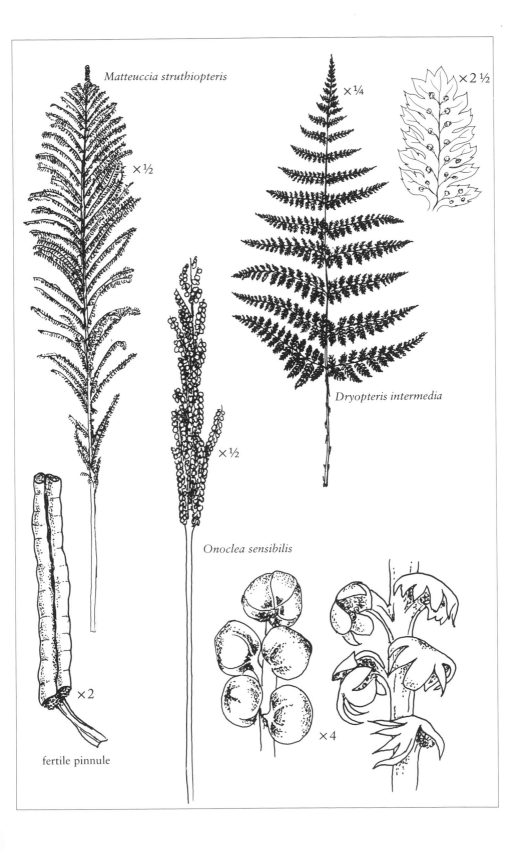

Matteuccia struthiopteris

×½

×¼

×2½

Dryopteris intermedia

×½

Onoclea sensibilis

×2

fertile pinnule

×4

Dryopteris marginalis (L.) A. Gray
Marginal shield fern, marginal wood-fern
Spleenwort Family (Aspleniaceae)

Leaves (fronds) grow 18–24in (45–60cm), 6–10in (15–25cm) wide. Stem (stipe) coarsely scaled, ½–⅓ frond length. Frond twice-cut, leathery, with coarser, less dissected appearance than in *D. intermedia.* Spore sacs (sori) near margins of leaflet backs. Rocky, wooded slopes. Ne. N. Am.

Polypodium virginianum L.
Common polypody
Polypody Family (Polypodiaceae)

Leaves (fronds) grow 4–14in (10–37cm). Stem (stipe) ⅓–½ frond length. Frond once-cut, with less dissected appearance than *D. marginalis.* Spore sacs (sori) large, round, on leaflet backs. On or among moist shaded rocks. E., c. N. Am.

Polystichum acrostichoides (Michx.) Schott.
Christmas-fern
Spleenwort Family (Aspleniaceae)

Leaves (fronds) grow 12–24in (30–60cm). Stem (stipe) scaly. Leaflets lobed at inner end, near stipe. Frond once-cut. Spore sacs (sori) found on undersides of leaflets at frond tip, giving appearance of brown undercoating. Moist woods. E. N. Am.

Fern Allies

Of fern allies present in the region, approximately 6 species of clubmoss (*Lycopodium*) and 1 species of horsetail (*Equisetum*) are commonly found in winter.

Clubmoss Family (Lycopodiaceae)

The Lycopodiaceae are evergreen plants that grow in patches low on the ground. Though they look like small evergreen conifers, they are more primitive plants, reproducing by spores, and are not related to the seed-bearing conifers. Most clubmosses found in the region bear spores above the top leaves on conelike strobili, which may or may not be stemmed, depending on the species. The numerous spores are almost microscopic.

Key to Clubmoss Family (Lycopodiaceae)

1a Strobili absent: Shining clubmoss (*L. lucidulum*) p. 260
1b Strobili present 2
  2a Strobili stemless 3
  2b Strobili stemmed 5
3a Branches erect, not spreading: Stiff clubmoss (*L. annotinum*) p. 258
3b Branches treelike, spreading 4

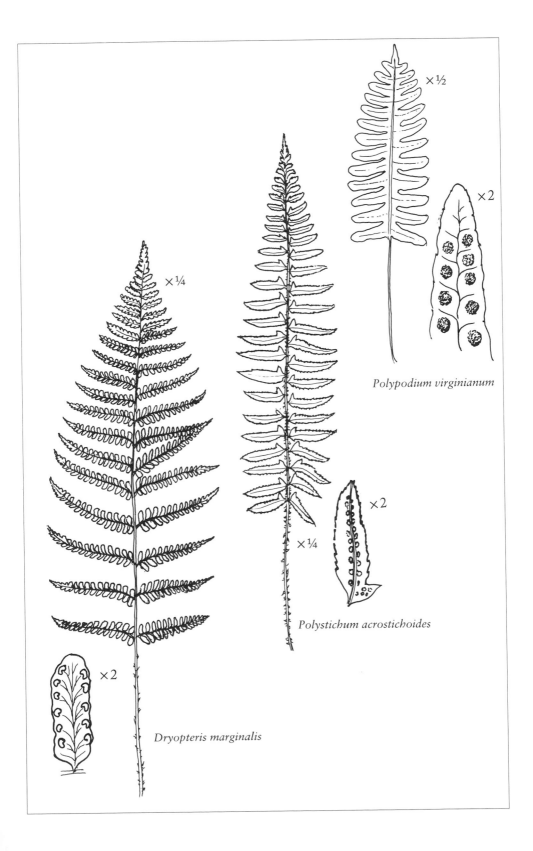

×½

×2

Polypodium virginianum

×¼

×2

×¼

Polystichum acrostichoides

×2

Dryopteris marginalis

4a Leaves of main stem appressed: Tree clubmoss (*L. obscurum*) p. 260
    4b Leaves of main stem broadly spreading: *L. dendroideum* p. 260
5a Strobili 2–3 per stem: Ground-pine (*L. clavatum*) p. 258
5b Strobili 4 per stem; stems twice-forked **6**
    6a Branchlets lack annual constrictions: Running cedar (*L. digitatum*) p. 258
    6b Branchlets have conspicuous annual constrictions: Ground cedar (*L. tristachyum*)
        p. 258

Lycopodium annotinum L.
Stiff clubmoss
Clubmoss Family (Lycopodiaceae)

Grows 4–8in (10–20cm). Branches erect, sometimes forked, never spreading. Branches arise from long, creeping stem (rhizome) on ground surface. Strobili about 1in (3cm), borne without stems on tips of erect branches. Coniferous woods, deciduous woods. N. N. Am.

Lycopodium clavatum L.
Ground-pine, staghorn clubmoss
Clubmoss Family (Lycopodiaceae)

Stems highly branched, widely creeping, forming extensive colonies. Leaves in many rows, each leaf with hairlike tip. Strobili 1½–3in (3–7cm) on stems 3–6in (7–15cm), usually 2–3 strobili per stem. Open woods to bogs. N. N. Am.

Lycopodium digitatum A. Braun
Running cedar
Clubmoss Family (Lycopodiaceae)

Grows 5–10in (13–25cm). Stems erect, repeatedly branched, strongly flattened, spreading fanlike. No annual constrictions on branchlets. Stems arise from long creeping stems (rhizomes) on soil surface or just beneath decayed litter. Leaves in 4 rows. Strobili 1–2in (2.5–5cm), often with tail-like sterile tip. Strobili stems 2–4in (5–10cm), usually twice-forked, bearing 4 strobili. Forkings close together, producing X-shape when viewed from above. Dry open woods, meadows. Ne. N. Am.

SIMILAR SPECIES

L. tristachyum Pursh   Ground cedar. Underground stems (rhizomes) deeply underground. Branchlets have conspicuous annual constrictions. Strobili stems twice-forked, bearing 4 strobili. Forkings separated, producing H-shape when viewed from above. Open woods, sandy meadows, rocky barrens. Ne. N. Am.

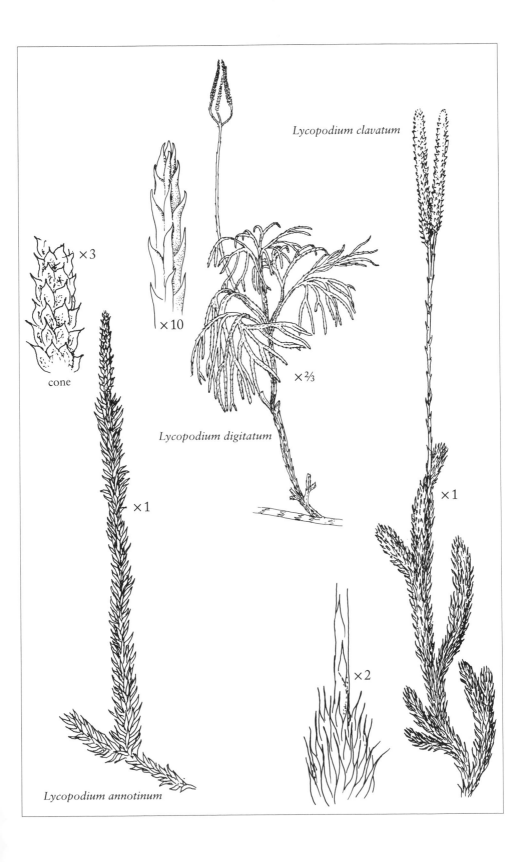

Lycopodium clavatum

×3

cone

×10

Lycopodium digitatum

×2/3

×1

×2

×1

Lycopodium annotinum

Lycopodium lucidulum Michx.

Shining clubmoss

Clubmoss Family (Lycopodiaceae)

Grows 6–8in (15–20cm). Stems erect, forming a clump. Older parts of stems lie down and root. Leaves in alternating bands of shorter and longer leaves. Strobili are absent. Rich moist woods. E. N.Am.

Lycopodium obscurum L.

Tree clubmoss, princess-pine

Clubmoss Family (Lycopodiaceae)

Grows 6–12in (15–30cm). Branches erect, treelike, spreading, growing from creeping underground stems (rhizomes) 1–2in (2.5–5cm) below ground. Leaves needlelike, appressed to ascending, in 6 rows. 1 row of leaves along branchtop. Strobili 1–2in (2.5–5cm), stemless. Moist evergreen or deciduous woods to bogs. N. N. Am.

SIMILAR SPECIES

L. dendroideum Michx. Leaves of main stem broadly spreading. 2 rows of leaves along branchtop. Leaves light green.

Horsetail Family (Equisetaceae)

Equisetum hyemale L.

Scouring-rush, common scouring-rush

Grows unbranched to 3½ft (1.1m). Stem dark green, rough, hollow, with 18–40 ridges. Cylindrical, ash-gray sheaths at stem joints banded black. Tiny, sharp teeth atop sheath, dark brown, narrow, soon withering. Strobilus sharp-pointed, at terminal stem end. Rootstock widely creeping, producing thicketlike growth. Varied damp habitats. Most of N. Am.

Grasses, Sedges, and Rushes: Introduction

Although at first glance the vegetative parts of grasses, sedges, and rushes appear quite similar, in fact differences in their floral structures separate them into 3 distinct families. The differences most obvious in winter are detailed below. Fruits are usually dispersed by winter but are described here in case they are clinging to the specimen.

Grass Family (Poaceae)

STEMS With some exceptions, mainly hollow, except at nodes (where leaves attach). Usually round, sometimes flattened, usually bulging at joints where leaf bases attach.

LEAVES Arranged in 2 rows on stem. Sheaths, which wrap around stem, open at least part way down back. Ligule projects from top of sheath on inside and is useful in identification.

INFLORESCENCE Spike, raceme, or panicle.

FLOWERS Arranged in spikelets; modified bracts without sepals or petals.

FRUIT Single grain of varied shape.

ANNUAL OR PERENNIAL

HABITAT More often in dry areas.

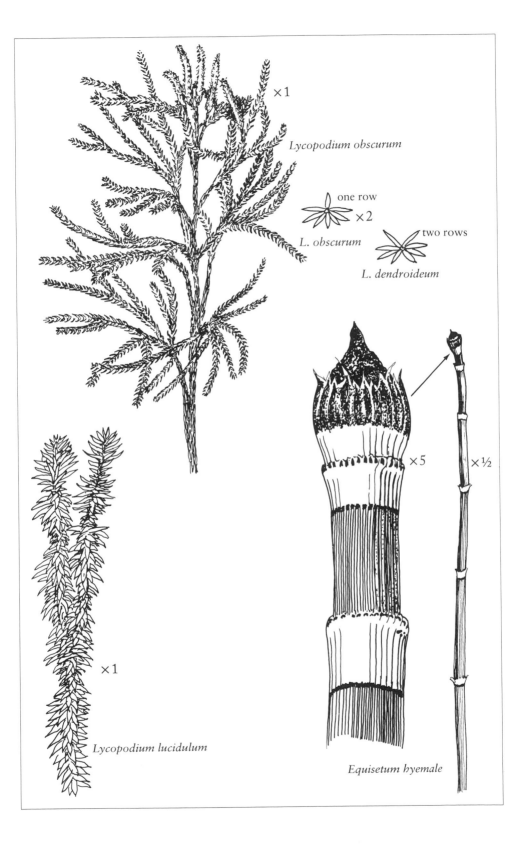

×1

Lycopodium obscurum

one row
×2
L. obscurum

two rows
L. dendroideum

×5

×½

×1

Lycopodium lucidulum

Equisetum hyemale

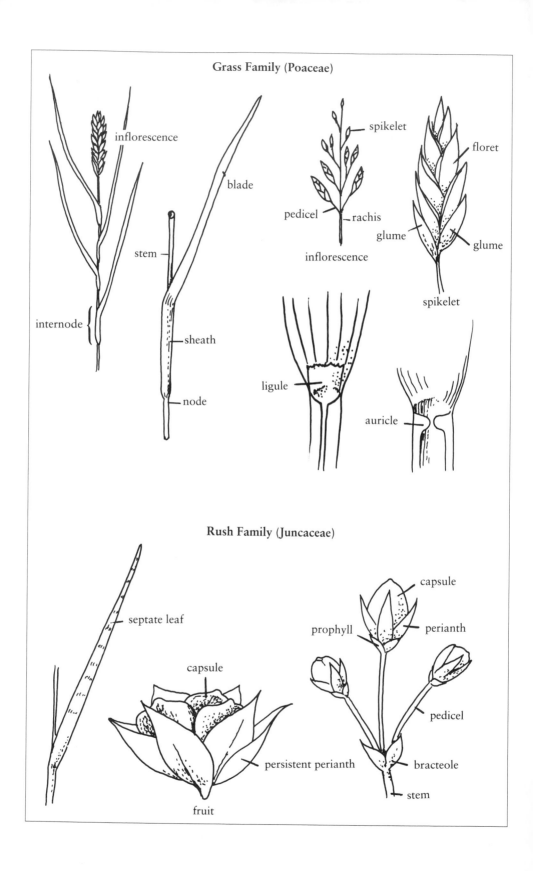

Grass Family (Poaceae)

inflorescence

blade

stem

spikelet

floret

pedicel

rachis

glume

glume

inflorescence

spikelet

internode

sheath

node

ligule

auricle

Rush Family (Juncaceae)

septate leaf

capsule

capsule

prophyll

perianth

pedicel

persistent perianth

bracteole

stem

fruit

Sedge Family (Cyperaceae)

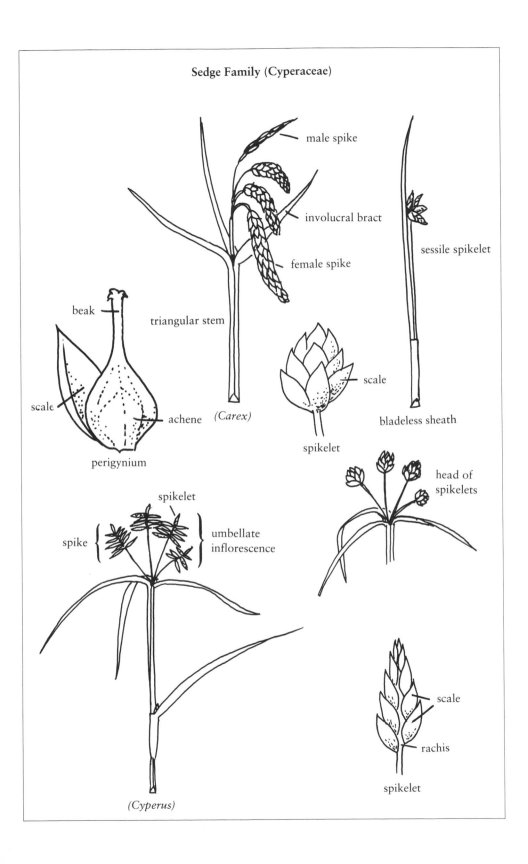

male spike

involucral bract

female spike

sessile spikelet

beak

triangular stem

scale

achene

(Carex)

scale

bladeless sheath

spikelet

perigynium

head of
spikelets

spikelet

spike

umbellate
inflorescence

scale

rachis

spikelet

(Cyperus)

Sedge Family (Cyperaceae)

STEMS Mostly solid (although a few species have hollow stems in winter), mostly triangular, some round. Not jointed.

LEAVES Arranged in 3 rows around stem. Sheaths closed in back.

INFLORESCENCE Umbels, heads, or panicles.

FLOWER Arranged in spikelets; 1 modified bract per flower without petals or sepals.

FRUIT Achenes, either 3-cornered or lens-shaped.

MAINLY PERENNIAL

HABITAT More often in damp to wet areas.

Rush Family (Juncaceae)

STEMS Solid, mostly round.

LEAVES Sometimes round and solid, otherwise flat.

INFLORESCENCE Umbels or heads.

FLOWERS Regular, with 3 small petals and 3 small sepals that are essentially alike but in 2 separate whorls. Some species have tiny bracts (prophylls) subtending flowers.

FRUIT Capsules, 1- to 3-chambered, many-seeded (except in *Luzula*, which have just 3 seeds). Seeds mostly dispersed in winter.

MAINLY PERENNIAL

HABITAT Mostly wet or damp habitats; sometimes on compacted soil.

Key to Grass Family (Poaceae)

1a No inflorescence in winter; leaves remaining: Bluegrass (*Poa* spp.) p. 290
1b Inflorescence remnant is visible 2
    2a Inflorescence spikelike 3
    2b Inflorescence in panicles, umbels, or branches along stem 4
3a Inflorescence spikelike, without bristles p. 276
3b Inflorescence spikelike, with bristles p. 280
    4a Inflorescence forms small branches along stem length p. 288
    4b Inflorescence in panicles or umbels 5
5a Inflorescence in panicles p. 264
5b Inflorescence in umbels p. 286

Grasses with Inflorescence in Panicles

Dactylis glomerata L.
Orchard-grass
Grass Family (Poaceae)

KEY IMPRESSIONS Grows 1½–5ft (.5–1.6m). Inflorescence an open panicle, erect or divergent, lower branches naked at base. Branches bear numerous short-stemmed spikelets on dense oval clusters near end.

Key to Grass Family (Poaceae)

1a

3a   3b

4a

5a

5b

×½

×5

Dactylis glomerata

SPIKELETS 3–6-flowered. Bristle to 1mm on flower bract.
LEAVES Blades 3–8mm wide, elongate.
LIGULES 5–7mm long.
PERENNIAL
HABITAT Very common in fields, meadows, lawns, roadsides.
RANGE Native to Europe; introduced throughout region.

Phragmites australis (Cav.) Trin. (*P. communis*)
Common reed
Grass Family (Poaceae)

KEY IMPRESSIONS Grows to 13ft (4.3m). Inflorescence a large, tawny, silky plumelike panicle at terminal stem end, subtended by tuft of silky hairs, tawny. Forms large, spreading colonies.
SPIKELETS Few-flowered.
LEAVES ¾–1¼in (2–3cm) wide, stiff, flat, long.
LIGULES Short, 1mm.
PERENNIAL From stout underground stems.
HABITAT Swamps, wet shores, ditches, ponds, edges of salt marshes; tolerates alkaline and brackish water.
RANGE Throughout region.

Eragrostis spectabilis (Pursh) Steudel
Purple lovegrass
Grass Family (Poaceae)

KEY IMPRESSIONS Grows 8–18in (20–45cm). Inflorescence a stiff, delicate panicle, first purple, then tan. Panicle ⅔ length of shoot. Inflorescence may break away and roll like tumbleweed.
SPIKELETS Flat, 7–11-flowered.
LEAVES Firm or stiff; may have hair tufts in axils.
LIGULES Band of short hairs.
PERENNIAL
HABITAT Dry soil, fields, open woods.
RANGE Maine to N.Dak., south to Fla. and Tex.

Panicum clandestinum L.
Deer-tongue grass
Grass Family (Poaceae)

KEY IMPRESSIONS Grows to 5ft (1.6m), but usually shorter. Often clusters in large colonies. Inflorescence a stiff panicle with 1 small oval flower at end of each branch. Inflorescence falls early, but leaf masses persist in winter. Stem usually roughly hairy.
SPIKELETS 1-flowered, oval.
LEAVES Broad, heart-shaped base, lance-tipped, rough. Sheaths bristly. Similar in shape to deer's tongue.
LIGULES Band of hairs or absent.
PERENNIAL
HABITAT Moist woods, thickets; abundant.
RANGE Que. to N.S. and Mich., Mo., and Okla., south to Fla. and Tex.

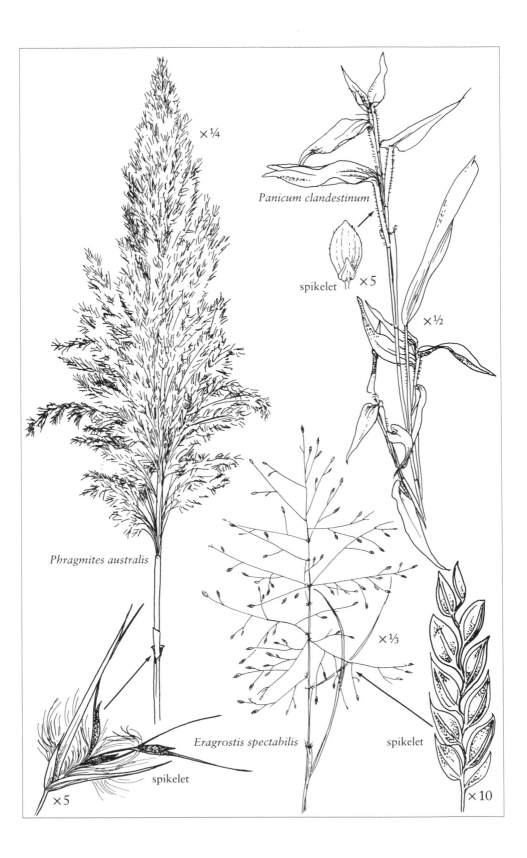

×¼

Panicum clandestinum

spikelet ×5

×½

Phragmites australis

Eragrostis spectabilis

×⅓

spikelet

spikelet

×5

×10

Echinochloa crusgalli (L.) P. Beauv.

Barnyard-grass

Grass Family (Poaceae)

KEY IMPRESSIONS Grows 4in–3½ft (.1–1.2m). Inflorescence crowded in thick, bristly, spikelike branches aggregated into terminal panicle.

SPIKELETS 1–2-flowered. Flower flat, with short bristles on outer scales and longer bristle at tip.

LEAVES 5–30mm wide.

LIGULES Absent.

ANNUAL

HABITAT Fields, roadsides, farmyards; widespread.

RANGE Native to Eurasia; widespread throughout N. Am.

Spartina pectinata Link.

Prairie cord-grass

Grass Family (Poaceae)

KEY IMPRESSIONS Grows 2–7ft (.6–2.3m). Inflorescence a panicle with stiff branches, widely spaced. Spikelets lined up along 1 side of branch.

SPIKELETS 1-flowered. Bristle 3–10mm on flower bract.

LEAVES 5–10mm wide; inrolled when dry.

LIGULES Band of hairs.

PERENNIAL From long, coarse underground stems.

HABITAT Marshes, shores, wet prairies.

RANGE Nfld. and Que. to Alb. and Wash., south to N.C. and Tex.; abundant in prairie states.

SIMILAR SPECIES

S. *cynosuroides* (L.) Roth Salt reed-grass, big cord-grass. Grows to 10ft (3.1m). Tall, bigger, more robust than *S. pectinata*. Generally grows in wetter habitats. No bristle on flower bract. Coastal salt or brackish marshes. Mass. to Fla. and Tex.

Phalaris arundinacea L.

Reed canary-grass

Grass Family (Poaceae)

KEY IMPRESSIONS Grows to 7ft (2.3m). Tall. Inflorescence in panicle opening in spring but then closing up tightly. Forms large colonies.

SPIKELETS 2-flowered, each with 2 scales of equal size.

LEAVES 10–15mm wide.

LIGULES Membranous, usually large.

PERENNIAL

HABITAT Streambanks, lakeshores, marshes, moist ground.

RANGE Circumboreal in N. Am. from Nfld. to Alaska, south to N.C., Kans., and Calif. More abundant westward.

SIMILAR SPECIES

Ribbon grass (*P. arundinacea* var. *picta* L.), with green-and-white striped leaves, is a horticultural variant.

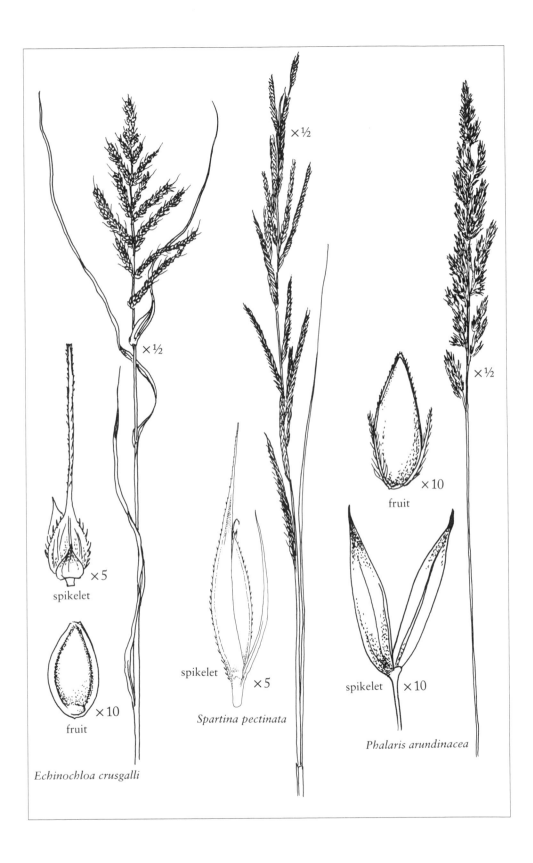

×½

×½

×½

×5
spikelet

×10
fruit

spikelet ×5

Spartina pectinata

×10
fruit

spikelet ×10

Phalaris arundinacea

Echinochloa crusgalli

Sorghastrum nutans (L.) Nash
Indian grass
Grass Family (Poaceae)

KEY IMPRESSIONS   Grows 2–9ft (.6–3m). Inflorescence a spreading panicle.
SPIKELETS   In pairs, one perfect, the other lacking florets, with only a hairy, sterile stem present. Spikelets 1-flowered. 1 flower scale terminates in a twisted bristle (awn), 9–15mm.
LEAVES   5–10mm wide.
LIGULES   Well-developed.
PERENNIAL
HABITAT   Moist or dry prairies, open woods, fields. Dominant species of tall-grass prairie but also found in fields, roadsides.
RANGE   Throughout region.

Panicum virgatum L.
Switchgrass
Grass Family (Poaceae)

KEY IMPRESSIONS   Grows to 7ft (2.3m). Smooth, growing in large leafy yellow clumps that last through winter. Inflorescence an upright panicle bearing spikelets singly at branch ends.
SPIKELETS   Oval, 1-flowered.
LEAVES   To 15mm wide.
LIGULES   Dense zone of silky hairs.
PERENNIAL
HABITAT   Open woods, prairies, dunes, shores, brackish marshes.
RANGE   N.S. and Que. to Man. and Mont., south to Ariz. and Mexico.

Panicum dichotomiflorum Michx.
Fall panicum
Grass Family (Poaceae)

KEY IMPRESSIONS   Grows to 7ft (2.3m). May grow in sprawling clumps. Inflorescence an upright panicle with many branches. Stems fat.
SPIKELETS   Oval, 1-flowered.
LEAVES   4–20mm wide.
LIGULES   Dense ring of white hairs, 1–2mm.
ANNUAL
HABITAT   Moist soil and shores; found as weed in cultivated land.
RANGE   N.S. and Que. to Minn. and S.Dak., south to Fla. and Tex.

Panicum capillare L.
Witch-grass
Grass Family (Poaceae)

KEY IMPRESSIONS   Grows to 2½ft (40cm). Coarse, hairy. Inflorescence large, almost ⅔ length of plant, and may break off and roll like tumbleweed.
SPIKELETS   Oval, on long stems, 1-flowered.
LEAVES   Fuzzy leaf sheaths.

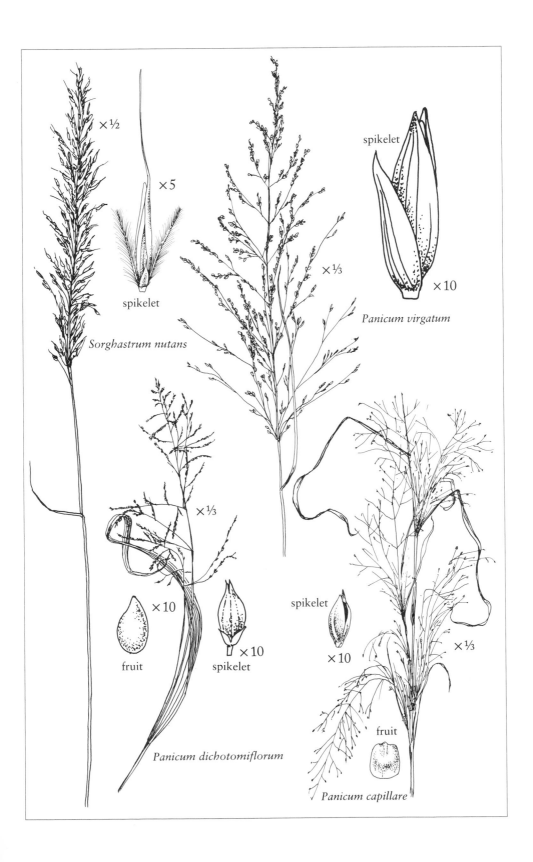

×½

×5

spikelet

Sorghastrum nutans

×⅓

spikelet

×10

Panicum virgatum

×⅓

×10

fruit

×10

spikelet

Panicum dichotomiflorum

spikelet

×10

×⅓

fruit

Panicum capillare

LIGULES 1–3mm.

ANNUAL

HABITAT Dry or moist soil; frequent weed in fields, gardens.

RANGE Throughout most of U.S. and s. Canada.

Cinna arundinacea L.
Common woodreed
Grass Family (Poaceae)

KEY IMPRESSIONS Grows 1½–5ft (45cm–1.6m). Inflorescence a large panicle, 4–16in (10–40cm), narrow, often somewhat drooping, with crowded ascending branches.

SPIKELETS 1-flowered.

LEAVES 6–12mm wide, flat, elongate.

LIGULES Membranous; reddish brown when fresh.

PERENNIAL

HABITAT Moist woods.

RANGE Maine to Ont., Minn. and N.Dak., south to Ga. and Tex.

SIMILAR SPECIES

 C. latifolia (Trevir) Griseb. Drooping woodreed. Panicle branches spreading or drooping, loosely flowered. Moist woods. Circumboreal south to Pa., n. Ill., Minn., and Colo.; in mountains to N.C.

Tridens flavus (L.) A. Hitchc. (*Triodia flavus*)
Purpletop
Grass Family (Poaceae)

KEY IMPRESSIONS Grows 2½–7ft (.75–2.3m). Inflorescence a large panicle with drooping branches, widely spaced. First purple, turning brown.

SPIKELETS 3–9-flowered.

LEAVES 3–8mm wide, elongate to slender tip, with hair tufts in axils. Sheaths bearded at top.

PERENNIAL Sometimes with very short underground stems.

HABITAT Fields, roadsides, open woods.

RANGE Mass. to s. Ont., s. Mich. and Nebr., south to Fla. and Tex.

Muhlenbergia schreberi J. F. Gmelin
Nimblewill
Grass Family (Poaceae)

KEY IMPRESSIONS Grows 8in–2ft (20–60cm). Inflorescence a long narrow panicle 2–8in (6–19cm). Falls over and sprawls, sometimes rooting at nodes.

SPIKELETS 1-flowered. Flower scale with bristle, 1.5–4mm, at tip.

LEAVES Sprawling, smooth, except around base of blade.

LIGULES Minute with short hairs, .1–.2mm.

PERENNIAL

HABITAT Disturbed moist or wet areas; often in lawns, gardens.

RANGE N.H. and Mass. to Minn. and Nebr., south to Fla. and Tex.

Inflorescence in Panicles

Tridens flavus

Cinna arundinacea

Muhlenbergia schreberi

×⅓

×⅓

×½

×10

×10

×10

Glyceria canadensis (Michx.) Trin.

Rattlesnake-mannagrass

Grass Family (Poaceae)

KEY IMPRESSIONS   Grows 1–3½ft (.3–1.1m). Inflorescence in drooping branches bearing spikelets mostly at tip. Leaf sheaths closed.

SPIKELETS   5–10-flowered.

LEAVES   Rough to the touch, 3–7mm or more wide.

LIGULES   2–6mm.

PERENNIAL

HABITAT   Swamps, bogs, wet woods.

RANGE   Nfld. to Minn., south to N.J. and Ill.

Chasmanthium latifolium (Michx.) Yates

Wild oats

Grass Family (Poaceae)

KEY IMPRESSIONS   Grows 3–5ft (1–1.6m). Inflorescence open, with nodding large, flat spikelets.

SPIKELETS   Large, 6–17-flowered.

LEAVES   Flat, narrowly lance-shaped, ½–¾in (1–2cm) wide.

LIGULES   Short, thin membrane with fringe of short hairs.

PERENNIAL

HABITAT   Moist woods, streambanks.

RANGE   N.J. to Ga., nw. Fla., west to Ohio, Ind., Ill., Kans., and Tex.

Agrostis gigantea Roth (*A. alba*)

Redtop

Grass Family (Poaceae)

KEY IMPRESSIONS   Grows 10in–4ft (.2–1.3m). Inflorescence opens at flowering but then may contract; very variable. Panicle branches in bunches. Flowers in late spring but may bloom into September.

SPIKELETS   Crowded, 1-flowered.

LEAVES   5–10mm wide, flat, stiff.

LIGULES   2.5–6mm, higher than wide.

PERENNIAL   From underground stems, forming dense mat and creating sod.

HABITAT   Moist meadows, shores, coastal marshes, other moist areas.

RANGE   Native to Europe; cultivated throughout most of U.S. and s. Canada.

Bromus inermis Leysser

Smooth brome

Grass Family (Poaceae)

KEY IMPRESSIONS   Grows 1½in–3½ft (.04–1.1m). Spring-blooming, but remnants may be found in winter. Inflorescence contracts after blooming.

SPIKELETS   15–30mm, 7–11-flowered. Flowers without bristle or with short bristle, 2.5mm.

LEAVES   8–15mm wide. Sheaths closed.

LIGULES   .5–1mm.

Inflorescence in Panicles

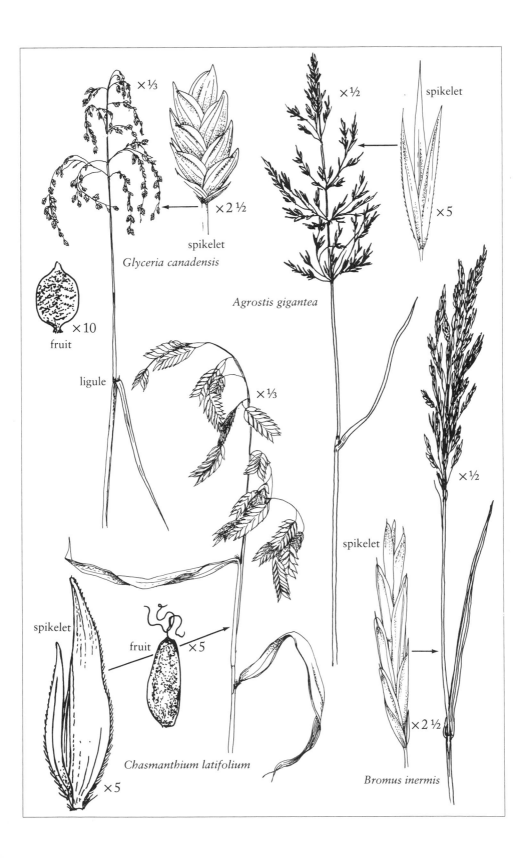

×⅓

×2½

spikelet

Glyceria canadensis

×10

fruit

ligule

×⅓

spikelet

fruit ×5

Chasmanthium latifolium

×5

spikelet

×½

spikelet

×5

×½

spikelet

×2½

Bromus inermis

Agrostis gigantea

PERENNIAL   From long underground stems.
HABITAT   Cultivated for forage; frequent escapee to roadsides, fields.
RANGE   Native to Europe; Que. to Minn. and Alb., south to Md., Ohio, Mo., and N.Mex.

Bromus tectorum L.
Downy chess, junegrass
Grass Family (Poaceae)

KEY IMPRESSIONS   Usually grows low to ground but may reach 3½ft (1.1m). Usually sprawling. Inflorescence drooping. Spring-blooming, but remnants may be found in late fall, especially at beaches.
SPIKELETS   3–8-flowered with long bristles, 10–17mm.
LEAVES   Blades 3–4mm wide, fuzzy. Sheaths closed.
LIGULES   1–2.5mm.
ANNUAL
HABITAT   Roadsides, waste areas, beaches; common.
RANGE   Native to Europe; throughout U.S.

Zizania aquatica L.
Wild rice
Grass Family (Poaceae)

KEY IMPRESSIONS   Grows to 10ft (3.3m). Very tall. Male and female flowers grow separately on large panicle. Male flower branches widely spreading on lower panicle; female branches above, ascending. Branches remain after flowers and fruit have fallen.
FRUIT   Rodlike grain.
SPIKELETS   1-flowered; female flowers erect at first, then drooping; males pendulous.
LEAVES   Wide, flat, soft.
LIGULES   Membranous.
ANNUAL
HABITAT   Marshes, shallow water, river mouths.
RANGE   S. Que., along coasts from Maine to Fla., n. Great Lakes, and irregularly inland in n. N.Y.

Grasses with Spikelike Inflorescence without Bristles

Spartina patens (Aiton) Muhl.
Salt-meadow cord-grass
Grass Family (Poaceae)

KEY IMPRESSIONS   Grows 1–2½ft (30–75cm). Inflorescence an upright spike with spikelets lined along 1 side of branch. Thin stems bend easily. Forms large, extended mats in salt marshes.
SPIKELETS   1-flowered, strongly flattened.
LEAVES   Inrolled, 1–4mm when flattened.
LIGULES   Band of hairs.
PERENNIAL
HABITAT   Salt marshes, wet beaches.
RANGE   Coastal Que. to Fla. and Tex.; inland in salty areas in c. N.Y., s. Ont., and c. Mich.

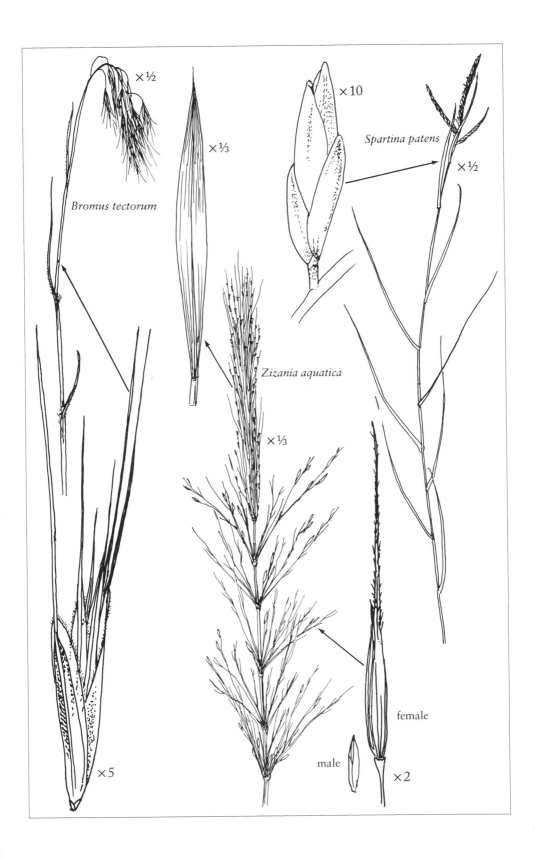

×½

Bromus tectorum

×⅓

×10

Spartina patens

×½

Zizania aquatica

×⅓

×5

male

female

×2

Spartina alterniflora Loisel

Saltwater cord-grass, smooth cord-grass

Grass Family (Poaceae)

KEY IMPRESSIONS Grows to 9ft (3m). Tall. Inflorescence narrow, spikelike, shaggy. Spikelets line up along 1 or 2 sides of spike. Grows in large masses on outer edges of salt marshes.

SPIKELETS 1-flowered.

LEAVES 5–15mm wide, elongate.

LIGULES Band of hairs.

PERENNIAL From elongated underground stems.

HABITAT Coastal, mainly intertidal salt marshes.

RANGE Que. and Nfld. to Fla. and Tex.

Ammophila breviligulata Fern.

Beach-grass, marram

Grass Family (Poaceae)

KEY IMPRESSIONS Grows to 3½ft (1.1m). Inflorescence a contracted spikelike panicle, about 12in (30cm), whitish, dense.

SPIKELETS 1-flowered.

LEAVES Basal, long, narrow. Flat at base, inrolled above.

LIGULES 1–3mm, membranous.

PERENNIAL From long underground stems.

HABITAT Dunes, dry sandy shores.

RANGE Along Great Lakes, Lake Champlain, and Atlantic coast from Nfld. to N.C.

Leymus mollis (Trin.) Pilger (*Elymus mollis*)

American dunegrass

Grass Family (Poaceae)

KEY IMPRESSIONS 20in–5ft (.6–1.6m). Inflorescence a stout, erect, dense spike.

SPIKELETS Coarse, 4–6-flowered, mostly paired at nodes.

LEAVES 6–15mm wide.

LIGULES Under 1mm.

PERENNIAL

HABITAT Sandy beaches, dunes.

RANGE Both coasts of N. Am., south to Mass. and Calif., shores of Great Lakes.

Tripsacum dactyloides (L.) L.

Gama-grass

Grass Family (Poaceae)

KEY IMPRESSIONS Grows 3½–8ft (1.1–2.6m). Spikes 4–10in (10–25cm).

SPIKELETS 7–10mm. Female and male spikelets separate. Male above, in pairs at nodes, 2-flowered; female single at nodes.

LEAVES Often to ⅔in (2cm) wide.

PERENNIAL Stout.

HABITAT Swamps, wet soil, salt marsh or wood edges.

RANGE Tropical Am. and north to Mass., s. Mich., Iowa, and Nebr.

Spikelike Inflorescence without Bristles

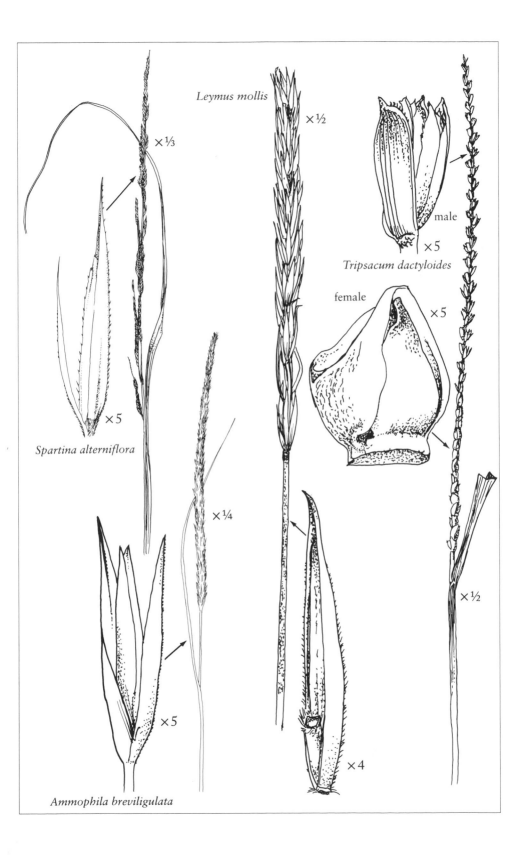

Leymus mollis

×½

Tripsacum dactyloides

male

×5

female

×5

×⅓

×5

Spartina alterniflora

×¼

×½

×4

×5

Ammophila breviligulata

Distichlis spicata (L.) Greene
Spike grass
Grass Family (Poaceae)

KEY IMPRESSIONS   Grows 4in–4ft (.1–1.3m). Sprawling, forming dense mats. Inflorescence a short, congested spike to 3½in (8cm).
SPIKELETS   Flattened, 4–19-flowered.
LEAVES   Rigid, inrolled, sheaths closely overlapping.
PERENNIAL
HABITAT   Salt marshes.
RANGE   Along coast from N.S. to tropical Am.

Grasses with Spikes with Flat Spikelets along Stem

Lolium perenne L.
Ryegrass
Grass Family (Poaceae)

KEY IMPRESSIONS   Grows 1–2ft (30–60cm). Stem single. Flat spikelets sideways on stem.
SPIKELETS   5–22-flowered, 1-scaled, large, on side away from stem.
LEAVES   Flat blades, 2–4mm wide.
PERENNIAL   Short-lived.
HABITAT   Meadows, lawns, roadsides, waste areas.
RANGE   Native to Europe; throughout region.

Elytrigia repens (L.) Nevski. (*Agropyron repens*)
Quack grass
Grass Family (Poaceae)

KEY IMPRESSIONS   Grows 1–4ft (.3–1.3m). Spikelets flat, with backs toward central stem.
SPIKELETS   3–8-flowered. Each with 2 scales of equal length at bottom.
LEAVES   Mostly flat, 3–10mm wide.
PERENNIAL
HABITAT   Disturbed sites.
RANGE   Native to Eurasia and possibly N. Am. Atlantic coast; widespread as weed throughout most of U.S. and Canada.

Grasses with Cylindrical Spikes with Bristles

Phleum pratense L.
Timothy
Grass Family (Poaceae)

KEY IMPRESSIONS   Grows 1–3½ft (.3–1.1m). Inflorescence narrow, dense, cylindrical, spikelike.
SPIKELETS   1-flowered. Bracts bristled, not united at base.

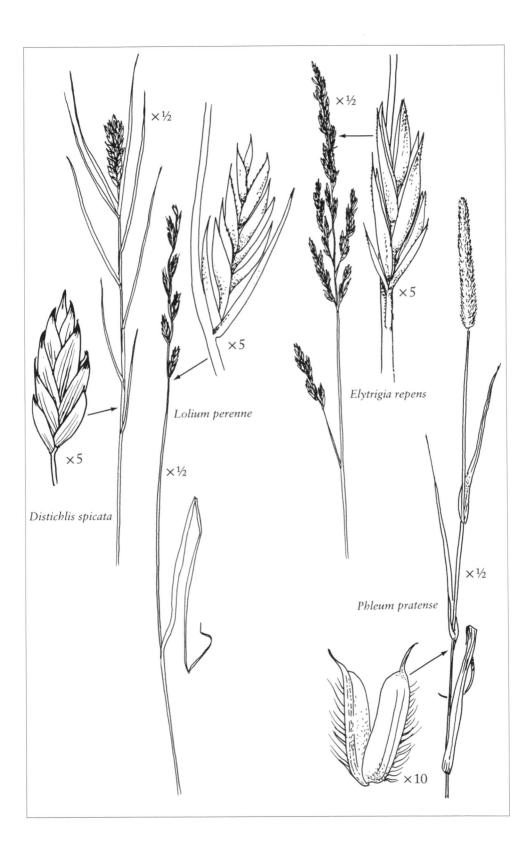

×½

×5

Elytrigia repens

×5

Lolium perenne

×5

×½

×5

Distichlis spicata

×½

×½

Phleum pratense

×10

LEAVES Flat.

LIGULES Membranous, elongate.

PERENNIAL

HABITAT Fields, roadsides; very common.

RANGE Native to Europe, cultivated for hay and pasture; escaped and naturalized throughout most of U.S. and Canada.

SIMILAR SPECIES

Alopecurus L. spp. Foxtail. Grows in tufts low to ground. Floral bracts united at base. Softer to touch than *Phleum* spp. Moist meadows, fields, waste areas. Throughout region.

Setaria P. Beauv., nom. conserv. spp. Foxtail-grass. Inflorescence cylindrical, flexible, spikelike, with dense fine bristles. Spikelets 1–2-flowered.

S. viridis (L.) P. Beauv. Green foxtail. Grows 4in–4ft (10cm–1.3m). Inflorescence slightly nodding or remaining upright. Spikelets subtended by 1–3 bristles. Annual. Fields, gardens, waste areas. Throughout region.

S. faberi R. Herrm. Nodding foxtail, giant foxtail. Grows to 6ft (2m). Largest of 3 *Setaria* described here. Inflorescence drooping. Spikelets subtended usually by 3 bristles but can be 1–6. Annual. Fields, waste areas. Native to e. Asia; throughout region.

S. glauca (L.) P. Beauv. Yellow foxtail. Grows 4in–4ft (.1–1.3m). Inflorescence stiff, straight. Hairs yellow-brown. Spikelets subtended by 4–12 bristles. Annual. Cultivated soil, waste areas. Native to Europe; throughout region.

Elymus canadensis L.
Canada wild rye
Grass Family (Poaceae)

KEY IMPRESSIONS Grows 2½–6ft (.75–2m). Inflorescence an erect spike, densely flowered.

SPIKELETS 3–4-flowered. Bristles 15–30mm, coarse, thick, curving outward.

LEAVES 3–12mm wide, 5–9 per stem.

LIGULES Short.

PERENNIAL

HABITAT Streambanks, dry to moist fields, meadows.

RANGE N.B. and Que. to Alaska, south to N.C., Tex., and Calif.

Elymus virginicus L.
Virginia wild rye
Grass Family (Poaceae)

KEY IMPRESSIONS Grows 1–5ft (.3–1.6m). Inflorescence stiff, upright, compact.

SPIKELETS 2–4-flowered, mostly paired. Bristles 2in (3.5cm), stiff, straight.

LEAVES 4–10mm wide, 6–10 per stem.

LIGULES Short.

PERENNIAL

HABITAT Moist woods, meadows, prairies.

RANGE Nfld. to Alb., south to Fla. and Ariz.

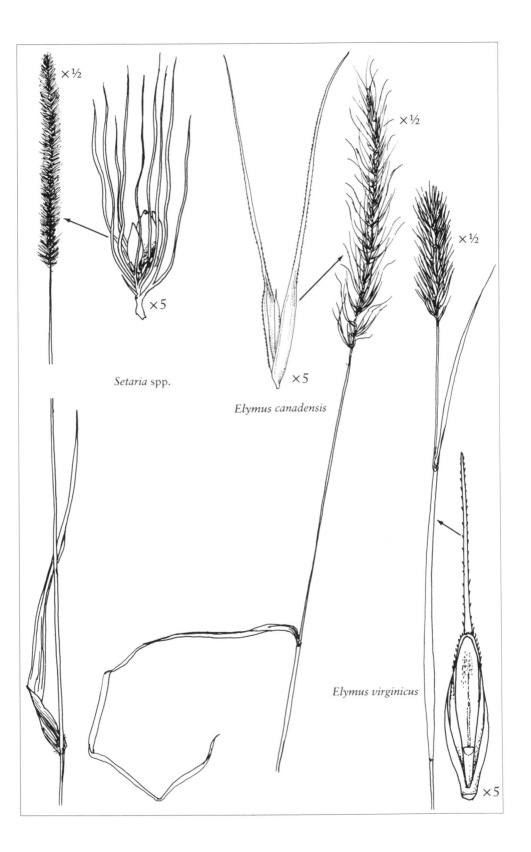

×½

×5

Setaria spp.

×½

×5

Elymus canadensis

×½

Elymus virginicus

×5

Hordeum vulgare L.
Barley
Grass Family (Poaceae)

KEY IMPRESSIONS   Grows 2–4ft (.6–1.3m). Inflorescence upright.
SPIKELETS   3 per node, dense, bristly. Bristles long, 2½–6¼in (6–16cm). Lower bristles longer than upper.
LEAVES   5–12mm wide.
LIGULES   Cut off at top.
ANNUAL
HABITAT   Along roads, railroads.
RANGE   Cultivated in Europe; occasional in region.

Secale cereale L.
Rye
Grass Family (Poaceae)

KEY IMPRESSIONS   Grows 2–3½ft (.6–1.1m). Inflorescence a stout, heavy spike often drooping when ripe.
SPIKELETS   2 per node, 2-flowered. Bristles 1–3in (2–7cm), stiff, all about same length.
LEAVES   3–7mm wide.
ANNUAL
HABITAT   Disturbed areas.
RANGE   Cultivated in Europe; throughout region.

Hordeum jubatum L.
Squirreltail-grass, foxtail-barley
Grass Family (Poaceae)

KEY IMPRESSIONS   Grows 1–2½ft (30–75cm). Grows low to ground. Spikes 1½–4in (4–10cm), nodding.
SPIKELETS   3 per node. Numerous long bristles, ½–2½in (1–6cm).
LEAVES   1.5–5mm wide.
LIGULES   Apex cut off (truncate).
PERENNIAL
HABITAT   Roadsides, fields, moist or wet woods.
RANGE   Nfld. to Alaska, south to Del., Ill., Mo., Tex., and Calif.

Elymus hystrix L. (*Hystrix patula*)
Bottlebrush grass
Grass Family (Poaceae)

KEY IMPRESSIONS   Grows 2–5ft (.6–1.6m). Inflorescence with obvious spaces between spikelets.
SPIKELETS   2 per node, fairly large, V-shaped, with long, stiff bristles, horizontally spreading. Bristles ½–1½in (1–4cm).
LEAVES   Flat, 8–15mm wide.
LIGULES   Short.
PERENNIAL
HABITAT   Woods.
RANGE   N.S. and Que. to N.Dak., south to Va. and Okla.

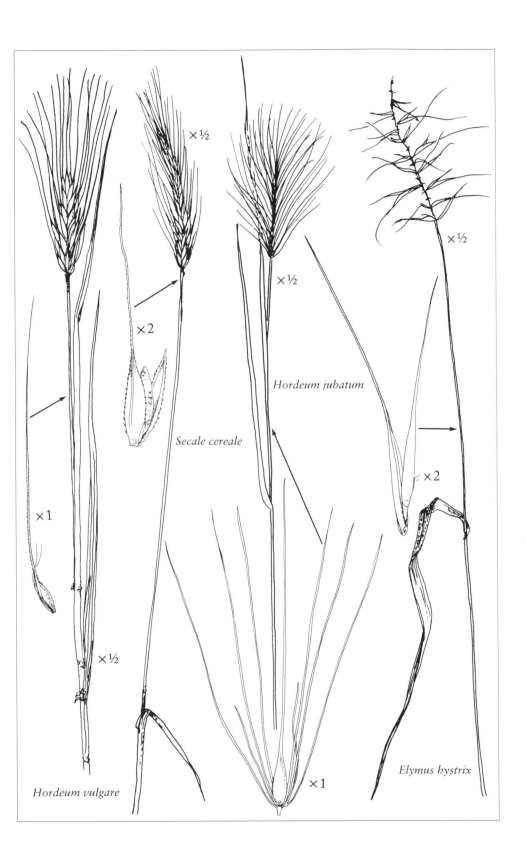

×½

×2

×½

×1

×1

×½

Hordeum jubatum

Secale cereale

Hordeum vulgare

×2

Elymus hystrix

Grasses with Inflorescence Resembling an Umbel

Andropogon gerardii Vitman
Big bluestem, beardgrass, turkey-claw
Grass Family (Poaceae)

KEY IMPRESSIONS   Grows 2½–5ft (.75–1.6m). Inflorescence of bristly racemes radiating umbel-like from terminal stem end.
SPIKELETS   1-flowered, paired, 1 stemless, with bristle 8–20mm, twisted below, other stemmed.
LEAVES   5–15mm wide. Stems leafy.
PERENNIAL   From short underground stems.
HABITAT   Moist or dry open areas, tall-grass prairies.
RANGE   Que. to Sask., south to Fla. and Ariz.

Digitaria sanguinalis (L.) Scop.
Northern crab-grass
Grass Family (Poaceae)

KEY IMPRESSIONS   Grows 1–4ft (.3–1.3m). Sprawling habit, with 3–6 racemelike branches spreading like fingers.
SPIKELETS   1 fertile flower per spikelet. Fruits smooth, oval.
LEAVES   5–10mm wide.
ANNUAL
HABITAT   Lawns, fields, gardens, waste areas.
RANGE   Native to Europe; established as weed throughout region.

Eleusine indica (L.) Gaertner
Yard-grass, goose-grass
Grass Family (Poaceae)

KEY IMPRESSIONS   Grows 1–2ft (30–60cm). Spikes look like a closed zipper. Grows in tufts. Flower clusters jagged.
SPIKELETS   3–6-flowered.
LEAVES   Flat or folded, 3–8mm wide.
LIGULES   Membranous, fringed.
ANNUAL
HABITAT   Lawns, gardens, waste areas.
RANGE   Pantropical extending north to Mass., S.Dak., and Utah.

Paspalum L. spp.
Bead-grass
Grass Family (Poaceae)

KEY IMPRESSIONS   Grows to 3½ft (1.1m). Flat, circular spikelets lined along 1 side of spike-like raceme. Terminal inflorescence 1 to many branched. Grows in tufts.
SPIKELETS   1-flowered.
LEAVES   Usually soft.
LIGULES   Membranous.

Eleusine indica

×½

×5

×⅓

×½

Digitaria sanguinalis

×½

×5

Andropogon gerardii

×5

Paspalum spp.

×10

ANNUAL OR PERENNIAL

HABITAT Dry or moist, open or lightly wooded places, often in sandy soil.

RANGE Mainly tropical and warm climates, but some species extend north to N.H.

Grasses with Inflorescence Forming Small Branches along Length of Stem

Schizachyrium scoparium (Michx.) Nash (*Andropogon scoparium*)
Little bluestem, broom beardgrass, prairie beardgrass
Grass Family (Poaceae)

KEY IMPRESSIONS Grows 1½–5ft (.45–1.6m). Bristly spikelets lined along branches, and branches extend beyond leaves. Branches ascend stem, mingled with leaves. Stalks tan-brown.

SPIKELETS 1-flowered, each flower with extending bristle and fuzzy sterile spikelet attached.

LEAVES 3–6mm wide.

PERENNIAL

HABITAT Abundant and highly varied; important part of tall- and mixed-grass prairies; dry soil, old fields, prairies, open woods.

RANGE N.B., Que., to Alb., south to Fla. and Tex.

Andropogon virginicus L.
Broom sedge
Grass Family (Poaceae)

KEY IMPRESSIONS Grows 20in–5ft (.5–1.6m). Very similar to *Schizachyrium scoparium,* above, but with spikelet branches tucked inside leafy bracts rather than extending beyond leaves.

SPIKELETS In pairs at joints, one stemless, the other with small stem.

LEAVES 3–8mm wide, sparsely hairy on ligule and sheath.

PERENNIAL

HABITAT Fields, open woods.

RANGE Along s. coastal plain northward to Mass., s. Ont., Ohio, Mo., and Kans., south to Fla. and Tex.

Bouteloua curtipendula (Michx.) Torr.
Tall gramma-grass, side-oats grass
Grass Family (Poaceae)

KEY IMPRESSIONS Grows 1–3½ft (.3–1.1m). Inflorescence of 15 or more short spikes, hanging mainly from 1 side of stem.

SPIKELETS 3–7 per node. 1 perfect flower, 1 or more sterile vestiges. Short bristles.

LEAVES Elongate, 2–7mm wide.

LIGULES Band of short hairs.

PERENNIAL from short, slender underground stems.

HABITAT Dry woods in e. states; dry prairies, sandhills in West.

RANGE Maine to Mont., south to Ala. and Calif.

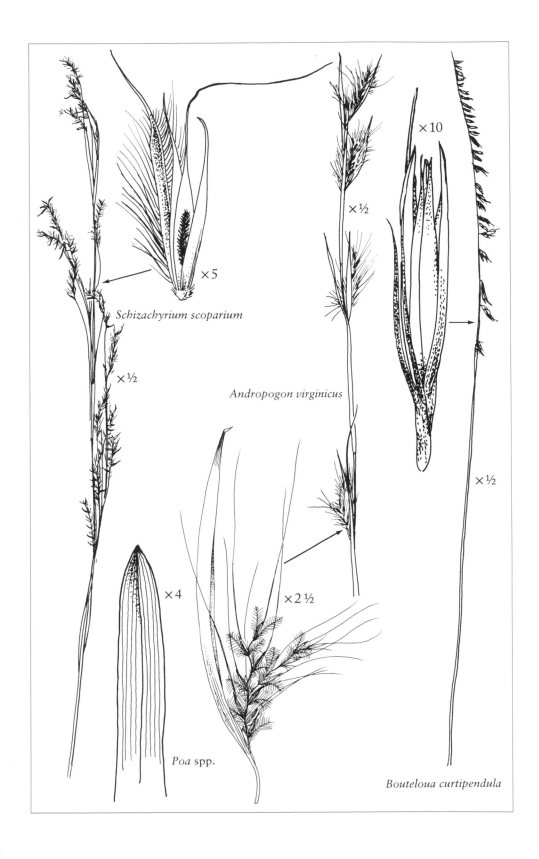

Schizachyrium scoparium

×5

×½

Andropogon virginicus

×10

×½

×½

×4

×2½

Poa spp.

Bouteloua curtipendula

Grasses without Inflorescence but with Leaves

Poa L. spp.
Bluegrass
Grass Family (Poaceae)

Many species of this genus are spring-blooming but have leaves that persist in winter. Look for leaves ending in a boat-shaped tip. Widespread, mostly in temperate and boreal zones.

Sedge Family (Cyperaceae)

Key to Sedge Family (Cyperaceae)

This key comprises only the most common genera and species. Before you use the key, look at your specimen and note whether the scales in the spikelet are arranged in 2 rows or on all sides of the axis. Try to isolate an achene and see whether it has bristles that surround it from the base or a beak on its apex and whether it is flat or 3-angled.

1a Achenes contained within sac (perigynium); spikelets of separate male and female flowers either on the same spikelets (⅓ of species) or on separate spikelets, lower flowers female and upper ones male; stems triangular in about ⅔ of species: *Carex* spp. pp. 298–300
1b Achenes not enclosed within perigynium; spikelets alike 2
   2a Stem leafless, bearing 1 or more spikelets at or near top 3
   2b Stem leafy 5
3a 1 spikelet, erect, at very top of stem: *Eleocharis* spp. p. 292
3b Few to several spikelets, lateral, near top of stem 4
   4a Stem round: Softstem-bulrush (*Scirpus validus*) p. 294
   4b Stem triangular: Three-square (*Scirpus americanus*) p. 292
5a Scales of spikelets in 2 rows, alternating on opposite sides of axis 6
5b Scales of spikelets on all sides of axis 7
   6a Flower clusters terminal on stem or branches: *Cyperus* spp. p. 292
   6b Flower clusters axillary along side of stem: Three-way sedge (*Dulichium arundinaceum*) p. 292
7a Achene with terminal beak: *Rhynchospora* spp. p. 296
7b Achene without beak 8
   8a Bristles present, more or less surrounding achene 9
   8b Bristles absent from around achene 10
9a Bristles abundant, silky (cottony in mass), more than 1cm: *Eriophorum* spp. p. 296
9b Bristles few, scarcely silky, brownish, less than 1cm: *Scirpus* spp. p. 294
   10a Spikelets in close headlike clusters: Twig-rush (*Cladium mariscoides*) p. 296
   10b Spikelets in loose panicled clusters 11
11a Achenes 3-cornered, with swollen, persistent style base: *Bulbostylis* spp. p. 296
11b Achenes lens-shaped, without swollen, persistent style base: *Fimbristylis* spp. p. 296

Key to Sedge Family (Cyperaceae)

1a

3a

4a   4b

6a   6b

7a

9a   9b

10a

11a 11b

×½

achene ×10

spike ×1

spikelet

×5

Dulichium arundinaceum

Dulichium arundinaceum (L.) Britton
Three-way sedge
Sedge Family (Cyperaceae)

Grows 8in–3½ft (.2–1.1m). Inflorescence in spikelike flat clusters arranged along length of stem. Achenes 2.5–3mm, oblong, flat, long-beaked. Leaves flat, grasslike, in 3 rows. Stem hollow, roundish. Swamps, marshes. Nfld. to Minn., south to Fla. and Tex.; in West, B.C. to Calif. and Mont.

Cyperus esculentus L.
Yellow nutsedge
Sedge Family (Cyperaceae)

Grows 8in–3ft (.2–1m). Inflorescence radiates in branches from top of stem. Flat, layered spikes perpendicular to branch. Leafy bracts extend beyond inflorescence. Achenes oblong, 3-cornered. Leaves basal. Stem triangular. Underground stems with hard little tubers. Damp or wet soil. Throughout most of region.

Cyperus strigosus L.
False nutsedge, umbrella sedge
Sedge Family (Cyperaceae)

Grows to 3½ft but usually 1ft (3.–1.1m). Similar to *C. esculentus* but without underground tubers. Flower scales keeled (ridged) unlike flower scales of *C. esculentus*. Moist fields, swamps, shores. Que. to Minn. and S.Dak., south to Fla. and Tex.

Eleocharis acicularis (L.) Roemer & Schultes
Spike-rush
Sedge Family (Cyperaceae)

Grows 1in–1ft (2.5–30cm). Small plant with thin, wiry stems. Several *Eleocharis* species are similar and variable. All have leafless stems and 1 conical inflorescence at terminal end. Achenes white to pale gray, 3-cornered with 3-cornered conical beak. Often forms large mats in mud. Marshes, muddy shores, other wet areas. Circumboreal south to Fla. and Mexico.

Scirpus americanus Pers.
Three-square, chairmakers rush
Sedge Family (Cyperaceae)

Grows 1¼in–5ft (.03–1.6m). Inflorescence appears to emerge from side of stem with no stalks; in fact, 1 bract extends above inflorescence and appears as continuation of stem. Spikelets oblong, several-scaled, with bristles. Achenes convex, 1.8–2.5mm, including .3mm beak. Leaves few, all on lower part of stem. Stem triangular, solid. Marshes, wet meadows, other wet, low areas; tolerates alkali. N.S. to Wash. south to S. Am.

Sedge Family

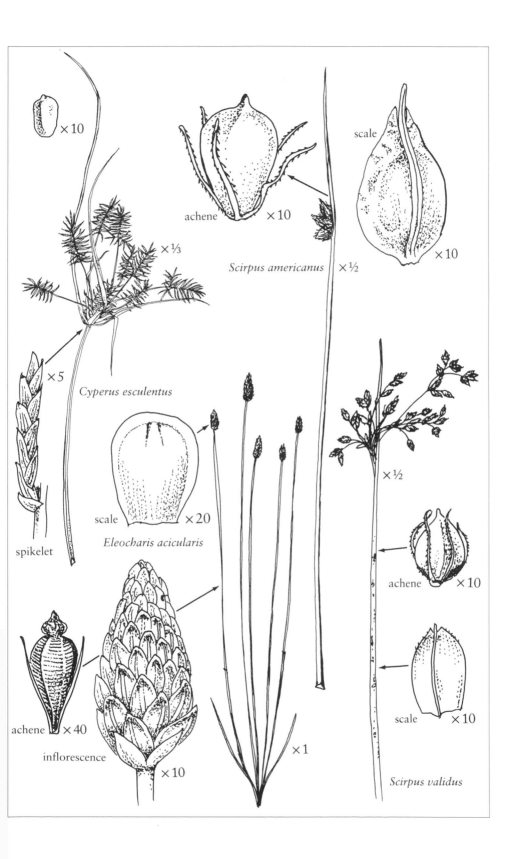

×10

achene ×10

Scirpus americanus ×½

scale

×10

×⅓

Cyperus esculentus

×5

scale ×20

Eleocharis acicularis

×½

spikelet

achene ×10

scale ×10

achene ×40

inflorescence

×10

×1

Scirpus validus

Scirpus validus Vahl.

Softstem-bulrush

Sedge Family (Cyperaceae)

Grows 1½–10ft (.45–3.3m). Inflorescence appears to emerge on branches from side of stem because principal bract extends above inflorescence as extension of stem. Spikelets less than 1cm, with scales 2.5–3mm. Achenes 1.8–2.3mm, unequally 3-cornered. Leaves few, mainly toward base. Stems round, easily squashed. Grows in clumps. Marshes, muddy shores of lakes and streams; tolerates alkali. Throughout temperate N. Am.

Scirpus cyperinus (L.) Kunth.

Wool-grass

Sedge Family (Cyperaceae)

Grows to 6ft (2m). Grows in clumps. Inflorescence woolly, brown, radiates from 1 point at end of stem, then radiates again and droops. Bracts long, leafy, spreading. Spikelets sub-tended by 6 bristles surpassing scales and giving woolly appearance. Achenes .7–1mm, pale, 3-cornered, short-beaked. Scales elliptic. Leaves long on stem. Grows in clumps. Bogs, marshes, wet meadows. Nfld. to B.C., south to Fla. and Tex.

Scirpus microcarpus C. Presl. (*S. rubrotinctus*)

Barberpole sedge

Sedge Family (Cyperaceae)

Grows 3½ft (1.1m). Inflorescence dense. Many-flowered, in gray-green clusters at terminal end, subtended by leafy bracts. Spikelets 4–6mm. Bristles 4–6, slightly surpassing achene. Achenes lens-shaped, some 3-cornered, slightly beaked. Leaf sheaths banded deep red. Stems triangular. Wet low ground. Nfld. to Alaska, south to W.Va., Iowa, N.Mex., and s. Calif.

SIMILAR SPECIES

S. atrovirens Willd. Black bulrush, dark green bulrush. Bigger than *S. microcarpus*. Flower clusters fewer, brown rather than green. No red on leaf sheath.

Scirpus robustus Pursh

Saltmarsh-bulrush

Sedge Family (Cyperaceae)

Grows 2½–5ft (.76–1.6m). Inflorescence unbranched or on short branches, on terminal stem end. Bracts long, leafy. Spikelets oblong. Achenes 3–3.5mm, dark brown to black, glossy, with minute beak. Scales brown, with bristle. Stem sharply triangular. Grows in patches. Perennial from stout underground stems with tubers. Coastal brackish or saline marshes. N.S. to Tex. and Calif.

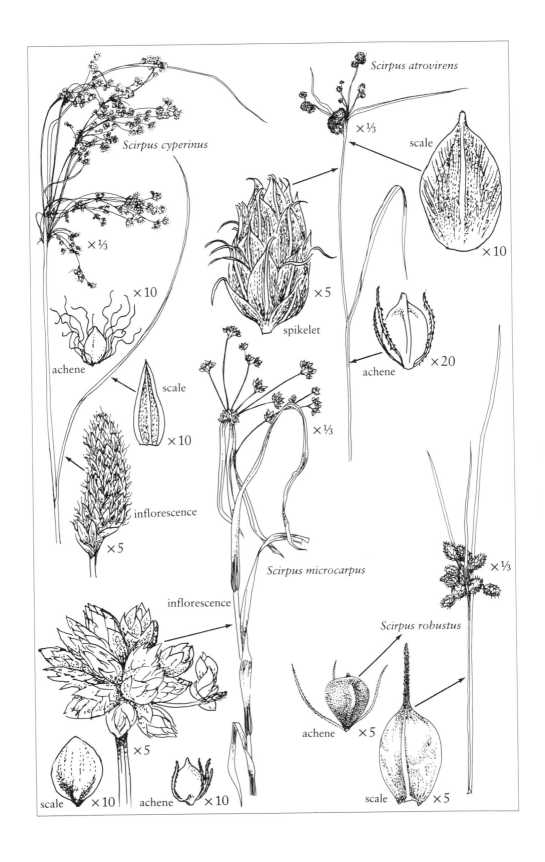

Scirpus cyperinus

×⅓

×10

achene

Scirpus atrovirens

×⅓

scale

×10

scale

×10

spikelet

×5

achene

×20

inflorescence

×5

×⅓

Scirpus microcarpus

inflorescence

×⅓

Scirpus robustus

achene

×5

×5

scale

×10

achene

×10

scale

×5

Bulbostylis capillaris (L.) C. B. Clarke
Fimbristylis autumnalis (L.) Roemer & Schultes
Sedge Family (Cyperaceae)

These 2 genera are hard to distinguish in winter. Short, 1–16in (2.5–40cm), growing in clumps. Both have wiry basal leaves. Many spikelets in umbel-type branches at terminal stem end. Inflorescence subtended by leaflike bracts. Scales on spikelets spirally layered. Wiry basal leaves and stems. *Bulbostylis* achenes 3-cornered, ribbed, beaked, with swollen base; leaf sheaths long-fringed. *Fimbristylis* achenes lens-shaped or 3-cornered, smooth, beakless, without swollen base; leaf sheaths either short-fringed or unfringed. *Fimbristylis* generally found in varied wet areas; *Bulbostylis* usually found in dry open rocky or sandy areas. Found throughout region.

Eriophorum virginicum L.
Tawny cotton-grass
Sedge Family (Cyperaceae)

Grows 1½–4ft (.45–1.3m). Stems solitary, erect, terminated by large clusters of white or tawny hairs attached to achenes. Leaves slender, threadlike, clustered at base. Forms large tussocks. Bogs, open conifer swamps. Circumboreal, s. to N.J., Pa., n. Ind., and Alb.

Rhynchospora Vahl, nom. conserv. spp.
Beak-rush
Sedge Family (Cyperaceae)

Grows to 5ft (1.6m); usually smaller. Inflorescence occupies upper ¼ of stem, irregularly shaped, with brownish spirally layered scales. Spikelets round, with bristles. Achenes lens-shaped, beaked at top. Leaves grasslike, with closed sheaths. Stems vaguely triangular, thin, weak. Wet places. Various species throughout region.

Cladium mariscoides (Muhl.) Torr.
Twig-rush
Sedge Family (Cyperaceae)

Similar to *Rhynchospora* but with stiffer, fatter stems. Achenes dull brown, sharply pointed, without beak (unlike those of *Rhynchospora*). Stem vaguely triangular. Wet places. N.S. to Minn., south to w. Fla., Ky., and e. Tex.

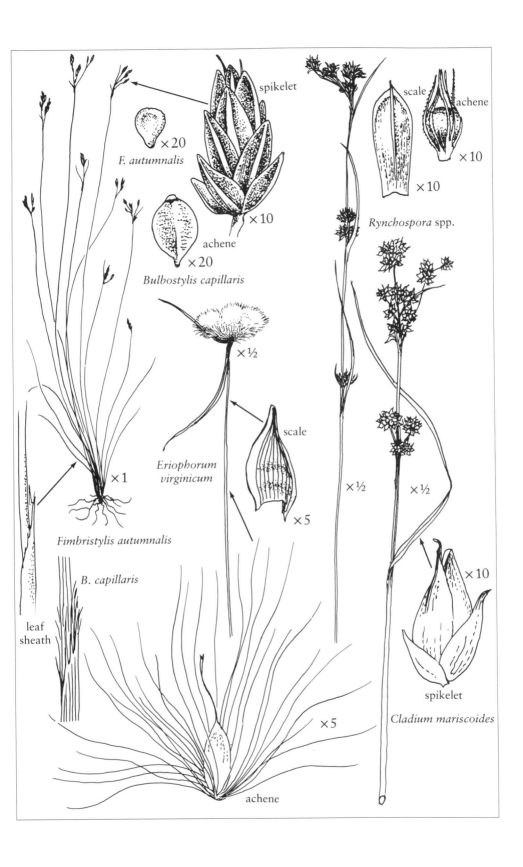

spikelet

×20

F. autumnalis

×10

achene

×20

Bulbostylis capillaris

scale

achene

×10

×10

Rynchospora spp.

×½

scale

Eriophorum virginicum

×5

×½

×½

×1

Fimbristylis autumnalis

×10

B. capillaris

leaf sheath

×5

achene

spikelet

Cladium mariscoides

Carex L. spp.

Sedge

Sedge Family (Cyperaceae)

Spikelets of male and female flowers on same or separate spikes. Achenes contained
within sac (perigynium).

Carex crinita Lam.

Sedge Family (Cyperaceae)

Grows 1–5½ ft (.3–1.7m). Female inflorescence of drooping cylindrical, bristly spikes. Male
inflorescence extends at terminal end. Stem triangular. Achenes lens-shaped, enclosed in
small-beaked pouch. Grows in clumps. Wet areas. Nfld. and Que. to Minn., south to Ga.
and Tex.

Carex lupulina Muhl.

Sedge Family (Cyperaceae)

Grows to 4ft (1.3m). Female inflorescence cylindrical, subtended by leafy bracts. Male inflorescence extends above female. Achenes triangular, enclosed in inflated sacs, long-
beaked, with 2 small teeth at top. Stem triangular. Grows in leafy tussocks. Moist to wet
woods, meadows, marshes. N.S. and N.B. to Minn. and Nebr., south to Fla. and Tex.

Carex lurida Wahlenb.

Sedge Family (Cyperaceae)

Grows 8in–3½ ft (.2–1.1m). Female inflorescence cylindrical, bristly, with many flower
sacs. Male inflorescence extends above female. Long, leafy bracts subtend inflorescence.
Flower sacs small, slightly inflated, with long, straight beak terminated by 2 teeth. Stem triangular. Achenes 3-cornered. Swamps, wet meadows, woods. N.S. to Minn., south to Fla.
and Mexico.

Carex scoparia Schk.

Sedge Family (Cyperaceae)

Grows 8in–3½ ft (.2–1.1m). Inflorescence composed of scaly, oval clusters at stem top. Male
flowers at base of female flowers; hard to distinguish. Stem thin, triangular. Flower sacs
very flat, wing-margined, with flat beak. Achenes lens-shaped. Open swamps, wet meadows, shores. Nfld. to Fla., west to B.C., Oreg., and N.Mex.

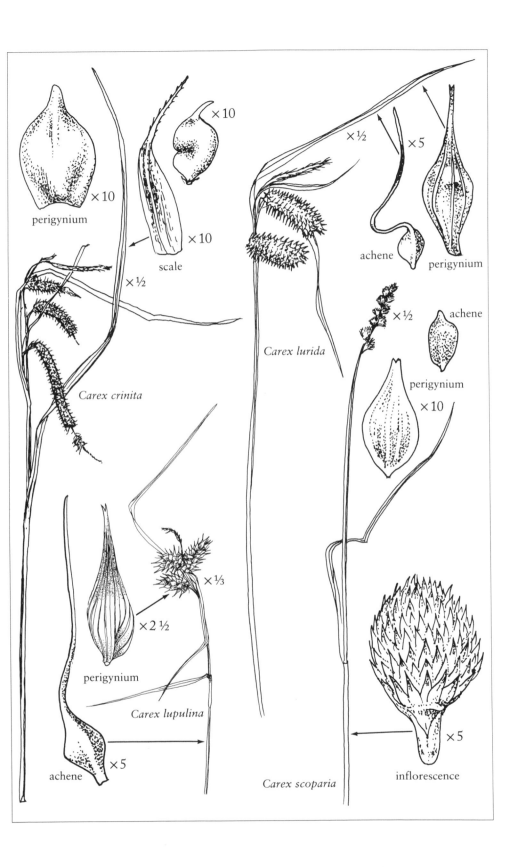

perigynium ×10

×10

scale ×10

×½

Carex crinita

perigynium ×2½

Carex lupulina

achene ×5

×½

×5

achene   perigynium

achene

perigynium ×10

Carex lurida

Carex scoparia

inflorescence ×5

Carex vulpinoidea Michx.
Sedge Family (Cyperaceae)

Grows 8–3½ft (.2–1.1m). Inflorescence an upright, narrow, asymmetical spike. Male and female flowers mixed; hard to distinguish. Bristlelike bracts under and throughout inflorescence. Flower sacs flattened. Achenes lens-shaped. Grows in clumps. Marshes, other wet low places. Nfld. to Fla., west to B.C., Wash., and Ariz.

Carex intumescens Rudge.
Sedge Family (Cyperaceae)

Grows 1–2½ft (30–75cm). Female inflorescence somewhat round in overall outline, subtended by leafy bracts. Male inflorescence extends above female. Achenes 3-cornered, enclosed in inflated shiny sacs with beaks terminating in 2 small teeth. Stem triangular. Grows in clumps. Moist or wet woods. Nfld. to se. Man., south to Fla. and Tex.

Carex stricta Lam.
Tussock sedge
Sedge Family (Cyperaceae)

Grows to 4½ft (1.4m); usually smaller. Forms large clumps of leafy tussocks in wet places. Tussocks usually solid enough to serve as stepping "stones" in swamps and marshes. Flowering stalks disintegrate quickly; not useful in winter identification. Swamps, marshes; abundant, especially where seasonally flooded. Que. to N.S. to Minn. and Man., south to Va. and Tex.

Carex pensylvanica Lam.
Pennsylvania sedge
Sedge Family (Cyperaceae)

Grows to 16in (40cm); small. Flowers early in spring, stalks disintegrating by late spring. Thin leaves remain throughout year. Tufts with reddish bases, surrounded by dried leaves of previous season. Female spikes, if present, round. Male spikes separate, ½–¾in (1–2cm). Achenes rounded, 3-cornered. Leaves 1.5–3mm wide. Long underground stems. Deciduous woods. N.S. to Minn., south to S.C., Ky., and Ark.

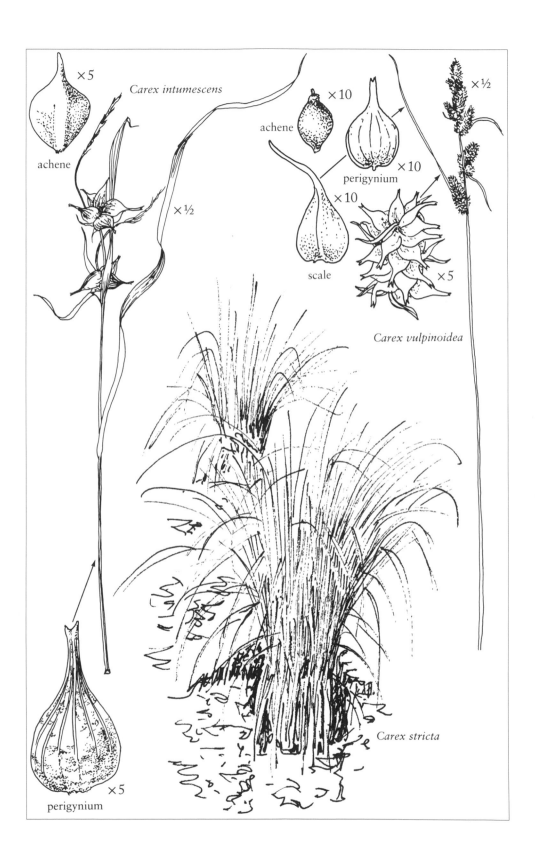

×5
Carex intumescens
achene

achene ×10

×10
perigynium

×10

×½

scale ×10

×5

Carex vulpinoidea

×½

×5
perigynium

Carex stricta

Rush Family (Juncaceae)

The sepals and petals of *Juncus* species are essentially alike, but in 2 separate whorls.
Some species have prophylls, small bracts subtending the flowers.
Several *Juncus* species are highly subject to gall formation. When an insect deposits eggs on a host
plant, the plant reacts by forming a gall, and the insect larva lives within, obtaining food
and shelter from the plant. In the example illustrated here, the incitant is a jumping
louse (psyllid), *Homoptera levia maculipennis*.

Juncus tenuis Willd.
Path-rush
Rush Family (Juncaceae)

Grows 4in–2ft (6–60cm). Inflorescence loosely branched at terminal stem end, subtended
by bracts that surpass it. Sepals and petals longer than sharp-pointed capsule. Flowers prophyllate. Capsules imperfectly 3-chambered. Seeds .3–.5mm, ribbed, with small beaks.
Leaves narrow, basal, flat, with auricle visible above sheath. Stems tough, leafless, round,
solid, wiry. Grows in clumps. Dry or moist compacted soil; abundant along forest paths,
often forming pure patches. Throughout N. Am.

Juncus canadensis J. Gay
Rush Family (Juncaceae)

Grows 8in–4ft (.2–1.3m). Great variation in size. Inflorescence in forking terminal
branches. Subtending bracts shorter than inflorescence. Flowers lack prophylls. Capsules
partially 3-chambered, in clusters. Seeds spindle-shaped, longitudinally ridged, with ap-
pendages ½ of length. Leaves basal and on stem, round, with faint, horizontal rings around
them (septate). Stems round. Swamps, marshes, wet shores. Que. and N.S. to Minn., south
to S.C., Ind., and Nebr.

Juncus effusus L.
Soft rush
Rush Family (Juncaceae)

Grows 16in–7ft (.4–2.3m). Inflorescence in panicle appearing to emerge from 1 point on
stem side, owing to subtending bract that seems to arise as continuation of stem. Flowers
prophyllate. Capsules 3-chambered. Basal sheaths bladeless. Stem round, leafless. Grows
in clumps. Open marshes, wet meadows. Throughout region.

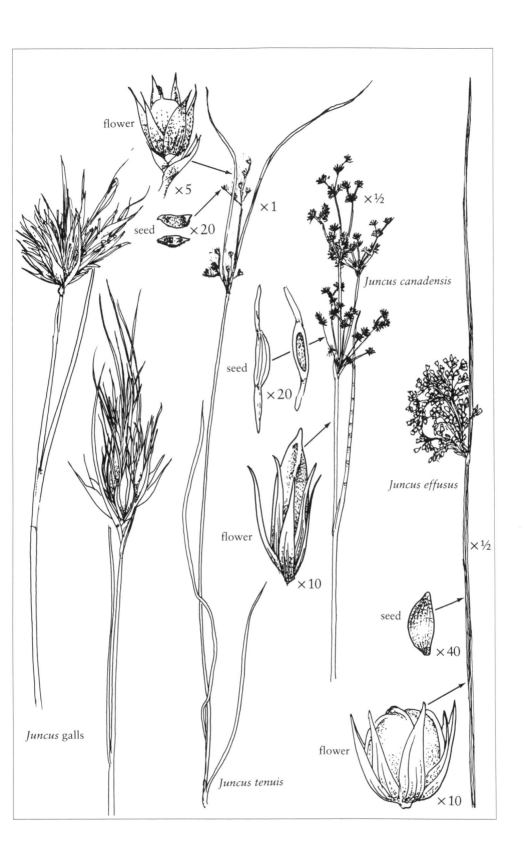

flower

×5

seed ×20

×1

Juncus canadensis

×½

seed

×20

Juncus effusus

flower

×10

×½

seed

×40

Juncus galls

flower

Juncus tenuis

×10

Juncus gerardii Loisel
Black grass
Rush Family (Juncaceae)

Grows 6in–2½ft (15–75cm). Similar to *J. tenuis* but with subtending bracts shorter than inflorescence. Sepals and petals shorter than capsule. Flowers prophyllate. Capsules 3-chambered, rounded above, with short beak. Seeds .5mm, lopsided, eplliptical, longitudinally ribbed, cross-lined. Leaves on stem. Salt marshes; inland in salty and nonsalty conditions. Circumboreal, south to Va.

Juncus acuminatus Michx.
Rush Family (Juncaceae)

Grows to 3in–2½ft (8–75cm). Inflorescence loose, spreading, with 5–20 rounded heads, 6–10mm thick. Flowers lack prophylls. Leaves round, septate (with horizontal rings around them). Capsules 1-chambered, short-pointed, equal in length to perianth. Stems tufted. Wet soil, meadows, shores, low woods. Maine and N.S. to Wis., south to Fla. and Mexico; B.C. to Oreg.

Luzula multiflora (Retz.) Lej.
Wood-rush
Rush Family (Juncaceae)

Grows to 2ft (60cm). Inflorescence blooms in spring, largely gone in winter. Any remaining fruit 1-chambered with just 3 seeds within. Leaves flat, grasslike, with closed sheath. Wispy, white, loose hairs scattered on stem and leaves. Forms dense clumps. Wooded or open disturbed places; widespread. Apparently native to most of region; south to Del., Ind., and Mo.

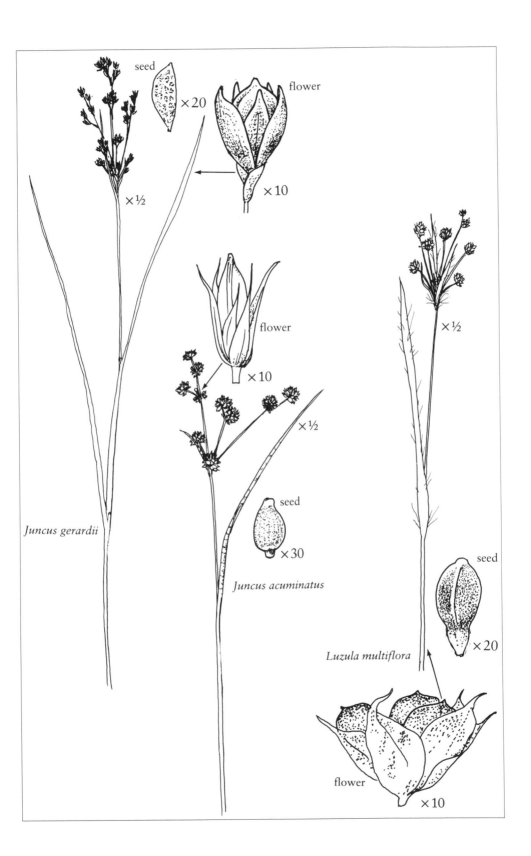

seed ×20

flower

×½

×10

flower

×10

×½

seed

×30

Juncus gerardii

Juncus acuminatus

×½

seed

×20

Luzula multiflora

flower

×10

Illustrated Glossary

Achene. A small, dry, one-celled, one-seeded fruit that does not open and looks like a seed itself.

Acute. Tapering to the apex.

Alternate. Borne singly and not opposite. Applies to leaves, stalks, and branches.

Annual. Completing the life-cycle in one growing season.

Armed. Provided with thorns, spines, or prickles.

Awn. Slender bristlelike part usually at the tip of a structure.

Axis. The angle between a branch or leaf and the portion of the plant from which it arises.

Beak. A long, pointed tip.

Bearded. With long or stiff hairs.

Berry. A fleshy fruit.

Biennial. A plant with a two-year life-cycle that produces leaves in its first year and flowers and leaves in its second year.

Bilabiate. Two-lipped.

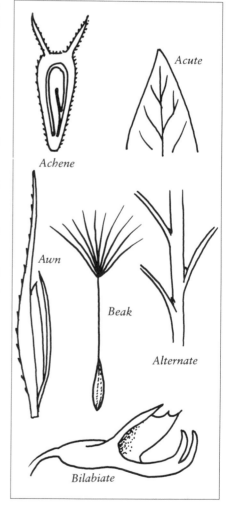

Bog. Wetland characterized by evergreen trees and shrubs, underlying peat deposits, and poor drainage, leading to highly acidic conditions.

Bract. A more or less modified leaf, often found under or surrounding the flower.

Bulb. An underground leaf bud with fleshy scales, e.g., an onion.

Bur. A seed or fruit bearing spines or prickles, usually hooked or barbed.

Calyx, calyxes. The sepals collectively; the outer series of floral leaves.

Campanulate. Bell-shaped.

Capsule. A dry fruit of more than one chamber that splits open.

Caudex. The persistent, often woody base of an herbaceous stem.

Chaff. A thin, dry scale or bract. One of the bracts between the individual flowers in a head in the Daisy Family (Asteraceae).

Clasping. Describing a sessile leaf with the lower edges of the blade partly surrounding the stem.

Coma. A tuft of hairs, especially at a seed tip.

Compound leaf. Made up of separate, smaller leaflets.

Corm. A thickened, vertical, solid underground stem.

Corolla. The petals collectively.

Corymb. A flat-topped or convex open inflorescence, technically a contracted raceme. The central flower blooms latest.

Corymbose. Borne in corymbs or corymblike.

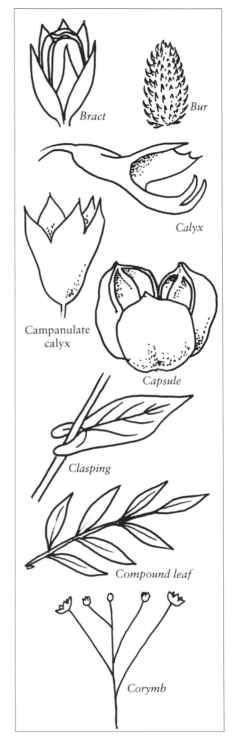

Bract

Bur

Calyx

Campanulate calyx

Capsule

Clasping

Compound leaf

Corymb

Crenate. Toothed, with teeth rounded at the apex.

Cyme. A flower cluster, often convex or flat-topped, in which the central flower blooms earliest.

Decumbent. Reclining on the ground but with an ascending apex, e.g., as a stem.

Decurrent. Extending downward from the point of insertion, e.g., a leaf decurrent on the stem.

Decussate. Arranged oppositely, with each pair set at right angles to the pair above and the pair below.

Dehiscent. Opening by definite pores or slits to discharge contents.

Dentate. Toothed, with teeth directed outward.

Dioecious. Flowers unisexual and borne on separate plants.

Dissected. Cut deeply into fine lobes; fern-like.

Endocarp. The inner part of the pericarp.

Entire. Margins without teeth or lobes.

Floret. A small flower, especially one in a dense cluster.

Follicle. A dry, one-chambered fruit, splitting down one side only.

Fruit. The ripened ovary and any other structures that enclose it at maturity.

Gall. A swelling of plant tissue usually caused by fungi or insect parasites.

Glabrous. No hairs present at all; smooth.

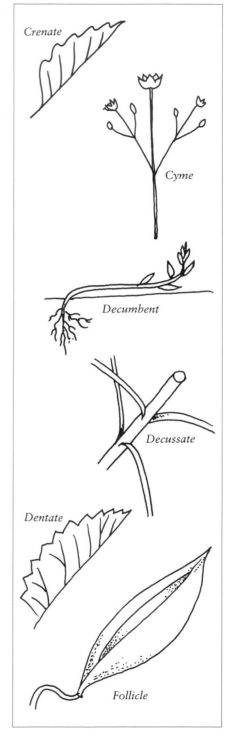

Crenate

Cyme

Decumbent

Decussate

Dentate

Follicle

Head. A tight cluster of stalkless or almost stalkless flowers or fruits at the tip of the stem.

Hirsute. With moderately coarse and stiff hairs.

Hispid. With stiff and rigid bristles or hairs.

Hypanthium. An enlargement or development of the receptacle under the calyx.

Imbricate. Partly overlapping, as shingles on a roof.

Indehiscent. Remaining persistently closed.

Inflorescence. The flowering part of the plant. A cluster of flowers.

Involucre. A whorl of distinct or united leaves or bracts subtending a flower or inflorescence.

Lanceolate. Lance-shaped. Several times longer than wide, broadest toward the base and tapering to the apex.

Legume. A fruit composed of one chamber and splitting open on two sides. Usually synonymous with pod. Characteristic fruit of the Pea or Bean Family (Fabaceae).

Ligule. A small projection at the top of the leaf sheath on the inside.

Linear. Narrow and flat, with sides parallel.

Lobe. A division of an organ, especially if rounded.

Locule. A cell or compartment of the ovary.

Loculicidal. A dehiscent fruit that splits down the center of a locule.

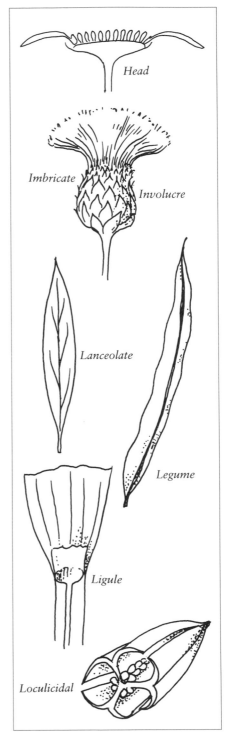

Loment. A leguminous fruit conspicuously constricted between the seeds.

Marsh. A wetland characterized by the absence of woody plants, with vegetation composed of herbaceous plants and with a water table at or above the ground most of the year.

Meadow. A tract of moist, low-lying, usually level land with grasses and herbaceous plants.

Monoecious. Bearing unisexual flowers, with both male and female flowers on the same plant.

Nerve. A simple or unbranched vein or slender rib.

Node. A point on the stem where branches or leaves originate.

Nut. A one-seeded, indehiscent fruit with a hard wall.

Oblong. Longer than wide, with sides usually parallel.

Obovate. Egg-shaped in outline; attached at the narrow end.

Ocrea. A tubular, sheathing stipule. Characteristic of the Smartweed Family (Polygonaceae).

Opposite. Paired and borne on the same level on the stem, as with leaves, stalks, and branches.

Ovary. That part of the pistil that contains the ovules.

Ovate. Egg-shaped in outline; attached at the wide end.

Ovule. The structure that develops into the seed.

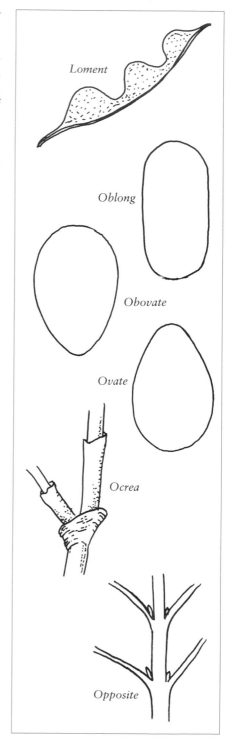

Loment

Oblong

Obovate

Ovate

Ocrea

Opposite

Palmate. The lobes that run downward toward one place at the base.

Panicle. A compound raceme. An inflorescence in which the flowers are borne on stalks that branch off larger stalks.

Pappus. The modified calyx in the Daisy Family (Asteraceae), forming a crown of fine hairs, bristles, or scales at the summit of the fruit, the achene.

Parasite. An organism that grows upon and obtains nourishment from another living organism and gives nothing to the survival of the host.

Pedicel. The stalk to a single flower of an inflorescence.

Peduncle. The stalk to a solitary flower or to an inflorescence.

Perennial. An herbaceous plant that dies back to the ground at the end of its growing season but survives underground by roots or a stem.

Perfoliate. Describing a leaf stem that passes through the leaf blade.

Pericarp. The matured ovary wall of a fruit.

Perigynium. A special sac that encloses the achene in the genus *Carex*.

Petiole. The stalk to a leaf.

Phyllotaxy. The arrangement of leaves on a stem.

Pinnate. A compound leaf with leaflets on 2 opposite sides of the axis.

Pinnatifid. Pinnately lobed or parted halfway or more into the midrib.

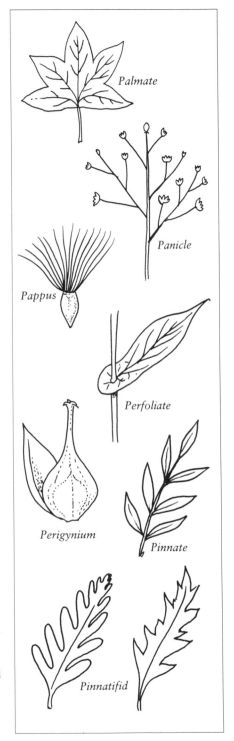

Palmate

Panicle

Pappus

Perfoliate

Perigynium

Pinnate

Pinnatifid

Pistil. The female part of the flower, consisting of stigma, style, and ovary.

Plumose. Hairs with side hairs along the main axis, as the plume of a feather.

Pod. A dry, dehiscent fruit that opens along two seams; often a synonym for legume.

Prickle. A small, sharp, pointed outgrowth of young bark.

Procumbent. Lying or trailing on the ground, usually not rooting at the nodes.

Prophyll. One of the pair of small bracts at the base of a flower, as in some species of *Juncus.*

Prostrate. Lying flat on the ground, sometimes rooting at the nodes.

Pubescent. Covered with short, soft hairs.

Raceme. An arrangement of stalked flowers along a central stem.

Receptacle. The more or less expanded portion of the flower stalk that bears either the organs of a flower or the collected flowers of a head, as in the Daisy Family (Asteraceae).

Reflexed. Abruptly bent or turned downward or backward.

Rhizome. An underground stem that sends out shoots and roots as it grows.

Root. The part of a plant that absorbs water and nutrients from the ground.

Rootstock. An underground stem, or rhizome; also any elongated underground structure through which a plant spreads.

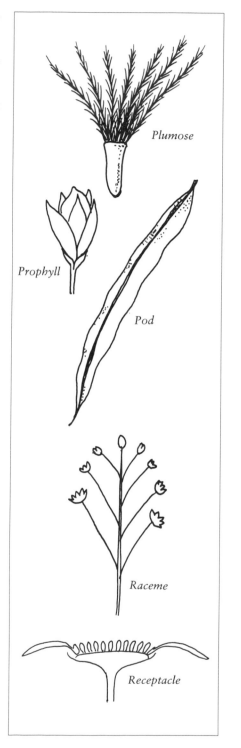

Plumose

Prophyll

Pod

Raceme

Receptacle

Rosette. A dense basal cluster of leaves in a circular pattern.

Samara. A dry, indehiscent winged fruit.

Saprophyte. A plant that obtains nourishment from dead organic matter.

Schizocarp. A dry fruit of two or more indehiscent one-seeded segments. Typical of the Carrot Family (Apiaceae).

Scorpioid. Coiled at the apex like a scorpion's tail, especially an inflorescence.

Seed. A fertilized ovule consisting of the embryo and a food supply.

Sepal. One of the parts of the outer whorl of the flower, usually green in color.

Septicidal. A capsule that splits down the septa, not through the locule. Compare to Loculicidal.

Septum, septa. A membranous, often translucent partition found within fruits and flowers.

Serrate. With sharp teeth directed forward.

Sessile. Attached directly to the base, lacking a stem.

Sheath. The lower part of the leaf that wraps around the stem.

Silicle. A short fruit of the Mustard Family (Brassicaceae), usually not more than twice as long as wide. *See also* Silique.

Silique. A long, narrow fruit of the Mustard Family (Brassicaceae). A two-parted fruit divided down the middle by a membrane that is often persistent after the outer walls and seeds have fallen away.

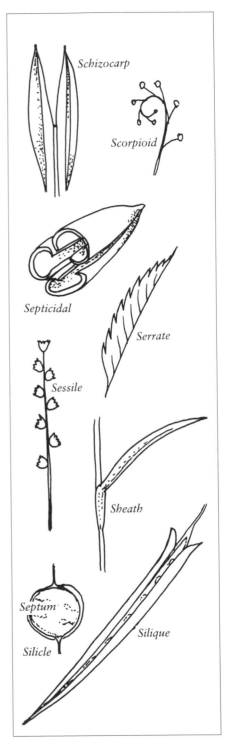

Schizocarp

Scorpioid

Septicidal

Serrate

Sessile

Sheath

Septum

Silicle

Silique

Sinus. The recess between two adjoining lobes.

Spike. An inflorescence with stalkless (sessile) flowers along a central stem.

Spine. A short-pointed outgrowth from the stem with an absence of vascular tissue. Compare to Thorn.

Stigma. The apex of the pistil, where the pollen lands.

Stipule. An appendage at the base of a leaf stalk, such as a small leaf or thorn.

Stolon. A trailing shoot above the ground, rooting at the nodes.

Strobilus, strobili. An aggregation of modified spore-bearing leaves that resembles a cone.

Style. The part of the pistil that connects the ovary to the stigma.

Subtend. To occur closely beneath something.

Suffruticose. A perennial in which the lower part of the stem is woody but the upper part is herbaceous.

Swamp. A wetland dominated by wetland trees and shrubs and a diversity of herbaceous plants.

Taproot. The primary root, continuing the axis of the plant downward.

Tendril. A slender branchlike structure that curls about and serves as an organ of support.

Thorn. A sharp-pointed protuberance that contains vascular tissue. Compare to Spine.

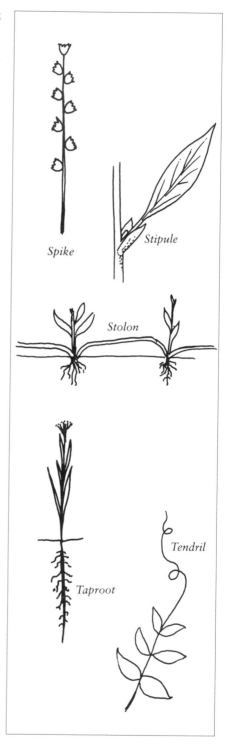

Spike

Stipule

Stolon

Taproot

Tendril

Tomentose. Covered by dense, woolly, entangled hairs.

Tuber. A thickened, short, subterranean stem having numerous buds.

Turbinate. Top-shaped; inversely conical.

Umbel. A convex or flat-topped inflorescence, the flowers all arising from one point.

Vernation. The particular arrangement of a leaf or its parts in the bud.

Verticillate. Three or more leaves arranged in a circle about a common axis. Also whorled.

Whorled. See Verticillate.

Wing. Any membranous or thin expansion bordering or surrounding an organ.

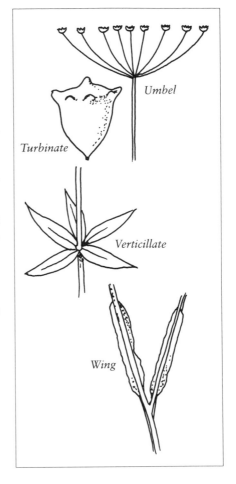

References

Beal, Ernest O. *A Manual of Marsh and Aquatic Vascular Plants of North Carolina with Habitat Data*. North Carolina Agricultural Experiment Station, 1977.

Brown, Lauren. *Weeds in Winter*. New York: W. W. Norton, 1976.

———. *Grasses: An Identification Guide*. Boston: Houghton Mifflin, 1979.

Delorit, R. J. *An Illustrated Taxonomy Manual of Weed Seeds*. River Falls, Wis.: Agronomy Publications, 1970.

Embertson, Jane. *Pods: Wildflowers and Weeds in Their Final Beauty*. New York: Charles Scribner and Sons, 1979.

Fassett, N. C. *The Manual of Aquatic Plants*. Madison: University of Wisconsin Press, 1980.

Felt, E. P. *Plant Galls and Gall Makers*. New York: Hafner, 1965.

Fernald, Merritt Lyndon. *Gray's Manual of Botany*. 8th ed. D. Van Nostrand, 1950.

Gleason, Henry A. *The New Britton and Brown Illustrated Flora of the Northeastern United States and Adjacent Canada*. 3d rev. ed. New York: Hafner, 1968.

Gleason, Henry A., and Arthur Cronquist. *Manual of Vascular Plants of Northeastern United States and Adjacent Canada*. 2d ed. Bronx, N.Y.: New York Botanical Garden, 1991.

Hitchcock, A. S. *Manual of the Grasses of the United States*. 2d ed., rev. Washington, D.C.: U.S. Government Printing Office, 1950.

Mickel, John T. *How to Know the Ferns and Fern Allies*. Dubuque, Iowa: W. C. Brown, 1979.

Montgomery, F. H. *Seeds and Fruits of Plants of Eastern Canada and Northeastern United States*. Toronto: University of Toronto Press, 1977.

Newcomb, Lawrence. *Newcomb's Wildflower Guide*. Boston: Little, Brown, 1977.

Peterson, Roger Tory, and Margaret McKenny. *A Field Guide to Wildflowers of Northeastern and North-central North America*. Boston: Houghton Mifflin, 1968.

Porter, C. L. *Taxonomy of Flowering Plants*. San Francisco: W. H. Freeman, 1967. (Reprinted by Dover, 1993.)

Rickett, H. N. *Wild Flowers of the United States: The Northeastern States*. New York: McGraw-Hill, 1966.

Smith, Helen V. *Winter Wildflowers*. Booklet of the Michigan Botanical Club. Special Publication no. 2, 1973.

Winterringer, G. S. *Some Plant Galls of Illinois*. Springfield: Illinois State Museum, Story of Illinois #12. 1961.

Zomlefer, Wendy. *Common Florida Angiosperm Families*. Parts I and II. Gainesville, Fla.: Storter Printing, 1983.

Index